LIBRARY OF HEBREW BIBLE/
OLD TESTAMENT STUDIES

481

Formerly Journal for the Study of the Old Testament Supplement Series

Editors
Claudia V. Camp, Texas Christian University
Andrew Mein, Westcott House, Cambridge

Founding Editors
David J. A. Clines, Philip R. Davies and David M. Gunn

Editorial Board
Richard J. Coggins, Alan Cooper, John Goldingay, Robert P. Gordon,
Norman K. Gottwald, Gina Hens-Piazza, John Jarick, Andrew D. H. Mayes,
Carol Meyers, Patrick D. Miller, Yvonne Sherwood

GOOD FIGS, BAD FIGS

Judicial Differentiation in the Book of Jeremiah

R. J. R. Plant

t&t clark

NEW YORK • LONDON

T & T Clark International, 80 Maiden Lane, New York, NY 10038

T & T Clark International, The Tower Building, 11 York Road, London SE1 7NX

T & T Clark International is a Continuum imprint.

Library of Congress Cataloging-in-Publication Data
Plant, R. J. R. (Robin J. R.)
  Good figs, bad figs : judicial differentiation in the book of Jeremiah / R.J.R. Plant.
    p. cm. -- (The library of Hebrew Bible/Old Testament studies ; #483)
  Includes bibliographical references and index.
  ISBN-13: 978-0-567-02687-3 (hardcover : alk. paper)
  ISBN-10: 0-567-02687-6 (hardcover : alk. paper)
  1. Bible. O.T. Jeremiah--Criticism, interpretation, etc. 2. Judgment--Biblical teaching. I.
Title. II. Series.

  BS1525.52.P53 2007
  224'.206--dc22

                              2007018009

    06 07 08 09 10   10 9 8 7 6 5 4 3 2 1

Extracts from Karl-Friedrich Pohlmann, *Studien zum Jeremiabuch. Ein Beitrag zur Frage nach der Entstehung des Jeremiabuches* (FRLANT 118; Göttingen: Vandenhoeck & Ruprecht, 1978), reprinted by permission of the publisher.

Extracts from Christopher R. Seitz, *Theology in Conflict: Reactions to the Exile in the Book of Jeremiah* (BZAW 176; Berlin and New York: W. de Gruyter, 1989), reprinted by permission of the publisher.

Extracts from Nelson Kilpp, *Niederreißen und aufbauen. Das Verhältnis von Heilsverheißung und Unheilsverkündigung bei Jeremia und im Jeremiabuch* (BThSt 13; Neukirchen–Vluyn: Neukirchener Verlag, 1990), reprinted by permission of the publisher.

Printed in Great Britain by Biddles Ltd, King's Lynn, Norfolk

To my father, Peter Plant
Who died shortly before this book went to print.

CONTENTS

PREFACE

The following study represents a substantial revision of a doctoral dissertation submitted to the University of Edinburgh in July 2003. At one level, therefore, it is intended as a contribution towards our understanding of the theology of Jeremiah. Naturally, the book comes bearing an invisible "work in progress" label. I am all too aware of questions raised and not resolved. If, however, it stimulates further thought and discussion, I shall be well satisfied.

Despite the academic nature of the work, the issues with which it grapples—national and individual culpability, divine justice and grace—are clearly of wider significance. One of the many gauntlets thrown down to religion in Richard Dawkins' recent best-seller, *The God Delusion* (London: Bantam, 2006), is the apparent inability of the biblical god to exercise judgment discriminately. Those (like me) who wish to promote the Christian faith in the contemporary world will want to take the challenge seriously. The book of Jeremiah, it seems to me, offers a valuable resource for doing so.

I should like to express my sincere thanks to Drs Andrew Mein and Claudia Camp for accepting this monograph into the LHBOTS series. I am also grateful to Gabriella Page-Fort and Katie Gallof at Continuum for their help throughout the production of the book, and to Duncan Burns for his expertise in typesetting the manuscript and for his frequent friendly advice. Whatever merit this book may have is due in no small part to the perceptive supervision and kind encouragement of Dr David Reimer and Professor Graeme Auld during my doctoral research, though neither should be held responsible for the views expressed in it. Professor Mary Smallwood also graciously shared her time and wisdom regarding the Greek text of Jeremiah. At various stages, Drs Harold Hoehner, Lazarus Phiri, Mark Garcia, Donald Fairbairn and Cherryl Hunt have supplied me with important articles that were not readily to hand. It is a happy duty also to mention Mr Stuart and Dr Dorothy Elford, not only for proofing the entire manuscript at short notice, but (even more) for their enriching friendship over four years. Citations from the works of Karl-Friedrich Pohlmann, Christopher R. Seitz and Nelson Kilpp are reproduced by permission of the publishers.

I should very much have liked to place this book in the hands of my parents, who for over forty years have constantly encouraged me both to study and to live out the Christian scriptures. Sadly, in the case of my father, that will now not be possible. To him this book is gratefully dedicated.

Finally, I owe a special debt to my wife, Danielle, for her constant support, computer literacy and calm head. Not even retyping large chunks of text in a new and exotic alphabet (Hebrew) fazed her. She will, however, be more relieved than anyone to see the project finished.

Robin Plant
Timişoara, Romania

ABBREVIATIONS

Journals, Reference Works, Series

AB	Anchor Bible
AnBib	Analecta Biblica
ANVAO	Avhandlinger utgitt av Det Norske Videnskaps-Akademi; Oslo
AOTC	Apollos Old Testament Commentary
ATANT	Abhandlungen zur Theologie des Alten und Neuen Testaments
ATSAT	Arbeiten zu Text und Sprache im Alten Testament
BDB	Francis Brown, S. R. Driver and Charles A. Briggs. *Hebrew and English Lexicon of the Old Testament*. Oxford, 1907
BETL	Bibliotheca ephemeridum theologicarum lovaniensium
BHS	*Biblia Hebraica Stuttgartensia*. Edited by K. Elliger and W. Rudolph. 5th rev. ed. Stuttgart, 1997
BKAT	Biblischer Kommentar, Altes Testament
BO	Biblica et Orientalia
BS	The Biblical Seminar
BST	Basel Studies of Theology
BTCL	Biblical and Theological Classics Library
BTS	Biblisch-Theologische Studien
BWANT	Beiträge zur Wissenschaft vom Alten und Neuen Testament
BZ	*Biblische Zeitschrift*
BZAW	Beihefte zur Zeitschrift für die alttestamentliche Wissenschaft
CB	Cambridge Bible for Schools and Colleges
CBC	Cambridge Bible Commentary
CBET	Contributions to Biblical Exegesis and Theology
CBQ	*Catholic Biblical Quarterly*
DIHGS	*Davidson's Introductory Hebrew Grammar: Syntax*. Edited by J. C. L. Gibson. 4th ed. Edinburgh, 1994
EvT	*Evangelische Theologie*
FRLANT	Forschungen zur Religion und Literatur des Alten und Neuen Testaments
GBH	T. Muraoka. *A Grammar of Biblical Hebrew*. 2 vols. SB 14. Rome, 1996. ET of P. Joüon, *Grammaire de l'Hébreu biblique*. Rome, 1923
GKC	*Gesenius' Hebrew Grammar*. Edited by E. Kautzsch. Revised and translated by A. E. Cowley. Oxford, 1910
GTA	Göttinger theologische Arbeiten

HALOT	*The Hebrew and Aramaic Lexicon of the Old Testament*. Edited by M. E. J. Richardson. 5 vols. Leiden, 1994–2000. ET of *Hebräisches und aramäisches Lexikon zum Alten Testament*. Edited by L. Koehler, W. Baumgartner and J. J. Stamm. 3d ed. 5 vols. Leiden, 1967–95
HAR	*Hebrew Annual Review*
HAT	Handbuch zum Alten Testament
HKAT	Handkommentar zum Alten Testament
HSM	Hebrew Semitic Monographs
IBH	Thomas O. Lambdin. *Introduction to Biblical Hebrew*. London: Darton, Longman & Todd, 1973
ICC	International Critical Commentary
JBL	*Journal of Biblical Literature*
JNES	*Journal of Near Eastern Studies*
JQR	*Jewish Quarterly Review*
JSJSup	*Journal for the Study of Judaism*: Supplement Series
JSOT	*Journal for the Study of the Old Testament*
JSOTSup	*Journal for the Study of the Old Testament*: Supplement Series
JTS	*Journal of Theological Studies*
KAT	Kommentar zum Alten Testament
KD	*Kerygma und Dogma*
KHAT	Kurzer Hand-Kommentar zum Alten Testament
LAI	Library of Ancient Israel
NCB	New Century Bible
NGB	Das Alte Testament Deutsch: Neues Göttinger Bibelwerk
NIBC	New International Biblical Commentary
NICOT	New International Commentary on the Old Testament
NIDOTTE	*New International Dictionary of Old Testament Theology and Exegesis*. Edited by Willem A. VanGemeren. 5 vols. Grand Rapids, 1997
NTL	New Testament Library
OBO	Orbis Biblicus et Orientalis
OBT	Overtures to Biblical Theology
OS	Oudtestamentische Studiën
OTG	Old Testament Guides
OTL	Old Testament Library
OTWSA	*Die Outestamentiese Werkgemeenskaap in Suid-Afrika*
PEQ	*Palestine Exploration Quarterly*
PTMS	Pittsburgh Theological Monograph Series
Rahlfs	*Septuaginta*. Edited by Alfred Rahlfs. Stuttgart, 1979
RQ	*Revue de Qumran*
SB	Subsidia Biblica
SBB	Stuttgarter biblische Beiträge
SBLDS	Society for Biblical Literature Dissertation Series
SBLMS	Society for Biblical Literature Monograph Series
SBLSBS	Society of Biblical Literature Sources for Biblical Study
SBT	Studies in Biblical Theology (Second Series)

SJOT	*Scandinavian Journal of Theology*
SOFSup	Symbolae Osloenses Fasc. Supplementary Series
SOTI	Studies in Old Testament Interpretation
ST	Studia Theologica
TBST	The Bible Speaks Today
TOTC	Tyndale Old Testament Commentaries
VSH	*Vanderbilt Studies in the Humanities*
VT	Vetus Testamentum
VTSup	Supplements to *Vetus Testamentum*
WBC	Word Biblical Commentary
WMANT	Wissenschaftliche Monographien zum Alten und Neuen Testament
ZAW	*Zeitschrift für die alttestamentliche Wissenschaft*
Ziegler	*Septuaginta. Vetus Testamentum Graecum*. Vol. 15. *Ieremias, Baruch, Threni, Epistula Ieremiae*. Edited by J. Ziegler. Göttingen: Vandenhoeck & Ruprecht, 1957
ZTK	*Zeitschrift für Theologie und Kirche*

Ancient Texts and Versions

LXX	Septuagint
LXX^A	Codex Alexandrinus
LXX^B	Codex Vaticanus
LXX^S	Codex Sinaiticus
LXX^Q	Codex Marchalianus
LXX^{Luc}	Lucianic recension of the Septuagint
LXX$^\alpha$	Aquila
LXX$^\sigma$	Symmachus
4QJer^d	Jeremiah scroll from Qumran Cave 4
V^P	The Petersburg Codex to the Prophets
Vulg.	Vulgate
Targ.	Targum Jonathan to the Prophets
Memorabilia	Xenophon, *Memorabilia and Oeconomicus*
pap. Mur	Papyrii from Wadi Murabbaᶜat

Other

DtrH	The Deuteronomistic History
EVV	English versions of the Bible
NIV	New International Version
REB	Revised English Bible
RSV	Revised Standard Version

INTRODUCTION: MORE THAN JUSTICE?

Two texts, which in most English Bibles happen to stand at opposite ends of the Old Testament canon, may be taken as providing a convenient point of entry to our survey of the concept of divine judgment and salvation in the Old Testament. The first is found in Gen 18, where YHWH's hint that he intends the wholesale destruction of Sodom and Gomorrah provokes Abraham's famous protest:

> Will you sweep away the righteous with the wicked? What if there are fifty righteous people in the city? Will you really sweep it away and not spare (ולא תשא) the place for the sake of the fifty righteous people in it? Far be it from you to do such a thing—to kill the righteous with the wicked, treating the righteous and the wicked alike. Far be it from you! Will not the judge of all the earth do right? (Gen 18:23–25 NIV)

As the words ולא תשא make clear, what Abraham is requesting is not that YHWH should exercise a more discriminate judgment, treating the righteous and the wicked separately, but rather that the entire city be pardoned for the sake of a righteous few.[1] In fact, the climax of the story presents precisely the former scenario, with Lot and his family being (forcibly) rescued prior to the obliteration of the two cities (Gen 19:16–25). The story thus strikes a somewhat enigmatic note concerning YHWH's practice of justice. Ultimately, in Abraham's terms, the judge of all the earth does right. At the same time, the preceding chapter implies that he might act otherwise; or as Walter Brueggemann puts it, "that at the edge of Yahweh's judicial work, more than justice is possible."[2]

From this story set in the days before Israel's existence, we fast forward to the time of their last recognized prophet. After reporting the post-exilic community's complaint that serving God was futile (Mal 3:14–15), the author describes the humble response of those who feared YHWH (יראי יהוה, v. 16), who put their names to a scroll of remembrance (ספר זכרון). This elicits the following oracle: "'They will be mine', says the LORD Almighty, 'in the day when I make up my treasured possession. I will spare them, just as a man spares his son who serves him. And you will again see the distinction between (וראיתם בין...ל) the righteous and the wicked, between those who serve God and those who do not'" (Mal 3:17–18 NIV).

---

1. Noted by Paul Joyce, "Individual and Community," in *Beginning Old Testament Study* (ed. John Rogerson; rev. ed.; London: SPCK, 1998), 74–89 (85). See too Gerhard von Rad, *Genesis: A Commentary* (trans. John H. Marks; OTL; London: SCM Press, 1972), 212–13.

2. Walter Brueggemann, *Old Testament Theology: Testimony, Dispute, Advocacy* (Minneapolis: Fortress, 1997), 274.

While no claim is being made here for any literary dependence between these passages, they both express a fundamental theological problem in the Old Testament; namely, YHWH's practice of salvation and judgment. The issue can be formulated more precisely. On the one hand, it has to do with the *scope* of divine wrath and favour. According to Gen 18–19, YHWH "does right" in this matter, which is to say that he distinguishes between different groups of people; yet it also suggests that such selectivity cannot be taken for granted. Likewise, Mal 3 promises that YHWH will differentiate between those who serve him and those who do not, but indicates that this is a future rather than a present reality.

Secondly, there is the question of the *rationale* for YHWH's judicial action. Both our passages speak of YHWH distinguishing between the righteous and wicked. Yet Gen 19 paints an ambiguous picture of Lot's moral fibre (vv. 6–8), and ultimately his vacillating family is pulled from the city simply because YHWH had pity on them (בחמלת יהוה, v. 16). Conversely, in Mal 3:18 the righteous whom YHWH will spare (חמל again) are identified with "those who feared YHWH" and thus seem to display a more obvious piety.

How does YHWH exercise judgment and salvation? Does he act destructively against whole communities, or does he make distinctions? Either way, do his actions involve justice, or something more? Clearly, to explore such complex and far-reaching questions with reference to the entire Old Testament could fill several volumes. In the study that follows, however, I will simply offer a general outline of Old Testament perspectives on this issue, before focussing specifically on how it is interpreted in the longest and (probably) most complex of the prophetic books, that of Jeremiah.

Chapter 1

JUDICIAL DIFFERENTIATION IN THE OLD TESTAMENT

1. *Introduction*

In the Preface, I suggested that the question of how YHWH practises justice in Israel—whether he differentiates between people, and if so, why—is one of the fundamental theological concerns of the Old Testament. The bulk of the study that follows will attempt to explore how this issue is handled specifically within the book of Jeremiah. In this first chapter, however, I will attempt to place the investigation on a broader canvas, by sketching the main ways in which YHWH's judicial action is interpreted elsewhere in the Old Testament. Since the prophetic literature adopts a distinctive outlook in this regard, as will become clear later, I will deal with this corpus separately from the rest of the Old Testament.

A few qualifying remarks are in order at the outset. First of all, space clearly precludes a comprehensive survey of all the Old Testament material that might be relevant to the question of judicial differentiation. My aim, however, is to identify and illustrate the principal textual voices, and to see how they relate to one another. Secondly, for the purposes of this chapter, the concept of judicial action is not restricted to specific Hebrew lexical fields (e.g. שפט, דין, ריב), but rather is defined in broad terms as signifying YHWH's blessing or wrath in response to the actions of his people. Thirdly, this part of the study will focus on the present form of the text, without attempting to allocate different perspectives to different redactional layers. Finally, the exercise is essentially a descriptive one. That is to say, the survey aims to see how salvation and judgment is interpreted in the text, without conjecture as to the historical or ideological factors in shaping those interpretations.

It is, of course, only with YHWH's exercise of judgment and salvation that this study is concerned. Much of Israel's legal code doubtless required justice to be applied on an individual basis, a principle most clearly formulated in Deut 24:16: "Fathers shall not be put to death on account of their children, nor children put to death on account of their fathers; each one shall die for his own sin." Such texts, however, fall outside the scope of this chapter since strictly speaking they deal with the administration of justice by Israel rather than by YHWH.[1] At

---

1. For this distinction, see Joyce, "Individual and Community," 83. Community actions such as the stoning of a blasphemer (Lev 25:10–23) and of a Sabbath breaker (Num 15:32–36) illustrate the point.

the same time, one should not make too rigid a distinction in this respect, and in some cases my study of YHWH's exercise of judgment will necessarily touch on its mediation through human agency.

2. *Judgment and Salvation Outside the Prophetic Corpus*

2.1. *Judgment and Salvation as Selective*

We can begin this survey of YHWH's judicial action by highlighting various passages that illustrate the principle of what I will call *selective* judgment; that is to say, cases in which divine retribution is both discriminate and related to human conduct. Broadly speaking, such action can take one of two forms. Where YHWH simultaneously deals favourably with some and punitively with others, judgment can be described as *antithetical*. Where, on the other hand, judgment simply involves the singling out of an individual or group for blessing or censure, it is more appropriately designated *single-sided*.

An obvious starting point is provided by the Wisdom tradition, the "International–Creation–Ethical" orientation of which emphasizes personal behaviour rather than communal existence. In particular, the book of Proverbs frequently affirms a direct link between conduct and consequence.[2] To be sure, at times this appears to be conceived in terms of "natural consequences"—the logical outworking of actions in a morally structured universe (e.g. Prov 6:9–11; 11:5–6).[3] Nevertheless, many passages interpret matters in explicitly theological terms: YHWH "stores up victory for the upright, he is a shield to those who walk blamelessly," writes the sage, "but the wicked will be cut off from the land, and the treacherous will be torn from it" (2:7, 22). Similarly, we are told that "a good man obtains favour from YHWH, but a crafty man he condemns" (12:2). Even though a righteous man may suffer and an evil man prosper, the former is assured of a future hope (אחרית) whereas the latter is not (23:18; 24:20). A somewhat different articulation of YHWH's judicial activity emerges later in Proverbs, where the writer warns against exploiting the poor (דל), the oppressed (עני) and the orphan (יתום, 22:22–23; 23:10–11). In the event of such injustice, YHWH himself will "argue their case" (יריב ריבם); indeed, he is described as the orphan's redeemer (גאל), though no indication is given as to *how* he will fulfil this judicial role.

---

2. Such a simple relationship was of course resisted by other voices in the Wisdom tradition, notably Job and Qoheleth; see further below.

3. See Klaus Koch, "Is There a Doctrine of Retribution in the Old Testament?," in *Theodicy in the Old Testament* (ed. James L. Crenshaw; Philadelphia: Fortress, 1983), 57–87. A distinction must be made, however, between describing retribution as *indirect* and as *impersonal*, the former term retaining room for the involvement of God in the natural world; on this point, see Walter Brueggemann, *Old Testament Theology: Testimony, Dispute, Advocacy* (Minneapolis: Fortress, 1997), 338. Cf. Walther Eichrodt's remarks, *Theology of the Old Testament*, vol. 2 (trans. J. A. Baker; OTL; London: SCM, 1967), 426: "From being a merely natural phenomenon, whereby the punishment reveals the inevitable natural consequence of the morbid sinful matter, *the correspondence has now become moral*, something based on the righteous purpose of the God of retribution" (italics original; cf. 423 n. 8).

Conversely, the Psalms mostly operate within an "Israel–Torah–Covenant" framework, but here too it is regularly assumed or asserted that YHWH judges his people discriminately. Precisely this conviction undergirds the Individual Laments (e.g. Pss 17; 35; 43; 54),[4] where the psalmist appeals for vindication (דין, שׁפט) against his enemies (איבים),[5] and it is stated as a more general truth in many of the Psalms of Trust (e.g. Pss 4; 23; 52; 62).[6] Even the contemplative Ps 139 contains an abrupt call for God to "slay the wicked" (v. 19). Then again, a number of Psalms are classified as Prophetic Judgment Oracles (e.g. Pss 12; 14; 50; 82), due to their vision of YHWH adjudicating among his assembled people. Indeed, the idea of judicial differentiation is stated succinctly in Ps 1, which bridges Wisdom and covenantal thinking: "YHWH knows the way of the righteous, but the way of the wicked will perish" (v. 6).[7]

In contrast to Proverbs, the Psalter offers various glimpses into how such selective judgment was envisaged. At one level, it could consist of the psalmist's victory over (or rescue from) his personal enemies, an interpretation suggested by those editorial superscriptions that key certain psalms to the life of David. On the other hand, Wisdom-type poems, such as Ps 1, may anticipate an eschatological judgment, either in the Messianic age or at the final resurrection.[8] In some cases, Israel's king is viewed as YHWH's agent in establishing justice (e.g. Pss 72; 101). A further clue as to *how* YHWH adjudicates was suggested by Weiser, who postulated an annual Covenant Festival of Yahweh as the Psalms' life setting.[9] This, he argued, involved a cultic re-enactment of Israel's *Heilsgeschichte*, in which YHWH's past judicial acts were appropriated and experienced afresh by those present: "Whilst the execution of Yahweh's judgment in the covenant cult signifies to the godly who are faithful to Yahweh that they will have a share in salvation…it has the opposite effect on the wicked, that is, on

---

4. O. M. T. O'Donovan, *The Desire of the Nations: Rediscovering the Roots of Political Theology* (Cambridge: Cambridge University Press, 1986), 74, referring to Ps 11: "No longer able to count on the processes of human judgment, the plaintiff appeals to the judgment-seat of Yhwh himself before whose narrowed eyes not only he, the righteous one, but also his detractor, 'the wicked one,' are reduced to singularity."

5. The term איבים is of course ambiguous, and sometimes denotes foreign nations rather than fellow Israelites (e.g. Pss 7; 9; 56; 59). See further Stephen J. L. Croft, *The Identity of the Individual in the Psalms* (JSOTSup 44; Sheffield: JSOT, 1987), 15–48; more briefly, Tyler F. Williams, s.v., איב, *NIDOTTE* 1:369, who argues that "the use of stereotypical language and a number of valid identifications makes it clear that no one identification is possible or desirable."

6. Ps 52 is sometimes classified as an Individual Lament (cf. vv. 1–4), but the dominant note appears to be one of confidence in the downfall of the wicked and the security of the righteous (vv. 5–9).

7. In Wisdom fashion, Ps 1 contrasts the two ways of the righteous and the wicked; however, the righteous man is precisely the one who meditates on the Torah of YHWH (1:2).

8. For a brief review of interpretations of the judgment in Ps 1:5, see A. A. Anderson, *The Book of Psalms*. Vol. 1, *Psalms 1–72* (NCB; London: Marshall, Morgan & Scott, 1972), 62.

9. Artur Weiser, *The Psalms: A Commentary* (trans. H. Hartwell; OTL; London: SCM, 1962), 23–52. H.-J. Kraus, *Worship in Israel: A Cultic History of the Old Testament* (Oxford: Blackwell, 1966), 136–41, 179–88, argues that the Feast of Tabernacles included several festivals, including a covenant renewal ceremony based on Josh 24.

enemies both of Yahweh and Israel and also of godly individuals."[10] Whether or not Weiser was right in his particular reconstruction of this festival, or in seeing it as the setting for "the vast majority of the individual psalms,"[11] passages such as Ps 50 demonstrate that the idea of YHWH adjudicating among his people played a significant role in Israel's worship.[12]

Before leaving the Psalms, we may note that in the process of appealing for justice, they sometimes view the various human parties through more than one interpretative paradigm. For instance, while the laments routinely employ the polarity of the righteous and the wicked, several of them also adopt the model (noted earlier in Proverbs) of the poor and the oppressor: "I know that YHWH works vindication for the oppressed (עני) and justice for the needy (אביונים)" (140:13 [12]; cf. 18:28 [27]; 35:10; 70:3–5 [2–4]; 86:1).[13] It is in fact unlikely that the writers of these psalms were themselves economically destitute.[14] Rather, the socio-economic categories of עני and אביונים provided them with a valuable hermeneutical lens. By interpreting themselves as the poor and their enemies as the oppressor, they could confidently call on YHWH to adjudicate in their favour. In a further hermeneutical move, other psalms adapt the language of older traditions in which YHWH differentiated between Israel and the nations. Thus the statement in Ps 34:8 (7) that "the angel of YHWH (מלאך יהוה) surrounds those who fear him and delivers them" recalls various salvific events in Israel's history (Exod 14:19; 23:20; 2 Sam 24:16; 2 Kgs 19:35), while the promise in Ps 37 that the righteous will possess the land (ירש ארץ, vv. 9, 11, 22, 29, 34) clearly echoes the conquest traditions. Since in both cases it is probably a post-exilic community that is being addressed, the language suggests a reinterpretation of YHWH's past judgments for a new context.[15]

Despite focussing on Israel as a community (קהל, עדה), the Pentateuchal narratives regularly portray YHWH as singling out individuals or groups for blessing or punishment.[16] A notable example occurs in the story of the golden

---

10.   Weiser, *Psalms*, 47.

11.   Ibid., 35.

12.   The belief that YHWH's judgment was mediated through the cult appears to be reflected in the Torah of Temple Entry psalms (e.g. Pss 15; 24), which call for self-examination before entering.

13.   Throughout this study, wherever chapter or verse numbers diverge between *BHS* and EVV, the latter are shown in square brackets.

14.   Indeed, in Ps 18 the persona of the author shifts to that of the king, victorious over his enemies (including other nations).

15.   According to Christopher J. H. Wright, s.v., ירש, *NIDOTTE* 2:548, "in the Psalms, it appears that the expression 'possess the land' has become virtually metaphorical for the hope of God's general blessing and vindication promised to righteous individuals within the community distinguished by their faithful obedience and humility from the wicked and oppressive, who are destined for extinction."

16.   Obviously, space precludes a comprehensive survey of the Pentateuch. Note, however, the remarks of David J. A. Clines, *The Theme of the Pentateuch* (JSOTSup 10; Sheffield: JSOT, 1978), 63–64, regarding the primeval history of Gen 1–11: "Where God's relationship with individuals is concerned, his dealing can be highly personalized (note especially the differing punishments for the three principal actors in the Fall story). But where a whole community's relationship with God is involved, the operation in justice can sometimes be undifferentiated, as in the 'Sons of God' episode, where all mankind's life-span…is shortened because of the sins of the 'Sons of God.'"

calf (Exod 32). Initially, the writer implicates all Israel in the apostasy, with the sole exception of Moses (vv. 1–6); consequently, YHWH's threat to destroy "this people" and make Moses into a great nation (vv. 9–10) constitutes a clear form of (antithetical) judicial differentiation, however asymmetrical. Later, however, a new distinction appears. Responding to Moses' call, מי ליהוה אלי (v. 26), the Levites go through the camp killing three thousand of their compatriots (vv. 27–29), thereby gaining appointment to priestly office: "You have ordained your-selves (מלאו ידכם) to YHWH today, for you were against your own sons and brothers, and he has blessed you this day" (v. 29). The shift in perspective has been well observed by Childs:

> Up until this point in the story no distinction had been made among the people. "All the people" had responded to Aaron's call for gold (v. 3) and had celebrated the worship of the calf. Consequently, "this people" as a collective entity received the divine con-demnation (v. 9). Suddenly a distinction within Israel is called for.[17]

Subsequently, when Moses offers to forfeit his life for the forgiveness of the people, YHWH refuses, emphasizing the individualism of his justice: מי אשר חטא לי אמחנו מספרי (v. 33). What is striking in this story, therefore, is the flexi-bility of its analysis of guilt and punishment. The same community of Israel is seen through different lenses, first as a single mass in opposition to YHWH/ Moses, and then in more nuanced terms. Still, elements of ambiguity remain. Had the Levites themselves participated in the earlier apostasy (as vv. 1–6 imply)? If so, their act of solidarity with Moses serves a double role, not only winning the blessing of v. 29, but also nullifying their liability to judgment. And of course, Aaron—clearly viewed by the narrator as at least partly culpable—emerges from the episode rebuked but otherwise unscathed.[18] Consequently, while the principle of selective judgment in v. 33 appears unambiguous and precise, correlating it to the preceding story is less straightforward.

The picture of YHWH exercising selective judgment in Israel emerges even more clearly in the book of Numbers. In the case of Nadab and Abihu, who are put to death for burning "unauthorized fire" before YHWH (Num 3:4; cf. Lev 10:1–2), the text illustrates what I earlier described as the single-sided model of judgment. Conversely, following the return of the twelve spies from Canaan (Num 13–14), judicial differentiation follows the more frequent antithetical pattern. Here, the people's decision to follow the majority report of the twelve spies, and not to enter the land, results in YHWH's declaration that every one of them will die in the desert, while the ten men responsible for inciting their rebellion are struck dead by plague. The faithful Joshua and Caleb, on the other hand, are not only spared the plague, but assured that they personally will enter the land (Num 14:22–35). Only in regard to the children of those who had dis-obeyed is the selectiveness of YHWH's judgment in any way qualified. Once the present adult generation had died, YHWH would indeed bring them into the land (והביאתי אתם, v. 31), but in the meantime they would "bear the unfaithfulness" of their parents (ונשאו את זנותיכם, v. 33), wandering as shepherds in the desert.

---

17. Brevard S. Childs, *Exodus: A Commentary* (OTL; London: SCM, 1974), 571.
18. On the subtle but unfavourable depiction of Aaron in this story, see ibid., 564–70.

Two other passages in Numbers deserve attention, the first occurring in ch. 16. The compositional history of this passage is complex, but as it stands it reports a challenge to the authority of Moses and Aaron by Korah, Dathan and Abiram, plus two hundred and fifty "leaders of the congregation" (v. 2).[19] The seriousness of the threat posed by their action, however, only becomes apparent from YHWH's command to Moses and Aaron in v. 21: "Separate yourselves from this congregation (העדה הזאת) so that I may consume them at once." Moses and Aaron immediately intercede: "O God, God of the spirits of all humanity, if one person sins will you be angry with the entire congregation (כל העדה)?" (v. 22). In response, YHWH isolates the three protagonists (and their families) for judgment (vv. 23–33), before consuming the 250 by fire (v. 35). As Noth remarks, "Yahweh thus makes a decision, in accordance with the objection of Moses and Aaron, in favour of 'individual requital.'"[20]

Secondly, Num 25 describes how a collective act of sexual immorality and idolatry incurs wrath against Israel (v. 3).[21] Two distinct responses follow. YHWH tells Moses to execute "the leaders of the people" (ראשי העם, v. 4) in order to divert his wrath, this group apparently being seen as representing the whole nation. Moses, for his part, instructs the judges to kill all those actively involved in the affair (v. 5). The decisive point, however, is when an Israelite man enters the camp with a Midianite woman, prompting Phinehas to follow both to their tent and drive a spear through them. In so doing, he not only halts the plague (מגפה, v. 9) that has killed 24,000 Israelites,[22] but also wins YHWH's pledge of a covenant of peace (בריתי שלום, v. 12). Within the one community of Israel, therefore, not only do we see separate acts of judgment upon the people and their leaders, but also YHWH's promise of personal blessing for one individual.

In various ways, Deuteronomy also endorses the principle of judicial selectivity. Early on, Moses recalls how Israel's rebellion at Kadesh Barnea (Deut 1:26–46; cf. Num 14) resulted in YHWH's judgment on that "evil generation"

---

19. Most scholars detect a conflation of two stories, one about Dathan and Abiram, the other about Korah. For a helpful discussion, see Eryl W. Davies, *Numbers* (NCB; London: HarperCollins, 1995), 162–68.

20. Martin Noth, *Numbers: A Commentary* (trans. James D. Martin; OTL; London: SCM, 1968), 127. My reading takes the האיש אחד / כל העדה contrast in v. 22 to be between Korah (and his followers) and the wider Israelite assembly; so Noth, *Numbers*, 127, and Gordon J. Wenham, *Numbers: An Introduction and Commentary* (TOTC; Leicester: IVP, 1981), 137 (the latter taking כל העדה as denoting "the representatives of all the nation"). Conversely, George W. Coats, *Rebellion in the Wilderness* (Nashville: Abingdon, 1968), 171–72, and Philip J. Budd, *Numbers* (WBC 5; Waco: Word, 1984), 188, see the contrast as between Korah and his followers. However, not only does כל העדה normally denote all Israel (cf. "his [= Korah's] congregation," vv. 5, 6, 11, 16), but also it is hard to see why Moses would have viewed Korah as the sole offender in this episode. Moreover, the references to the elders of Israel (v. 25) and all Israel (v. 34) implies a general gathering in vv. 21–22.

21. Again, most scholars see here two originally distinct stories, the first of which (vv. 1–5) focussed on Israel's adoption of Canaanite fertility cults, while the second (vv. 6–18) told the story of Phinehas.

22. Although a plague has not previously been mentioned, it may be implied in v. 3, ויחר אף יהוה בישראל; cf. the association of wrath (קצף) and plague (נגף) in Num 17:11.

(Deut 1:35), with the exception of Caleb and Joshua (1:36, 38) and the children "who do not yet know good and evil" (אשר לא ידעו היום טוב ורע, 1:39). Towards the end of the book, we find a litany of curses against wicked individuals (ארור + masc. sing. ptc.) pronounced on Mount Ebal (27:15–26).[23] Moreover, while Deuteronomy for the most part regards social justice as the responsibility of the Israelite community, here too it occasionally hints at the direct judicial activity of YHWH. At this point, the perspective is remarkably similar to that which we noted in Prov 22 and 23. Those denied justice may "cry to YHWH against you and YHWH will hold you guilty" (והיה בך חטא, 15:9; 24:14–15). YHWH "works justice (עשה משפט) for the orphan and the widow" (10:18). Likewise, YHWH warns that if anyone does not listen to his words as spoken by a prophet, "I myself will hold him accountable" (אנכי אדרש מעמו, 18:18–19). As in Proverbs, exactly how these selective judicial actions will be performed is not said.

Finally, we may highlight three passages in the Former Prophets, usually seen as either written or shaped by the Deuteronomistic editor, which depict varied modes of judicial differentiation in Israel. The first occurs in the prophetic oracle against Eli (1 Sam 2:27–36; cf. 3:12–14). After affirming as a general principle that "those who honour me I will honour but those who despise me will be of little account" (v. 30), YHWH's announcement of judgment sharply distinguishes between Eli's house and the nation: "Good will be done (ייטיב) to Israel but there will never be an old man in your house all the days" (v. 32).[24] The polarity here, of course, is clearly antithetical. Conversely, 2 Kings describes the contrasting responses of Ahaziah and Hezekiah to personal suffering. The decision of the former to consult Baal-Zebub, rather than YHWH, incurs his death-sentence (2 Kgs 1:16–17), whereas the latter's humble prayer results in healing (2 Kgs 20:1–7). In both cases, YHWH's judicial action follows the single-sided model, being directed solely towards the individual concerned.

In summary, the belief that YHWH exercises selective judgment finds widespread support in the Old Testament. The basic concept can be expressed within diverse theological frameworks (e.g. Wisdom, Covenantal), literary genres, putative sources and social contexts, and in a variety of modes. Broadly speaking, the rationale for YHWH's action may be framed either in terms of the righteous and the wicked (variously understood) or of the poor and their oppressors. Two further points may be underlined. First, we have seen that more than one judicial polarity can operate in the same passage (Exod 32; Num 25). In other words, the lines demarcating the wicked from the righteous can be drawn in different ways within a very small biblical unit. Secondly, textual affirmations of selectivity are not always perfectly assimilated with other elements in the text. Thus, both

23. Robert P. Gordon, "Curse, Malediction," *NIDOTTE* 4:491–93 (492), notes that "even where the reference is not explicit, an implied appeal to divine authority can often be assumed."

24. The use of יטב Hiph. (plus accusative) to describe YHWH's good purposes for Israel is characteristic of the Deuteronomistic texts; see Deut 8:16; 28:63; 30:5; Jer 18:10; Zech 8:15. H.W. Hertzberg, *I and II Samuel. A Commentary* (trans. J. S. Bowden; OTL; London: SCM, 1964), 38, sees here "a speech constructed by the deuteronomistic compiler which describes the downfall of the sons of Eli to the advantage of the Zadokite priesthood."

Exod 32 and 1 Sam 2 contain quasi-formulaic statements of individual responsibility (Exod 32:33; 1 Sam 2:30); yet in the former passage Aaron is curiously
exempt from punishment, while the latter predicts disaster for Eli's descendants.
With more self-awareness, perhaps, Num 14:31–33 concedes that the children
will suffer for the disobedience of their parents. These qualifying elements are
discrete, but they indicate that the (textual) worlds created by their authors were
more complex than any one formulation of judicial selectivity.

2.2. *Judgment and Salvation as Unselective*

Having seen how several quite diverse strands of the Old Testament portray
YHWH as judging selectively, we can now consider the textual witness to the
contrary, that is, cases where his wrath affects a group wider than that which has
been indicted for an offence. The *threat* of such a scenario has, of course,
already emerged in Num 16:21–22, where Moses' and Aaron's intercession is
prompted by YHWH's threat to destroy the rest of the community. However,
leaving aside for now the Prophetic literature, how far does the Old Testament
represent YHWH as implementing such indiscriminate judgment?

The counter-testimonial nature of such an idea naturally points us to the book
of Job.[25] Here, the orthodox position is voiced by Bildad: "Surely God does not
reject a blameless person (תם) or strengthen the hand of the wicked" (מרעים,
8:20). Job initially accepts this, at least in theory (9:1), but appears to see sheer
power, rather than justice, as God's chief activity. Consequently, even though
he is blameless (תם אני, v. 21), he will never receive a hearing. From this, Job
moves to an explicit rejection of the idea of judicial selectivity. Human conduct
is immaterial (אחת היא), in that YHWH "destroys both the blameless and the
wicked" (תם ורשע הוא מכלה, v. 22). The realities of natural disaster (v. 23) and
social injustice (v. 24) prove the point, given Job's double premise that both
inflict suffering on the blameless (which is incontestable) and that both are the
work of God—any denial of which must face his final gauntlet, "If it is not he,
then who is it?" (אם לא אפוא מי הוא, v. 24). Job here affirms clearly enough the
principle of unselective judgment. The status of this affirmation within the book
as a whole, however, is much less clear, since it may not represent Job's final
perspective (cf. 42:5–6) or that of the narrator.

At the outer theological margins of the Old Testament, Qoheleth's concept of
God's judicial activity is characteristically elusive. On the one hand, he appears
to affirm the orthodox *credo*: "God will judge both the righteous and the
wicked" (3:16 [17]; similarly 8:12–13; 11:9; 12:14).[26] Alongside these statements, however, Qoheleth offers a counter-creed based on empirical reality.
There is no one to comfort the oppressed (4:1), and longevity bears no relation
to righteousness (7:15; cf. 8:14). Indeed, the ultimate reality of death envelops
everyone: "To all one destiny (מקרה אחד)—the righteous and the wicked, the

---

25.   For the use of "testimony" and "counter-testimony" as a hermeneutical model for exploring
the Old Testament, see Brueggemann, *Old Testament Theology*, xvi–xvii.

26.   The editorial epilogue of 12:9–14 is widely seen as giving the book a more orthodox gloss.
Yet it is hard to see in 12:14 anything that has not been said already.

good and the bad, the clean and the unclean, those who offer sacrifices and those who do not... One destiny to all" (9:2–3; cf. 2:14, 15; 3:19). The words here echo those of Job, but with a crucial difference; "destiny" has replaced the active retribution of YHWH. That is to say, Qoheleth's counter-creed is not so much one of indiscriminate judgment, but rather one of no judgment at all.[27] The picture would of course be different if it could be established that Qoheleth believed in some form of adjudication after death, but such an outlook is at best unproven.[28] Whether it is possible to synthesize these affirmations of Qoheleth is doubtful, though it is probably too simplistic to regard the more orthodox statements as merely ironic.[29] Fox gives perhaps the best statement of the matter: "Qohelet sees the tension as a clash between two truths, neither of which he dismisses or ascribes to another form of wisdom. Nor does he reconcile the tension by abandoning belief in divine justice or by embracing a theodicy... Qohelet does not choose any way out."[30]

Closer to the theological mainstream of the Old Testament, the idea of non-selective judgment is often linked to passages exhibiting the concept of collective liability. As Eichrodt puts it, "that for the sin of the individual not only he himself but also his family and clan—and, if he occupies an exalted position, then also his tribe and his nation—must be liable is a view understandable on the basis of the strong collective sense of the early period."[31] In fact, we have already seen this principle illustrated in regard to the families of Korah, Dathan and Abiram (Num 16) and the house of Eli (1 Sam 2:31–36). Elsewhere in the Former Prophets, disobedience on the part of a king frequently incurs judgment

27.   Deryck Sheriffs, *The Friendship of the Lord: An Old Testament Spirituality* (Carlisle: Paternoster, 1996), 184–85, contrasts the observations of Eccl 4:1–3; 7:15 and 8:14, where social injustice goes unchecked, with the promises of Prov 22:22–23 and 23:10–11.

28.   Michael A. Eaton, *Ecclesiastes: An Introduction and Commentary* (TOTC; Leicester: IVP, 1983), 84, takes the final שם of 3:16 to denote an afterlife setting for the judgment described in the first part of the verse. Robert Gordis, *Koheleth—The Man and His World: A Study of Ecclesiastes* (New York: Schocken, 1968), 235, also sees here an allusion to judgment after death, but argues that Qoheleth is in fact satirizing such an idea. However, his paraphrase—"There is a time for every event and every deed—over there!"—implies an ironic attitude towards justice in *this* life, rather than in the next. According to Michael V. Fox, *A Time to Tear Down and a Time to Build: A Rereading of Ecclesiastes* (Grand Rapids: Eerdmans, 1999), 215, "Qohelet does not have enough of a belief in judgement after death to say that there is a time for 'everything' in the afterlife." However, "the sentence affirms a time of judgement for all deeds" (216).

29.   The idea that Qoheleth cites traditional proverbs primarily in order to refute them was advanced by Gordis, *Koheleth*, 95–108. Others regard Qoheleth as conducting a more subtle "Yes, but" dialogue with Wisdom; see, e.g., J. Loader, *Polar Structures in the Book of Qoheleth* (BZAW 152; Berlin: de Gruyter, 1979); Roland E. Murphy, *Ecclesiastes* (WBC 23A; Dallas: Word, 1992), lxiii–lxiv, 22. Both approaches are criticized by Fox, *Rereading*, 15–26.

30.   Fox, *Rereading*, 68. Similarly, replying to the view of James L. Crenshaw, *A Whirlpool of Torment: Israelite Traditions of God as an Oppressive Presence* (OBT; Philadelphia: Fortress, 1984), 91, that "it was Qoheleth's special burden to be unable to believe in divine justice," Sheriffs, *Friendship of the Lord*, 180 n. 2, states that this "eliminates a tension in the book...that we must retain as a characteristic of this work."

31.   Eichrodt, *Theology*, 2:429. The story of Achan (Josh 7) is of course often seen as the parade example of the idea of collective liability; I will return to this later.

on his dynasty. Following Solomon's apostasy (1 Kgs 11:1–8), YHWH declares that he will tear the kingdom "out of the hand of your son" (v. 12).[32] Judgment oracles are also delivered against the houses of Jeroboam (1 Kgs 14:10–16), Baasha (1 Kgs 16:1–4) and Ahab (1 Kgs 21:21–22; 2 Kgs 9:8–9).[33] Especially striking is the prophecy that even Jeroboam's son Abijah—"in whom YHWH, the God of Israel, has found something good (דבר טוב)"—will also die (1 Kgs 14:12–13). At this point, however, the text moves to limit the undifferentiating nature of the judicial action. Precisely because of Abijah's goodness, "all Israel will mourn for him and bury him; he is the only one (זה לבדו) belonging to Jeroboam who will have a burial" (v. 13). Thus, although YHWH's death sentence here carries no exemptions, in the matter of burial and lament an element of selectivity is retained, apparently based on the moral quality of the individuals concerned.[34]

Two other passages which imply some form of undifferentiated judgment form a balancing pair in the Samuel Appendix of 2 Sam 21–24,[35] where they both depict situations of natural disorder in Israel. In the first (21:1–14), a three year famine prompts David to seek YHWH regarding its cause. In one sense, the answer is clear: "It is because of Saul and his blood-stained house; it is because he killed the Gibeonites" (v. 1). Since no further direction is given as to how to remedy the situation, David asks the surviving Gibeonites what he should do "so that you will bless YHWH's inheritance" (וברכו את נחלת יהוה, v. 3). In the events that follow, the narrator's perspective remains opaque. David's decision to hand over seven sons of Saul to be killed (vv. 7–9a) triggers the resumption of harvest and rain (vv. 9b–10); yet it is only after he has recovered the bones of Saul and Jonathan from Jabesh-gilead, plus those of the seven sons, and given them proper burial (vv. 11–13), that we are explicitly told of the restoration of divine favour on the land (ויעתר אלהים לארץ אחרי כן, v. 14). The underlying assumptions in the text are elusive, but they seem to reflect the view, found elsewhere in

---

32.   Later in 1 Kgs 11, when Jeroboam is told that he will rule the ten tribes, MT relates YHWH's action to the apostasy of Israel as a whole: יען אשר עזבוני וישתחוו לעשתרת...ולא הלכו בדרכי (v. 33). In LXX and the other ancient versions, however, the verbs are third person singular; that this probably reflects the earlier reading is supported by the concluding words in MT, כדוד אביו, "like David his father."

33.   In the case of Jeroboam and Ahab, it is added that YHWH will cut off משתין בקיר עצור ועזוב בישראל, "he who urinates against a wall, slave and free in Israel" (1 Kgs 14:10; 21:21; 2 Kgs 9:8). However, the context precludes a reference to the entire male population. On the cryptic expression עצור ועזוב, see John Gray, *I and II Kings: A Commentary* (OTL; London: SCM, 1964), 307–8, and Simon J. DeVries, *1 Kings* (WBC 12; Waco: Word, 1985), 179; the latter takes it to mean "helpless and abandoned."

34.   The significance of this promise should not be overlooked; proper burial and mourning (or the lack of it) were indicative of the honour placed upon the person concerned, and were greatly desired. Cf. the response of the prophet of Bethel to the death of the "man of God" (1 Kgs 13:30–31), Jeremiah's promise to Zedekiah (Jer 34:5) and, conversely, his judgment oracle on Jehoiakim (Jer 22:18).

35.   On the unity of this section, see Brevard S. Childs, *Introduction to the Old Testament as Scripture* (London: SCM, 1979), 273–75; Robert P. Gordon, *1 and 2 Samuel: A Commentary* (Exeter: Paternoster, 1986), 45.

the Old Testament, that Yʜᴡʜ, land and people stand in symbiotic relation-ship.[36] Consequently, how we interpret the correlation of sin, judgment and guilt in this passage needs to be carefully nuanced. Nowhere is the famine said to have been directly sent by Yʜᴡʜ. Rather, *under* Yʜᴡʜ (since it is his נחלה, and he hears prayer concerning it), the land responds both to human violence (v. 1) and human blessing (v. 3). When it does so, all its inhabitants are naturally affected.

By contrast, in the counterbalancing story in 2 Sam 24 Israel experiences calamity directly at the hands of Yʜᴡʜ, following David's sin—however we understand this—of conducting a census (vv. 2–9). Presented with the choice of famine, fleeing from his enemies, or plague (v. 13), David opts for the last, with the result that 70,000 people "from Dan to Beersheba" (v. 15) die. As Jerusalem is about to be destroyed, Yʜᴡʜ relents (וינחם, v. 16), on the grounds that the disaster already inflicted is sufficient (רב). However, the prayer of David that follows reveals a highly personalized concept of guilt and punishment: "'I am the one who has sinned and done wrong. These are sheep—what have they done? Let your hand be against me and my family'" (v. 17).

Both these passages, therefore, depict situations in which all Israel suffers natural calamity as a result of the guilt of one person. Although in the first of them Yʜᴡʜ's judicial role is somewhat elusive and indirect, in the second it is quite unambiguous; indeed, David's prayer emphasizes the point.

We have thus looked at a number of passages that might be thought to affirm a non-selective dimension to Yʜᴡʜ's judicial action. In the case of Qoheleth, I have argued, the counter-creed is one of no justice rather than rough justice. Job certainly indicts God for destroying people indiscriminately, but the status of this claim in the wider framework of the book is uncertain. Clearer testimony to the idea of non-selective judgment emerges in oracles against the families of culpable individuals, though in the case of Jeroboam this is mitigated by the promise concerning Abijah. Finally, two passages in 2 Sam 21–24 depict indi-vidual sin leading to famine and plague across the land. In the first, however, Yʜᴡʜ's involvement appears to be more indirect, while in the second he relents and David protests (in that order). In short, the idea of undifferentiated judgment is far less prevalent in the Old Testament than that of selective judgment. Where it does appear, some sort of qualification or question is often placed against it.

2.3. *Judgment and Salvation as National*
In addition to these two interpretations of Yʜᴡʜ's judicial action, that is, as selective and as unselective, certain parts of the Old Testament also offer a third

---

36. E.g. Gen 4:11; Job 31:38–40. On this idea, see especially H. Wheeler Robinson, *Inspiration and Revelation in the Old Testament* (Oxford: Oxford University Press, 1946), 1–48. According to Robinson, "nature is alive through and through, and therefore the more capable of sympathy with man, and of response to the rule of its Creator and upholder, on whom it directly depends" (p. 16). Similar ideas have been traced in the Exodus plague narrative by Terence E. Fretheim, "The Plagues as Ecological Signs of Historical Disaster," *JBL* 110 (1991): 385–96, and in Jeremiah by Norman C. Habel, *The Land is Mine* (Minneapolis: Fortress, 1995), 75–91.

perspective, which can best be described as *national, but not unselective*. The basis of this lies in a particular vision of Israel found especially within the book of Deuteronomy.

I noted earlier how Deuteronomy occasionally envisages Israel as a mixed community, comprising obedient and disobedient alike (e.g. especially Deut 27:15–26).[37] More typically, however, the book operates with a strongly unified concept of Israel, corporately personified as YHWH's son (8:5; 32:6) and inheritance (נחלה, 4:20; 9:26, 29).[38] As a single people they are addressed and called to respond (4:1–40; 5:1, 32–33; 6:1–25, etc.), and as a single people they will prosper (15:4–6) or be destroyed (7:4; 8:19–20). It is tempting, perhaps, to regard this vision as a natural (or even necessary) corollary of the Sinai covenant (5:2–33),[39] in which YHWH is Israel's undifferentiated partner (6:4), and the land is the undifferentiated inheritance of both. Such an extrapolation, however, would be inferential rather than exegetical.

The all-Israel paradigm finds its classic expression in Deut 28, where vv. 1–14 set out the blessings for obedience, and vv. 15–68 the curses for disobedience. Two points deserve note. First, throughout the chapter Israel is envisaged as acting *in unison*; nowhere is the prospect raised of some obeying and others disobeying. Secondly, almost all the blessings and curses are related either to land fertility (rain, harvest, drought, etc.) or to land security (peace, war, invasion, etc.), and are therefore almost *inescapably* national in character. Similar promises and warnings relating to the fruitfulness and tenure of the land occur elsewhere in the book (4:25–27; 6:3, 15; 7:12–15; 11:13–17).

Consequently, although YHWH's acts of blessing or judgment pertain to all Israel, from Deuteronomy's perspective they are neither selective nor unselective, since the whole nation is either obedient or disobedient. To be sure, disobedience by individuals or small groups is anticipated (13:1–18; 17:2–7; 21:18–21, etc.), but in such cases it is usually the community which exercises retribution, rather than YHWH himself. Indeed, by decisively punishing such acts, Israel demonstrates its coherence and unity; especially significant is the exhortation to "burn out the evil from among you" (13:6; 17:7, 12; 19:13, etc.).[40] Conversely, while several passages anticipate rebellion from Israel *as a whole* (8:12–20; 28:15; 31:16–21, etc.), none of them entertain the prospect of individuals or

---

37. At a rhetorical level, of course, the structure of the book sets Moses apart from the rest of the nation, and the sense of disparity is reinforced by their contrasting dispositions towards YHWH— a point underlined when Moses recounts the story of the golden calf (Deut 9:7–21; cf. Exod 32).

38. J. G. McConville, *Deuteronomy* (AOTC; Leicester: IVP/Apollos, 2002), 155, refers to "Deuteronomy's idea of the whole people as an integrated entity before God." The well-known alternation of singular and plural address in the book does not affect this point.

39. From an extensive literature on this topic, see especially E. W. Nicholson, *God and His People: Covenant and Theology in the Old Testament* (Oxford: Clarendon, 1986); William J. Dumbrell, *Covenant and Creation: A Theology of the Old Testament Covenants* (BTCL; Carlisle: Paternoster, 1997), 80–126.

40. On Deut 13:5, see McConville, *Deuteronomy*, 238, who states: "The threat to the solidarity of Israel in the present case has as its background the concept of a united covenant people... This being so, rebellion (even of a few) strikes at the heart of the true nature of Israel."

small groups remaining faithful to YHWH. In short, the all-Israel paradigm represented in much of Deuteronomy inevitably results in a concept of national but not indiscriminate judgment.

This distinctive perspective is reflected elsewhere in the Deuteronomistic History (DtrH). The paradigmatic sermons of Joshua (Josh 23–24) and Samuel (1 Sam 12) set out two alternative paths: Israel will either obey or disobey (with the corresponding response from YHWH). Similarly, the editor of Judges describes the people's apostasy and punishment (Judg 2:10–19) as all-inclusive acts. Somewhat more complex is the picture in the book of Kings. Though ultimately concerned with the judgment of exile on the *people* of Israel and Judah, the narrative leading up to these events focuses on their *leaders*.[41] Nevertheless, here too disobedience and judgment are both conceived in national terms. Israel is banished because their kings "walked in the way of Jeroboam *and the sin which he caused Israel to commit*" (וּבְחַטֹּאתוֹ אֲשֶׁר הֶחֱטִיא אֶת יִשְׂרָאֵל, 1 Kgs 15:26, 34; 16:19, 26, etc.), the phrase implying that leader and people together were culpable. This is made explicit in 2 Kgs 13:6, and reiterated at length in the editorial review of 2 Kgs 17:7–23. As far as judgment on Judah is concerned, the decisive factor is the idolatry and bloodshed committed by Manasseh (2 Kgs 21:1–16; 23:26–27), but here too the text unambiguously implicates the whole nation (2 Kgs 21:9).[42] Taken as a whole, the book of Kings appears to offer a dual perspective, in which the sin and judgment of the people is epitomized by the sin and judgment of their rulers.[43]

Within the Old Testament, this concept of Israel—acting and being judged as one—emerges first in Deuteronomy. As we have seen, earlier sections of the Pentateuch, while aware of the people's propensity for apostasy, regularly highlight faithful exceptions. Since Deuteronomy's more unified model of Israel continues into DtrH, we might regard it as 'Deuteronomistic'—were it not for the fact that other passages which are regularly ascribed to the Deuteronomist (e.g. 1 Sam 2:27–36; 2 Kgs 1:16–17; 20:1–7) allow for a more pluralistic view of the nation. It thus seems preferable to regard this all-Israel vision as *one* aspect of Deuteronomistic thought. Likewise, although it is clearly not unconnected with the Sinai covenant, the fact that Exodus and Numbers depict a more diverse community precludes us designating it "covenantal" *per se*. In fact, these different models of Israel may be shaped more by two other factors; Israel's relationship to the land on the one hand, and the end-point perspective of the respective texts on the other. In Exodus–Numbers, Israel is a journeying community, moving towards the moment of entry into the land. Such a frame of

41. This shift of focus away from "the people" in Kings is in striking contrast to Numbers and Deuteronomy.

42. McConville, *Deuteronomy*, 127, sees 2 Kgs 23:26–27 as "the closest approximation to the principle of an extended, and thus undeserved, retribution," but adds that "those who fell to Babylon are shown to have actually participated in the guilt." Cf. the sweeping indictment of Judah's sin in 1 Kgs 14:22–24.

43. Iain W. Provan, *1 and 2 Kings* (NIBC; Carlisle: Paternoster, 1995), 95, notes how "in the book of Kings, kings are characteristically models for and representative of the behaviour of their subjects."

reference readily permits a pluralistic concept of Israel, a generation of which has perished *en route*. In Deuteronomy and DtrH, by contrast, a new trajectory begins which will culminate in exile.[44] However, since Israel's identity is now tied to the land, internal differentiation is less possible, and land-loss inevitably means the end of the entire nation.[45]

2.4. *Perspectives in Conflict: Three Case Studies*

So far, then, we have identified three broad perspectives within the Old Testament concerning the way in which YHWH exercises judgment in Israel. I have termed them "selective," "unselective" and "national" interpretations. We have also noticed that more than one of these may be represented within the same book or (presumed) editorial strand. In order to illustrate further the potential for diversity within the Old Testament in its analysis of divine judgment, I will conclude this section by looking at three cases in which the same incident is viewed through more than one of these three perspectives.

In the first place, we may consider the well-known story of Achan (Josh 7), whose theft of items that were under the *ḥērem* brings disaster upon the entire nation. Here, it is vital to note that the very brief report of Achan's action is sandwiched between the statements that "the Israelites acted unfaithfully (וימעלו בני ישראל מעל)...so YHWH's anger burned against Israel" (v. 1). This analysis is later reiterated at length by YHWH, a series of plural verbs emphasizing the point: חטא ישראל וגם עברו את בריתי...וגם לקחו מן החרם וגם גנבו וגם כחשו וגם שמו בכליהם (v. 11). Nowhere, of course, does the narrator *explain* this indictment of the entire community.[46] Granted his perspective, however, Israel's rout by the men of Ai (vv. 3–5) is only to be expected. That is to say, Josh 7 appears to adopt the national view of judgment that we found in Deuteronomy and other parts of DtrH. Later in the book, however, a different perspective is articulated, when the Israelites confront the eastern tribes for erecting an altar by the Jordan: "Did not Achan son of Zerah act unfaithfully (הלוא עכן בן זרח מעל מעל)... Did not wrath come upon the whole community, and was he the only one who died for his sin?" (22:20). Particularly significant here is the substitution of Achan

---

44. In one sense, Clines, *Theme of the Pentateuch*, 53, is right to say of both Numbers and Deuteronomy that "their orientation and movement is towards the land, the promise of which is—by the end of these books—partly and proleptically fulfilled, but to a large extent unfulfilled." Nevertheless, it is clear that Deuteronomy looks beyond entry into the land in a way that the preceding books do not. See further Walter Brueggemann, *The Land: Place as Gift, Promise and Challenge in Biblical Faith* (OBT; Philadelphia: Fortress, 1977), 45–70 (Chapter 4, "Reflections at the Boundary").

45. "Given its intimate relationship to both Yahweh and Israel (described, e.g., as the 'inheritance' of both), the land functions as a midterm in the relationship between them."—Christopher J. H. Wright, s.v., ארץ, *NIDOTTE* 1:523.

46. Cf. Eichrodt, *Theology*, 2:429 n. 4, states: "It would be short-sighted to discover in this close connection of the individual with the community simply evidence of a low level of moral thinking...the members of a family or clan are far more seriously induced to watch over each other, and to bring the erring back to the right path, if they know that they will all be held responsible together for the offence of a fellow member of the group... On the other hand, however, it cannot be denied that at this stage the right relationship between the community and the individual person has not yet been discovered."

for Israel as the subject of מעל. The book of Joshua, therefore, presents two responses to the disaster that befell Israel following the sin of Achan. One insists that the whole nation was culpable, while the other concludes that wrath fell on the entire community (כל עדת ישראל) for the sin of one man (איש אחד). The story of Achan thus generates both national and unselective interpretations of YHWH's judicial action.

Divergent interpretations of a single issue also emerge in Deuteronomy, in regard to the question (of some importance in the book) as to why Moses himself will not enter the land. Three times in the opening chapters Moses explains that this is because YHWH was angry with him on account of the people (בגללכם, 1:37; למענכם, 3:26; על דבריכם, 4:21). Uniquely within Deuteronomy, these verses clearly imply an unselective aspect to YHWH's judicial decision.[47] At the end of the book, however, Moses highlights his own culpability by recalling YHWH's anger with him at Meribah Kadesh (32:50–52; cf. Num 20:1–13): "Because you broke faith with me...because you did not sanctify me" (על אשר מעלתם בי...אשר לא קדשתם אותי, v. 51). Consequently, alongside Deuteronomy's governing model of national judgment for a unified nation, its subtext relating to Moses' non-entry into Canaan reveals both selective and unselective notions of judgment. We may recall at this point how, in Exod 32:33, YHWH explicitly refused Moses' request to substitute his life for that of the people on the grounds that "he who sins against me I will erase from my book."

Thirdly, a brief but significant passage near the end of Deuteronomy (29:17–20 [18–21]) strikingly combines selective and national concepts of judgment. Having reminded the people of the idolatry of the nations through which they had passed, Moses sounds a note of warning: "Lest there is among you a man or woman, clan or tribe, whose heart turns aside this day from YHWH our God to worship the gods of the nations; lest there is among you a bitter root of poison and bitterness" (v. 17 [18]). This person may think the covenant guarantees his personal wellbeing: "It will be well with me even though I live in the stubbornness of my heart" (שלום יהיה לי כי בשררות לבי אלך, v. 18 [19]).[48] Such presumption will be severely punished by YHWH (v. 19 [20]): He will "never be willing to forgive him" (לא יאבה יהוה סלח לו); his wrath will burn against "that man" (באיש ההוא); he will "blot out his name" (ומחה יהוה את שמו) from under heaven. Most notably, YHWH "will single him out (בדל, Hiph.) from all the tribes of Israel for disaster" (v. 20 [21]). A clearer affirmation of selective judgment would be hard to imagine.[49]

---

47. According to McConville, *Deuteronomy*, 71, there is in Deuteronomy "no very specific reason for the exclusion, beyond a kind of solidarity with the people, who have deserved it"; similarly Peter C. Craigie, *The Book of Deuteronomy* (NICOT; Grand Rapids: Eerdmans, 1976), 105.

48. This translation of שררות is implied by the immediate context and the usage of the term elsewhere; so Craigie, *Deuteronomy*, 355; S. R. Driver, *A Critical and Exegetical Commentary on Deuteronomy* (ICC; Edinburgh: T. & T. Clark, 1895), 325; Michael A. Grisanti, s.v., שרירות, *NIDOTTE* 4:254. An alternative rendition as "self-reliance, resoluteness" is suggested by A. Spencer, "שרירות as Self-Reliance," *JBL* 100 (1981): 247–48; it is also accepted here by McConville, *Deuteronomy*, 412.

49. So Eichrodt, *Theology*, 2:440, who thus judged these verses a late addition.

Yet the passage reveals a more complex situation. The very fact that this solemn warning is addressed to the nation (note the double פֶּן יֵשׁ בָּכֶם of v. 17 [18]) implies that the presence of a wicked individual or tribe may have wider repercussions, while in the same verse the imagery of "a root bearing poison and wormwood" (שֹׁרֶשׁ פֹּרֶה רֹאשׁ וְלַעֲנָה) leaves little doubt as to the potential infective influence of such people on the community.[50] Consequently, the most likely meaning of the proverbial conclusion to v. 18 [19], "so as to sweep away the moist [ground] with the dry" (לְמַעַן סְפוֹת הָרָוָה אֶת הַצְּמֵאָה), is that the sin of one will bring judgment on all.[51] What is less clear is whether individual apostasy *by itself* incurs YHWH's wrath on the nation (thus implying unselective judgment), or does so only by first corrupting it and making it liable to judgment.[52] The metaphor of "poison" in v. 17 (18), however, rather points in the latter direction. In addition, the scenario at the end of v. 18 (19) may presuppose that all Israel is culpable, inasmuch as it has failed to prevent apostasy from taking root. Taken as a whole, therefore, the passage affirms that YHWH may single out an individual for wrath, while retaining the vision of national judgment for national guilt.

2.5. *Conclusions*

So far, I have concentrated on how YHWH's judicial action is interpreted in the Torah and the Writings. Three distinct interpretations of judgment have been identified, which I have termed selective, unselective and national. Of these, the first has been found to be the most frequent and widespread.

In the process, the present study has highlighted the significance of metaphor and model in shaping the way in which the text interprets YHWH's exercise of judgment. Thus, language from the exodus and conquest which originally served to differentiate Israel from the nations is used to distinguish pious and impious communities within post-exilic Judah, while the "the poor and the oppressed" becomes a lens through which to appeal for justice against personal enemies. In Deuteronomy and DtrH, a unitary model of the nation (itself shaped by other factors) naturally yields a national conception of sin and judgment; on the other hand, in 1 Sam 21 a quasi-psychical relationship of YHWH, land and people results in judgment taking on an unselective dimension.

Moreover, we have seen how conflicting analyses of YHWH's judicial action may be juxtaposed. Where, for example, a single passage affirms the principle of selective judgment, it may still offer more than one delineation of the culpable and the innocent. Even more striking are cases in which a small textual unit, or a larger unit dealing with the same subject, combines selective, non-selective and

---

50. Craigie, *Deuteronomy*, 358.
51. So ibid., 358; Driver, *Deuteronomy*, 325. Alternatively, McConville, *Deuteronomy*, 412, renders the phrase "so that plenty of water may put an end to drought"; this, he argues, expresses the man's optimism concerning his preferred fertility religion. The more usual reading seems preferable, however, and even McConville admits that "the immediate context contains two somewhat contrasting ideas" (p. 417).
52. This question is noted (though not answered) by Driver, *Deuteronomy*, 325.

national interpretations of judgment. Such juxtaposition of ideas may suggest a degree of intentionality—or an inability to synthesize every aspect of the material.

3. *Judgment and Salvation in the Prophetic Corpus*

3.1. *National Judgment in the Prophets*

Having explored the idea of divine retribution in the Law and the Writings, we can now turn to consider how this issue is understood in the prophetic literature. Naturally, due account must be taken of the diversity of this corpus, both in its authorship and historical context. Nevertheless, it is fair to say that the dominant impression of YHWH's judicial action in the prophets is its sweeping, comprehensive character. Whether the vision is one of retribution or restoration, its scope embraces all Israel. Indeed, this observation provides the starting point for Klaus Koenen's important study of the subject:

> Die klassischen Propheten Israels sehen das Volk als Einheit. Die Gerichtsprophetie kündet dem Volk Jahwes mit allem ihr zur Verfügung stehenden Sprachgewalt den Untergang an. Selbst wenn in den Anklagereden nur das Verhalten einzelner Exponenten oder Gruppen des Volkes, besonders der Oberschicht, angeprangert wird, gilt die Unheilsankündigung doch letztlich dem ganzen Volk... Auf der anderen Seite gelten auch die Heilsankündigungen—man denke an Hosea wie an Deuterojesaja—dem ganzen Volk. Den Propheten geht es nicht um ein individuelles, den jeweiligen Taten entsprechendes Ergehen, sondern um die Zukunft, die das Volk als Ganzes trifft.[53]

I will return to discuss Koenen's work in more detail shortly. For now, a small sample of texts will serve to corroborate his observation concerning the prophetic emphasis on "the people as a whole." In the eighth century, Amos predicted the collapse of the northern kingdom,[54] with the wry assurance that "as a shepherd saves from the lion's mouth two legs or a piece of an ear, so will the Israelites be saved" (Amos 3:12). The severity of the tone intensifies when YHWH calls for the pillar of the sanctuary to be brought down "on the heads of all the people":

> Those who are left I will kill with the sword;
> > no fugitive among them will flee,
> > no refugee among them will escape.
> If they dig down to Sheol,
> > from there my hand will take them...
> If they go into exile pursued by their enemies,
> > from there I will command the sword to kill them. (Amos 9:1–4)

---

53. Klaus Koenen, *Heil den Gerechten—Unheil den Sündern! Ein Beitrag zur Theologie der Prophetenbücher* (BZAW 229; Berlin: de Gruyter, 1994), 1–2. Koenen adds that this emphasis on "the people as a whole" is largely peculiar to the prophets; the legal, cultic and wisdom traditions show far more interest in the conduct of the individual, and its consequences for that individual.

54. According to Hans Walter Wolff, *Joel and Amos: A Commentary on the Books of the Prophets Joel and Amos* (trans. W. Janzen; Hermeneia; Philadelphia: Fortress, 1977), 105, Amos' idea of *national* disaster is "the provocatively new dimension in his message. The older maledictions did not dare express this, even conditionally, for Israel as a whole." See too Klaus Koch, *The Prophets*. Vol. 1, *The Assyrian Period* (trans. Margaret Kohl; London: SCM, 1982), 41.

Likewise, following Isaiah's commission as a prophet (Isa 6:1–10), 6:11–12 YHWH warns him that there can be no salvation for Judah:

> Until the cities lie in ruins,
>   without inhabitant,
> and the houses are unoccupied,
>   and the fields ruined and devastated,
> and YHWH has sent everyone far away
>   and the land is utterly desolate.

As the last two passages suggest, military aggression by foreign nations is the most characteristic mode of judgment in the prophets, whether the scenario envisaged is simply invasion (e.g. Isa 8:6–8; Jer 1:14–16; Hab 1:5–11) or invasion culminating in exile (e.g. Jer 10:17–18; Amos 6:7; Mic 1:8–16). The totality of such disaster is well encapsulated in the "sword, famine and plague" motif of Jeremiah and Ezekiel (Jer 14:12–13; Ezek 6:11–12, etc). At other times, divine wrath is expressed through natural disorder; several passages (Jer 3:3; 12:4; 14:2–6; 23:10; Hos 4:3)[55] describe a drought in the land, causing both human and ecological suffering, while Joel (1:2–20) graphically depicts the catastrophe inflicted by a plague of locusts. Either way, the entire land and the entire population are affected.[56]

As the above citation from Koenen indicates, the same all-inclusive rhetoric also applies to many of the prophetic oracles of salvation. Numerous passages announce God's mercy and restoration for the nation as a whole, whether personified as an individual (Isa 12:1–3) or seen as made up of diverse groups (Jer 31:8–9). The concluding verse of Amos, 9:14, may be taken as representative:

> I will restore the fortunes of my people Israel;
>   they will rebuild the ruined cities and live in them.
> They will plant vineyards and drink their wine;
>   they will make gardens and eat their fruit.
> I will plant them in their own land,
>   and they will never again be uprooted from the land I have given them.

Allowing for the cursory nature of this overview, we may nevertheless provisionally accept Koenen's claim that the prophets typically portray judgment

---

55. Here again, ecological disorder may be depicted as nature's own response to human evil. Concerning Hos 4:1–3, Hans Walter Wolff, *Hosea: A Commentary on the Book of the Prophet Hosea* (trans. Gary Stansell; Hermeneia; Philadelphia: Fortress, 1974), 68, writes: "It is noticeable that the judgment results not from the direct actions of Yahweh himself, but from an 'organic structure of order,' 'a sphere in which one's actions have fateful consequences,' which Yahweh puts into effect." Similarly, Brueggemann, *Old Testament Theology*, 541–42, sees here "a second form of curse, in which creation by itself turns deathly (without the disruptive agency of Yahweh) in response to recalcitrance, abuse, disobedience, and oppression. That is, the uncompromising requirements of creation are self-actualizing in their sanctions."

56. A notable exception occurs in Amos 4:7: "I sent rain on one town, but on another I sent no rain. One field had rain; the field that had no rain dried up." The context suggests, however, that this selective action was (as in Goshen) revelatory rather than judicial; such unusual phenomena, like the withholding of rain three months before harvest, were intended to rouse Israel to repentance.

and salvation as pertaining to "the people as a whole." Highly significant in the light of the preceding discussion, however, is Koenen's further remark that this holds true *even when only certain individuals or groups are indicted*. Given the distinction that was made earlier between unselective and national judgment, we must now ask how the prophets construed the extent of Israel's guilt. In other words, does their estimate of disaster correspond to their estimate of sin?

For the most part, the answer has to be affirmative. One has only to read the opening verses of Isaiah, the gateway to the prophetic corpus,[57] to gauge the extent of the prophet's indictment of Judah:

> Woe, sinful nation, people burdened with guilt,
> > offspring of evildoers, corrupt children!
> They have forsaken YHWH, they have spurned the Holy One of Israel
> > and turned their backs on him. (Isa 1:4)

Isaiah's contemporary, Micah of Moresheth, describes the situation even more graphically:

> The godly have perished from the land;
> > there is not one upright person.
> All of them lie in wait to shed blood;
> > each one hunts his brother with a net.
> Both hands are skilled in evil;
> > the ruler seeks bribes and the judge accepts them...
> The best of them is a brier,
> > the upright worse than a thorn hedge. (Mic 7:2–4)

At around the same time, Hosea was portraying the northern kingdom of Israel in similar terms:

> There is no faithfulness, no love,
> > no knowledge of God in the land.
> Just cursing, lying and murder,
> > stealing and adultery;
> They use violence,
> > and bloodshed follows bloodshed.
> Therefore the land mourns,
> > and all who live in it waste away. (Hos 4:1–3)

Given the close linguistic and theological connections between Hosea and Jeremiah, it is not surprising to find the latter, a hundred years later, using similar language to depict the southern kingdom (12:1–4; 23:9–10). In fact, Jeremiah goes even further than his predecessor in emphasizing the ubiquity of his people's guilt, as we will see later.

Probably the most searing critique of Israel's apostasy, however, occurs in the book of Ezekiel, where it is seen in historical terms. As Zimmerli points out, Ezekiel (unlike Hosea and Jeremiah) has no concept of an earlier golden age in

---

57. That is, of course, in the Masoretic canon. In the Talmud, Isaiah is preceded by Jeremiah and Ezekiel, while the Septuagint places the twelve "Minor Prophets" first.

Israel's history; rather, she is seen as one disobedient mass from birth.[58] This emerges most emphatically in chs. 16, 20 and 23, but is also stated more succinctly in YHWH's initial words to the prophet:

> Son of man, I am sending you to the Israelites, to a rebellious nation that has rebelled against me; they and their fathers have been in revolt against me to this day. I am sending to you to people who are stubborn and obstinate. (Ezek 2:3–4)

Consequently, both in their indictment of the nation and their vision of its impending punishment, the prophetic oracles are couched in uncompromisingly all-Israel terms.[59] Their refusal to allow any exceptions in either respect is summed up in Isaiah's words:

> Those who guide this people mislead them,
>   and those who are guided are confused.
> Therefore the Lord will take no pleasure in the young men,
>   nor show compassion to their orphans and widows.
> For all are ungodly and wicked,
>   every mouth speaks vileness. (Isa 9:15–16 [16–17])

Over against this insistence on Israel's all-pervasive guilt, however, the prophetic texts occasionally sound a note of dissonance. Minor textual voices are heard which seem, at least by implication, to qualify the scope of the charge. Thus, although both Amos and Micah address the whole nation, their critique (as Koenen noted) focuses on the social and economic elite (Amos 4:1–4; 5:7–13; 6:1–6; 8:4–6; Mic 3:1–12; 6:9–16), and Amos actually recognizes an element within the land to whom he refers as "the righteous" (Amos 2:6; 5:12; cf. 4:1; 8:6). Also striking is the way in which Zephaniah's onslaught against Judah (Zeph 1:4–18) gives way to a call to "seek YHWH, all you humble of the land (ענוי הארץ), you who keep his commands" (Zeph 2:3). Isaiah 3:15 also mentions "the humble" (ענויים), pairing the term with "my people" (עמי). However, it is the presence of the prophets themselves that most lends itself to deconstructing their indictment of Israel.[60] By the very act of reporting YHWH's commission (Isa 6:1–7; Jer 1:4–19; Ezek 2:3–8; Amos 7:14–15) and proclaiming his word, they tacitly depict themselves as faithful (if reluctant) servants. Moreover, we occasionally read of other individuals who identify with the prophets (Isa 8:18; Jer 26:24; 36:4–26).

---

58. Walther Zimmerli, "The Message of the Prophet Ezekiel," *Interpretation* 23 (1969): 131–57 (143): "Ezekiel takes up the images of the earlier prophets, but with terrifying rigor forms them in a message that the people of Yahweh are radically corrupt…that is, from the roots."

59. Eichrodt's conclusion, *Theology*, 2:435, seems well founded: "This expectation of the coming judgement of wrath also explains why the prophets pay no attention to the problem of the collective liability of the community, in which no exception is made for the individual. In view of the indisputable importance of prophetism for the development of religious individuality, one might have thought that a detailed treatment of this question would be an indispensable requirement in their work. Nevertheless, it is quite obvious that the prophets themselves did not feel this necessity; and the decisive reason was their conviction that every member of the nation was involved in the mountainous corporate guilt."

60. That is, whether we think of the prophets as a presence in the community, or simply in the text.

Whether either the prophets or their editors were aware of the formal disparity between these hints of a faithful presence in Israel, and the overriding accusation of national guilt, is hard to gauge. If taken seriously, however, these textual counter-claims quietly imply that YHWH's judicial action against Israel, as announced by the prophets, has an indiscriminate dimension. In fact, in two places in the prophetic literature this is openly conceded. The point slips out, albeit retrospectively and parenthetically, in Jeremiah's oracle against Edom: "Those who did not deserve (אשר אין משפטם) to drink the cup had to drink it, and will you not be punished?" (Jer 49:12).[61] It is expressed more explicitly, however, in Ezek 21:8–9 (3–4), where YHWH declares his intention to "cut off from you the righteous and wicked" (הכרתי ממך צדיק ורשע).[62] Such a harsh voicing of this concept is unparalleled in the prophetic literature, but it may indicate a more general awareness of an uncomfortable reality.

On the other hand, the prophets never appear to question the legitimacy of YHWH's sweeping retribution, in a manner comparable to Abraham (Gen 18:23–25) or David (2 Sam 24:17). This is not to say they do not protest at all. Amos calls on YHWH to "cease!" (חדל, 7:5) from destroying Israel by fire; however, his appeal rests on the fact that Israel is small (כי קטן הוא), rather than on any righteous community within it (cf. his plea in v. 2 for YHWH to forgive, סלח). Similarly, Ezekiel twice asks in dismay if YHWH intends to destroy all Israel (המשחית אתה את כל שארית ישראל בשפכך את חמתך על ירושלם, 9:8; כלה אתה עשה את שארית ישראל, 11:13), but again, it is not divine justice as such that is at issue; YHWH has already commanded that those who grieve over the abomina- tions (תועבות) in the city are to be spared (Ezek 9:4). Rather, in each of these texts, the prophetic protest appears to spring more from horrified incredulity,[63] rather than from belief in a faithful remnant. Probably the most direct challenge to YHWH's judgment on the nation comes from Habakkuk: "Why are you silent when the wicked swallows up those more righteous than himself?" (Hab 1:13). Even so, his objection is not so much to the indiscriminate destruction of Judah, as to the agency of a nation (Babylon) that is even more culpable.[64]

Thus, the dominant picture that emerges from the prophets is one of "national" judgment; comprehensive punishment for comprehensive guilt. It

---

61.   Some interpreters think the reference is to Judah; so W. Rudolph, *Jeremia* (HAT 12; Tübingen: Mohr [Paul Siebeck], 1947), 269; Gerald L. Keown, Pamela J. Scalise and Thomas G. Smothers, *Jeremiah 26–52* (WBC 27; Dallas: Word, 1995), 329. Alternatively, they may simply be "innocent peoples…caught in the flow of international upheaval caused by Yahweh," as Walter Brueggemann, *A Commentary on Jeremiah: Exile and Homecoming* (Grand Rapids: Eerdmans, 1998), 457, believes; similarly Derek Kidner, *The Message of Jeremiah: Against Wind and Tide* (TBST; Leicester: IVP, 1987), 145.

62.   An evidently perplexed Greek translator rendered the text ἄδικον καὶ ἄνομον (Ezek 21:8).

63.   Or possibly from disbelief that YHWH could put an end to his covenant community.

64.   For this traditional reading of Hab 1, see, e.g., J. Lindblom, *Prophecy in Ancient Israel* (Philadelphia: Fortress, 1962), 254; William Sanford LaSor, David Allan Hubbard and Frederic William Bush, *Old Testament Survey: The Message, Form and Background of the Old Testament* (Grand Rapids: Eerdmans, 1982), 450–51; Peter J. M. Southwell, "Habakkuk: Theology of," *NIDOTTE* 4:689. It is, however, by no means certain. Some, e.g., E. Nielsen, "The Righteous and the Wicked in Habaqquq," *ST* 6 (1953): 54–78, argue that "the wicked one" in 1:13 is Jehoiakim.

would be easy, therefore, to conclude that, in this respect, prophetic thinking was influenced by the all-Israel paradigm which we identified earlier in Deuteronomy and DtrH. Without ruling out some such connection, however, we should note that many of the sweeping judgment oracles of Amos, Isaiah and Jeremiah, for example, are couched not in Deuteronomistic terms, but rather in the distinctive poetry of the prophets. Indeed, it is at just such points that scholars are most ready to judge the material authentic. Alongside this governing analysis of sin and judgment, however, we also find occasional hints of a faithful presence in Israel, and (very rarely) an assertion that YHWH's retribution is unselective. As elsewhere in the Old Testament, therefore, certain tensions remain in the prophetic interpretation of YHWH's judicial action.

3.2. *Selective Judgment and Salvation in the Prophets*

At the start of this section, I cited Koenen's observation that the characteristic prophetic emphasis on judgment and salvation for "the people as a whole" is quite distinctive within the Old Testament. However, Koenen notes that even in the prophetic corpus, "Es gibt Texte, die nicht vom Heil oder Unheil des ganzen Volkes sprechen, sondern im Blick auf die Zukunft zwischen Gerechten und Sündern—wie immer diese im einzelnen beschrieben sein mögen—unterscheiden. Den Gerechten wird es gut gehen, den Sündern dagegen schlecht."[65]

In the rest of his book, Koenen identifies and discusses examples of these *selective* prophetic judgment and salvation oracles. He is careful at the outset to delimit the scope of his enquiry.[66] "Deuteronomistic alternatives," which set out two options along with their respective consequences, are excluded, since (as I noted earlier) these still view the people as a single entity. Also set aside are passages in which a single individual is exempt from judgment on a wider group. The chief criterion in Koenen's selection of texts, however, is that they allocate salvation and judgment according to the *ethical profile* of the respective groups. Consequently, he excludes promises of salvation for a remnant predicated solely on YHWH's sovereign decision, and passages in which salvation depends on specific "here and now" actions. In neither case, he argues, does salvation depend on the "right conduct" (*recht Verhalten*)[67] of the group in question.

On the basis of this approach, Koenen concludes that the relevant prophetic oracles fall into two broad categories. In the first, salvation for the righteous follows the eschatological destruction of the wicked (e.g. Ezek 34:17–22; Zeph 2:1–11; 3:11–13; Mal 3:13–21), while in the second, salvation and judgment occur simultaneously. Neither concept, he argues, is present in the earlier prophets.[68] Rather, Koenen sees the book of Habakkuk as marking the watershed in this area of prophetic thinking:

---

65.   Koenen, *Heil den Gerechten*, 3.
66.   Ibid., 5.
67.   Ibid.
68.   The only passages from Amos and Hosea discussed by Koenen occur at the end of each book (Amos 9:7–10; Hos 14:10), and both are widely judged to be later additions. Micah is not mentioned at all. Various Isaianic texts are discussed, but again these are from sections of the book thought to be much later than Isaiah himself (e.g. Isa 25:1–5; 26:1–12; 65:8–16).

Mit der differenzierten Ankündigung von Heil und Unheil für die in einem Konflikt
gegenüberstehenden Gruppen unterscheidet sich Habakuk von den klassischen Propheten, die bei ihrer Ankündigung immer das ganze Volk im Blick haben. Habakuk macht
den verschiedenen Gruppen des Volkes erstmals unterschiedliche Ankündigung.[69]

While allowing for different redactional layers within Habakkuk, Koenen attributes this ground-breaking theological concept to its earliest literary stratum,
which he dates to the start of the sixth century.[70] In fact, his work as a whole
suggests that the idea of differentiated judgment and salvation received a significant impetus during the decades leading up to the fall of Jerusalem in 587.

Other scholars have reached similar conclusions regarding the importance of
the sixth century for the concept of selective judgment and salvation within
Judah. Emmerson, for example, notes how conflict within the post-exilic community is reflected in the judgment and salvation oracle of Isa 65:8–16 (cf.
66:5), with its dichotomy between "my servants" and "you who forsake YHWH."
"In this dual orientation," writes Emmerson, "it differs in a remarkable fashion
from the traditional forms of pre-exilic prophecy in which the nation is treated
as a corporate entity whether for judgment or salvation."[71] In Ezekiel, we have
already seen how those who grieved over Jerusalem's idolatry were specifically
excluded from the otherwise indiscriminate slaughter (9:3–6). Working from a
different angle, Duguid explores the stance taken by this book towards the leaders of Israel—kings and princes, priests and Levites, prophets, and lay leadership—and finds a striking corollary between what each group is promised and
their past conduct.[72] There is, he argues, "a coherent and connected attitude
taken toward these leadership groups throughout the book: those singled out for
the most reproach in Ezekiel's critique of the past are marginalized in his plan
for the future, while those who escape blame are assigned positions of honour."[73]

At this point, we can return to the passage in Mal 3 with which this study
began. Here, the prophet's audience are rebuked for their cynical assertion that
"even those who do evil prosper, even those who challenge God escape" (v. 15).
However, the humble response of a select group (v. 16) elicits YHWH's pledge
of future salvation (v. 17), along with an assurance that "you will again see the
distinction between the righteous and the wicked, between those who serve God
and those who do not" (v. 18). Clearly this constitutes selective judgment, even
if it awaits eschatological fulfilment (cf. 3:19–21 [4:1–3]). It is therefore all the

69. Koenen, *Heil den Gerechten*, 164.
70. Ibid., 146. Scholars generally date most or all of Habakkuk to the late seventh or early sixth
century; see Nielsen, "The Righteous and the Wicked"; E. Otto, "Die Theologie des Buches
Habakkuk," *VT* 35 (1985): 274–95; Robert D. Haak, *Habakkuk* (VTSup 44; Leiden: Brill, 1992),
133; R. Mason, *Zephaniah, Habakkuk, Joel* (OTG; Sheffield: JSOT, 1994).
71. Grace I. Emmerson, *Isaiah 56–66* (OTG; Sheffield: Sheffield Academic Press, 1992), 31–
32; see further pp. 81–94 on the background to this passage. Discussing the significance of the
ownership of the land in Isa 56–66, Wright, *NIDOTTE* 2:548, remarks that "rightful possession of
the land is one of the distinguishing marks of those counted worthy to belong to the confessional
community of the righteous."
72. Iain M. Duguid, *Ezekiel and the Leaders of Israel* (VTSup 56; Leiden: Brill, 1994).
73. Ibid., 1.

more striking that the preceding verses adopt a vision of the people and of YHWH's judicial action that is explicitly national: "The whole nation" (הגוי כלו, v. 9) is under a curse for defaulting on its tithes and offerings; repentance, however, will result in the blessings of fertility promised in Deuteronomy: "Then all the nations will bless you, for you will have a delightful land" (v. 12). This juxtaposing of selective and national concepts of judgment, of course, parallels what we have seen elsewhere. More importantly, it demonstrates that the older idea of judgment continued to have currency in Judah long after the sixth century.[74]

4. *Conclusions*

This survey has identified three broad interpretations of YHWH's judicial action in the Old Testament. In the Torah and the Writings, what I have termed the selective principle is the most prevalent, while the prophets generally depict sin, salvation and judgment in national terms. In neither corpus, however, does the dominant interpretation have exclusive status; indeed, divergent analyses of divine judgment sometimes occur in close proximity.

To some extent, this plurality of perspectives is due to the nature of language as a hermeneutical system *through which* one sees.[75] Since the terminology used in judicial polarities is frequently either ambiguous (e.g. the poor/the oppressor) or general (the righteous/the wicked), it readily lends itself to reinterpretation; we saw earlier how both Proverbs and the Psalms apply such categories to different situations. Such an interpretative manoeuvre may be a fairly simple one ("the poor" = me, "the oppressor" = my enemy). On the other hand, to substitute one part of a polarity may alter the entire paradigm. Habakkuk illustrates this point well. Initially, "the wicked" and "the righteous" are used as categories by which the prophet sees his own nation of Judah as morally pluralist (Hab 1:4). In *this* situation, justice means retribution against certain Judean wrongdoers. When, however, "the wicked" is identified with Babylon, such internal distinctions (and indeed, those between Judah and other nations; cf. 1:17) fade from view; the invader's victims now form a single entity, "one more righteous than he" (1:13). In other words, the lines demarcating the guilty and the innocent vary, *depending on the overall frame of reference.*

74.　Steven L. McKenzie and Howard N. Wallace, "Covenant Themes in Malachi," *CBQ* 45 (1983): 549–63 (563), argue that Mal 3:13–21 is a redactional reinterpretation of the original message of the book: "The covenant people are narrowed to include only a segment of the postexilic community... No longer is the entire community indicted but only a part of it."

75.　On this point, see the discussion of Wittgenstein's concept of language games in Anthony C. Thiselton, *The Two Horizons: New Testament Hermeneutics and Philosophical Description with Special Reference to Heidegger, Bultmann, Gadamer and Wittgenstein* (Exeter: Paternoster, 1980), especially 373–79, 417–19. Thiselton summarizes: "*What* is seen remains the same; *how* it is seen depends on the significance or function of the phenomenon within a given system, frame of reference, or setting in life" (p. 418).

The significance of the writer's broader frame of reference for his interpretation of YHWH's judicial action is also illustrated in the Pentateuch. As we have seen, the model of Israel presented in Exodus–Numbers of a people still journeying towards the land, is one which facilitates their depiction as a mixed company who experience selective judgment. Israel being what it is (or was), even the loss of a generation does not preclude their children from arriving in Canaan. In Deuteronomy and DtrH, however, Israel becomes a nation whose very identity is bound up with the land, from which, moreover, the editor knows it will ultimately be expelled. Within this model, conduct and consequence are naturally seen in national terms.

Other factors are also at work in the diverse perspectives on YHWH's judicial action, not least of which is the fact that salvation and judgment can signify different things. Where judgment involves ecological disorder, inevitably the entire nation suffers; to this extent, it can be interpreted only in national or unselective terms. Even in this situation, however, 1 Kgs 17 indicates that in *other* respects (i.e. the provision of food and resuscitation of a dead child) an element of selectivity is still possible. Again, YHWH's words concerning the children of the Israelites in the desert (Num 14) illustrate judicial differentiation to the extent that they themselves will enter the land, but non-differentiation to the extent that they must "bear the sin" of their parents for forty years in the wilderness. Perhaps the clearest example of different analyses being possible, depending on the judicial act in question, emerges in the case of Ahijah (1 Kgs 14). Inasmuch as the boy dies, one can only speak of unselective judgment; inasmuch as he will be mourned and buried, however, judgment takes on a selective aspect.

Finally, it may be said that the variety of judicial interpretations demonstrates the resistance of the biblical traditions to a single model. That is to say, the texts create (or reflect) situations more complex than any one polarity can express. Thus, the author of Exod 32 is able to illustrate in broad terms YHWH's stated principle of individual retribution, but the tradition also knows that Aaron himself does not die (yet). Numbers can affirm that YHWH singled out Joshua and Caleb for special commendation and blessing, but cannot avoid the fact that they (like the next generation) had to "bear the sin" of the rest of Israel. The Deuteronomist, meanwhile, favours the all-Israel model of judgment and salvation, but also retains (or creates) traditions depicting the blessing or punishment of specific kings.

Certainly, the proximity of diverse interpretations creates logical gaps and tensions. Different judicial models either clash or cut across each other. To add one example to those already discussed, Deuteronomy and the prophets both insist that YHWH requires justice for the widow and orphan, *and* warn of national disaster if such covenant requirements are flouted. The logical dilemma that arises—namely, the fate of the widow and the orphan in the event of such calamity—is left unvoiced and unresolved. Are the widow and the orphan themselves guilty? If they are not, will they somehow be spared when the nation is punished? If the answer to both questions is no, does that not mean that

YHWH's judgment is indiscriminate? In fact, in one small nook of the prophetic corpus—where in fact the focus moves outside of Israel—this particular gap is closed. In Jeremiah's oracle against Edom (Jer 49:7–11), the message of devastation coming on the nation is followed by an unexpected promise: "Leave your orphans; I will protect their lives. Your widows too can trust in me" (v. 11).[76] Since within a wider canonical context these same social groups are those for whom YHWH pledges to "work justice," the point is not simply that the text qualifies its message of national judgment, but rather does so in the light of a different judicial paradigm.

Our discussion of selective judgment has given rather slight attention to its rationale. Two points have emerged, however, that will be significant for our study of Jeremiah. In the first place, the Old Testament often speaks very generally of salvation for the righteous and punishment for the wicked; where such language is filled out, it is usually in such familiar terms as proper worship of YHWH, devotion to the Torah, generosity to the poor, sexual propriety, and so on (and their opposites). Occasionally, though, the stated rationale is more specific. We have seen that in Exod 32:29 and Num 25:6–13, showing solidarity with YHWH in his wrath earns his particular blessing, while in Ezek 9:3–6, those who grieve over Jerusalem's idolatry are spared execution. Secondly, there is a certain flexibility in the logical structure of the antithetical judgment model. In some instances this carries a corresponding dual rationale; the Levites and Phinehas are blessed for their devotion to YHWH while their apostate compatriots perish (Exod 32; Num 25). In other cases, however, antithetical judgment models offer one-sided rationales. The context of 1 Sam 2:32 clearly explains YHWH's judgment against the house of Eli, but no reason is given for the promise that "good will be done to Israel." A somewhat analogous situation arises where YHWH takes up the case of the poor against their oppressors. While social injustice clearly constitutes violation of the covenant, no *necessary* moral virtue attaches to the victims of injustice. In sum, both the mode and the rationale of judicial differentiation in the Old Testament are capable of considerable diversity of expression.

---

76. See Brueggemann, *Exile and Homecoming*, 457, who refers to "this exceptional note." Many scholars, however, add ואין אמר, "with no one to say," at the end of v. 10, so that v. 11 contains the compassionate words that will *not* be spoken; so Rudolph, *Jeremia*, 266; John Bright, *Jeremiah: Introduction, Translation and Notes* (AB 21; New York: Doubleday, 1965), 328; J. A. Thompson, *The Book of Jeremiah* (NICOT; Grand Rapids: Eerdmans, 1980), 721; William L. Holladay, *Jeremiah 2: A Commentary on the Book of the Prophet Jeremiah, Chapters 26–52* (Minneapolis: Fortress, 1989), 376; Keown, Scalise and Smothers, *Jeremiah 26–52*, 330.

Chapter 2

JUDICIAL DIFFERENTIATION IN JEREMIAH

1. *Introduction*

In the previous chapter I outlined the principal ways in which the Old Testament interprets YHWH's exercise of judgment in Israel. Against this general background, our enquiry can now begin to focus specifically on the book of Jeremiah. This chapter aims to set out the rationale and the methodological basis for doing so. I will begin by reviewing the work of Klaus Koenen in relation to Jeremiah, before moving on to discuss three other monographs which all help shed light on the notion of judicial differentiation in this prophetic book. An engagement with these studies will also serve to define more precisely the issues, and suggest the methodology, for the present enquiry.

2. *Klaus Koenen and the Book of Jeremiah*

In the last chapter, it was noted that Koenen regards Habakkuk, in the late seventh century, as the first of the classical prophets to proclaim "salvation for the righteous and judgment for the wicked" within Judah. We also saw how other scholars have identified this idea of judicial differentiation as an emerging feature of prophecy during the exilic period. Given such observations, we might well expect to find the same concept in one of Habakkuk and Ezekiel's close contemporaries, Jeremiah of Anathoth.[1] Apart from Jeremiah's chronological proximity to these prophets, two other historical factors encourage the thought that he may have proclaimed some form of selective judgment. First, irrespective of when his ministry began, it spanned a period in which Judah twice suffered invasion and deportation (597 and 587). The fact that certain groups

---

1.   On the basis of Jer 1:2, most scholars trace the start of Jeremiah's ministry to the thirteenth year of Josiah, that is, to 627–626; so Bright, *Jeremiah*, xxix; Thompson, *The Book of Jeremiah*, 10–11; H. Cazelles, "La Vie de Jérémie dans son Contexte National et International," in *Le Livre de Jérémie. le prophète et son milieu, les oracles et leur transmission* (ed. P.-M. Bogaert; Leuven: Leuven University Press, 1981), 24–25, 29–32; Peter C. Craigie, Page H. Kelley and Joel F. Drinkard, Jr., *Jeremiah 1–25* (WBC 26; Dallas: Word, 1991), xlv. Some, however, maintain that this was the year of his birth, and that he did not begin preaching until 609; see J. Philip Hyatt, "The Beginning of Jeremiah's Prophecy," *ZAW* 78 (1966): 204–14; Holladay, *Jeremiah 2*, 25–26; Norman K. Gottwald, *The Hebrew Bible: A Socio-Literary Introduction* (Philadelphia: Fortress, 1985), 395–96.

were taken away while others were left might easily lend itself to being interpreted in terms of salvation for some and judgment for others. Secondly, Jeremiah, more than any other prophetic book, witnesses to the plurality of political factions within Judah prior to 587. Not only so, it strongly suggests that Jeremiah himself was no mere outsider in Jerusalem, but rather was associated with certain prominent individuals, especially the scribal family of Shaphan (Jer 26:24; 29:3; 36:10–19; 39:14).[2] To the extent that theology is shaped by socio-political factors,[3] it would not be surprising if Jeremiah had entertained a hope that some would be spared YHWH's judgment, and maybe even rewarded for their faithfulness. In fact, Parke-Taylor connects the relative frequency of the term "remnant" (שְׁאֵרִית) in Jeremiah with the existence of Jeremiah's loyal support group.[4]

How far, and in what way, Jeremiah does reflect ideas of judicial differentiation will form the focus of the following study. Without prejudging the results, it may simply be noted at this point that several passages immediately suggest themselves as relevant. YHWH will distinguish between those exiled to Babylon and those left behind in Jerusalem (chs. 24 and 29), between the people and their leaders (23:1–8) and between those who flee the city and those who remain in it (21:8–10; 38:1–3). Individual salvation oracles are also addressed to Ebed-Melech and Baruch (38:15–18; 45:1–5).

None of these passages, however, are discussed by Koenen. In fact, the only Jeremianic texts he examines are the psalm-like 17:5–8 ("Cursed is he who trusts in a man… Blessed is he who trusts in YHWH") and the oracle of 30:23–24 ("Behold, the storm of YHWH…on the head of the wicked"). At first sight this might seem reasonable, given the strict terms of his enquiry noted in the previous chapter. YHWH's promises to the exiles are predicated on his sovereign decision, rather than on their conduct, while the offer of "life as booty" in chs. 21 and 38 requires only the specific action of abandoning the city. In the case of the oracles to Baruch and Ebed-Melech, it is a matter of individuals being exempt from judgment on a wider group. On closer reflection, however, the omission of these (and other) Jeremianic passages from Koenen's discussion would seem to point up certain flaws in his approach.

In the first place, Koenen's decision to exclude from his study oracles of individual salvation is methodologically curious, a point highlighted by the fact

2. For a helpful discussion of the evidence for Jeremiah's scribal support group, see J. Andrew Dearman, "My Servants the Scribes: Composition and Context in Jeremiah 36," *JBL* 109 (1990): 408–20. Burke O. Long, "Social Dimensions of Prophetic Conflict," *Semeia* 21 (1981): 31–53 (46), writes of "a network of family relationships supportive of Jeremiah, and extending into the highest levels of royal and cultic service."

3. Long, "Social Dimensions," 31–32, highlights the "societal" and "highly situational" nature of prophetic conflict. See further R. R. Wilson, *Prophecy and Society in Ancient Israel* (Philadelphia: Fortress, 1980), 241–51; David J. Reimer, "Political Prophets? Political Exegesis and Prophetic Theology," in *Intertextuality in Ugarit and Israel* (ed. Johannes C. de Moor; Leiden: Brill, 1998), 126–42.

4. Geoffrey H. Parke-Taylor, *The Formation of the Book of Jeremiah: Doublets and Recurring Phrases* (SBLMS 51; Atlanta: Scholars Press, 2000), 264.

that the promise of deliverance for Ebed-Melech is explicitly grounded in the fact that he trusted in YHWH (38:18).[5] It thereby echoes (perhaps deliberately) the benediction on such a person in 17:7–8.[6] A single individual still constitutes a party over against another (much larger) party, and an oracle guaranteeing that individual's exemption from disaster still represents an act of selective judgment and salvation within the nation. If one thinks in terms of the reception-history of the book, of course, a textual individual may well represent a wider group of readers.[7]

Secondly, Koenen's criterion of "right conduct" (*recht Verhalten*) in selecting his material is problematic. Nowhere is this phrase clearly defined, and indeed, Koenen's qualifying remark concerning the terms "the righteous" and "the sinners"—"wie immer diese im einzelnen beschrieben sein mögen"[8]—indicates that these are distinctly slippery concepts. *Prima facie*, one could argue that even very specific actions such as surrender to the Babylonians, or listening to Jeremiah rather than another prophet, are seen within the text as right conduct, at least to the extent that they display trust in YHWH rather than someone else (the very point at issue in Jer 17:5–8). Moreover, Koenen appears to overlook the possibility that divine grace and human conduct may *both* be factors in judgment and salvation prophecy. For example, he does not address Jer 23:1–8, presumably because this is a "remnant" prophecy based on YHWH's gracious initiative; yet it begins by announcing judgment on Judah's leaders precisely because of their past misconduct.[9] Here, it will be noticed, the logical structure of the oracle resembles that of 1 Sam 2:32, where YHWH's sentence on the house of Eli is predicated on its wickedness, but his benevolence towards Israel is unexplained. Likewise, although Jeremiah's promise of restoration for the exiles (29:10–14) is grounded in divine initiative, it expressly anticipates their seeking and praying to YHWH,[10] and is followed by judgment oracles against three individuals for prophesying lies (29:23, 31). In both cases, the promise of salvation for some and not others has an ethical aspect, although it is not the *only* aspect.

5. Koenen concedes this point in a footnote, *Heil den Gerechten*, 5 n. 11, but otherwise makes no mention of it.

6. One might point out that, formally speaking, Jer 17:5–8 also addresses individuals: אָרוּר הַגֶּבֶר...בָּרוּךְ הַגֶּבֶר.

7. Concerning individuals such as Ebed-Melech and Baruch, Christopher R. Seitz, "Isaiah in Parish Bible Study: The Question of the Place of the Reader in Biblical Texts," in *Word Without End: The Old Testament as Abiding Theological Witness* (ed. Christopher R. Seitz; Waco: Baylor University Press, 2004), 194–212 (202), remarks: "Their potential function as paradigms for a remnant in need of hope and forgiveness—a remnant confronted not by Jeremiah himself, but by the book of Jeremiah as a word of scripture—seems clear."

8. Koenen, *Heil den Gerechten*, 3.

9. A similar point could be made regarding Ezek 34:1–16, also largely ignored by Koenen. His claim, *Heil den Gerechten*, 74, that "nach [Ezek 34] vv. 1–16 gehört das ganze Volk Israel zur Herde Jahwes," leaves the identity of the "shepherds" a mystery.

10. Indeed, in the Greek text these verbs are imperatives. As will be seen later, the degree of conditionality in 29:13 depends on how we interpret כִּי.

Finally, Koenen's work is weakened by focussing entirely on short, discrete oracles, thereby overlooking judgment and salvation polarities that may emerge from much larger blocks of text. It was noted in the previous chapter how Duguid's study of Ezekiel *as a whole* reveals modes of inner-Judean differentiation that are not immediately obvious. And, as we will see in the next chapter, when YHWH's promise of his presence and protection for Jeremiah (1:8, 19) is seen in the wider context of chs. 1–20, a distinctive polarity of judgment and salvation emerges, configured around prophet and nation. Indeed, when Jeremiah is read as a whole, it becomes clear that no fewer than *three* individuals— Jeremiah, Ebed-Melech and Baruch—are to be exempt from YHWH's wrath on Judah.

It may be argued that these criticisms relate more to the *limitations*, rather than the *incoherence*, of Koenen's enquiry, and that it is unfair to fault him for not doing what he does not set out to do. In one sense this is true. As a study of self-contained oracles announcing salvation to the (collective) pious and judgment to the (collective) impious, Koenen's work has value. My argument, however, is that such a tightly defined approach is *a priori* somewhat artificial. That is to say, the prophetic concept of "salvation for the righteous, judgment for the wicked" may be more varied in its form and more nuanced in its rationale than Koenen's very precise categories allow us to appreciate. To gain a fuller and clearer picture of how this idea is interpreted in Jeremiah (or any of the prophets), larger units of text, oracles addressed to individuals and cases where YHWH's grace and human conduct intertwine, must all be taken into account.

3. Three Studies of Jeremiah: Pohlmann, Seitz and Kilpp

3.1. The Work of Karl-Friedrich Pohlmann

One of the most significant milestones in Jeremiah studies was set down in 1978 with the monograph of Karl-Friedrich Pohlmann.[11] According to Pohlmann, the final form of Jeremiah reflects the bitter rivalry between the descendants of those exiled to Babylon in 597, and those who were left in Judah.[12] The dominant voice in the book now is that of the former group. They alone constitute Israel and they alone will enjoy YHWH's future blessings.[13] In order to promote this ideology, the editors have sought (tendentiously) to portray Jeremiah as prophesying only disaster for those who remained in the land after 597 (as in 21:1–10; 38:23; and 42:17–21). Indeed, their outlook is reflected in the very structure of Jeremiah. Chapter 24 concludes the first part by announcing YHWH's rejection of Zedekiah and his countrymen, but his favour toward the *Golah*

---

11.   Karl-Friedrich Pohlmann, *Studien zum Jeremiabuch. Ein Beitrag zur Frage nach der Entstehung des Jeremiabuches* (FRLANT 118; Göttingen: Vandenhoeck & Ruprecht, 1978).

12.   Ibid., 191. As evidence for the emergence of the pro-*Golah* party in Judah, Pohlmann points to the pre-eminence of Zerubbabel, Ezra and Nehemiah (p. 191 n. 21).

13.   Ibid., 183. Pohlmann describes this claim to be the exclusive representatives of Israel as an *Alleinvertretungsanspruch* (p. 144).

community in Babylon. This message is then developed at length; chs. 26–34 describe the hopeful future of the exiles (cf. 24:3–7), while chs. 37–44 emphasize the fate of those who remained behind (cf. 24:8–10). Consequently, Pohlmann describes the rationale behind the present arrangement of Jer 21–45 as one of prophecy and fulfilment.[14] This editorial reworking of Jeremiah he terms "*die golaorientierte Redaktion*" (GR), tracing it to the fourth century BC (probably in Judah).[15]

Alongside this exclusivist claim for the Babylonian *Golah*, however, Pohlmann detects in Jer 37–44 traces of an older base narrative (*Grundtext*), reflecting a very different outlook.[16] According to the Jeremiah depicted in this document, those who had not been deported in 597 could still live peacefully in the land if Zedekiah would submit to the Babylonians (38:17, 19–22). His refusal to do so, and the subsequent fall of Jerusalem, naturally prompted a crisis of faith among those left in Judah after 587. Had YHWH finally abandoned them? The answer of the author of the *Grundtext* was "no." Since the catastrophe was the fault of the leadership ("auf das Konto derer, die sich weigerten, auf Jahwe zu hören, die Stadt der Oberherrschaft der Babylonier auszuliefern"),[17] and since the land itself belonged to YHWH, an ongoing relationship between YHWH and the Judean remnant was still possible.[18] This, however, depended upon their remaining in the land, and not, as some were already doing, fleeing to Egypt (42:9–11, 13–14).

Pohlmann's thesis amplified and developed certain ideas that had been mooted by earlier scholars,[19] and has subsequently had considerable influence. In particular, his belief that the pro-*Golah* message of Jeremiah reflects a political power claim within fourth-century Judah, rather than the outlook of the sixth-century prophet, anticipated a trend in the following two decades towards ideological readings of Jeremiah.[20] His description of ch. 24 as programmatic for

14. Ibid., 185.

15. Ibid., 190–91.

16. Ibid., 186–87, 198–200. See his appendix (pp. 208–23) for a synopsis of the original and the redactional material.

17. Ibid., 198.

18. Ibid., 188–89.

19. See, e.g., Herbert Gordon May, "Towards an Objective Approach to the Book of Jeremiah: The Biographer," *JBL* 61 (1942): 139–53 (148–49); J. Philip Hyatt, "The Deuteronomic Edition of the Book of Jeremiah," *VSH* 1 (1951): 71–95, republished in Leo G. Perdue and Brian W. Kovacs, eds., *A Prophet to the Nations: Essays in Jeremiah Studies* (Winona Lake: Eisenbrauns, 1984), 247–67 (all subsequent citations of this essay are from the Perdue and Kovacs volume); Peter R. Ackroyd, *Exile and Restoration: A Study of Hebrew Thought of the Sixth Century B.C.* (OTL; London: SCM, 1968), 243–44, especially n. 43; E. W. Nicholson, *Preaching to the Exiles: A Study of the Prose Tradition in the Book of Jeremiah* (Oxford: Blackwell, 1970), 110.

20. See especially Robert P. Carroll, *Jeremiah: A Commentary* (OTL; London: SCM, 1986), 65–82; also Roy D. Wells, "The Amplification of the Expectations of the Exiles in the MT Revision of Jeremiah," in *Troubling Jeremiah* (ed. A.R. Pete Diamond, Kathleen M. O'Connor and Louis Stulman; JSOTSup 260; Sheffield: Sheffield Academic Press, 1999), 272–92; Carolyn J. Sharp, "The Call of Jeremiah and Diaspora Politics," *JBL* 119 (2000): 421–38.

the book as a whole is also echoed by others.[21] Methodologically, Pohlmann's argument benefits from its attention to conceptual (rather than simply lexical) aspects of the text; in this respect, it marks an important advance on the work of Thiel.[22]

I will, of course, discuss specific aspects of Pohlmann's argument in later chapters, but two general criticisms may be offered at this stage. First, while his focus on conceptual distinctions within texts is welcome, it sometimes lapses into hyper-criticism. Perspectives that may be complementary are too often assumed (rather than shown) to be incompatible, and thus allocated to different editorial hands. His identification of no fewer than four redactional strata in Jer 42, for example, is both implausible and unnecessary. Moreover, his readiness to designate material as redactional means that, in his analysis, very little is left of the *Grundtext*; as Seitz remarks, "Pohlmann's *Vorlage* is barely a torso."[23] Pohlmann himself admits that its introduction has been lost altogether.[24]

Secondly, Pohlmann's fourth-century dating of GR is problematic. As several commentators have pointed out, if the redaction is as late as this, it is far from clear why it *exclusively* champions the 597 exiles. As McKane remarks, "All that is needed…is a simple antithesis between those who went into exile, whether in 597 or 586, and those who did not go into exile. What interest could he possibly have had in the middle of the fifth century or later in asserting that the only bearers of Judaism were those who had been deported with Jehoiachin in 597?"[25] Again, Pohlmann himself acknowledges the problem: "Wie die Redaktion dazu kommt, von einer der Gola von Jahwe gewährten Vorrangstellung auszugehen, bleibt allerdings unklar."[26]

The more immediate concern, however, is what light Pohlmann's thesis sheds on the idea of selective judgment and salvation in Jeremiah. Although he did not frame his enquiry in these terms, several of his findings are nonetheless significant for the present study. First, and most obviously, he has identified within the GR material a clear mode of inner-Judean differentiation, that is, "Salvation for the 597 exiles/Judgment for everyone else." More significantly, in the light of our discussion of Koenen's work, Pohlmann traces this polarity not merely

21. E.g. McConville, *Judgment and Promise*, 111–13; Konrad Schmid, *Buchgestalten des Jeremiabuches: Untersuchungen zur Redaktions- und Rezeptionsgeschichte von Jer 30–33 im Kontext des Buches* (WMANT 72; Neukirchen–Vluyn: Neukirchener, 1996), 255–62.

22. Winfried Thiel, *Die deuteronomistische Redaktion von Jeremia 1–25* (WMANT 41; Neukirchen–Vluyn: Neukirchener, 1973), and *Die deuteronomistische Redaktion von Jeremia 26–45. Mit einer Gesamtbeurteilung der deuteronomistischen Redaktion des Buches Jeremias* (WMANT 52; Neukirchen–Vluyn: Neukirchener, 1981). See, for example, Pohlmann's emphasis on the conceptual differences between Jer 24:6 and 42:10, despite their verbal similarities (*Studien*, 130–31).

23. Christopher R. Seitz, *Theology in Conflict: Reactions to the Exile in the Book of Jeremiah* (BZAW 176; Berlin: de Gruyter, 1989), 239.

24. Pohlmann, *Studien*, 208.

25. William McKane, *A Critical and Exegetical Commentary on Jeremiah.* Vol. 1, *Introduction and Commentary on Jeremiah I–XXV* (ICC New Series; Edinburgh: T. & T. Clark, 1986), 614. See too Hermann-Josef Stipp, "Zedekiah in the Book of Jeremiah: On the Formation of a Biblical Character," *CBQ* 58 (1996): 627–48 (642–43); Sharp, "Call of Jeremiah," 438 n. 33.

26. Pohlmann, *Studien*, 189.

to one or two specific passages, but to Jeremiah *as a whole*. That is to say, although it is stated programmatically in ch. 24, it is then developed and reinforced throughout the book, not only in poetry and sermons but also in narrative material.

Such an approach, I suggested earlier, is from the outset likely to be more fruitful in exploring the prophetic concept of judicial differentiation than one which deals solely with individual oracles. The present enquiry, therefore, will interact carefully with Pohlmann's work. Nevertheless, his claim that the judgment/salvation polarity reflected in Jer 24 has final status in the book is questionable, inasmuch as it overlooks several passages that offer a more inclusive vision. One immediately thinks, for example, of the salvation oracles in chs. 30–33. Pohlmann (tellingly) gives little attention to this section, but argues that its original all-Israel scope has been deliberately narrowed by its present placement.[27] He then seeks to buttress this claim by arguing that 32:16–44 repeats the pro-*Golah* outlook of 24:1–10.[28] This, however, will not do; as Schmid points out, there is no evidence anywhere in chs. 30–33 of a 597-exclusive voice.[29] But similar objections are also raised by 23:1–8, where YHWH promises to scatter the shepherds but bring back his flock "from all the lands where I scattered them" (23:3). It is hard to see how this can be subsumed within the GR perspective, and indeed, Pohlmann completely overlooks this passage (as he does all the material between 21:10 and 24:1). Nor does he discuss the individual salvation oracles to Ebed-Melech and Baruch.

Even in those passages Pohlmann assigns to GR, it is not certain that the pattern of differentiation is as uniform as he suggests. Although, for instance, Jer 21:1–10 and 24:1–10 are similar in many respects, the former passage allows for the possibility of survivors among the people of Jerusalem in a way that the latter passage does not. Then again, while ch. 24 configures the 597 exiles as a unity, ch. 29 highlights internal distinctions among them. In fact, it is noticeable that despite Pohlmann's claim that ch. 29 endorses the pro-*Golah* viewpoint of ch. 24, he actually says little about ch. 29, and even less about its relationship to chs. 27–28.

As a final observation concerning Pohlmann's analysis of GR, it is significant that nowhere does he identify any textual *rationale* for its polarity of "Salvation for the 597 exiles/Judgment for everyone else." To be sure, he regards this ideology as reflecting a political power claim in post-exilic Judah. Even if this is so, however, one might have expected its proponents to have supplied some sort of theological basis for their outlook. But as Pohlmann presents things, YHWH's choice of one group of exiles for blessing and their compatriots for disaster is wholly arbitrary. At this point, his reading of Jer 24 coincides with that of Koenen; salvation is grounded simply in YHWH's sovereign decree.

---

27.   Pohlmann, *Studien*, 30–31 n. 61 (see also p. 46): "Da in Jer 29 im wesentlichen die gleiche Auffassung wie in Jer 24 und Jer 44 zu Grunde liegt, können die folgenden Heilsweissagungen in Jer 30ff jetzt nur noch mit der babylonischen Gola in Verbindung gebracht werden."

28.   Ibid., *Studien*, 46–47.

29.   Schmid, *Buchgestalten*, 177 n. 607; he specifically criticizes Pohlmann on this point.

This brings us to Pohlmann's analysis of the *Grundtext*. Here, as we have seen, the prophet's message is quite different. Up until the fall of Jerusalem, the Judean community are presented with the dual alternatives of blessing (if they submit to the Babylonians) or ruin (if they do not). Even after 587, however, those left in the land still had the option of a hopeful future, since the fall of the city was due to the obstinacy of its leaders. On this reading, therefore, the *Grundtext* operates with its own distinctive mode of judicial differentiation: "Judgment for the leadership/Judgment or salvation for the remnant."[30]

Two points deserve comment. First, we saw earlier that Koenen excluded from his study texts setting out dual alternatives, since (he argued) these still envisaged the people as a unity. Pohlmann's reading of Jeremiah, however, suggests that such passages may still be relevant to the issue of selective judgment and salvation, *if they are addressed to a restricted audience*. That is to say, if one group is presented with alternatives, leading to blessing or disaster, while another group is offered no such choice, then a significant form of judicial differentiation is implied. Whether or not one accepts Pohlmann's theory of the *Grundtext*, he has identified a textual voice according to which Judah's leaders have been judged, while the remnant may still choose life. Once again, it may be added that such a judicial polarity is likely to emerge only within the context of an extended textual unit.

Secondly, it is noticeable that Pohlmann regards the *Grundtext*, unlike GR, as having an ethical/theological rationale for its perspective. The fall of Judah and the exile of its people is attributed to the failure of Zedekiah and his advisors to hear YHWH's word through Jeremiah. Conversely, since those left in Judah played no part in such rebellion, they could still have a hopeful future. In other words, judgment and salvation in Pohlmann's *Grundtext* is by no means arbitrary, but clearly related to matters of human culpability.

As I have said, Pohlmann was not seeking to interpret Jeremiah in terms of judicial differentiation. Nevertheless, his study has suggested several potentially fruitful lines of enquiry. As well as identifying two distinct judgment and salvation polarities in Jeremiah (between the 597 exiles and everyone else in Judah, and between the post-587 community and their former leaders), he has demonstrated the value of attending to larger textual units, rather than just to isolated oracles. At the same time, I have suggested that Pohlmann's thesis is open to question at various points. In particular, he appears to have overstated the extent to which the judicial polarity in Jer 24 governs the entire book. This point could be rephrased in the form of a question: Does this exclusive claim in favour of the 597 *Golah* community really have the final word in Jeremiah, or is it simply juxtaposed alongside other polarities? To answer this question, we will need to examine a number of passages that Pohlmann overlooks, as well as probing more closely the rationale underlying Jer 24.

---

30. Such a perspective contrasts with that observed earlier in the book of Kings, where monarch and people together are seen as culpable for the fall of the nation.

3.2. *The Work of Christopher R. Seitz*

While accepting the main lines of Pohlmann's argument, the 1989 study of Christopher R. Seitz adopts both a wider perspective and a different starting point.[31] Seitz begins by noting that prior to 597, Jeremiah's preaching (as reflected in chs. 1–20) was one of wholesale judgment: "Up to this point in time, the powerful imagery of military destruction and deportation had dominated the prophet's description of impending judgment."[32] The deportation of Jehoiachin and others to Babylon, however, brought about a significant change in the prophet's thinking:

> The concrete circumstances of 597 gave the prophet Jeremiah and his message a startling and forceful validation; at the same time, those circumstances gave rise to a distinct transformation of that message... This transformation included a new focus directed toward the necessity of Judah's submission to Babylon... Because Jeremiah was not deported, his message to the post-597 community had to address the altered circumstances of this "remnant" community.[33]

It is against this backdrop that Seitz explores subsequent responses to exile in the central chapters of Jeremiah. Here, like Pohlmann, he finds two very different viewpoints. The first, which is also that of the post-597 Jeremiah, Seitz characterizes as "submit and live."[34] If Zedekiah and his people accepted the suzerainty of Babylon, YHWH would allow them to live peacefully in their own land, and would show them favour. This message was promulgated in a document Seitz calls the Scribal Chronicle (SC). While sections of this are found in chs. 21–24, 27–29 and 32–34, SC is most evident between chs. 37–43. Noting the repeated references in these chapters to scribes and other individuals from the family of Shaphan, Seitz surmises that the author of SC himself belonged to this circle.[35]

At the same time, Seitz argues that SC was reworked and supplemented by what he calls the Exilic Redaction (ER). In many respects, Seitz's ER is similar to Pohlmann's GR, although he traces it to sixth-century Babylon, rather than fourth-century Judah;[36] indeed, it has strong affinities with the theological traditions in Ezekiel.[37] From the standpoint of its editors, the disobedience and destruction of the Judean remnant was inevitable from the outset and in line with Jeremiah's earlier preaching. According to Seitz,

> It is to be emphasized that those deported in 597 were familiar in a direct way only with the pre-597 message of Jeremiah... A different line was adopted in the post-597 Jeremiah traditions, with an emphasis upon submission of king and community in the

31. Seitz, *Theology in Conflict*, 205–91; see too his earlier essay, "The Crisis of Interpretation Over the Meaning and Purpose of the Exile," *VT* 35 (1985): 78–97.

32. Seitz, *Theology in Conflict*, 207.

33. Ibid., 207.

34. Ibid., 205–7.

35. Ibid., 215–16, 285.

36. Ibid., 212–14. Seitz also strikes a more sympathetic tone towards ER than Pohlmann does to GR: "Since they knew of the ultimate fate of Zedekiah (see xxxix 7ff.) and the city (xxxix 8–10), theirs was a thoroughly justifiable and accurate interpretation" ("Crisis of Interpretation," 92).

37. Seitz, *Theology in Conflict*, 213–14.

land. However, for the post-597 exilic community, the ongoing Jeremiah traditions were either unavailable...irrelevant...eclipsed...or, most likely, open to gross misinterpretation.[38]

ER expresses its theological stance by supplementing SC with material pronouncing YHWH's wrath against Zedekiah and his people (24:1–10; 29:16–19) and against the post-587 Judean remnant (42:13–22; 44:1–28). A key manoeuvre in this editorial process is what Seitz calls "foreclosing"; that is, placing a conditional promise of hope in a new context so that a negative response appears certain from the start. In this way, Seitz concludes,

> The sense of continuity the Exilic Redaction seeks to establish between all levels of Jeremiah tradition, regardless of provenance or temporal circumstances (pre-597, post-597, post-587) is underscored... Put another way, though it may appear in the Scribal Chronicle that Yahweh can "build and plant" when the post-597 (27.1–11) and post-587 remnant (40.9–12; 42.10–12) submits to Babylonian rule...the Exilic Redaction anticipates a greater judgment awaiting both Judah and "the whole land" (45.4–5).[39]

In several respects, Seitz has offered a more satisfying analysis than Pohlmann. It is able to take account of material that Pohlmann either ignored or skated over (e.g. 23:1–8; 27:1–29:32), while avoiding the multiplicity of sources proposed by the German scholar. Nevertheless, there are problematic areas, not least in Seitz's interpretation of SC. Its characteristic "submit and live" message, he believes, comes to expression in 27:12–17 and 42:10–12, where Jeremiah assures the people that by serving the king of Babylon, they may live peacefully in Judah. However, Seitz also ascribes to SC 21:8–10 and 38:1–3, where the promise is one of mere survival, and YHWH's tone markedly more severe. Irrespective of whether we accept Seitz's hypothesis of the Scribal Chronicle, therefore, or his analysis of its contents, we need to define more carefully what the call to "submit and live" means in different contexts.[40]

Clearly, the polarities of judgment and salvation implied by Seitz's thesis are broadly comparable to those we saw in the work of Pohlmann. Crucially, however, Seitz's ER has a wider salvific vision than Pohlmann's GR, since it holds out a message of ultimate hope to *all* who experience exile. Granted, Seitz is not always clear on this point; in one place he states that ER "presses for...a judgment which will bring about the final elimination of the post-597 remnant."[41] Elsewhere, however, it becomes clear that in Seitz's view, ER regards judgment on the whole land not as final, but rather as the necessary prelude to salvation. He writes: "Only after this judgment is accomplished can restoration be considered (Jer 52.31–34). Throughout the book of Jeremiah, the Exilic Redaction makes clear that the restoration of Israel involves Yahweh's returning of a deported people."[42]

---

38.   Ibid., 227–28.

39.   Ibid., 291.

40.   A further blurring of issues seems to occur when Seitz, *Theology in Conflict*, 210 n. 8 (cf. p. 283), designates 29:10–14 as ER, despite the fact that part of this material is an MT plus.

41.   Ibid., 224.

42.   Ibid., 291.

In keeping with this interpretation of ER, Seitz also ascribes to it such passages as 23:1–8 and 29:10–14, which are generally seen as envisaging the return of a general *Diaspora*.[43] The resulting polarity is thus one of "Salvation for the exiles/Judgment for the non-exiles," without a bias toward any *particular* group of exiles.

This broader conception of ER points up a further significant difference between Seitz's approach and that of Pohlmann. Whereas the latter saw GR's exclusive claim for the 597 *Golah* as grounded simply in YHWH's sovereign decree (masking the political motives of its editors), Seitz's remark—"only after this judgment is accomplished can restoration be considered"—hints at a rationale rooted in what one might call a theology of exile. Although he does not develop this idea, he clearly interprets ER as viewing exile as the necessary precursor to salvation.

Seitz reiterates both these points in a separate article written the same year.[44] "There are no sub-groups within Jeremiah's generation to be given special treatment," he writes, before adding, "at least until they are exiled."[45] Likewise, in connection with the vision of Jer 24 he refers to YHWH's promise of salvation for "the already-punished good figs of exile."[46] In this article, however, Seitz focuses attention on the (textual) figures of Jeremiah, Baruch and Ebed-Melech —all of whom, we noted earlier, are conspicuously absent from the discussions of Koenen and Pohlmann. Seitz argues that Jeremiah has been deliberately shaped by its Deuteronomistic editors so as to highlight parallels between these three individuals and Moses, Caleb and Joshua. Like the prototypical prophet Moses, who died outside the promised land, Jeremiah suffers undeservedly in God's judgment on the nation: "Between God and Jeremiah there is no rider for personal exemption. He must die in the wilderness like Moses before him. And in the logic of Deuteronomy, he is judged not for his own disobedience, but because of his own generation."[47]

At this point, Seitz's words recall Koenen's description of the typical prophetic view of judgment. It soon emerges, however, that this picture of indiscriminate judgment is not the whole story. Like Caleb and Joshua in the wilderness, the faithful Ebed-Melech and Baruch receive personal assurances of exemption from YHWH's impending wrath. Seitz concludes that "Ebed-Melech and Baruch are types modelled on Caleb and Joshua in the canonical movement of the Book of Jeremiah. All four figures are contrasted with the generations of which they were a part."[48]

---

43. Whether 29:10–14 should in fact be interpreted in this way is a point I shall return to in Chapter 6.

44. Christopher R. Seitz, "The Prophet Moses and the Canonical Shape of Jeremiah," *ZAW* 101 (1989): 3–27. Seitz's reference to "the logic of Deuteronomy" is significant, in the light of our earlier discussion of the different perspectives on culpability and judgment in that book.

45. Ibid., 13.

46. Ibid.

47. Ibid., 11.

48. Ibid., 17–18.

Although this analysis is attractively neat, it might be pointed out that Baruch shares exactly the same end as Jeremiah, taken off to Egypt in despair (45:1–5). Moreover, if Ebed-Melech and Baruch are indeed to be spared the coming wrath, how does this relate to the theology of ER, in which YHWH's salvation is contingent upon the prior experience of his judgment? Nevertheless, however we assess this typological paralleling of Moses, Caleb and Joshua/Jeremiah, Ebed-Melech and Baruch, Seitz has certainly helped our understanding of Jeremiah by highlighting the significance of the latter three individuals within the book, over against their "generation."[49] In so doing, of course, he has provided us with a fresh and thought-provoking polarity of salvation and judgment. Later in this study I shall explore in more detail this way of construing the nation.

3.3. *The Work of Nelson Kilpp*

In some ways, the work that comes closest to the present enquiry is the 1990 monograph of Nelson Kilpp, which explores the relationship between judgment and salvation prophecy in Jeremiah.[50] In the second part of this study, Kilpp examines the salvation oracles in chs. 3 and 30–31, concluding that they probably reflect Jeremiah's preaching to the inhabitants of the former northern kingdom.[51] More relevant to our concerns, however, is the first part of the book, which deals with messages of hope to a Judean audience.[52] Here Kilpp gives special attention to ch. 24 ("Heil und Unheil im Nebeneinander"), ch. 29 ("Heil im fremden Land") and ch. 32 ("Heil für das Land Juda"), but he also devotes a chapter to oracles addressed to individuals and small groups; namely, Zedekiah (34:1–5; 38:14–23), Ebed-Melech (39:15–18), Baruch (45:1–5) and the Rechabites (ch. 35). Like Pohlmann and Seitz, Kilpp distinguishes between authentic and redactional material; the latter, however, is identified by its (future-orientated) view of salvation rather than by its stance towards particular Judean groups.

Two features of Kilpp's analysis are of particular interest. First, he is careful to attend to the *meaning* of the terms "judgment" and "salvation." These can either be distinct acts in their own right (e.g. death by sword, famine and plague, or restoration to the land), or one can simply entail exemption (*die Aussonderung*) from the other. In the authentic oracles to communities (29:5–7; 32:15), Kilpp argues, salvation is of the first type. YHWH guarantees his blessing on the people's everyday lives—family, harvest, and so on—with fruitfulness replacing futility.[53] At the same time, what is promised is not simply a return to how things were, but rather a new era in which geographical dislocation, and the loss of religious and political institutions, are irrelevant.[54]

---

49. This word recurs repeatedly in Seitz's discussion.

50. Nelson Kilpp, *Niederreißen und aufbauen. Das Verhältnis von Heilsverheißung und Unheilsverkündigung bei Jeremia und im Jeremiabuch* (BTS 13; Neukirchen–Vluyn: Neukirchener, 1990).

51. Ibid., 99–176.

52. Ibid., 30–98.

53. Ibid., 56–58, 81.

54. Ibid., 38, 60. Only in the redactional material of 24:6 and 29:10–14, Kilpp (ibid., 40, 67) maintains, is restoration to the land seen as a prerequisite of salvation.

On the other hand, Kilpp points out, Jeremiah's salvation oracles to individuals and small groups are much more modest in their scope. All that is promised to such people is personal survival, exemption from the catastrophe about to fall on Judah.[55] Meanwhile, the (redactional) judgment prophecy against Shemaiah, that "he will not see the good which I will do for my people" (29:32), constitutes a reverse form of *Aussonderung*, in which an individual is excluded from a general announcement of divine blessing.[56]

The second point of interest in Kilpp's study is his interpretation of the rationale underlying Jeremiah's preaching of salvation. Commenting on the vision of two baskets of figs (ch. 24), Kilpp notes that no explanation is given for YHWH's favour towards those Judeans who had been taken to Babylon.[57] Rather than seeing this either as arbitrary or as ideological prejudice, however, he remarks, "Das einzig sichtbare Merkmal, das die beiden Gruppen im ursprünglichen Visionsbericht Jer 24 unterscheidet, ist ihre Situation. Dabei geht es nicht an erster Stelle um den Wohnort, sondern um das eingetroffene bzw. nicht eingetroffene Gericht."[58]

In other words, salvation can be offered to the exiles precisely because they *are* exiles, while those in Judah have yet to experience YHWH's wrath. The same principle undergirds Jeremiah's letter to the *Golah* community in 29:4–7. It also emerges, albeit in a slightly different form, in ch. 32, where Jeremiah's purchase of land is the symbolic basis for a prophecy of hope. While Jerusalem continued to hold out against the Babylonians, the inhabitants of the rest of Judah (*die Landbewohner*) were already suffering the effects of invasion and occupation.[59] Kilpp sums up the matter thus: "Dem Volksteil, der das Unheil erfahren hat und noch erlebt, wird Heil zugesagt. Sind es Jer 24; 29 die 597 Deportierten im Gegensatz zu den Zurückgebliebenen, so in Jer 32,15 die Landbewohner im Gegensatz zu dem Jerusalemern."[60]

---

55. Ibid., 93: "Die Lebenszusage schränkt die äußerste Auswirkung des Unheils für einzelne ein: eine karge Heilsverheißung, die noch zurückhaltender als Jer 29,5–7 und Jer 32,15 ist."

56. Ibid., 61: "Jeremia kennt die Aussonderung einzelner oder kleinerer Gruppen vom künftigen Unheil (Baruch, Ebed-Melech, Rechabiten); eine Aussonderung einzelner aus dem zukünftigen Heil ist sonst bei Jeremia nicht bekannt. Die Perspektive von Jer 29,32 ist anders als die Jeremias: Das Heil geschieht prinzipiell dem Volk, doch gibt es Ausnahmen."

57. Ibid., 36, 38.

58. Ibid., 38. On the same page, he remarks, "Damit ist Heil Kritik an Bestehendem."

59. Ibid., 79: "Ein gewisser Gegensatz zwischen Jerusalem und Land Juda macht sich bemerkbar... Damit träfe das verheißene Heil nicht allgemein all diejenigen, die irgendwann in der Zukunft im Lande Juda leben werden, sondern die in der Gegenwart lebende Landbevölkerung Judas, die dem Gericht schon ausgesetzt ist."

60. Ibid., 80. Kilpp's thinking was anticipated in two works by Thomas M. Raitt, "Jeremiah's Deliverance Message to Judah," in *Rhetorical Criticism: Essays in Honor of James Muilenburg* (ed. J. J. Jackson and M. Kessler; PTMS 1; Pittsburgh: Pickwick, 1974), 166–85; *A Theology of Exile: Judgment/Deliverance in Jeremiah and Ezekiel* (Philadelphia: Fortress, 1977). According to Raitt, "the people's accountability for their sin together with God's attitude and intention toward them are radically shifted when the exile becomes a fact. The punishment itself creates an entirely new situation" ("Jeremiah's Deliverance Message," 171).

Clearly, this understanding of the philosophy of judgment and salvation in Jeremiah's preaching both echoes and develops the notion of restoration after judgment touched on by Seitz in his discussion of ER. It will be noted, however, that Kilpp defines judgment more broadly, to include not only exile but also the experience of YHWH's wrath in Judah.

Kilpp has offered us a rewarding study. By attending to the meaning of "salvation" in different contexts, he achieves a more nuanced analysis than those of Pohlmann and Seitz. Moreover, his interpretation of the rationale for the salvation oracles enables him to account for the proclamation of hope to certain audiences, and judgment to others, in terms of Jeremiah's own understanding, rather than that of later editors. Relating his work to our own enquiry, we find two distinct polarities: (1) "Judgment for all/Salvation (= blessing on daily life) for those judged" (2) "Judgment for all/Salvation (= exemption from judgment) for individuals."

There remains, however, a degree of ambiguity in Kilpp's analysis. For if the criteria for YHWH's renewed favour is the experience of his judgment—whether in a foreign land or in Judah—then it is hard to see how *any* could ultimately be excluded.[61] Yet according to Kilpp, one of the defining features of the coming salvation is a wholly new *modus operandi* in YHWH's way of relating to his people. Whereas previously judgment was executed on the entire nation, in future "Jahwe handelt nun nicht mehr an dem Volk, sondern an den Volksteilen."[62] In fact, when Kilpp describes YHWH's new community as independent of the sort of geographical and political structures (such as land and temple) that create an undifferentiated *Volk*, he seems to be hinting at a principle of confessional voluntarism.[63] We are left wondering, therefore, whether Jeremiah's announcement of salvation has a conditional dimension, beyond the involuntary experience of judgment.

Kilpp's study is also somewhat selective. Notably, he takes no account of those passages (so important for Pohlmann and Seitz) in which Jeremiah invites the post-597/587 Judean community to "submit and live" (chs. 27–28 and 42:10–18), nor of the oracles in 21:8–10 or 38:1–3, even though these would seem to fall into his category of prophecies of individual survival. Also absent is any discussion of the prophecy regarding "shepherds and sheep" in 23:1–8.

4. *Judicial Differentiation in Jeremiah: A Fresh Approach*

How, then, have these four studies helped our understanding of judicial differentiation in Jeremiah? We have seen that Koenen's analysis of the concept in the

---

61. Including those who eventually fled to Judah (43:5–7), since they too had suffered the disaster of 587.

62. Kilpp, *Niederreißen*, 38. Later he writes: "Wurde von Jeremia dem ganzen Volk und dem ganzen Land das Gericht angekündigt, geschieht in den Heilsweissagungen das Gegenteil: Nicht mehr das Volksganze, sondern nur Teile davon werden betroffen. Dem Volksteil, der das Unheil erfahren hat und noch erlebt, wird Heil zugesagt" (p. 80).

63. But then in this case it is hard to see why Kilpp should regard as inauthentic passages that announce the exclusion of rebellious individuals from YHWH's salvation (e.g. Jer 29:32).

prophetic corpus generally found little evidence for it in Jeremiah itself. This, I suggested, was due to an artificially narrow definition of the idea. We then considered the monographs by Pohlmann, Seitz and Kilpp. For the most part these highlight the polarity of "Salvation for exiles/Judgment for others" in Jer 24 and 29, a verdict deemed arbitrary by Pohlmann, but which Seitz and Kilpp see as rooted in a theology of exile. Elsewhere in Jeremiah, however, Pohlmann identifies a polarity of "Judgment for the leaders/Judgment or salvation for the remnant," which is obviously related to the conduct of each group. Seitz and Kilpp observe how Baruch and Ebed-Melech are exempt from judgment, while Kilpp also notes the exclusion of Shemaiah from YHWH's salvation. That there is an ethical aspect to these individual oracles is clear.

Might there, however, be other judicial polarities in Jeremiah? It has already been noted that Pohlmann, Seitz and Kilpp overlook certain passages that would *prima facie* seem to be relevant, such as 23:1–8. Indeed, we might ask how the prophet himself fits into the drama of judgment and salvation. Seitz sees Jeremiah, like his prototype Moses, as suffering unjustly in YHWH's wrath against the nation,[64] but his remarks leave room for further study of this idea. In short, there would seem to be scope for an investigation of *all* the different modes of judicial differentiation in Jeremiah, carefully describing the form and rationale of each.

Secondly, might there be a fruitful alternative to the essentially diachronic methodology of the scholars we have looked at? Differences in detail notwithstanding, the studies of Pohlmann, Seitz and Kilpp all rest on redaction-critical foundations. Such an approach is (in principle) perfectly valid, but one of the occupational hazards of redaction criticism is a tendency towards circular argument; texts are allocated to a particular editorial strand, the (purported) theological perspective of which is then attributed to each text. I have argued that Pohlmann and Seitz at times fall into just this trap; that is, their interpretation of the *overall* viewpoint of a given redactor controls their reading of the *particular* passages they allocate to him. In so doing, they may be blurring crucial distinctions between Jeremiah's preaching in different contexts.

An alternative approach to the concept of judicial differentiation in Jeremiah would be to explore the various polarities synchronically. Indeed, the very shape of the book invites us to do so.[65] Whereas the first twenty chapters are dominated by the threat of disaster for the entire land, from ch. 21 onwards we encounter a series of oracles announcing judgment for some and salvation for others.[66]

---

64. It is noticeable that at just this point, Seitz ("Canonical Shape," 11) moves outside Jeremiah for theological explication: "in the logic of Deuteronomy, [Jeremiah] is judged not for his own disobedience, but because of his generation—in the idiom of Deuteronomy, 'on your account' (Deut 1,37; 3,26)."

65. The different textual sequences of Jeremiah MT and Jeremiah OG do not affect this particular point.

66. Seitz, "Isaiah in Parish Bible Study," 201, remarks that in Jer 21–45 "the situation of unmitigated judgment changes…the reader sees the emergence of a small but courageous remnant, who in the midst of hardship and a sentence of divine judgment are still able to trust in God's infinite mercy."

Consequently, the issue of selective or non-selective judgment is highlighted by the overall structure of Jeremiah. Furthermore, the passages that we will examine are not randomly scattered, but rather counter-balance each other within well-defined literary units. For example, Jer 21–24 contains three prophecies of judgment and salvation—for those who leave the city and those who stay (21:1–10), for "the shepherds and the sheep" (23:1–8) and for the exiled and non-exiled communities (24:1–10)—and these stand at the opening, centre and conclusion of the unit respectively. The Judean and *Golah* communities are juxtaposed again, albeit in a more nuanced way, in Jer 27–29, while the individual salvation oracles to Ebed-Melech and Baruch counter-balance each other in the macro-section Jer 37–45.

The aim of the following study, therefore, is twofold. First, it attempts the *descriptive* task of identifying and describing the various judicial polarities in Jeremiah within their present literary units. Who is differentiated from whom in each passage? What is the rationale for YHWH's judgment? Secondly, it explores the *hermeneutical* issues arising from the juxtaposition of different polarities within the same literary units. How do these relate to one another? Does any one form of judicial differentiation have the dominant voice? It is in the latter regard, I believe, that this study breaks new ground.

The course can be charted as follows. Two brief chapters deal with sections of Jeremiah which, so far as YHWH's judgment and salvation are concerned, form opposite poles within the book. Chapter 3 explores the macro-section Jer 1–20, where the picture is (almost) completely one of national judgment. This provides the counterpoint to Chapter 7, which highlights the vision of all-Israel salvation in Jer 30–31.

Chapters 4, 5 and 6, which focus attention on Jer 21–24, 27–29 and 37–45, form the heart of this study. Each of these literary units will be placed in its *Sitz im Buch*, prior to an exegetical study of the relevant passages and discussion of the questions outlined above. Finally, in Chapter 8, I will reflect on the hermeneutical and theological implications of the enquiry.

A few procedural comments are in order. First, for each passage examined I have set out in parallel columns the relevant Hebrew and Greek texts, that is, the consonantal base of the Masoretic Text (MT) and the Old Greek Text (OG). For the former, I have followed *Codex Leningradensis* (B19ᴬ) as provided in *BHS*; in the passages we shall be discussing, this is identical with the text of the *Aleppo Codex*.[67] For OG, I have followed J. Ziegler's eclectic Göttingen text.[68] Quantitative and content variants are underlined.

Each passage is followed by "Textual Notes." It should be emphasized that these are not intended to provide comprehensive textual commentary, but simply to highlight points that will have a bearing on subsequent discussion. Traditionally, the goal of text criticism has been defined as the recovery of "the original

67. This provides the base text in C. Rabin et al., eds., *The Hebrew University Bible: The Book of Jeremiah* (Jerusalem: Magnes, 1997).

68. J. Ziegler, ed., *Septuaginta. Vetus Testamentum Graecum, Vol. XV: Ieremias, Baruch, Threni, Epistula Ieremiae* (Göttingen: Vandenhoeck & Ruprecht, 1957).

text."[69] Such a notion is problematic,[70] not least in the case of Jeremiah where MT and OG diverge so significantly.[71] While it is generally accepted that OG reflects a Hebrew text significantly different to that contained in MT, it is far less clear when and how the two traditions (or editions) diverged.[72] Certainly, we should not automatically assume that a reading peculiar to MT is late (still less, "inferior").[73] Consequently, where I have marked a given reading as "MT plus," this means no more than that the reading was probably absent from the OG *Vorlage*. A quantitative variant (i.e. a reading in one text that is absent from another) is indicated by the symbol >. In the case of content variants, the Greek reading is followed by a Hebrew equivalent. Such a retroversion is not necessarily being equated with the translator's *Vorlage*; a decision on that point will be indicated in the subsequent discussion.

The Hebrew text which will function as the basis for "Exegesis" is that of the (unpointed) MT, except in those few places where textual *error* (as opposed to modification or expansion) has occurred (e.g. the reading יהויקים in 27:1). Here too, I have not attempted to provide a detailed verse-by-verse commentary. Naturally, there will be some overlap between "Textual Notes" and "Exegesis."

In the "Coherence and Redaction" sections, attention is given to the literary and conceptual unity of the passage under review, rather than to its authorship.

---

69. So B. J. Roberts, *The Old Testament Text and Versions: The Hebrew Text in Transmission and the History of the Ancient Versions* (Cardiff: University of Wales Press, 1951), xi; D. Winton Thomas, "The Textual Criticism of the Old Testament," in *The Old Testament and Modern Study: A Generation of Discovery and Research* (ed. H. H. Rowley; Oxford: Oxford University Press, 1951), 238–59 (259); Ralph W. Klein, *Textual Criticism of the Old Testament: From the Septuagint to Qumran* (Philadelphia: Fortress, 1974), vii.

70. See A. P. Hayman, "The 'Original Text': A Scholarly Illusion," in *Words Remembered, Texts Renewed: Essays in Honour of John F. A. Sawyer* (ed. Jon Davies, Graham Harvey and Wilfred G. E. Watson; JSOTSup 195; Sheffield: Sheffield Academic Press, 1995), 434–49.

71. Jeremiah MT is now thought to exceed Jeremiah OG by some 3,097 words; so Y.-J. Min, "The Minuses and Pluses of the LXX Translation of Jeremiah as Compared with the Massoretic Text" (Ph.D diss., Jerusalem: Hebrew University, 1977), 159; cited by Sven Soderlund, *The Greek Text of Jeremiah: A Revised Hypothesis* (JSOTSup 47; Sheffield: JSOT, 1985), 11; cf. the older estimate of F. Giesebrecht, *Das Buch Jeremia, übersetzt und erklärt* (HKAT; Göttingen: Vandenhoeck & Ruprecht, 1894), xix, of 2,700 extra words.

72. J. Gerald Janzen, *Studies in the Text of Jeremiah* (HSM 6; Cambridge, Mass.: Harvard University Press, 1973), 134, dates the divergence to the mid-fifth or early fourth century, while P.-M. Bogaert, "De Baruch à Jérémie. Les Deux Rédactions Conservées du Livre de Jérémie," in Bogaert, ed., *Le Livre de Jérémie*, 168–73 (168 n. 1), puts it around 300. However, Frank M. Cross, "The Evolution of a Theory of Local Texts," in *Qumran and the History of the Biblical Text* (ed. Frank M. Cross and Shemaryahu Talmon; Cambridge, Mass.: Harvard University Press, 1975), 306–20 (309), believes that both textual traditions may have existed from the fifth or even the sixth century; cf. David J. Reimer, *The Oracles Against Babylon in Jeremiah 50–51: A Horror Among the Nations* (San Francisco: Mellen Research University Press, 1993), 112.

73. See Emanuel Tov, "Some Aspects of the Textual and Literary History of the Book of Jeremiah," in Bogaert, ed., *Le Livre de Jérémie*, 147–67 (150); Craigie, Kelley and Drinkard, *Jeremiah 1–25*, xliii. Nor can it be assumed that the Hebrew *Vorlage* of OG was itself a pristine text; see Janzen, *Studies*, 117–20; Jack R. Lundbom, *Jeremiah 1–20: A New Translation with Introduction and Commentary* (AB 21A; New York: Doubleday, 1999), 61–62, 885–87.

At the very least, this discussion will serve to highlight some of the key issues for interpretation. As will become apparent, I am often sceptical of claims for multiple redactional layers within a given text. Such hypotheses, it seems to me, tend to underestimate the capacity of the biblical writer (or prophet) for subtlety of thinking, paradox and irony.[74] Even if a text can be shown to display internal dissonance, this does not of itself indicate a plurality of speakers; an individual is perfectly capable of being inconsistent. It may, therefore, be better to speak of different *voices* in a text, without necessarily implying different *authors*.

---

74. On this point, see Jeremiah Unterman, *From Repentance to Redemption: Jeremiah's Thought in Transition* (JSOTSup 54; Sheffield: Sheffield Academic Press, 1987), 18; McConville, *Judgment and Promise*, 22–26.

Chapter 3

JUDICIAL DIFFERENTIATION IN JEREMIAH 1–20

1. Introduction: The Literary Cohesion of Jeremiah 1–20

With good reason, Jeremiah scholarship has long regarded chs. 1–25 as comprising part one of the entire book.[1] Despite its mixture of prose sermons, poetic oracles and laments, this macro-section is dominated by the threat of YHWH's impending judgment against Judah. Admittedly, its precise terminus varies, depending on whether we are reading MT or OG. In the former, the image of Jeremiah giving the cup of wrath to the foreign kings and announcing YHWH's judgment against the whole earth (25:15–38) brings to fulfilment Jeremiah's commission as "a prophet to the nations" (1:5–10). However, the first section of Jeremiah OG ends with the prophet's sermon in the fourth year of Jehoiakim (25:3–13; cf. the retrospective ἐν τρισκαιδεκάτῳ ἔτει τοῦ Ιωσια...καὶ ἕως τῆς ἡμέρας ταύτης, v. 3), with the Oracles against the Nations (OAN) forming the second major section (25:14–32:24).[2] Either way, some scholars believe that these 25 chapters (or parts of them) reflect an early edition of the book: "Cap. 1–25 bildet, wenn auch vielleicht in etwas kürzerer Form als der jetzigen, sozusagen die Urgestalt des Jeremiabuches...und scheint eine gewisse Zeit für sich existiert zu haben," wrote Duhm.[3] More recently, Clements has stated that

1. See B. Duhm, *Das Buch Jeremia* (KHAT; Tübingen: Mohr [Paul Siebeck], 1901), xxi; Paul Volz, *Der Prophet Jeremia. Übersetzt und erklärt* (2d ed.; KAT; Leipzig: Deichert, 1928), xliv. Ronald E. Clements, "Jeremiah 1–25 and the Deuteronomistic History," in *Old Testament Prophecy: From Oracles to Canon* (ed. Ronald E. Clements; Louisville: Westminster John Knox, 1996), 107–22, reads Jer 1–25 as an exposition of the main themes of the Deuteronomistic History, while Louis Stulman, *Order Amid Chaos: Jeremiah as Symbolic Tapestry* (BS 57; Sheffield: Sheffield Academic Press, 1998), 31, sees them as "dismantling Judah's first principles." Most two-volume commentaries on Jeremiah also divide after ch. 25.

2. See Artur Weiser, *Introduction to the Old Testament* (trans. D. M. Barton; London: Darton, Longman & Todd, 1961), 213, and Schmid, *Buchgestalten*, 7; cf. Rudolph, *Jeremia*, 139. This structural division is highlighted in v. 13, where πάντα τὰ γεγραμμένα ἐν τῷ βιβλίῳ τούτῳ (כל הכתוב בספר הזה) clearly indicates the conclusion of a major literary unit. Lundbom, *Jeremiah 1–20*, 93, believes that "these words make better sense when taken as a pointer to what originally lay ahead—and what in LXX still does lie ahead—viz., the oracles against Babylon." However, the preceding phrase, כל דברי אשר דברתי עליה, strongly suggests that in the OG *Vorlage*, כל הכתוב בספר הזה was retrospective; so Bright, *Jeremiah*, 163. The same is probably true of τῷ βιβλίῳ τούτῳ in OG.

3. Duhm, *Jeremia*, xxi; similarly Bright, *Jeremiah*, lvii–lviii.

the phrase כל הכתוב בספר הזה (25:13) "clearly betrays its role as a formal ending to a *literary collection*."[4] Many commentators have identified this ספר with Baruch's second (and enlarged) scroll of 605 BC (36:32).

Equally, however, several factors suggest that Jer 1–20 has a literary integrity of its own. In his seminal study in 1966, Rietzschel argued that these chapters originally formed a "traditions block" (*Überlieferungsblock*), concluding in what is now ch. 45.[5] Thus, Jeremiah's final lament (20:7–18) led straight into Baruch's, linked by the catchword יגון, "sorrow" (20:18; 45:3).[6] Rietzschel's analysis has more recently been taken up by Lundbom, as reflected in the arrangement of his three-volume commentary on Jeremiah.[7] Lundbom notes that the prophet's anguished cry in 20:18, למה זה מרחם יצאתי לראות עמל ויגון, creates an unmistakeable *inclusio* with YHWH's words of commission in 1:5, בטרם תצא מרחם הקדשתיך.[8] Whether or not we accept his conclusion that "chs. 1–20 can be designated the First Edition of the book of Jeremiah,"[9] it is clear that 20:18 marks a definite pause in the flow of the text.

To this we may add the observation that, in contrast to later chapters, Jer 1–20 is conspicuous for its lack of historical or circumstantial detail. After the opening superscription (1:1–3), listing the various reigns during which Jeremiah prophesied, not a single king is mentioned, other than the brief reference to Josiah in 3:6. Especially striking in this regard is the unspecified date of the temple sermon in ch. 7 (cf. 26:1!) and the plural vocative in 19:3, "Hear the word of YHWH, O *kings* of Judah." A similar vagueness is evident in relation to the prophet's audience, addressed simply as "Judah" (2:28); "Jerusalem" (4:14; 6:8; 15:5); "men of Judah and Jerusalem" (4:3; 11:2; 18:11); "this people" (7:16; 11:14; 15:1); "the house of Israel" (9:26; 10:1; 18:6), and so on. Even when particular groups (e.g. kings, prophets and priests) are referred to, they are piled up without distinction (1:18; 2:26; 4:9; 8:1; 13:13). Only with the men of Anathoth (11:21–23) and Pashhur ben Immer (20:1–6) do the targets of criticism become more specific. All in all, Jer 1–20 seems to be drawing a portrait of Judah in which historical and audience-critical distinctions simply do not matter.

---

4. Clements, "Jeremiah 1–25," 109 (italics mine).

5. Claus Rietzschel, *Das Problem der Urrolle. Ein Beitrag zur Redaktionsgeschichte des Jeremiabuches* (Gütersloh: Gütersloher Verlagshaus/Gerd Mohn, 1966), 128–29. Rietzschel believed that chs. 21–24 were added later to this "traditions block."

6. This verbal echo may well be intentional, although 45:1b clearly presupposes the narrative of ch. 36.

7. In addition to his commentary on Jer 1–20, see now Jack R. Lundbom, *Jeremiah 21–36: A New Translation with Introduction and Commentary* (AB 21B; New York: Doubleday, 2004), and *Jeremiah 37–52: A New Translation with Introduction and Commentary* (AB 21C; New York: Doubleday, 2004). Kidner, *The Message of Jeremiah*, 29, also regards chs. 2–20 and 21–45 respectively as parts one and two of the book.

8. Lundbom, *Jeremiah 1–20*, 93.

9. Ibid., 94.

2. *Judicial Non-differentiation in Jeremiah 1–20*

Given what has just been said, it comes as no surprise to discover that the message of divine judgment in Jer 1–20 is against the entire land. When it falls, no one will be safe (12:12), for YHWH's wrath will be poured out on man and beast (על האדם ועל הבהמה, 7:20). YHWH has rejected the generation of his wrath (דור עברתו, 7:29). Especially comprehensive is the language of 6:11–15, where, having described himself as full of the wrath of YHWH (6:11), Jeremiah cries:

> Pour it out on the children in the street and on the young men assembling together; both husband and wife will be caught in it, and the old, full of years. Their houses will be turned over to others, together with their fields and their wives... They will fall with the fallen; in the time when I visit them they will be brought down.

Commenting on this passage, Brueggemann notes: "The (people's) failure occasions the full, powerful release of YHWH's wrath against every part of the city. This passage, unlike others that indict the leadership, includes all in the scope of disobedience—children, young men, husbands, wives, old folk (v. 11)."[10]

Granted, there is some variation regarding the *nature* of judgment, since alongside the prophecy that Judah will be carried into exile (הגלת יהודה כלה, 13:19) is the claim that both great and small (גדלים וקטנים, 16:6) will die in the land. The scope of the disaster, however, is not in doubt, and hints that any might survive are few. Jeremiah 6:9 speaks of the remnant of Israel (שארית ישראל), a phrase that is unique within the book, but the ultimate fate even of this group seems to be annihilation rather than salvation.[11] An ominous future for השארית is also anticipated in 8:3 and 15:9. In 4:27, a warning of devastation on Judah is followed by the words כלה לא אעשה ("but I will not make an end of her"),[12] and a similar caveat occurs in 5:10, עלו בשרותיה ושחתו וכלה אל תעשו.[13]

10. Brueggemann, *Exile and Homecoming*, 72.
11. So McKane, *Jeremiah 1*, 144–45; Carroll, *Jeremiah*, 195; William L. Holladay, *Jeremiah 1: A Commentary on the Book of the Prophet Jeremiah, Chapters 1–25* (Philadelphia: Fortress, 1986), 213; Craigie, Kelley and Drinkard, *Jeremiah 1–25*, 102–3; Brueggemann, *Exile and Homecoming*, 71–72; contra Duhm, *Jeremia*, 68; Rudolph, *Jeremia*, 38–39; John M. Berridge, *People, Prophet, and the Word of YHWH: An Examination of Form and Content in the Proclamation of the Prophet Jeremiah* (BST 4; Zurich: EVZ, 1970), 79. If we follow MT, עולל יעוללו, the subject must be Israel's enemies and the verb given an ominous sense. Following OG, Rudolph, *Jeremia*, 36, and Bright, *Jeremiah*, 44, emend to עולל עולל, so that Jeremiah is being addressed. But it is still not certain that gleaning means saving; see John Skinner, *Prophecy and Religion: Studies in the Life of Jeremiah* (Cambridge: Cambridge University Press, 1922), 156–57; Thompson, *Jeremiah*, 257.
12. Some scholars (e.g. Rudolph, *Jeremia*, 30; McKane, *Jeremiah 1*, 109) avoid the problem by emending to וכלה הלה אעשה ("and I will make an end of her"), but against this see Brueggemann, *Exile and Homecoming*, 60–61. John Calvin, *Commentaries on the Book of the Prophet Jeremiah and the Lamentations*, vol. 1 (trans. J. Owen; Edinburgh: Calvin Translation Society, 1852), 241, takes the words to mean that God "would observe no moderation in executing his vengeance," while Craigie, Kelley and Drinkard, *Jeremiah 1–25*, 80, translate them "I will not *yet* have brought the end."
13. אל is deleted by Duhm, *Jeremia*, 59; Rudolph, *Jeremia*, 33; McKane, *Jeremiah 1*, 120; Carroll, *Jeremiah*, 181; contra Thompson, *Jeremiah*, 243; Craigie, Kelley and Drinkard, *Jeremiah 1–25*, 90. According to the latter, "the notion of pruning (v 10b) and the notion of exile (v 19) seem

The meaning of כלה לא עשׂה, however, becomes clear after its third occurrence in 5:18; those who are spared will be taken to a foreign land (כן תעבדו זרים בארץ לא לכם, 5:19).

In fact, the only real note of hope in Jer 1–20 comes in prophecies of restoration, which necessarily assume the disaster of exile (3:14–18; 12:14–16; 16:14–15). To be sure, the first of these forms part of a wider unit (3:1–4:2), often thought to contain some of the prophet's earliest oracles, in which he appears to hold out the possibility of forgiveness and restoration, conditional on genuine repentance (e.g. 3:12aβ–13, 19–25; 4:1–2). Indeed, Skinner detected in these particular verses a theology of *undifferentiated salvation* similar to that described by Koenen: "We are led to regard it as an ideal picture of national conversion, setting forth the condition of restoration to Yahweh's favour as a change of heart, expressing itself in a corporate act of confession in which the whole nation is conceived as taking part... [Jeremiah's] thought still moves on the plane of national religion."[14]

Whether this was in fact the perspective of the young prophet is impossible to say. The interpretation (both diachronic and synchronic) of 3:1–4:2 is remarkably complex, due to the alternation of poetry and prose (and deciding which is which), the difficulty of delimiting the various literary units, and the ambiguity of צפונה and משׁבה ישׂראל in v. 12.[15] What is clear, however, is that the final horizon of the present text lies in 3:18: "Together they will come from the land of the north to the land I gave your fathers as an inheritance." This perspective thus serves to underline the more sombre view of Jer 1–20, that no restoration to YHWH will be possible prior to the judgment of exile. On this basis, McConville interprets the appeal to Israel to return (3:12) as "a way of conceptualizing before Judah the idea that for her too there lies a way back to God beyond an exile which she in turn must endure."[16] A few scholars have even argued that 3:14–18 (and other parts of this section) were addressed to Israelites of the former northern kingdom, already exiled in Assyria.[17]

---

to support the notion that '*not* a final end' is in the prophet's mind, but only a terrible act of judgment that will seem like the end."

14.　Skinner, *Prophecy and Religion*, 87.

15.　Ibid., 79–88, saw here an authentic poem addressed to Judah (vv. 1–5, 12aβ–13, 21–25), interrupted by later oracles to Israel (vv. 6–11) and the post-exilic community (vv. 14–18). Very similar are the analyses of McKane, *Jeremiah 1*, 69–71, and Carroll, *Jeremiah*, 145–47, who argue however that the addition of vv. 6–11, 12aα, was due to a misreading of the earlier material as referring to Israel. By contrast, Bright, *Jeremiah*, 25–27, treats the northern kingdom as the subject of vv. 6–13, and probably of vv. 14–15 as well.

16.　McConville, *Judgment and Promise*, 35–39.

17.　So Moshe Weinfeld, "Jeremiah and the Spiritual Metamorphosis of Israel," *ZAW* 88 (1976): 17–56 (23); Thompson, *Jeremiah*, 199–200. However, even if vv. 12–13 do address Israel as distinct from Judah (*pace* Skinner, McKane and Carroll), they may have in view Israelites still living in their former territory, rather than those in exile; so H. Cazelles, "Israël du nord et arche d"alliance (Jér. III 16)," *VT* 18 (1968): 149–58 (who reads 3:12–17 as an appeal to this remnant to reunite with their southern compatriots under Josiah); Craigie, Kelley and Drinkard, *Jeremiah 1–25*, 57; Brueggemann, *Exile and Homecoming*, 45.

Taken as a whole, therefore, Jer 1–20 announces comprehensive disaster for Judah. However, to use the terms that I introduced in my opening chapter, it is clear that this constitutes an act of national rather than undifferentiated judgment. For Judah's guilt is equally comprehensive. From the least to the greatest (מקטן ועד גדול), all (כלו) are greedy for gain and practice deceit (6:13 = 8:10). All of them (כלם) are rebels (6:28) and adulterers (9:1), and within Jerusalem all is oppression (כלה עשק, 6:6). No one (אין איש) repents of his wickedness (8:6) or takes YHWH's judgment to heart (12:11). In fact, in 9:25–26 YHWH refuses even to differentiate Judah from the other nations, since "the whole house of Israel (כל בית ישראל) is uncircumcised in heart."[18]

This picture of unqualified guilt and judgment is encapsulated in Jer 5. The chapter opens with YHWH challenging Jeremiah to find one person in Jerusalem "who does justice and seeks truth" (v. 1). Although the prophet concedes that the poor (דלים) are ignorant of YHWH's ways (v. 4a), he has higher expectations of the leaders (הגדלים, v. 5a). But he is disappointed; they have *as one* (המה יחדו, v. 5b) rejected YHWH's yoke. Later on, the chapter briefly hints at a more nuanced view (vv. 26–31). Here, YHWH refers to the entire nation as "my people" (עמי, vv. 26, 31),[19] but singles out for condemnation those whom he terms "the wicked" (רשעים, v. 26)—powerful and rich men (גדלו ויעשירו, v. 27) who have failed to defend the poor (אביונים) and the orphan (יתום, v. 28). At this point, the textual construal of Judah appears more differentiating, with "the wicked" defined as a particular group of people.[20] This is of course a familiar social polarity in the Old Testament, and one in which (as we have seen) YHWH often sides with the poor; indeed, אביונים sometimes stands in synonymous parallelism with צדיק, "the righteous" (Amos 2:6; 5:12). Thus, we would most naturally take YHWH's question, "Shall I not punish *these people*?" (העל אלה לא אפקד, v. 29) as referring specifically to the רשעים of vv. 26–28. However, the following clause—"In a nation (בגוי אשר כזה) such as this, shall I not vindicate myself?"—makes the divine wrath sound less discriminating, and the shift back towards a unitary view of the people is completed in v. 31: "The prophets prophesy lies, the priests rule by their own hand, and my people love it this way."[21] Consequently, although 5:26–28 briefly suggests viewing guilt and judgment in selective terms, the present form of the text subordinates such distinctions to a more comprehensive analysis of sin and judgment, akin to that seen earlier in Deuteronomy.[22]

---

18. On this depiction of Judah as wholly evil, see further Robert P. Carroll, *From Chaos to Covenant: Uses of Prophecy in the Book of Jeremiah* (London: SCM, 1981), 67–68.

19. As Lundbom, *Jeremiah 1–20*, 406, observes, the term forms an *inclusio*.

20. Berridge, *People, Prophet, and the Word of YHWH*, 163 n. 260.

21. While McKane, *Jeremiah 1*, 136, and Rudolph, *Jeremia*, 35, see vv. 30–31 as originally independent, Lundbom, *Jeremiah 1–20*, 406, sees v. 29 as the intrusive element: "Without vv 30–31 the indictment in vv 26–28 remains flat, which may account for the need to bring in the stereotyped v 29; with these verses, the false prophets are blamed, the puppet priests are blamed, but the real culprit turns out to be the people."

22. Parke-Taylor, *Formation*, 88, argues that in 5:26, רשעים must "typify the people as a whole, when one considers the total pericope 5:20–29, addressed to 'the house of Jacob,' 'Judah' (5:20)."

Granted, this idea of national guilt may have been heightened redactionally. In his study of Jer 11–20, Mark Smith argues that the laments have been placed in carefully constructed literary units (chs. 11–12; 13–15; 16–17; and 19–20), each of which also contains a prose story about the prophet.[23] As a result, Smith remarks:

> There is a shift from the laments' original purpose to their main function in context. In their original usage, they serve to defend Jeremiah's prophetic mission against unnamed enemies. In context, however, the laments stress the guilt of the prophet's foes and extend their identity to include Judah and Jerusalem, in short all the people and its leadership.[24]

Again, it is not to be thought that in *literary* terms "Jerusalem" constitutes a uniform entity. As Biddle has shown, Jer 1–20 contains "a virtual chorus of voices in dialogue,"[25] in which the persona of Lady Jerusalem, for example, is quite distinct from that of the people of Judah. The former voices a spontaneous emotional response to disaster (e.g. 4:19–21; 10:19–22), while the latter express confusion and despair at YHWH's unwillingness to forgive (e.g. 14:7–9; 19–22). Nevertheless, while we encounter a variety of responses to the coming disaster, there is no indication that any of these personae are less culpable or less liable to judgment than others.

3. *Judicial Differentiation in Jeremiah 1–20: Jeremiah/the Nation*

Thus far, then, Koenen's claim regarding the undifferentiating perspective of the prophets finds considerable support in Jer 1–20. There is, though, one highly significant judicial polarity here, to which I have already alluded in connection with the laments; namely, that between the nation(s) and the prophet himself. This is established in the very first chapter: Jeremiah has been set apart (קדש Hiph.) as "a prophet to the nations" (v. 5). Indeed, he is given authority over them, in language that will be paradigmatic in the book: לנתוש ולנתוץ ולהאביד ולהרוס לבנות ולנטוע (v. 10). Moreover, accompanying this commission is an individual salvation oracle: "Do not be afraid of them, for I am with you to save you (כי אתך אני להצלך)" (v. 8). Rhetorically, therefore, YHWH's address creates just two parties: Jeremiah ("you") and the nations ("them"). Later in the chapter, however, the scope of this differentiation is narrowed, as the emphasis falls on Jeremiah as a prophet to his own country: "But look, I have made you today a fortified city, an iron pillar, and a bronze wall, against the whole land (על כל הארץ)—against the kings of Judah, her princes, her priests, and the people of the

---

23.   Mark S. Smith, *The Laments of Jeremiah and Their Contexts: A Literary and Redactional Study of Jeremiah 11–20* (SBLMS 42; Atlanta: Scholars Press, 1990), 43–64.

24.   Ibid., 39. Putting this same observation in reverse, Parke-Taylor, *Formation*, 88, argues that in 12:1, the term "the wicked" "has a wide application," but the literary context ("the men of Anathoth") makes it more specific (11:21–23).

25.   Mark E. Biddle, *Polyphony and Symphony in Prophetic Literature: Rereading Jeremiah 7–20* (SOTI 2; Macon, Ga.: Mercer University Press, 1996), 115.

land. They will fight against you but will not overcome you, for I am with you, says YHWH, to rescue you" (vv. 18–19).[26]

Thus, the plurality of social groups which constitute Judah are here bracketed together in (anticipated) opposition to Jeremiah. In the ongoing life of the book, of course, it may well be that the prophet is representative of a wider group of readers.[27] Nevertheless, according to the lines drawn by the text there only two categories of people: Jeremiah of Anathoth, and the nation to which he will speak.

The sense of conflict between these two groups becomes pronounced in chs. 11–20, the tension being highlighted by Jeremiah's laments. Following the second of these (15:15–18), YHWH reassures the prophet of his security in terms almost identical to those of 1:8, 18–19: "'I will make you to this people like a wall, a fortified wall of bronze. They will fight against you but will not overcome you, for I am with you to save you and rescue you,' declares YHWH. 'I will rescue you from the hands of the wicked and redeem you from the hand of the cruel.'" (15:20–21).

Now it may be argued that while the salvation oracles in chs. 1 and 15 guarantee Jeremiah's salvation in respect to the hostility of his people, they say nothing about his fate when YHWH finally visits Judah in judgment. Consequently, they do not provide a true parallel to the antithetical judgment oracles discussed in ch. 1. However, it has already been noted that YHWH's promise in 1:8, כי אתך אני להצלך, relates to the threat posed by the *nations*, and as chs. 1–20 unfold it becomes clear that it is they who will be the agent of YHWH's wrath (4:5–7, 19–21, 29; 5:15–17; 6:1–8, 22–23; 8:14–16). Thus, to be saved from the nations implies some sort of exemption (as yet unexplained) from YHWH's judgment on Judah. Of particular significance is the image of Jeremiah as a fortified city (עיר מבצר, 1:18), in contrast to the fortified cities of Judah (4:5; 5:17; 8:14; 34:7) which will fall to the invading armies. Indeed, in the context of the wider book, with its strong narrative interest in the Babylonian siege of *the city* (Jerusalem), the description of Jeremiah as עיר מבצר can scarcely be coincidental.

With the reaffirmation of YHWH's personal salvation in 15:20–21, however, the aspect of *conditionality*—hinted at only briefly in 1:17—emerges as a critical issue. Although Jeremiah has indeed been chosen before his birth and set apart from the rest of the nation, the certainty of deliverance requires the prophet's continued acceptance of his calling. Consequently, the oracle is preceded by a

---

26.   OG does not reflect על כל הארץ.

27.   Brueggemann, *Exile and Homecoming*, 30, writes: "The God of this oracle is not indiscriminate… An important distinction is made between the majority, who are unresponsive and so under threat, and this minority voice (Jeremiah), who holds faithfully to the purpose of Yahweh." Noting the emphatic ואתה in 1:17 and 45:5, he adds: "Indeed, these two 'but you' speeches in 1:17–19 and 45:5 may at one time have formed an envelope for the entire text. These two promises may provide a clue to the editorial history of the book of Jeremiah. That editorial work was done by those who came after Jeremiah, who lived in the Exile and who took the text seriously. These faithful people understood themselves to be recipients of the same 'but you' assurances" (p. 30).

double imperative to Jeremiah that is unique within the book. The first clause, אם תשוב ואשיבך (v. 19b), constitutes nothing less than a blunt call to repentance: "If you return, I will restore you."[28] What this repentance must involve is then indicated by the following clause, ואם תוציא יקר מזולל, "If you speak what is precious rather than what is worthless."[29] Although by itself the injunction is somewhat opaque, the context relates Jeremiah's "worthless" words to his charge of YHWH's unreliability: היו תהיה לי כמו אכזב מים לא נאמנו (v. 18). Not only does such an allegation challenge YHWH's description of himself (2:13; cf. 17:8, 13), it simultaneously prevents Jeremiah from speaking the divine word and thus being YHWH's spokesman.[30]

The significance of this imperative for Jeremiah himself to return to YHWH lies in the fact that although chs. 1–20 include several calls for Judah to repent (e.g. 3:1–4:4; 7:1–8; 18:5–11), its final verdict seems to be that Judah is in fact unable to do so;[31] indeed, an apparently contrite *corporate* prayer has just been emphatically rejected by YHWH (14:19–15:4). By implication, therefore, 15:19b raises the question as to whether Jeremiah, unlike the rest of his compatriots, is capable of a genuine act of repentance. Having raised the question, however, the remainder of chs. 1–20 offers an ambiguous answer. Jeremiah continues to proclaim the word given him by YHWH, as shown in the narrative material of 18:1–20:6, but in the final lament that closes this macro-unit, he lapses again into bitterness and rejection of his calling (20:14–18). This being so, the judicial polarity governing Jer 1–20, that of "Jeremiah/The nation," would seem to be of a type described in the previous chapter—that is, where salvation is held out as a *possibility* to one party, but not at all to the other. Judah's fate is certain; that of the prophet is still in the balance.

---

28. Or, as Brueggemann, *Exile and Homecoming*, 148, neatly translates, "If you return, I will return you."

29. For this meaning of יצא Hiph., see Job 8:10; 15:3; Isa 48:20; cf. Jer 51:10, where it carries the sense "report, announce."

30. Craigie, Kelley and Drinkard, *Jeremiah 1–25*, 211: "He must purge his words of worthless and bitter elements before he can speak the divine words"; similarly Thompson, *Jeremiah*, 398; McKane, *Jeremiah 1*, 357, and most commentators. Quite differently, Edgar W. Conrad, *Reading the Latter Prophets: Towards a New Canonical Criticism* (JSOTSup 376; London: Continuum, 2003), 127–28, argues that Jeremiah is called to repent of his attempts to mediate for the people (12:1–4; 14:7–9, 19–22), against YHWH's express prohibition: "The impression is that in earlier turning to intercession for his people, Jeremiah had been turning away from Yahweh" (p. 127). Not only does this seem an implausible reading of 15:19, in two of the passages Conrad cites (14:7–9, 19–22) it is far from certain that the speaker is Jeremiah; see further Biddle, *Polyphony and Symphony*, 38–41.

31. The appeal in 3:22, שובו בנים שובבים ארפה משובתיכם, encapsulates rather than solves the problem. See further McConville, *Judgment and Promise*, 28–39. According to McConville, the overall arrangement of Jeremiah "testifies to the abandonment of hope that the exile might be averted by repentance" (p. 25); cf. Unterman, *Repentance to Redemption*, 176–79. The closest parallel to 15:19b comes in Ephraim's prayer (31:18), where however the requisite sequence of human and divine turning is reversed: השיבני ואשובה.

Chapter 4

JUDICIAL DIFFERENTIATION IN JEREMIAH 21–24

1. *Introduction to Jeremiah 21–24*

1.1. *Jeremiah 21–24 as a Literary Unit*

Jeremiah 21–24 forms the last major unit in what is generally seen as part one of the book, chs. 1–25.[1] Stulman describes it as "the final macro-unit of the first scroll,"[2] while Carroll and O'Connor both designate it an "appendix" to chs. 1–20.[3] Indirectly, this demarcation is supported by the literary cohesion of the first twenty chapters, as described earlier. In addition, several scholars have shown how Jer 11–20 forms a distinct sub-section structured around the confessions.[4] Jeremiah 25, meanwhile, has its own character as a review of the first part of the book. Within chs. 21–24 themselves, the first indication that we are dealing with a new literary unit lies in the opening formula, הדבר אשר היה אל ירמיהו מאת יהוה (21:1).[5] Previously (7:1; 11:1; 18:1; also 30:1), this expression, in

---

1. T. R. Hobbs, "Some Remarks on the Composition and Structure of the Book of Jeremiah," in Perdue and Kovacs, eds., *A Prophet to the Nations*, 175–99 (192), believes that part one of Jeremiah ends with ch. 24, since ch. 25 shares with the OAN "a common ideology, namely, the defeat of Israel's enemies." This surely misreads 25:1–11. A. Rofé's argument, "The Arrangement of the Book of Jeremiah," *ZAW* 101 (1989): 394–95, that chs. 1–24 are distinguished from chs. 25–52 by using undated material, is weakened not only by the exception of 24:1 (which he acknowledges) but also that of 21:1 (which he does not).

2. Stulman, *Order Amid Chaos*, 49.

3. Carroll, *Jeremiah*, 404; Kathleen M. O'Connor, *The Confessions of Jeremiah: Their Interpretation and Role in Chapters 1–25* (SBLDS 94; Atlanta: Scholars Press, 1988), 158. Similarly, Rietzschel, *Urrolle*, 128, saw chs. 21–24 as expanding an earlier "traditions block" (*Überlieferungsblock*) of chs. 1–20. See too Rudolph, *Jeremia*, 115; Craigie, Kelley and Drinkard, *Jeremiah 1–25*, 283; McConville, *Judgment and Promise*, 54. Among the few dissenters, Thompson, *Jeremiah*, 127–28, detaches chs. 21–23 ("Kings and false prophets denounced") from chs. 24–25 ("Two visions and a summary"), though note his disclaimer (p. 125). Lundbom, *Jeremiah 1–20*, 95–97, designates chs. 21–23 "The king and prophet appendix," and sees ch. 24 as introducing chs. 24–45. Brueggemann, *Exile and Homecoming*, 188, brackets chs. 21–25 together, adding the caveat that "it is difficult to detect an intentional ordering."

4. See A. R. Diamond, *The Confessions of Jeremiah in Context: Scenes of Prophetic Drama* (JSOTSup 45; Sheffield: JSOT, 1987), 177–88; O'Connor, *Confessions*, 130–46; Smith, *Laments*, 43–60. Lundbom, *Jeremiah 1–20*, 869, notes that the end of ch. 20 repeats terms from the end of ch. 10 (אשר, 11:3; 20:15) and the beginning of ch. 11 (כלה, 10:25; 20:18).

5. Strictly speaking, this formula marks a new *episode*, rather than a new *unit*; hence, it occurs three times between 34:1 and 35:1, while 26:1 and 36:1—generally seen as inaugurating new macro-sections—begin with the somewhat different היה הדבר הזה (אל ירמיהו) מאת יהוה לאמר.

conjunction with לאמר, has served to introduce a specific command from YHWH to Jeremiah ("Stand!" "Go!" "Rise!"). Here, no such instruction follows, and precisely what הדבר refers to is left unclear (see section 4.3, "Exegesis").

Two internal features of chs. 21–24 confirm their distinctiveness. First, in contrast to chs. 1–20, these four chapters are striking in their use of historical annotation. Here again, the opening formula of 21:1 is significant, since for the first time in the book it is linked to a particular context (בשלח אליו המלך צדקיהו את פשחור), thereby setting the subsequent pattern for this formula (cf. 32:1; 34:1, 8; 35:1; 40:1).[6] Moreover, chs. 21–24 regularly refer to specific kings and dates. Oracles addressed to Shallum, Jehoiakim and Jehoiachin (22:10–30) are framed by material set in the reign of Zedekiah (21:1–10 and 24:1–10). In keeping with this is the observation that chs. 21–24 contain the first messages of hope for particular groups of people (21:8–9; 23:1–8; 24:5–7). While there have been promises of restoration before now (3:14–18; 12:14–17; 16:14–16), these have been of a pan-Israel, and even international, character.

Secondly, chs. 21–24 are defined by their internal literary structure, which can be outlined as follows:

A.   Judgment on Zedekiah and Jerusalem; hope for those who go out to Babylon (21:1–10)

B.   Oracles against the kings (21:11–22:30)

C.   Promises of restoration and of a new king (23:1–8)

B′.   Oracles against the prophets (23:9–40)

A′.   Judgment on Zedekiah and Jerusalem; hope for those in Babylon (24:1–10)

21:1–10 and 24:1–10 form an *inclusio*. Both warn of judgment on Jerusalem and its king, but offer hope to those who identify with Babylon.[7] Verbally, this theology is expressed in similar terms; compare שמתי פני בעיר הזאת לרעה ולא (21:10) and שמתי עיני עליהם לטובה (24:6). Another link lies in the trilogy דבר, חרב, רעב (21:7, 9; 24:9). Pohlmann terms 21:1–10 and 24:1–10 a frame composition (*Rahmenkomposition*),[8] while Schmid refers to "die Klammerstellung um den Komplex 21–24."[9] Within this frame are two anthologies, castigating the kings (21:11–22:30) and the prophets (23:9–39), highlighted by their superscriptions, ולבית מלך יהודה[10] and לנבאים. Sandwiched between them is the literary and theological heart of the unit, 23:1–8. Here, YHWH promises to raise

---

6.   See further Pohlmann, *Studien*, 32 n. 63.

7.   Stulman, *Order Amid Chaos*, 51: "The prose discourse (of 21:1–10) declares that the destiny of Judah as a reimaged community depends in large measure on its response to Babylonian subjugation."

8.   Pohlmann, *Studien*, 184.

9.   Schmid, *Buchgestalten*, 261. Seitz, *Theology in Conflict*, 84, speaks of "an even larger section on Judahite/Davidic kingship (chs. 21–24) framed by judgment oracles against Zedekiah (21:1–10; 24:8–10)."

10.   OG ὁ οἶκος βασιλέως Ιουδα suggests that the *Vorlage* contained vocative address rather than a superscription. Possibly MT added the preposition ל to counterbalance לנבאים in 23:9. Duhm, *Jeremia*, 171; Rudolph, *Jeremia*, 116; McKane, *Jeremiah 1*, 506, all take ו as an MT plus but retain the preposition.

up a new king (יהוה צדקנו), so echoing the name of Zedekiah (צדקיהו) with whom chs. 21–24 begin and end. Without claiming that the second half of the unit is a perfect mirror image of the first, the overall pattern is too clear to be fortuitous.

What exactly is meant by describing chs. 21–24 as a "unit" is a moot point. Arguably, this section is a *compositional* unity; that is, it existed independently before being added *en bloc* to the developing book. Rudolph saw these four chapters as a separate literary cycle that was then inserted between chs. 20 and 25,[11] while Rietzschel saw them as an oral "tradition complex" (*Überlieferungskomplex*) that evolved in the exilic synagogues, before being added to the "tradition block" of chs. 1–20.[12] Both views are attractive, but inevitably speculative. It is possible, for example, that 21:1–23:8 ('Oracles about kings') was added first, and supplemented later by 23:9–39 and 24:1–10. All we can say with certainty is that chs. 21–24 constitute a *literary* unit within the present book.

This is not to deny their diversity. The anthological nature of the oracles against the kings and the prophets is apparent not only from their headings, but also by the mixture of poetry (e.g. 22:20–23; 23:9–14) and prose (e.g. 22:1–5; 23:33–39)—and, in the case of the first collection, by the fact that three different kings are addressed. Literary and historical differences are also evident in the two passages set in the reign of Zedekiah; 21:1–10 records Jeremiah's message to king and city during the siege of 588–587, while ch. 24 describes a private vision-experience of the prophet shortly after 597. More important is the *conceptual* diversity of this unit. Granted, the critique of Judah's leadership is a prominent theme; Thiel summarizes chs. 21–24 as "hauptsächlich Worte über die politischen und geistigen Führer des Volkes, Könige und Propheten,"[13] while Stulman entitles them "the dismantling of royal ideology."[14] But can *all* of chs. 21–24 be subsumed under this rubric (note Thiel's qualifying "hauptsächlich")? As we will see, 21:1–10 contains an indictment of the entire city *plus* a message of (qualified) hope to the people. Moreover, in ch. 24 judgment and hope appear totally unrelated to the issue of leadership. Thiel attempts to link YHWH's condemnation of Jerusalem here to the preceding critique: "das Gericht mit dem Versagen der Führer des Volkes und wohl auch mit dem blinden Vertrauen des Volkes auf seine Leiter (vgl. 14:14–16) begründet."[15] This, though, is

---

11. Rudolph, *Jeremia*, xviii.

12. Rietzschel, *Urrolle*, 127–36. By "tradition complexes," Rietzschel meant small collections of poetry and prose arranged according to their "thematischen Gesichspunkten oder Stichwortverknüpfungen" (p. 24). This approach is broadly accepted by Douglas Rawlinson Jones, *Jeremiah* (NCB; London: Marshall Pickering, 1992), 29–31.

13. Thiel, *Redaktion 1–25*, 230. Cf. Schmid, *Buchgestalten*, 261: "21:1–10 vertritt eine sehr königs– und führungskritische Sicht: Der Abschnitt ist der nachfolgenden Königsspruchsammlung vorgeschaltet worden und macht klar, daß der nationale Untergang auf das Konto Zedekias und der Fürsten ging: Sie waren rechtzeitig informiert und hätten sich den Babyloniern ergeben können."

14. Stulman, *Order Amid Chaos*, 31, 49–52.

15. Thiel, *Redaktion 1–25*, 260.

unconvincing;[16] as Carroll observes, ch. 24 "belongs to a rather different strand in that it distinguishes between two groups, those deported in 597 and those who remained behind in the city."[17]

1.2. *Jeremiah 21–24 in Its Literary Context*

If Jer 21–24 does form a distinct unit (and possibly a late addition), the question arises as to why it has been placed at this point in the text. Holladay's explanation—"because סבב Hiph., 'turn around', in v. 4 shares the same semantic field as הפך in 20:16"[18]—is hardly convincing. Nor is it clear, as Clines and Gunn believe, that "the self-curse and the 'why' question (20:18) are *naturally* understood as representing the prophet's personal reaction to the impending destruction which he will share with his people."[19] Possibly the name "Pashhur" (20:1–6; 21:1) functioned as a catchword,[20] though we might have expected a more substantial connection. Rudolph offers some help here by contrasting the rough treatment meted out to Jeremiah by Pashhur in ch. 20 and the humble demeanour of his namesake in ch. 21.[21] For his part, Pohlmann simply notes that "eine Anknüpfung an den vorausgehenden Kontext ist nicht erkennbar."[22]

There are, however, several lines of continuity between chs. 21–24 and what precedes which seem to have been strangely overlooked. First, the military crisis facing Jerusalem in 21:1–10 is in two respects clearly anticipated in chs. 19–20, which explicitly state that the city will be placed under *siege* (מצור, 19:9; cf. 21:4, 9), and that the enemy will be *Babylon* (20:4–6; cf. 21:1–10)—the first time this identification has been made in the book. We might also note how the warning in 20:4 that the king of Babylon will strike them with the sword (והכם בחרב) finds an echo in 21:7, והכם לפי חרב.

Secondly, the double prediction in ch. 20 that Judah will be exiled (גלה, v. 4) to Babylon,[23] and that Pashhur and his family will go into captivity there (הלך בשבי, v. 6), heralds a marked emphasis in chs. 21–24 on *deportation*. Though only hinted at in 21:1–10, it emerges clearly in the oracles against the kings: Shallum has already been exiled (גלה, 22:12), Jehoiakim's allies will go into captivity (הלך בשבי, 22:22) and Jehoiachin will be "hurled" (טול) into another land

---

16.   See Pohlmann's criticisms of Thiel on this point in his *Studien*, 184.

17.   Carroll, *Jeremiah*, 404.

18.   Holladay, *Jeremiah 1*, 569.

19.   David J. A. Clines and David M. Gunn, "Form, Occasion and Redaction in Jeremiah 20," *ZAW* 88 (1976): 390–409 (408, italics mine).

20.   So J. Philip Hyatt, "The Book of Jeremiah," in *The Interpreter's Bible*. Vol. 5, *Ecclesiastes, Song of Songs, Isaiah, Jeremiah* (ed. G. A. Buttrick; Nashville: Abingdon, 1956), 775–1142 (976); J. Paterson, "Jeremiah," in *Peake's Commentary on the Bible* (ed. M. Black and H.H. Rowley; London: Thomas Nelson & Sons, 1962), 537–62 (550).

21.   Rudolph, *Jeremia*, 116.

22.   Pohlmann, *Studien*, 32.

23.   This is "the first explicit reference to the place of exile in the book" (Craigie, Kelley and Drinkard, *Jeremiah 1*, 268), and (after 13:19, הגלת יהודה כלה הגלת שלומים) only the second reference to exile at all.

(על הארץ אחרת, 22:26).[24] The promise of restoration in 23:1–8 presupposes a general *Diaspora*, while 24:1–7 offers hope to those exiled (גלה) to Babylon in 587.

A third point relates to what was said earlier about the focus in chs. 21–24 on specific kings and groups of people. As see in the previous chapter, in chs. 1–19 the targets of Jeremiah's denunciations are of a very general nature. Chapter 20 breaks the pattern, however, by singling out for criticism a particular individual, Pashhur ben Immer. Thus it provides a transition between the generality of chs. 1–19 and the specificity of chs. 21–24. The rhetorical impact of this movement has been noted by Mark Smith: "Chapters 11–20 dramatize the guilt of the enemies in great detail, but leave them largely nameless. Through this mode of presentation, the audience is predisposed to accept the guilt of the enemies before their identity is unveiled, which takes place beginning in chapter 20 and is advanced in great detail in chapters 21–25."[25] Smith's comments about "the guilt of the enemies" are particularly significant for our own concerns, and I will return to them at the end of this chapter.

Granted, the juxtaposition of chs. 21–24 with ch. 20 raises a problem. Since Jeremiah's confrontation with Pashhur almost certainly took place before 597,[26] one would assume Pashhur was among those exiled with Jehoiachin in that year. Consequently, the negative tone of 20:1–6 is in tension with ch. 24, which (if taken at face value) assures the 597 exiles *without exception* of YHWH's favour. But as we will see, the same tension applies to chs. 21–24 internally as well.

2. *Jeremiah 21:1–10*

2.1. *Text*

הדבר אשר היה אל ירמיהו מאת 1 יהוה בשלח אליו המלך צדקיהו את פשחור בן מלכיה ואת צפניה בן מעשיה הכהן לאמר	ὁ λόγος ὁ γενόμενος παρὰ κυρίου πρὸς Ιερεμιαν ὅτε ἀπέστειλε πρὸς αὐτὸν ὁ βασιλεὺς Σεδεκιας τὸν Πασχωρ υἱὸν Μελχιου καὶ Σοφονιαν υἱὸν Μαασαιου τὸν ἱερέα λέγων
דרש נא בעדנו את יהוה כי 2 נבוכדראצר מלך בבל נלחם עלינו אולי יעשה יהוה אותנו ככל נפלאתיו ויעלה מעלינו	ἐπερώτησον περὶ ἡμῶν τὸν κύριον ὅτι βασιλεὺς Βαβυλῶνος ἐφέστηκεν ἐφ' ἡμᾶς εἰ ποιήσει κύριος κατὰ πάντα τὰ θαυμάσια αὐτοῦ καὶ ἀπελεύσεται ἀφ' ἡμῶν
ויאמר ירמיהו אליהם כה תאמרן 3 אל צדקיהו	καὶ εἶπε πρὸς αὐτοὺς Ιερεμιας οὕτως ἐρεῖτε πρὸς Σεδεκιαν <u>βασιλέα Ιουδα</u>
כה אמר יהוה אלהי ישראל הנני 4 מסב את כלי המלחמה אשר בידכם אשר אתם נלחמים בם את מלך בבל ואת הכשדים הצרים עליכם מחוץ לחומה ואספתי אותם אל תוך העיר הזאת	τάδε λέγει κύριος ἰδοὺ ἐγὼ μεταστρέφω τὰ ὅπλα τὰ πολεμικὰ ἐν οἷς ὑμεῖς πολεμεῖτε ἐν αὐτοῖς πρὸς τοὺς Χαλδαίους τοὺς συγκεκλεικότας ὑμᾶς ἔξωθεν τοῦ τείχους εἰς τὸ μέσον τῆς πόλεως ταύτης

24. Or, as OG presupposes, על ארץ אשר לא ילדתם.

25. Smith, *Laments*, 66.

26. The incident is undated, but since Pashhur is described as פקיד נגיד בבית יהוה (20:1), and since by the time of Jeremiah's letter to the exiles this position was held by Zephaniah (29:26), a date before 597 is likely. Thompson, *Jeremiah*, 445–46, and Lundbom, *Jeremiah 1–20*, 850, suggest a date between 609 and 605.

ונלחמתי אני אתכם ביד נטויה	5	καὶ πολεμήσω ἐγὼ ὑμᾶς ἐν χειρὶ
ובזרוע חזקה <u>ובאף</u> ובחמה ובקצף		ἐκτεταμένῃ καὶ ἐν βραχίονι κραταιῷ μετὰ
גדול		θυμοῦ καὶ ὀργῆς μεγάλης
והכיתי את ישבי העיר הזאת	6	καὶ πατάξω <u>πάντας</u> τοὺς κατοικοῦντας ἐν
את האדם ואת הבהמה בדבר		τῇ πόλει ταύτῃ τοὺς ἀνθρώπους <u>καὶ</u> τὰ
גדול ימתו		κτήνη ἐν θανάτῳ μεγάλῳ καὶ
		ἀποθανοῦνται
ואחרי כן נאם יהוה ואתן את	7	καὶ μετὰ ταῦτα λέγει κύριος δώσω τὸν
צדקיהו מלך יהודה ואת עבדיו		Σεδεκιαν βασιλέα Ιουδα καὶ τοὺς παῖδας
ואת העם <u>ואת</u> הנשארים בעיר		αὐτοῦ καὶ τὸν λαὸν τὸν καταλειφθέντα ἐν
הזאת מן הדבר מן החרב ומן		τῇ πόλει ταύτῃ ἀπὸ τοῦ θανάτου καὶ ἀπὸ
הרעב ביד <u>נבוכדראצר מלך</u>		τοῦ λιμοῦ καὶ ἀπὸ τῆς μαχαίρας εἰς
<u>בבל וביד</u> איביהם <u>וביד מבקשי</u>		χεῖρας ἐχθρῶν αὐτῶν <u>τῶν ζητούντων</u> τὰς
נפשם והכם לפי חרב לא <u>יחום</u>		ψυχὰς αὐτῶν καὶ κατακόψουσιν αὐτοὺς ἐν
עליהם ולא יחמל ולא ירחם		στόματι μαχαίρας οὐ <u>φείσομαι</u> ἐπ' αὐτοῖς
		καὶ οὐ μὴ <u>οἰκτιρήσω</u> αὐτούς
ואל העם הזה תאמר כה אמר	8	καὶ πρὸς τὸν λαὸν τοῦτον ἐρεῖς τάδε λέγει
יהוה הנני נתן לפניכם את דרך		κύριος ἰδοὺ ἐγὼ δέδωκα πρὸ προσώπου
החיים ואת דרך המות		ὑμῶν τὴν ὁδὸν τῆς ζωῆς καὶ τὴν ὁδὸν τοῦ
		θανάτου
הישב בעיר הזאת ימות בחרב	9	ὁ καθήμενος ἐν τῇ πόλει ταύτῃ
וברעב <u>ובדבר והיוצא ונפל</u> על		ἀποθανεῖται ἐν μαχαίρᾳ καὶ ἐν λιμῷ καὶ ὁ
המשדים הצרים עליכם יחיה		ἐκπορευόμενος <u>προσχωρῆσαι</u> πρὸς τοὺς
והיתה לו נפשו לשלל		Χαλδαίους τοὺς συγκεκλεικότας ὑμᾶς
		ζήσεται καὶ ἔσται ἡ ψυχὴ αὐτοῦ εἰς σκῦλα
		<u>καὶ ζήσεται</u>
כי שמתי פני בעיר הזאת לרעה	10	διότι ἐστήρικα τὸ πρόσωπόν μου ἐπὶ τὴν
ולא לטובה <u>נאם יהוה</u> ביד מלך		πόλιν ταύτην εἰς κακὰ καὶ οὐκ εἰς ἀγαθά
בבל תנתן ושרפה באש		εἰς χεῖρας βασιλέως Βαβυλῶνος
		παραδοθήσεται καὶ κατακαύσει αὐτὴν
		ἐν πυρί

2.2. *Textual Notes*

v. 3. OG βασιλέα Ιουδα = מלך יהודה >MT. This is unlikely to be a gloss by the translator, since he has already (v. 1) referred simply to ὁ βασιλεὺς Σεδεκιας. It thus suggests a longer reading in his Hebrew *Vorlage*. The wider significance of this is that it tells against the theory that the OG translator regularly abbreviated such details.

v. 4. MT אשר בידכם >OG. ואספתי אותם; את מלך בבל ו; אשר בידכם could be absent from OG or its *Vorlage* by haplography (repetition of אשר).[27] The same may apply to את מלך בבל ו (repetition of את); however, MT also gives extra prominence to the Babylonian king in v. 7, and though haplography is possible there too, its occurrence in two verses on the same point would be rather coincidental. ואספתי אותם also appears expansionary; leaving aside the lengthy subordinate clause (אשר אתם...לחומה), the *Vorlage* would have read מסב את כלי המלחמה...אל תוך העיר הזאת (for סבב [+ direct object] אל, see 2 Kgs 20:2).

---

27. So Janzen, *Studies*, 43.

Some have argued that OG has shortened its *Vorlage* for the sake of clarity,[28] but as Janzen remarks, MT is if anything clearer than OG.[29]

v. 5. ובאף >OG. MT plus; throughout this passage MT shows an impulse towards verbal trilogies (cf. ולא ירחם, v. 7; ובדבר, v. 9).

v. 6. MT ימתו; OG καὶ ἀποθανοῦνται. The conjunction affects the syntax of the whole verse: MT, "and I will strike down the inhabitants of this city…by a great plague they will die"; OG, "and I will strike down those who live in this city…with a great death, and they will die."

v. 7. MT ואת (הנשארים) >OG. Probable MT plus; this distinction between העם and הנשארים is unparalleled in Jeremiah, while העם הנשארים occurs five times (39:9 [×2]; 40:6; 41:10; 52:15).[30] MT may have added ואת in order to emphasize the totality of YHWH's judgment.[31]

MT נבוכדראצר מלך בבל וביד >OG. Haplography (either in OG or its *Vorlage*) is possible (repetition of ביד), but the fact that MT also contains a reference to Nebuchadrezzar in v. 4 that is lacking in OG suggests both are MT plusses.[32] The crucial point is that MT *requires* this reference to Nebuchadrezzar to facilitate its variant readings in the rest of the verse; without it, we are obliged to follow OG.

MT וביד מבקשי; OG τῶν ζητούντων. Not only does OG not represent וביד, it suggests an underlying (ביד איביהם (המבקשים (נפשם); for a similar construction, see Exod 4:19; Jer 11:21. However, it is unlikely that MT intends to imply a second group of people (who would they be?); rather, this is a case of hendiadys, "their enemies seeking their lives" (a form of *waw explicativum*).[33]

MT הכם; OG κατακόψουσιν αὐτοὺς = הכם. MT focuses on Nebuchadrezzar as the agent of judgment, while the plural form of the verb in OG connects it to "their enemies seeking their lives." The subject of הכם בחרב in 20:4 is (in both texts) the king of Babylon, but if we are right to view ביד נבוכדראצר מלך בבל as an MT plus, OG's κατακόψουσιν accurately interprets its *Vorlage*.

MT לא יחום עליהם ולא יחמל; OG οὐ φείσομαι ἐπ' αὐτοῖς καὶ οὐ μὴ οἰκτιρήσω αὐτούς. While MT keeps the focus on Nebuchadrezzar, OG makes YHWH the subject. Here too, the change can be ascribed to the translator only if we think his *Vorlage* contained an antecedent reference to Nebuchadrezzar; as has already

---

28. So Rudolph, *Jeremia*, 114; Helga Weippert, "Jahwekrieg und Bundesfluch in Jer 21 1–7," *ZAW* 82 (1970): 396–409 (398 n. 11).

29. Janzen, *Studies*, 43.

30. Contra C. F. Keil, *Biblischer Kommentar über den Propheten Jeremia und die Klageliede* (BKAT 2/3; Leipzig: Dörffling & Franke, 1872), 243, who saw here a further example of *waw explicativum*.

31. So Craigie, Kelley and Drinkard, *Jeremiah 1–25*, 28.

32. So Janzen, *Studies*, 4; Holladay, *Jeremiah 1*, 568 (though both concede haplography is possible).

33. See *GKC* §154 n. 1b; David W. Baker, "Further Examples of the Waw Explicativum," *VT* 30 (1980): 129–36. Rudolph, *Jeremia*, 234, renders Jer 46:26, ביד מבקשי נפשם וביד נבוכדראצר, "in die Hand derer, die ihnen nach dem Leben trachten, *nämlich* in die Hand Nebukadnezars" (italics mine). Note that wherever MT Jeremiah mentions מבקשי נפש and איבים together, it connects them with ו (19:7, 9; 34:20, 21; 44:30 [×2]; 49:37), while OG alternates between inserting καὶ (19:7; 51:30 [×2]) and omitting it (21:7; 25:17).

been suggested, this seems on balance unlikely. Since this is the end of the oracle, a summary statement by YHWH is appropriate (cf. 13:14).

2.3. *Exegesis*

v. 1. הדבר אשר היה אל ירמיהו מאת יהוה might denote the entire incident recorded here, but more probably refers to the oracle which Jeremiah sent to Zedekiah.

v. 2. דרש את יהוה (בעד) (like התפלל בעד) denotes prophetic intercession.[34] Whether the subject is the king or the people, consulting YHWH requires the mediation of a prophet (see Ezek 14:10; 20:1).[35] The desired response may simply be information or direction (8:2; 10:21), but often the underlying hope is for some divine act of salvation, preceded perhaps by a שלום oracle (29:7; 38:4).[36] Here, the ensuing אולי יעשה יהוה...ככל נפלאתיו makes this hope explicit. Zedekiah (and/or the writer) may be thinking of YHWH's deliverance of Judah during the Assyrian crisis (Isa 37); both Zedekiah and Hezekiah send a delegation to the prophet (v. 1; Isa 37:2), emphasize the gravity of the situation (v. 2a; Isa 37:3), refer *hopefully* to the prospect of YHWH's assistance (v. 2b; Isa 37:4a; note the use of אולי in both) and request intercession (v. 2a; Isa 37:4b).

v. 3. האמרן. Pohlmann finds the form remarkable,[37] but כה תאמרון is in fact more common than כה תאמרו.[38] Whether this is a deliberate allusion to Isaiah's use of כה תאמרון in addressing Hezekiah's delegation (Isa 37:6) is therefore uncertain.

v. 4. Knowing exactly what is envisaged here is complicated by the textual difficulties and the ambiguity of the wording and syntax. In OG it is the Judean כלי המלחמה (rather than the Babylonians) which YHWH will turn back (סבב) towards the city. This may also be the sense of MT, if ואספתי (אותם) relates to את כלי המלחמה,[39] but אספתי (אותם) might also denote את הכשדים הצרים עליהם.[40] The כלי המלחמה could be either the Judean troops or their weapons,[41] while סבב might mean turn back (in defeat or victory?) or surround (to protect or to blunt?). Thus, it is not immediately obvious whether YHWH is promising salvation or doom. Weippert interprets v. 4 as predicting that YHWH will cause

---

34.   התפלל (בעד) and דרש can be used synonymously; see 29:11, and also 37:3–7, where following the request התפלל נא בעדנו אל יהוה (v. 3), Jeremiah refers to שלח אתכם אלי לדרשני (v. 7).

35.   See Claus Westermann, "Die Begriffe für Fragen und Suchen im Alten Testament," *KD* 6 (1960): 16–22.

36.   See Jonathan Paige Sisson, "Jeremiah and the Jerusalemite Conception of Peace," *JBL* 105 (1986): 429–42.

37.   Pohlmann, *Studien*, 33.

38.   The former occurs in Gen 32:5; 1 Sam 11:9; 2 Kgs 19:6, 10; 37:6, 10; Isa 37:6, 10; the latter occurs in Gen 50:17; 1 Sam 18:25; 2 Kgs 22:18; Jer 23:35; 27:4; 37:7; 2 Chr 34:26. For תאמרון (without כה) see 2 Kgs 18:22; Isa 8:12; Jer 10:11.

39.   So Rudolph, *Jeremia*, 114; Pohlmann, *Studien*, 34.

40.   Volz, *Jeremia*, 216.

41.   כלי המלחמה usually means "weapons" (Deut 1:41; Judg 18:11; 1 Sam 8:12), but in 2 Sam 1:27 is synonymous with גבורים; cf. Jer 51:20. The addition of אשר בידכם in MT might seem to settle the matter in favour of "weapons," but cf. Num 31:49, אנשי המלחמה אשר בידנו, "the men of war at our disposal."

the Judaen troops to turn on one another in confusion (cf. Judg 7:22; 1 Sam 14:20; Zech 14:13), thereby leaving the city open to the Babylonians.[42]

v. 5. ונלחמתי אני אתכם again leaves some doubt as to who YHWH is fighting for.[43] The expression ביד חזקה ובזרוע נטויה often describes YHWH's deliverance of Israel from Egypt (Deut 4:34; 5:15; 2 Kgs 17:36, etc.). Here, however, the adjectives are transposed, perhaps as a further hint that YHWH has switched sides.[44]

v. 6. In the context of a prolonged siege, with diminishing food supplies, the prediction that the people will die בדבר גדול, "by a great plague," is historically realistic. By contrast, the mention of survivors מן הדבר מן החרב ומן הרעב (v. 7) is more stylized, and formally in tension with v. 6. Compare 42:16–17, where Jeremiah's warning against fleeing to Egypt initially has a rather matter of fact explanation, והיתה החרב אשר אתם יראים ממנה שם תשיג אתכם...והרעב אשר אתם דאגים ממנו שם ידבק אחריכם, but is followed by the more generalized claim, כל האנשים אשר שמו את פניהם לבוא מצרים ימותו בחרב ברעב ובדבר.

v. 7. The implications of the different readings in MT and OG have already been noted. The identity of מבקשי נפשם is unclear. The phrase מבקשי נפש is a distinctive of the Jeremiah prose tradition,[45] occurring in 11:21; 19:7, 9; 21:7; 22:25; 34:20, 21; 38:16; 44:30 (×2); 46:26; 49:37. Those whose life is sought vary,[46] but the identity of the מבקשי is stated only in 11:21 (the men of Anathoth). That the phrase here refers to the Babylonians is a reasonable inference, but internal enemies (deserters?) may also be in mind; see Zedekiah's admission, אני דאג את היהודים אשר נפלו אל הכשדים פן יתנו אתי בידם (38:19).[47]

v. 8. הנני נתן לפניכם את דרך החיים ואת דרך המות. The declaration recalls Moses' words to Israel, ראה נתתי לפניך היום את החיים ואת הטוב ואת המות ואת הרע (Deut 30:15). In that passage, "life" means YHWH's rich blessing (cf. v. 19) in the land Israel is about to enter. As v. 9 makes clear, however, what is on offer here is far more modest, making the allusion highly ironic. The terms "good" and "evil" from Deut 30:15 are taken up in v. 10, where YHWH states that he has set his face against the city לרעה ולא לטובה.[48]

---

42. Weippert, "Jahwekrieg," 407–8; followed by Pohlmann, *Studien*, 34.

43. Craigie, Kelley and Drinkard, *Jeremiah 1–25*, 287: "The ambiguity would be precisely that of the English, 'I am going to fight with you.'"

44. So Weippert, "Jahwekrieg," 399 n. 20; Holladay, *Jeremiah 1*, 571–72.

45. Elsewhere it occurs only in Samuel (1 Sam 20:1; 2 Sam 16:11) and Psalms (35:4; 38:13; 40:15; 70:3).

46. Jeremiah (11:21; 38:16), Jehoiachin (22:25), Zedekiah and his officials (21:7; 34:21; 44:30), the people of Judah and Jerusalem (19:7, 9; 21:7; 34:20), Pharaoh Hophra (44:30) and Elam (49:37).

47. Pohlmann, *Studien*, 36, argues that since Nebuchadrezzar is mentioned before "the enemies," he cannot be identified with them, and concludes that "Jahwes Gerichtshandeln mit der Eroberung Jerusalems durch den König von Babel für die im Lande Übriggebliebenen noch nicht abgeschlossen ist, sondern weitergeht." Obviously, this can only apply to MT, since OG makes no reference to the Babylonian king.

48. The use of דרך in conjunction with חיים and מות is characteristic of the wisdom literature; see Prov 6:23; 12:28; 14:12; 16:25. In Jer 21:8, however, דרך seems to have a more literal meaning; the way of life is the road out of the city.

v. 9. היוצא. Occasionally in Jeremiah יצא signifies "go *into exile*," though this is made explicit by the addition of בגולה (29:16; 48:7; also Zech 14:2).[49] Here, however, it means "surrender" (1 Sam 11:3; 2 Kgs 18:31 = Isa 36:16; 24:12; Jer 38:2, 17, 18, 21). It is thus related to, but not identical with, נפל, which has here the sense "go over to another side, defect" (1 Sam 29:3; 2 Kgs 7:4; Jer 37:13–14; 38:19; 39:9 = 2 Kgs 25:11; 52:15; 1 Chr 12:20; 2 Chr 15:9). Interestingly, while this is how NIV translates נפל in almost all these references, in Jer 21:9 (and 2 Kgs 7:4) it reads "surrender"—thereby glossing the potentially subversive aspect of the word. Such a translational decision highlights how, in the crisis of 587, Jeremiah's message could be framed in different ways: as cowardly desertion (cf. 37:13–14), pragmatic realism (cf. 2 Kgs 7:3–4) or courageous obedience to YHWH.[50]

והיתה לו נפשו לשלל. While the individual terms are clear enough (שלל denotes plunder in battle), the meaning of the expression, which is limited to Jeremiah (cf. 38:2; 39:18; 45:5),[51] is disputed. Most scholars interpret it as an ironic promise of survival *and no more*: "Vielleicht ein altes, gutmütig spottendes Sprichwort; wenn ein Besiegter entronnen war und sein nacktes Leben gerettet hatte, so hatte er wenigstens das als 'Beute.'"[52] Conversely, Parke-Taylor maintains that the contrast of דרך המות and דרך החיים implies "more than bare survival, and points to the blessing of Yahweh as promised in Deut 30:15–20."[53] Indeed, as will be seen later, the phrase נפש לשלל reappears in the oracles to Ebed-Melech (39:17–18) and Baruch (45:5), which carry an unmistakable note of personal blessing. However, what gives those oracles a positive aspect is not the phrase נפש לשלל *per se*, but the words and phrases that surround it. By contrast, in 21:9 there is nothing to suggest that anything beyond the avoidance of death is on offer (cf. 38:2, where והיתה לו נפשו לשלל is explained epexegetically by the ensuing וחי, "and he will live").

Weippert and Pohlmann have argued convincingly that Jer 21:1–10 depicts YHWH's judgment upon Israel as holy war in reverse.[54] Indicative of this change in his stance towards them are the phrases אתן...ביד (v. 5), ונלחמתי אתכם and והכם לפי בחרב (v. 7), which are paralleled elsewhere in relation to Israel's conquest of the land, and especially the *ḥērem* (see Deut 20:13; Josh 6:2, 21; 10:28). Less convincing is Pohlmann's claim that שלל (v. 9) and שרף באש (v. 10) also belong to this *ḥērem* language. As we have seen, the former is part of a characteristically Jeremianic expression (which concerns the actions of the

49.   In 22:11 and 29:2, however, יצא appears in an exilic sense without בגולה.
50.   Cf. Brueggemann, *Exile and Homecoming*, 190–91.
51.   This strongly suggests its authenticity; so Parke-Taylor, *Formation*, 202.
52.   Volz, *Jeremia*, 219; similarly Rudolph, *Jeremia*, 117; Bright, *Jeremiah*, 185; Holladay, *Jeremiah 1*, 574; Thompson, *Jeremiah*, 469; McKane, *Jeremiah 1*, 502.
53.   Parke-Taylor, *Formation*, 203.
54.   Weippert, "Jahwekrieg," esp. 398–402; Pohlmann, *Studien*, 34–39. Pohlmann argues (p. 39) that the concept of *ḥērem* "als Leitgedanken bei der Abfassung dieses Abschnitts, besonders der Verse 7–10 zugrunde gelegen haben müssen."

Judaens, not the Babylonians!), while the warning that Nebuchadrezzar would burn the city is also well established in Jeremiah (32:29; 34:2; 37:8, 10; 38:18; cf. 39:8).

2.4. *Coherence and Redaction*

Since 21:1–10 share the same historical setting, and since the stance taken by YHWH towards Jerusalem is consistently negative, it may seem natural to read these verses as a coherent whole.[55] At the same time, there is some tension between the two messages spoken by Jeremiah. While vv. 4–7 announce unqualified destruction on the city and those in it, vv. 8–10 introduce an exceptive element: those who surrender to the Babylonians will live. Given the nature of our overall enquiry, we need to explore further the relationship between these two messages.

The simplest solution might be to explain the disaster/hope distinction in audience-critical terms. Since the rhetorical markers כה תאמרן אל צדקיהו (v. 3) and ואל העם הזה תאמר (v. 8)[56] clearly distinguish between the king and the people, we might conclude that judgment is now inevitable for Zedekiah (and his royal court?), but may yet be averted by the ordinary people of Jerusalem. Brueggemann writes:

> The judgment is against the arrogant temple and the self-serving monarchy. It is as though a distinction is made between "people" and "government," as we often do with reference to "the Russian people" or "the Cuban people"... That is why vv. 8–10 are addressed to people, unlike vv. 3–7, which are addressed to the king.[57]

The problem with this analysis, however, is that the message sent to Zedekiah (vv. 4–7) makes no distinction at all between people and government. YHWH will strike down "the inhabitants of this city, both man and beast" (v. 6), and those who survive (העם הנשארים) will die at the hands of the king of Babylon (v. 7). Only when Jeremiah speaks to the people (vv. 8–10) does he suggest that some of them may live. Consequently, the audience/message correlation is not as neat as Brueggemann implies.[58] Putting the matter in somewhat formulaic terms, what we see is *not* audience A being told that A will be destroyed, and

---

55. So, e.g., Rudolph, *Jeremia*, 115–17. Volz, *Jeremia*, 218, and Bright, *Jeremiah*, 217, see vv. 8–10 as originally separate from vv. 1–7, though equally authentic and from the same historical context.

56. The singular תאמר indicates that YHWH is here addressing Jeremiah rather than the delegation.

57. Brueggemann, *Exile and Homecoming*, 191; Stulman, *Order Amid Chaos*, 50, agrees.

58. One might argue that Jeremiah's audience influenced the *rhetoric*, as much as the *content*, of his preaching. Consequently, a message of total disaster addressed to one party is more nuanced when addressed to another. This might not make for formal consistency, but is historically plausible; thus, Joel Rosenberg, "Jeremiah and Ezekiel," in *The Literary Guide to the Bible* (ed. Robert Alter and Frank Kermode; London: Fontana, 1987), 184–206 (194), refers to "the alteration of preachment to context and circumstance" in Jeremiah. But, as will be argued below, vv. 8–10 do not so much qualify the indiscriminate nature of vv. 4–7 as introduce a different scenario.

audience B being told that B has a choice; rather, we have audience A being told that A and B will be destroyed, and audience B being told that B has a choice.

Others seek to explain the tension between vv. 4–7 and 8–10 by ascribing them to different redactional layers. Seitz, for example, argues that, in its present form, 21:1–10 is "a redactional piece meant to foreclose on the possibility of ongoing life in the land."[59] It has thus been shaped by the ER, which sought to portray Judah's disobedience and destruction as inevitable (see Chapter 2). However, while Seitz attributes vv. 1–7 to ER, he believes that vv. 8–10 reflect the authentic "submit and live" preaching of Jeremiah, preserved in the Scribal Chronicle (SC). What we see in 21:1–10, therefore, is a classic example of ER's practice of foreclosing an offer of hope to Zedekiah and his people: "Within 21,1–7, v. 7 eliminates the possibility of survival after 587 B.C., even as 21,8–10 counsels surrender that 'you might live and have your life as prize of war.'"[60]

Clearly, such redaction-critical hypotheses satisfy only if they convincingly account for the present form of the text; that is to say, if the reshaped text actually conveys the viewpoint that has supposedly led the editor to reshape it. Whether 21:1–10 does in fact support a 'foreclosing' ideology is a question we will return to shortly. For now, we should note that, as a solution to the tension between vv. 1–7 and 8–10, Seitz's attractively simple, two-part division of the text is something of a chimera. McKane agrees that the contents of v. 7 "do not allow for any survivors to whom the prophet could have spoken in the terms of vv. 8–10,"[61] but also recognizes that—if taken literally—v. 6 allows no survivors to whom the prophet could speak as he does in v. 7: "The contents of vv. 5–6 will not allow the continuation in v. 7 indicated by ואחרי כן, and the contents of v. 7 will not allow the continuation in vv. 8–10."[62] Consequently, McKane has to posit *three* redactional strata in this passage. His explanation for this awkward amalgam of material—"the editor of 21:1–10 has attempted to portray a sequence of events corresponding imperfectly with the sequence in Jer 52:4–16"[63]—fails to convince, however. At this point, the redaction-critical approach to the problem of 21:1–10 begins to look suspect.[64]

In fact, the formal contradiction noted by McKane between vv. 6 and 7 is easily explicable by allowing for an element of hyperbole. Logically inconsistent statements are not uncommon in prophetic judgment oracles, as the following examples show:[65]

59. Seitz, *Theology in Conflict*, 253.

60. Ibid., 161 n. 130.

61. McKane, *Jeremiah 1*, 494.

62. Ibid., 494; similarly Carroll, *Jeremiah*, 409–10.

63. McKane, *Jeremiah 1*, 494.

64. Craigie, Kelley and Drinkard, *Jeremiah 1–25*, 287, rightly remark that to dismiss v. 7 as redundant "places too much rigidity on the oracular form." See too John Applegate, "The Fate of Zedekiah. Redactional Debate in the Book of Jeremiah: Part 1," *VT* 48 (1998): 137–60 (147–49), for criticisms of McKane's "rather rationalistic" (p. 147) reading of 21:1–10.

65. Cf. Hans M. Barstad, *The Myth of the Empty Land: A Study in the History and Archaeology of Judah During the "Exilic" Period* (SOFSup 28; Oslo: Scandinavian University Press, 1996), 31,

If ten men are left in one house, they will die. And his friend who is to burn the remains will come to carry them out of the house, and he will ask *anyone in the recesses of the house*, "Is anyone still with you?" and he will say "No one." Then he will say, "Quiet! We must not mention the name of the LORD." (Amos 6:9–10)

Outside is the sword, inside are plague and famine; those in the field will die by the sword, and those in the city will be consumed by famine and plague. *Their refugees will escape* and will be in the mountains, like doves mourning. (Ezek 7:15–16)

Perhaps, then, the assumption of hyperbole can also resolve the tension between vv. 4–7 and vv. 8–10. What is meant by the former is the death of great numbers during the siege (through disease and hunger) and afterwards (at the hand of the Babylonians), rather than the death of every single individual. Yet while there may indeed be an element of exaggeration in vv. 4–7, it is important to observe that the potential survivors in vv. 8–10 are not people who somehow *live through* the coming disaster (as in the Amos and Ezekiel passages above); rather, they are people who *leave* the city before the disaster falls.

I suggest, rather, that the key to the coherence of 21:1–10 lies in understanding the basic principle underlying it. This is stated clearly in v. 10: "For (כי) I have set my face against this city for evil and not for good." That is to say, YHWH's wrath is fundamentally against *Jerusalem*, rather than any particular group or individual. Accordingly, the fate of the people turns on their relationship to the city, a point highlighted by the term ישב. It is ישבי העיר whom YHWH will strike down (v. 6), and it is הישב בעיר who will die by the sword, famine, and plague (v. 9). ישב thus seems to denote affinity with, or even commitment to, Jerusalem,[66] a stance which both vv. 4–7 and 8–10 dismiss as futile. What vv. 8–9 offer "this people" (העם הזה, v. 8), however, is the chance to redefine their relationship to the doomed city by "going out" (יצא, v. 9) from it, and so to live. In more concrete terms, this suggests that the way of life is only a temporary option (note the brief pause implied by הנני מסב, v. 4),[67] and that once YHWH has begun to wage war on Jerusalem, it will be too late.[68]

If this is the underlying rationale of the passage, one might ask whether even Zedekiah's fate is utterly inevitable. The judgment oracle of vv. 4–7, unqualified though it is, must be understood in relation to its purpose. The situation presupposed is that of Judean resistance to the Babylonians (cf. "the weapons

---

on the repeated references to the deportation of "all the people" in 2 Kgs 24: "We might wonder: who are all these people who seem to surface all the time, when, allegedly, there is no one left in the country? The answer to this question is simple enough. When the ancient writer says 'all the people' he does not mean 'all the people,' but a large number. And when he refers to a large number, this may simply be because he wants to make a point with regard to the importance of what had happened."

66. This emerges more clearly if ישב is understood to mean "remain, stay, continue" (cf. Gen 24:55; Lev 12:4; 1 Sam 7:2; Mic 5:3, etc.); this is implied in v. 9 by the contrast with יצא.

67. On הנה + participle to signify "the event as imminent, or at least near at hand," see *GKC* §116p.

68. For the motif of coming out (יצא) from the doomed city, see Josh 6:23; Jer 50:8; 51:6–10; Isa 52:11.

of war with which you are fighting," v. 4) and at the same time hope for YHWH's assistance (v. 2). Jeremiah's reply is intended to destroy both strategies. So far from fighting for the city, YHWH is fighting against them (v. 5); consequently, military resistance and prophetic intercession are futile. The idea that Zedekiah might live if he too surrenders to the Babylonians (see 38:17) is not so much precluded as ignored, since it lies beyond the intention of the oracle.[69] This question will re-emerge explicitly, however, when we come to 38:14–28.

2.5. *Judicial Differentiation in Jeremiah 21:1–10:* הישבים / היצאים

The present study of 21:1–10 has revealed that, while the different audience markers in vv. 3 and 8 initially suggest that the key distinction is between the royal court and the ordinary people, a closer analysis of both messages (vv. 4–7 and 9–10) reveals that in terms of judgment and hope, the fundamental distinction is between the inhabitants and non-inhabitants of Jerusalem: those who stay, and those who go out. While the city is doomed, there is still the opportunity for its people to surrender (to disaffiliate from it, so to speak) and thereby live.

In the light of our discussion, we can now consider the arguments of Pohlmann and Seitz regarding this passage. Unlike Seitz (and McKane), Pohlmann accepts that the entire pericope derives from a single author, pointing to its pervasive holy war imagery: "Daß der ganze Abschnitt die einheitliche Komposition eines Verfassers ist, belegen die zahlreichen und durchgehend verwendeten formelhaften Wendungen aus dem Vorstellungsbereich eines Jahwekrieges oder Bannvollzuges und die konsequente Umkehrung dieser Aussagen gegen Jerusalem."[70] Since the predominant message is clearly one of judgment on Jerusalem, Pohlmann allocates the pericope to the *golaorientierte Redaktion*.

It is at just this point, however, that Pohlmann's argument runs into trouble, since, as we have seen, vv. 8–10 do hold out a *limited* hope to people who had not been deported with Jehoiachin. These verses would in fact seem to have more in common with the older redactional layer which Pohlmann identifies, which allowed for the people's continued existence if they surrendered to the Babylonians. Pohlmann seeks to counter this by minimizing the scope of the offer in vv. 9–10; the author, he argues, has deliberately used indirect language in v. 9 (הישב...היוצא), partly to avoid having Jeremiah address *all* the people,[71]

---

69. Oracles of doom did not *necessarily* preclude repentance and hope. See Walter Houston, "What Did the Prophets Think They Were Doing? Speech Acts and Prophetic Discourse in the Old Testament," *Biblical Interpretation* 1, 2 (1993): 167–88, who emphasizes the ambiguity of many of the responses to such pronouncements (e.g. mourning, prayer and fasting): "On the one hand…the hearers react to the word of doom in the same way as to a death; on the other, they do not assume that their doom is inexorable, but that there is a possibility of mercy" (p. 183).

70. Pohlmann, *Studien*, 39.

71. Ibid., 38: "Die Formulierung…הישב (vgl. Jer 38,2) scheint bewußt gewählt, um die direkte Anrede des ganzen Volkes zu vermeiden." Pohlmann's explanation—"weil sonst eine Spannung zu den vorausgegangenen allgemeinen und uneingeschränkten Unheilsankündigungen entstanden wäre" (ibid.; see too n. 113)—shows that he is uncomfortably aware of the tension between vv. 4–7 and 8–10.

and partly to imply that only a few would escape the destruction.[72] But this will not do; v. 8 clearly indicates that Jeremiah's announcement was public (יֹאמֶר הָעָם הַזֶּה תֹאמַר), while v. 9 leaves open the question of how many would surrender and so live; the terms הַיֹּשֵׁב...הַיּוֹצֵא express precisely this uncertainty.

Seitz, on the other hand, is fully aware of the significant shift that occurs after v. 7. Consequently, as we have seen, he attributes vv. 1–7 to SC and vv. 8–10 to ER. Such a conclusion is, however, questionable at two points. First, whether vv. 8–10 refer to life in the land or in exile, it is far from clear how vv. 1–7 foreclose on the possibility of survival, as he claims. Rather, vv. 8–10 assume precisely the destruction of the city that is prophesied in vv. 1–7 and offer the only way of escape. Had it been the editor's intention to blunt the force of vv. 8–10, the most obvious solution would have been to omit them altogether.[73]

Secondly, Seitz understands Jeremiah's message in 21:9–10 as akin to his "submit and live" preaching as found in 27:12–18 and 42:10–12 (both SC).[74] In so doing, however, he blurs some important differences between these three passages. Whereas in 27:11 and 42:10–12 the promise for those who submit to the Babylonians is, specifically, life *in the land*, the offer in 21:9 is ambiguous on this point; deportation is now at least a real danger. Then again, in contrast to the hopeful tone of 27:17—"Why should this city become a ruin?"—21:9–10 accepts Jerusalem's destruction as utterly inevitable. In other words, we can characterize the message of these three passages as "submit and live" only if we recognize that they define these terms quite differently. That being so, 21:8–10 turns out not to be in such sharp tension with 21:1–7 as Seitz assumes.[75] In short, the conditional offer of life held out to the people of Jerusalem in 21:8–10 is more sincere than Pohlmann admits, but less optimistic than Seitz imagines.

This brings us to one final remark in connection with 21:1–10. As we have seen, the offer of "life as booty" for those who leave the city is limited and undefined. In particular, it is unclear whether it will involve deportation or not.[76] If one assumes the authenticity of this declaration, the most likely explanation is that Jeremiah himself did not know what the outcome of surrender to the Babylonians would be.

72. Ibid.: "Nur wenige werden der umfassenden Vernichtung entgehen."

73. Seitz (*Theology in Conflict*, 240) makes precisely this point in criticizing Pohlmann's methodology: "If such priority is given to the freedom of secondary redactors, one begins to wonder why seams, narrative tensions, and the like are obvious in the present form of the text at all. Put bluntly, if the *Vorlage* was such a torso, and at such odds with the redactional position secondarily supplied, why did secondary redactors not drop it altogether?".

74. Ibid., 206: "In the post-597 years in Judah...Jeremiah consistently counsels those who remain in the land to go out and submit to Nebuchadnezzar."

75. To be sure, 21:8–10 can be understood as a *re-application* of earlier principles to address a changed historical situation. In fact, the notion that Jeremiah's outlook was not static is central to Seitz's argument that the prophet's message changed significantly after the deportation of Jehoiachin in 597; see especially ibid., 207.

76. Seitz (ibid., 206. n. 1) cautiously remarks that "it does not sound as though such action necessitates deportation."

3. *Jeremiah 23:1–8*

3.1. *Text*

הוי רעים מאבדים ומפצים את צאן מרעיתי נאם יהוה	1	ὦ οἱ ποιμένες οἱ ἀπολλύοντες καὶ διασκορπίζοντες τὰ πρόβατα τῆς <u>νομῆς αὐτῶν</u>
לכן כה אמר יהוה <u>אלהי ישראל</u> על הרעים <u>הרעים</u> את עמי אתם הפצתם את צאני ותדחום ולא פקדתם אתם הנני פקד עליכם את רע מעלליכם <u>נאם יהוה</u>	2	διὰ τοῦτο τάδε λέγει κύριος ἐπὶ τοὺς ποιμαίνοντας τὸν λαόν μου ὑμεῖς διεσκορπίσατε τὰ πρόβατά μου καὶ ἐξώσατε αὐτὰ καὶ οὐκ ἐπεσκέψασθε αὐτά ἰδοὺ ἐγὼ ἐκδικῶ ἐφ' ὑμᾶς κατὰ τὰ πονηρὰ ἐπιτηδεύματα ὑμῶν
ואני אקבץ את שארית <u>צאני</u> מכל <u>הארצות</u> אשר הדחתי אתם שם והשבתי אתהן על נוהן ופרו ורבו	3	καὶ ἐγὼ εἰσδέξομαι τοὺς καταλοίπους τοῦ <u>λαοῦ μου</u> ἀπὸ πάσης τῆς <u>γῆς</u> οὗ ἐξῶσα αὐτοὺς ἐκεῖ καὶ καταστήσω αὐτοὺς εἰς τὴν νομὴν αὐτῶν καὶ αὐξηθήσονται καὶ πληθυνθήσονται
והקמתי עליהם רעים ורעום ולא ייראו עוד ולא יחתו <u>ולא יפקדו</u> נאם יהוה	4	καὶ ἀναστήσω αὐτοῖς ποιμένας οἳ ποιμανοῦσιν αὐτούς καὶ οὐ φοβηθήσονται ἔτι οὐδὲ πτοηθήσονται λέγει κύριος
הנה ימים באים נאם יהוה והקמתי לדוד צמח צדיק ומלך מלך והשכיל ועשה משפט וצדקה בארץ	5	ἰδοὺ ἡμέραι ἔρχονται λέγει κύριος καὶ ἀναστήσω τῷ Δαυιδ ἀνατολὴν δικαίαν καὶ βασιλεύσει βασιλεὺς καὶ συνήσει καὶ ποιήσει κρίμα καὶ δικαιοσύνην ἐπὶ τῆς γῆς
בימיו תושע יהודה וישראל ישכן לבטח וזה שמו אשר יקראו יהוה צדקנו	6	ἐν ταῖς ἡμέραις αὐτοῦ σωθήσεται Ιουδας καὶ Ισραηλ κατασκηνώσει πεποιθώς καὶ τοῦτο τὸ ὄνομα ὃ καλέσει αὐτὸν κύριος <u>Ιωσεδεκ</u>
לכן הנה ימים באים נאם יהוה ולא יאמרו עוד חי יהוה אשר העלה את <u>בני</u> ישראל מארץ מצרים	7	διὰ τοῦτο ἰδοὺ ἡμέραι ἔρχονται λέγει κύριος καὶ οὐκ ἐροῦσιν ἔτι ζῇ κύριος ὃς ἀνήγαγε τὸν <u>οἶκον</u> Ισραηλ ἐκ γῆς Αἰγύπτου
כי אם חי יהוה <u>אשר העלה</u> ואשר הביא את זרע <u>בית</u> ישראל מארץ צפונה ומכל הארצות אשר <u>הדחתים</u> שם וישבו על אדמתם	8	ἀλλὰ ζῇ κύριος ὃς συνήγαγεν <u>ἅπαν</u> τὸ σπέρμα Ισραηλ ἀπὸ γῆς βορρᾶ καὶ ἀπὸ πασῶν τῶν χωρῶν οὗ <u>ἐξῶσεν αὐτοὺς</u> ἐκεῖ καὶ ἀπεκατέστησεν αὐτοὺς εἰς τὴν γῆν αὐτῶν

3.2. *Textual Notes*

v. 1. MT מרעיתי, "my pasture"; OG τῆς νομῆς αὐτῶν = מרעיתם, "their pasture."[77] Both readings make good sense contextually. MT provides the rationale for YHWH's action in vv. 2–3, while OG highlights the shepherds' abdication of responsibility. "The sheep of YHWH's pasture" is an established idiom in the Psalms (74:1; 79:13; 100:3).

v. 2. MT על הרעים הרעים; OG ἐπὶ τοὺς ποιμαίνοντας = על הרעים. OG may be paraphrasing the Hebrew idiom for stylistic reasons, although haplography in its *Vorlage* is also possible;[78] cf. v. 25, where OG renders הנבאים הנבאים with οἱ προφῆται οἱ προφητεύσιν.

v. 3. MT צאני; OG τοῦ λαοῦ μου may be paraphrasing its *Vorlage*, or rendering עמי.

MT הארצות; OG τῆς γῆς = הארץ. OG may reflect a content variant in its *Vorlage*, but a specific referent (i.e. Babylon) is unlikely. In 50(27):23; 51(28):25,

---

77. Following (with Ziegler) LXX[B], S; LXX[A] (followed by Rahlfs) reads τῆς νομῆς μου.
78. So Janzen, *Studies*, 117.

41, 49, πάσης τῆς γῆς renders כל הארץ, but in context both clearly mean "the whole earth." Elsewhere in Jeremiah the terms נדח and קבץ always imply a general *Diaspora* and are collocated with the plurals ארצות, גוים and מקומות (16:15; 23:8; 29:14; 32:37; cf. 40:11–12).

v. 4. MT ולא יפקדו >OG. For the meaning "be lacking" for פקד Niph., see Num 31:49; 1 Sam 20:18; 25:7; 1 Kgs 20:39; 2 Kgs 10:19. After יחתו and ייראו, therefore, יפקדו introduces a somewhat new idea.[79] Once again (cf. 21:5, 7, 9), MT prefers a trilogy of terms where OG contains only two.

v. 6. MT יִקְרָאוֹ ("he will call him") probably combines יִקְרָאוּ and יִקְרָאוֹ.[80] OG καλέσει αὐτόν also reads the term as third person singular (cf. Targ., Vulg., which presuppose יִקְרָאוֹ). MT leaves the subject of the verb ambiguous; either "one" (i.e. people in general) or YHWH himself. The latter is explicit in OG, if καλέσει αὐτόν κύριος Ιωσεδεκ means "the Lord will call him, 'Josedek,'"[81] but κύριος may also be a doublet of Ιωσεδεκ.[82]

MT צדקנו (cf. Vulg., *iustus noster*); OG Ιωσεδεκ. The Greek text probably reflects a variant reading in its *Vorlage* (יהוצדק or יוצדק), although צדקנו may just have been sufficiently enigmatic to prompt the translator to make the change.

vv. 7–8. OG places this oracle after the polemic against the prophets (vv. 9–40), clearly due to a similar arrangement in its *Vorlage*.

v. 7. MT בני ישראל; OG τὸν οἶκον Ισραηλ = בית ישראל. A probable case of equally ancient textual variants.[83] However, MT is supported by the corresponding בני (reflected by OG σπέρμα) in v. 8.

v. 8. MT אשר העלה ו >OG. Probably MT conflation from the parallel passage in 16:15.[84]

MT הדחתים, "I have driven them"; OG ἐξῶσεν αὐτούς = הדיחם, "he has driven them." By maintaining the third person language, OG gives a more consistent reading (which also corresponds to 16:15), but since we are dealing with human speech contained with divine speech, some formal inconsistency is not surprising and need not be secondary.

3.3. *Exegesis*

v. 1. The image of Israel as YHWH's flock (צאן) occurs frequently in the Old Testament (Num 27:17; 1 Kgs 22:17; Ps 95:7; Jer 31:10), as does the description of the nation's rulers as shepherds (רעים) of the people (Jer 3:15; Mic 5:4; cf. 2 Sam 5:2; 7:7; Ps 78:71, where David shepherds the nation). However, the use

79.　Duhm, *Jeremia*, 181, emends to יפחדו, "terrified."

80.　For this "doubly odd" form, see *GKC* §60c, 74e; Rudolph, *Jeremia*, 124.

81.　So Duhm, *Jeremia*, 181; Carroll, *Jeremiah*, 446; McKane, *Jeremiah 1*, 564. Craigie, Kelley and Drinkard, *Jeremiah 1–25*, 330, take this as the likely meaning of MT as well.

82.　J. Ziegler, *Beiträge zur Ieremias–Septuaginta. Nachrichten der Akademie der Wissenschaften in Göttingen*. Vol. 1. *Philologisch–Historische Klasse* (Göttingen: Vandenhoeck & Ruprecht, 1958), 92; Janzen, *Studies*, 32.

83.　See McKane, *Jeremiah 1*, 374.

84.　Bright, *Jeremiah*, 140; Holladay, *Jeremiah 1*, 621.

of רעים and צאן *together* as a metaphor for Israel's leaders and people is confined to the exilic and post-exilic prophetic corpus (Jer 10:21; 50:6; Ezek 34:1–10; Isa 63:11; Zech 10:2–3). For the most part, such רעים are *political* leaders. That this is the case in these verses is clear from their context, following the oracles against the kings of Judah (who are also described as רעים in 22:22) and preceding the prophecy of a rightful king (vv. 5–6).[85] Nevertheless, the term can also signify *spiritual* leaders. In Isa 63:11, Moses is the shepherd of Israel, while in Zech 11:4–9, 15–16, the prophet himself is given this role.[86] It is arguable that in Jer 2:8, הרעים stands in synonymous parallelism with הנביאים,[87] while in 10:21, the רעים who do not enquire (לא דרשו) of YHWH might also include prophets.[88] Since 23:1–8 is followed by the extended section לנבאים (23:9–40), the רעים *might* therefore include the prophets, at least in a secondary sense.[89]

מאבדים (אבד, Pi.) is most naturally rendered "destroying." Since this disrupts the general emphasis on "scattering" (פוץ, נדח) in vv. 1–4, some take the term to mean "lose, cause to go astray";[90] note the antithesis of אבד (Pi.) and בקש (Pi.) in Eccl 3:6. Conversely, this may weaken an intentionally forceful word; abusive rule by the leaders could explain why YHWH's promise of new shepherds (v. 4) is followed by the statement that his people "will not be afraid again" (compare the accusation against the shepherds in Ezek 34:4, בחזקה רדיתם אתם, "you have ruled them with violence"). But in what sense are the leaders destroying the people? One answer would be that by leading them away from YHWH, they have brought the disaster of exile upon the nation (cf. 50:6–7).[91] However, given the emphasis on social injustice in the previous chapter (22:3, 13–17), מאבדים might denote oppressive rule *in Israel*, and the same could even be true of מפצים, and ותדחום in v. 2.[92] On this view, the idea of exile is not

---

85. So Volz, *Jeremia*, 232; McKane, *Jeremiah 1*, 555; Craigie, Kelley and Drinkard, *Jeremiah 1–25*, 326; Brueggemann, *Exile and Homecoming*, 205. However, Rudolph, *Jeremia*, 125, and Bright, *Jeremiah*, 143, believe that royal officials generally are in view.

86. See Mike Butterworth, *Structure and the Book of Zechariah* (JSOTSup 130; Sheffield: JSOT Press, 1992), 204–5.

87. Especially if הכהנים is here synonymous with תפשי התורה; so Berridge, *People, Prophet, and the Word of YHWH*, 140. The terminology may, however, signify four different groups. Rudolph, *Jeremia*, 12, equates הכהנים with תפשי התורה, but distinguishes between הרעים and הנביאים.

88. So William L. Holladay, *Jeremiah: Spokesman Out of Time* (Philadelphia: United Church Press, 1974), 57; more recently, however, he takes it to mean "civil leaders" (*Jeremiah 1*, 342).

89. Cf. Joyce G. Baldwin, "*Ṣemaḥ* as a Technical Term in the Prophets," *VT* 16 (1964): 93–97 (94): "The message of ch. 23 suggests that by 'shepherds' the prophet means rulers in general; prophets and priests (v. 11) as well as kings." Cf. Thompson, *Jeremiah*, 335.

90. A. B. Ehrlich, *Randglossen zur Hebräischen Bibel: textkritisches, sprachliches und sachliches*. Vol. 4, *Jesia, Jeremia* (Leipzig: Hinrichs, 1912), 302; Rudolph, *Jeremia*, 125; Bright, *Jeremiah*, 139; McKane, *Jeremiah 1*, 554.

91. "The implication here is that neglect leaves the sheep as dead as if they have been deliberately killed" (Holladay, *Jeremiah 1*, 614); similarly Carroll, *Jeremiah*, 444.

92. According to Rudolph, *Jeremia*, 125, the three verbs in vv. 1–2 "malen also nur die mangelnde Fürsorge der Hirten…und sind nicht auf Gefangenschaft und Zersprengung unter die Völker auszudeuten."

introduced until v. 3, where, however, YHWH is the subject of נדח. Clearly, though, the language of v. 1 is flexible enough to allow both meanings.

v. 2. אתם הפצתם את צאני ותדחום. This emphatic assertion that it is the leaders of Israel who are responsible for the nation's demise is almost unparalleled in Jeremiah. We may compare YHWH's statement in 50:6, צאן אבדות היה עמי רעיהם התעום, though the following וצריהם אמרו לא נאשם תחת אשר חטאו ליהוה (v. 7) hints at a more general culpability.[93]

ולא פקדתם אתם הנני פקד עליהם. Most commentators see here an ironic word-play, with פקד meaning "attend to," initially in a positive sense ("care for") and then in a negative sense ("punish").[94] Recently, however, Auld has argued that both here and in v. 4, פקד should be given the meaning "count," there being a conscious allusion to the story of David's counting the Israelites (2 Sam 24:1–10).[95] Certainly, the meaning "(not) counted" fits the context well in v. 4 (cf. ופרו ורבו, v. 3), but whether פקד means "count" in v. 2 is unlikely; even if the author doubted that David's census really amounted to a sin, it is hard to see why he would have fastened on the kings' failure to count the people as particularly worthy of censure.[96]

v. 3. ופרו ורבו ("they will be fruitful and multiply") echoes 3:16, והיה כי תרבו ופריתם בארץ (the only other occurrence of פרה in Jeremiah). In both passages, this re-enactment of the creation mandate follows YHWH's restoration of the people to their land; by contrast, 29:6 (רבו שם ואל תמעטו) commands the exiles to multiply in Babylon.

v. 4. The parallels with 3:14–18 become even clearer. With והקמתי עליהם רעים ורעום, compare 3:15, ונתתי לכם רעים כלבי ורעו אתכם דעה והשכיל. Given the frequency of the 'shepherd' motif in Jeremiah, it is striking that only in these two verses does YHWH promise to provide the people with new shepherds. Also common to both passages are the expressions עוד...לא and ולא יפקדו (3:16), though the latter is pointed differently. But there are also connections to the thought-world of chs. 30–33; the use of לא עוד to describe Israel's transformation is prominent there too (30:8; 31:12, 29, 34, 40; 33:24), while the combination ירא/חתת occurs elsewhere in Jeremiah only in 30:10 (= 46:27).

Verses 5–6 occur in a very similar form in 33:15–16: the main differences are the use of בימים ההם ובעת ההיא (33:15aα) instead of הנה ימים באים נאם יהוה (23:5aα); אצמיח (33:15aα) instead of והקמתי (23:5aβ); ירושלם (33:16aβ) for ישראל (23:6aβ); וזה אשר יקרא לה (33:16bα) for וזה שמו אשר יקראו (23:6bα);

---

93. Since these are the words of Israel's enemies, it is hard to know how far they represent the perspective of the author.

94. E.g. Bright, *Jeremiah*, 143; Carroll, *Jeremiah*, 443; McKane, *Jeremiah 1*, 553; Thompson, *Jeremiah*, 487; Craigie, Kelley and Drinkard, *Jeremiah 1–25*, 326.

95. A. G. Auld, "Counting Sheep, Sins and Sour Grapes: The Primacy of the Primary History?," in *Sense and Sensitivity: Essays on Reading the Bible in Memory of Robert Carroll* (ed. Alastair G. Hunter and Philip R. Davies; JSOTSup 348; London: Sheffield Academic Press, 2002), 63–72 (65). Auld claims (p. 66) that "the tradition in Jer is deliberately encouraging reflection on that mysterious conclusion to the story of the first David."

96. Auld points to the prophecy in Jer 33:13 that in the restored Judah, the sheep will again be "counted," but here מנה rather than פקד is used.

and the absence in 33:15–16 of וּמָלַךְ מֶלֶךְ וְהִשְׂכִּיל (23:5bα). Consequently, the later passage is more focussed on the city of Jerusalem.

v. 5. צֶמַח צַדִּיק. Both terms must be considered together. Elsewhere in the Old Testament (e.g. Zech 3:8; 6:12), צֶמַח denotes a messianic figure, and some believe this to be the sense here.[97] If צַדִּיק is then interpreted to mean "righteous,"[98] the prophesied king stands in contrast to the unrighteous kings of ch. 22. However, the use of צֶמַח צַדִּיק in third-century BC Phoenician inscriptions to mean "rightful scion" has led scholars to see the same meaning here.[99] According to Holladay, "there is no plausible way in which one can assume that the Phoenician phrase somehow stems from a Hebrew phrase having a specific messianic nuance; one must conclude that Jeremiah is here using a general Northwest Semitic term for the legitimate king."[100] This, however, is to create a false dichotomy; v. 5b, וְעָשָׂה מִשְׁפָּט וּצְדָקָה בָּאָרֶץ, makes it clear that righteousness is the basis of rightfulness. Moreover, while the Phoenician inscriptions shed light on the origin of the expression, they do not exhaust its meaning in its present context. Whether צֶמַח is thought to be messianic depends partly on how we define the latter term.

v. 6. יְהוָה צִדְקֵנוּ. Most commentators see this as a deliberate word-play on צִדְקִיָּהוּ.[101] Less clear is its significance. Some see the allusion as positive; according to Clements, "there is no clear indication that it is intended to be an ironic dismissal of Zedekiah."[102] Others see the new name as contrasting with that of the present evil king: "das Programm, das im Namen des letzten Königs lag und dem dieser so wenig nachkam, wird unter dem neuen König erfüllt werden."[103] Some go further and see here an implicit critique of Zedekiah, thus supplying the oracle on his kingship that is otherwise lacking in this section. The oracle may well have undergone a semantic shift during its transition from *Sitz im Leben* to *Sitz im Buch*.

---

97. E.g. Baldwin, "*Ṣemaḥ* as a Technical Term," 93–97; Bright, *Jeremiah*, 143; Martin G. Abegg, Jr., s.v. צמח, *NIDOTTE* 3:816 ("there can be no doubt that צמח denotes the Messiah, the branch of David, in Jer 23:5 and 33:15.").

98. Rudolph, *Jeremia*, 125–26, allows that צדיק in v. 5b may be translated "echter" (true) or "gerecht" (righteous), but leans toward the latter.

99. See James Swetnam, "Some Observations on the Background of צדיק in Jeremias 23,5a," *Biblica* 46 (1965): 29–40 (38–40), who sets this promise against a background of tension regarding Zedekiah's instatement as king. Similarly, Bright, *Jeremiah*, 144; McKane, *Jeremiah 1*, 561; David J. Reimer, s.v. צדק, *NIDOTTE* 3: 764.

100. Holladay, *Jeremiah 1*, 618. In fact, Abegg, *NIDOTTE* 3:816, concedes that the Phoenician inscriptions provide a parallel to Jer 23:5.

101. In addition to those cited below, see Thompson, *Jeremiah*, 491. Exceptions are McKane, *Jeremiah 1*, 564, and A. Malamat, "Jeremiah and the Last Two Kings of Judah," *PEQ* 83 (1951): 81–87 (84), who argues that "the change of the name Mattaniah to Zedekiah upon his ascent to the throne was a subsequent result of Jeremiah's prophecy on King Messiah."

102. Ronald E. Clements, "Jeremiah: Prophet of Hope," in Clements, ed., *Old Testament Prophecy*, 123–41 (127). Carroll, *Jeremiah*, 446, suggests that this was a poem for Zedekiah's coronation.

103. Rudolph, *Jeremia*, 136; similarly, Bright, *Jeremiah*, 143; Craigie, Kelley and Drinkard, *Jeremiah 1–25*, 329; cautiously, Brueggemann, *Exile and Homecoming*, 207.

v. 8. Whether בית ישראל denotes the people of the former northern kingdom or Judeans exiled in the sixth century is uncertain, since the phrase "the land of the north" (ארץ צפונה) might be either Assyria or Babylon. Either way, the subsequent מכל הארצות אשר הדחתים שם (cf. v. 3) universalizes the promise.

3.4. *Coherence and Redaction*

Although I have identified 23:1–8 as a literary unit, it comprises three clearly distinct oracles: vv. 1–4, 5–6 and 7–8. Formally, these are demarcated by their respective introductions: the first by the "Woe!" formula (cf. 22:13), and the second and the third by the declaration, "Look, the days are coming," otherwise restricted to the Book of Consolation (30:3; 31:27, 38; 33:14).[104] Each oracle, moreover, has its own dominant imagery, namely, 'shepherd/flock' (vv. 1–4), 'the righteous king' (vv. 5–6) and 'new exodus' (vv. 7–8; note the twofold use of העלה). The fact that the second and third oracles occur almost verbatim in other contexts (vv. 5–6 = 33:15–16; vv. 7–8 = 16:14–15) also demonstrates their original independence; this is underlined in respect to vv. 7–8 by its different placement in MT and OG.

In addition, several scholars have questioned the original integrity of vv. 1–4. Rudolph saw v. 3 as a post-exilic gloss because (unlike vv. 1–2, 4) it explicitly assumes a worldwide *Diaspora*.[105] McKane, however, argues that we should detach vv. 1–2 from vv. 3–4: "There are two separate worlds of ideas: on the one hand the community disintegrated because its leaders were negligent, and, on the other, the community exiled by Yahweh as a judgment for its sins."[106] Certainly there is a progression of thought from v. 2 to v. 3, but it is hard to see why the same person should not be author of both.

Whatever their literary history, these oracles have been intelligently combined. Despite the unifying 'shepherd/flock' imagery, vv. 1–4 actually contain two separate promises for YHWH's people: restoration to their homeland (v. 3), and new shepherds for their protection (v. 4). The function of the second and third oracles is to develop each of these promises. Thus, vv. 5–6 interpret the promise of new shepherds by prophesying a particular king who will reign for the benefit of Judah and Israel; note the use of הקמתי as the connecting word (vv. 4, 5). Then, vv. 6–7 take up the promise of homecoming by anticipating a return that will replace the exodus as the definitive act of YHWH's salvation; note how v. 8 repeats מכל הארצות אשר הדחתים שם from v. 3.

3.5. *Judicial Differentiation in Jeremiah 23:1–8:* הרעים / הצאן

Within 23:1–8, the crucial section for our purposes is the opening oracle in vv. 1–4. Here, the metaphor of shepherds (רעים) and flock (צאן) creates a sharp

---

104. Note too the shift to poetic parallelism in the middle of the second oracle (vv. 5b, 6a).

105. Rudolph, *Jeremia*, 125. A similar conclusion is reached by J. Lust, "'Gathering and Return' in Jeremiah and Ezekiel," in Bogaert, ed., *Le Livre de Jérémie*, 117–42 (134–35), partly because v. 3 states that YHWH (rather than the shepherds) scattered the sheep, and partly because the language of multiplying "betrays a redaction influenced by a priestly style, unusual for Jeremiah" (p. 135).

106. McKane, *Jeremiah 1*, 557; similarly, Carroll, *Jeremiah*, 445.

inner-Judean distinction upon which the following judgment and salvation oracles are based. The shepherds are singled out for criticism. Instead of tending and overseeing (רעה and פקד) the flock, they have destroyed (אבד, v. 1) and scattered them (פוץ, vv. 1, 2; נדח, Hiph. v. 2). Consequently, YHWH will repay them in kind: הנני פקד עליכם את רע מעלליכם (v. 2; cf. 21:14). By contrast, in vv. 3–4 he promises to intervene on the flock's behalf, restoring them מכל הארצות אשר הדחתי אתם שם to security in their own land, and raising up (הקמתי) new shepherds to care for them. Equally striking is the affirmation of YHWH's relationship with the people; they are "my people" (עמי, v. 2), "my flock" (צאני, v. 2), "the flock of my pasture" (מרעיתי, v. 1). At the same time, the language throughout is historically and geographically non-specific; as we have seen, in vv. 5–8 even the Judah/Israel distinction is obliterated.

Within this oracle, judgment and salvation are closely linked to the question of culpability. In this respect, the adoption of "shepherds and sheep" as the controlling metaphor is crucial. For by viewing the kings as shepherds, the text automatically presents them as morally responsible agents, deserving of YHWH's punishment (פקד); scattering sheep is as reprehensible for a shepherd as it is for a king. What the metaphor does not permit is for blame to be attached to the people, because the people are simply sheep; indeed, throughout vv. 1–4 the flock remain entirely passive. In other words, framing the issue in terms of shepherds and sheep inevitably places the moral burden on the shepherds.

Naturally, the metaphor has its limits, and it should not be seen as implying that the people are guiltless. On the contrary, the wording of YHWH's pledge in vv. 3 and 8 to gather them "from all the places where *I* scattered them" (אשר הדחתי אתם), with its overtones of his personal wrath, hints at the opposite. We can say, however, that Jer 23:1–8 attaches greater culpability to Israel's leaders. Not only does this explain why the promise of restoration is limited to the people, it also accounts for the content of vv. 5–6. What YHWH promises here is not (as in ch. 24) the gift of a new heart and a new relationship; the terms עמי and צאני (v. 2) suggest this relationship is already established. Instead, since the chief problem has been their former leaders, what they are promised is a *new* leader, who will rule wisely and in righteousness.

This distinction between leaders and people in a combined judgment and salvation oracle is unique within Jeremiah. It is important to bear this in mind, since 23:1–8 is sometimes bracketed together with other promises of return for the *Diaspora*, such as 16:14–15; 29:14 and 32:37.[107] Crucially, though, none of these other promises distinguish between different Judean or Israelite groups; *all*, without exception, will be saved. As we have seen, the closest parallel to 23:1–8 is in 3:14–18; there, however, while YHWH promises to provide the people with new shepherds "after my own heart" (כלבי, v. 14), there is no message of blame or judgment on their former shepherds. Indeed, 3:14–18 explicitly refers to the nation as a whole as בנים שובבים (v. 14), and contains the pointed prophecy, ולא ילכו עוד אחרי שררות לבם הרע (v. 17). For a genuine parallel to the shepherd and flock polarity in Jer 23:1–8, we have to look to Ezek 34.

---

107. See, e.g., Schmid, *Buchgestalten*, 269–74.

4. *Jeremiah 24:1–10*

4.1. *Text*

הראני יהוה והנה שני דודאי האנים מועדים לפני היכל יהוה אחרי הגלות נבוכדראצר מלך בבל את יכניהו בן יהויקים מלך יהודה ואת שרי יהודה ואת החרש ואת המסגר מירושלם ויבאם בבל	1	ἔδειξέ μοι κύριος δύο καλάθους σύκων κειμένους κατὰ πρόσωπον ναοῦ κυρίου μετὰ τὸ ἀποικίσαι Ναβουχοδονοσορ βασιλέα Βαβυλῶνος τὸν Ιεχονιαν υἱὸν Ιωακιμ βασιλέα Ιουδα καὶ τοὺς ἄρχοντας καὶ τοὺς τεχνίτας καὶ τοὺς δεσμώτας καὶ τοὺς πλουσίους ἐξ Ιερουσαλημ καὶ ἤγαγεν αὐτοὺς εἰς Βαβυλῶνα
הדוד אחד האנים טבות מאד כתאני הבכרות והדוד אחד האנים רעות מאד אשר לא תאכלנה מרע	2	ὁ κάλαθος ὁ εἷς σύκων χρηστῶν σφόδρα ὡς τὰ σῦκα τὰ πρόιμα καὶ ὁ κάλαθος ὁ ἕτερος σύκων πονηρῶν σφόδρα ἃ οὐ βρωθήσεται ἀπὸ πονηρίας αὐτῶν
ויאמר יהוה אלי מה אתה ראה ירמיהו ואמר האנים התאנים הטבות טבות מאד והרעות רעות מאד אשר לא תאכלנה מרע	3	καὶ εἶπε κύριος πρός με τί σὺ ὁρᾷς Ιερεμια καὶ εἶπα σῦκα τὰ χρηστὰ χρηστὰ λίαν καὶ τὰ πονηρὰ πονηρὰ λίαν ἃ οὐ βρωθήσεται ἀπὸ πονηρίας αὐτῶν
ויהי דבר יהוה אלי לאמר	4	καὶ ἐγένετο λόγος κυρίου πρός με λέγων
כה אמר יהוה אלהי ישראל כתאנים הטבות האלה כן אכיר את גלות יהודה אשר שלחתי מן המקום הזה ארץ כשדים לטובה	5	τάδε λέγει κύριος ὁ θεὸς Ισραηλ ὡς τὰ σῦκα τὰ χρηστὰ ταῦτα οὕτως ἐπιγνώσομαι τοὺς ἀποικισθέντας Ιουδα οὓς ἐξαπέσταλκα ἐκ τοῦ τόπου τούτου εἰς γῆν Χαλδαίων εἰς ἀγαθὰ
ושמתי עיני עליהם לטובה והשבתים על הארץ הזאת ובניתים ולא אהרס ונטעתים ולא אתוש	6	καὶ στηριῶ τοὺς ὀφθαλμούς μου ἐπ' αὐτοὺς εἰς ἀγαθὰ καὶ ἀποκαταστήσω αὐτοὺς εἰς τὴν γῆν ταύτην καὶ ἀνοικοδομήσω αὐτοὺς καὶ οὐ μὴ καθελῶ καὶ καταφυτεύσω αὐτοὺς καὶ οὐ μὴ ἐκτίλω
ונתתי להם לב לדעת אתי כי אני יהוה והיו לי לעם ואנכי אהיה להם לאלהים כי ישבו אלי בכל לבם	7	καὶ δώσω αὐτοῖς καρδίαν τοῦ εἰδέναι αὐτοὺς ἐμὲ ὅτι ἐγώ εἰμι κύριος καὶ ἔσονταί μοι εἰς λαὸν καὶ ἐγὼ ἔσομαι αὐτοῖς εἰς θεόν ὅτι ἐπιστραφήσονται ἐπ' ἐμὲ ἐξ ὅλης τῆς καρδίας αὐτῶν
וכהאנים הרעות אשר לא תאכלנה מרע כי כה אמר יהוה כן אתן את צדקיהו מלך יהודה ואת שריו ואת שארית ירושלם הנשארים בארץ הזאת והישבים בארץ מצרים	8	καὶ ὡς τὰ σῦκα τὰ πονηρὰ ἃ οὐ βρωθήσεται ἀπὸ πονηρίας αὐτῶν τάδε λέγει κύριος οὕτως παραδώσω τὸν Σεδεκιαν βασιλέα Ιουδα καὶ τοὺς μεγιστᾶνας αὐτοῦ καὶ το κατάλοιπον Ιερουσαλημ τοὺς ὑπολελειμμένους ἐν τῇ γῇ ταύτῃ καὶ τοὺς κατοικοῦντας ἐν Αἰγύπτῳ
ונתתים לזועה לרעה לכל ממלכות הארץ לחרפה ולמשל לשנינה ולקללה בכל המקמות אשר אדיחם שם	9	καὶ δώσω αὐτοὺς εἰς διασκορπισμὸν εἰς πάσας τὰς βασιλείας τῆς γῆς καὶ εἰς ὀνειδισμὸν καὶ εἰς παραβολὴν καὶ εἰς μῖσος καὶ εἰς κατάραν ἐν παντὶ τόπῳ οὗ ἐξῶσα αὐτοὺς ἐκεῖ
ושלחתי בם את החרב את הרעב ואת הדבר עד תמם מעל האדמה אשר נתתי להם ולאבותיהם	10	καὶ ἀποστελῶ εἰς αὐτοὺς τὸν λιμὸν καὶ τὸν θάνατον καὶ τὴν μάχαιραν ἕως ἂν ἐκλίπωσιν ἀπὸ τῆς γῆς ἧς ἔδωκα αὐτοῖς

4.2. *Textual Notes*

v. 1. MT והנה >OG (making καλάθους the object of ἔδειξε). OG may either reflect a shorter *Vorlage* (cf. Jer 38[45]:22; Amos 7:1, 4, 5; 8:1, where it renders והנה with καὶ ἰδοὺ) or be haplographic, due to the juxtaposition of יהוה והנה.[108]

v. 5. MT גלות, "exiles"; OG ἀποικισθέντας, "colony" (cf. ἀποικία in 29[36]:1).

v. 8. MT כי >OG. Even if כי carries an emphatic sense ("ah!"),[109] it is almost certainly an MT plus; elsewhere Jeremiah OG consistently represents כי כה with ὅτι οὕτως (29[36]:10, etc.) or (δι)ὅτι τάδε (22:6, 11, etc.).

v. 9. MT לזועה, "object of terror"; OG, διασκορπισμὸν, "a scattering." The translator has probably guessed at a term that was unclear to him.[110]

לרעה >OG. Quite apart from the lack of a conjunction, MT is obscure. Relocating לרעה to the end of v. 8,[111] so that it balances לטובה at the end of v. 5, is attractive, but does not explain its omission in OG. It is lacking in the similar 15:4 and 29:18, and may be the result of conflation after one faulty manuscript read only רעה.[112]

v. 10. ולאבותיהם >OG. Possible haplography due to homoioteleuton (cf. the ending הם of the last two words), but probably an MT plus, since similar phrases in 7:14; 23:39 and 25:5 are represented by OG.

4.3. *Exegesis*

v. 1. הראני יהוה והנה. The use of ראה Hiph. + הנה is typical of the vision report, found elsewhere in the Old Testament; see especially Amos 7:1, 4, 7, where both elements are present.[113] However, the lack of an initial כה, otherwise typical of this genre, is striking.

מועדים is pointed by MT as מוּעָדִים (Hoph. ptc. pl. יעד). The only other Old Testament instance of יעד Hoph. is in Ezek 21:21(16), where it appears to mean "summoned" or "appointed" (i.e. to inflict judgment).[114] Since neither term is

---

108.   So Janzen, *Studies*, 117, 119.

109.   So Bright, *Jeremiah*, 193; Craigie, Kelley and Drinkard, *Jeremiah 1–25*, 360. See, however, Anneli Aejmelaeus, "The Function and Interpretation of כי in Biblical Hebrew," *JBL* 105 (1986): 193–209, who concludes that only exceptionally does the particle carry an emphatic sense (208).

110.   So Emanuel Tov, "Did the Septuagint Translators Always Understand Their Hebrew Text?," in his *The Greek and Hebrew Bible: Collected Essays on the Septuagint* (Leiden: Brill, 1999), 203–18 (208). Tov notes that elsewhere in Jeremiah זועה is rendered variously as ἀνάγκας, "punishment" (15:4) and διασπορά, "scattering" (34[41]:17), while in 2 Chr 29:8, ἔκστασις, "astonishment" is used.

111.   Volz, *Jeremia*, 247; Holladay, *Jeremiah 1*, 655; tentatively, Rudolph, *Jeremia*, 134; Bright, *Jeremiah*, 192 n. a.

112.   So Duhm, *Jeremia*, 199; Ziegler, *Beiträge*, 87; Janzen, *Studies*, 12–13; McKane, *Jeremiah 1*, 617.

113.   Cf. Zech 1:8; 2:1, 5; 5:1 (ראה Qal + הנה) and 2 Kgs 8:13; Zech 2:3; 3:1 (ראה Hiph. without והנה).

114.   For יעד Hiph. = "summon," see Jer 49:19; 50:44; Job 9:19. On Ezek 21:21, see Walther Zimmerli, *Ezekiel 1: A Commentary on the Book of the Prophet Ezekiel, Chapters 1–24* (Hermeneia; Philadelphia: Fortress, 1979), 431, and Moshe Greenberg, *Ezekiel 21–37: A New Translation with Introduction and Commentary* (AB 22A; New York: Doubleday, 1997), 426.

readily applicable to jars of figs, most commentaries and EVV read "placed, set." Whether יֻעַד Hoph. can bear this meaning is doubtful,[115] but it can also be obtained by emending to מָעֳמָדִים (Hoph. ptc. עמד),[116] or to מוּדָעִים (Hoph. ptc. of a proposed ידע, "place").[117] The latter is the simpler, though Old Testament evidence for ידע = "place" is lacking. "Placed" is clearly understood by Targ. (מַחֲתִין) and Vulg. (*positi*), though whether they assumed מוּעָדִים, מֻעֳמָדִים or מוּדָעִים is uncertain. OG κειμένους is of little help, since this can mean both "placed, deposited"[118] and "appointed."[119] It may be preferable to retain MT and read "summoned." Granted, the idea of figs being summoned before the temple is odd, but not impossible (see further below); indeed, the substitution of an expected עמדים with the more cryptic מועדים may be a deliberate device to seize our attention and heighten our alertness to what will follow.

היכל יהוה occurs elsewhere in Jeremiah only in 7:4. Most commentators see this as a reference to the temple in Jerusalem, and possibly, as in 1 Kgs 6 and Ezek 41, the inner sanctuary in particular (cf. the alleged cultic associations of הבכרות in v. 2). The preferred term in Jeremiah for the temple, however, is בית יהוה, and Calvin argued that "the temple…is to be taken here for the tribunal of God,"[120] citing Isa 26:21 and Mic 1:2–3 for the same idea.[121] Further support for this view comes from the emphasis in the preceding chapter on the סוד יהוה (23:18, 22), the heavenly council from which YHWH *sees* and *judges* (23:13–14, 23–24). This judicial aspect to היכל יהוה coheres well with the interpretation of מועדים suggested above; the figs are not being presented as an offering, but summoned and scrutinized for judgment.

The date rubric אחרי הגלות נבוכדראצר...ויבאם בבל is widely regarded as secondary, due its parenthetical nature, but a syntactic parenthesis should not automatically be equated with a redactional gloss.[122] Without v. 1b not only would the historical allusions in vv. 5 and 8 be highly abrupt, the vision as a whole would lose the key to its interpretation.[123] One might reasonably ask how

115.   Such a translation is rejected by Giesebrecht, *Jeremia*, 133, and D. Winton Thomas, "A Note on מועדים in Jeremiah 24,1," *JTS* 3 (1952): 55.

116.   Duhm, *Jeremia*, 197; Volz, *Jeremia*, 247; Pohlmann, *Studien*, 21 n. 8.

117.   So Winton Thomas, "Note on מועדים," 55; see further D. Winton Thomas, "The Root ידע in Hebrew," *JTS* 35 (1934): 298–306.

118.   E.g. Sir 22:18, χάρακες ἐπὶ μετεώρου κείμενοι; 2 Esd 6:1, ἐν ταῖς βιβλιοθήκαις ὅπου ἡ γάζα κεῖται ἐν Βαβυλῶνι.

119.   Cf. *Memorabilia* 4.4.21: οἱ παραβαίνοντες τοὺς ὑπὸ τῶν Θεῶν κειμένους νόμους.

120.   John Calvin, *Commentaries on the Book of the Prophet Jeremiah and the Lamentations*, vol. 3 (trans. J. Owen; Edinburgh: Calvin Translation Society, 1852), 221. Cf. Volz, *Jeremia*, 249: "nicht als 'Tempel,' sondern als 'Wohnort' Jahwes."

121.   Although Isa 26:21 refers not to היכל יהוה but to ממקומו.

122.   Cf. the opening double subordinate clause in Jer 40:1: הדבר אשר היה אל ירמיהו מאת יהוה. אחר שלח אתו נבוזראדן רב טבחים מן הרמה בקחתו אתו... The subsequent והוא אסור creates a further subsidiary clause, which is, however, probably secondary.

123.   Calvin, *Jeremiah and Lamentations 3*, 221: "Had not this been added, the vision would have been obscure." Pohlmann, *Studien*, 21, admits that v. 1b appears to interrupt, but adds: "Trotzdem handelt es sich hier kaum um eine nachträgliche Einschaltung; die Zeitbestimmung charakterisiert nämlich das ganze Kapitel dem Inhalt entsprechend als einen Bericht über eine 'neue'

a biblical writer could supply such a detail without it being suspected of being secondary.[124]

המסגר resists translation, though most agree that the root is סגר, "to close" (cf. Vulg., *inclusorem*). Its association with חרש (Jer 29:2; 2 Kgs 24:14, 16) suggests that מסגר is a craftsman of some sort, though as McKane remarks, "the form מסגר remains a problem, since we might have expected a formation of the same type as חרש (סגר)."[125] OG δεσμώτας ("prisoners") apparently understands המסגר to mean "the enclosed ones," an interpretation Bright deems "not impossible."[126] Alternatively, המסגר might denote *people who enclose*, that is, "guards" (cf. Targ., תרעיא; Ezra 7:24).

v. 2. As the root suggests, בכורה (Isa 28:4; Mic 7:1; Hos 9:10) implies fruit that ripens early. Some commentators have seen here an allusion to בכורים, "firstfruits."[127] However, OG τὰ σῦκα τὰ πρόιμα clearly takes הבכרות to mean simply "early fruit," and if the presentation of firstfruits was in mind we might have expected the cultic term רצה (לא) (Lev 1:4, 22:25; Jer 14:10, 12; Mal 1:10, 13), rather than טוב.

v. 5. The use of the messenger formula, כה אמר יהוה אלהי ישראל, here and in v. 8 is often seen as incongruous in a private vision report, and thus redactional. Craigie et al. argue for its retention on the ground that the vision was for the benefit of the king and people,[128] but the text is silent regarding any third-party audience. More significantly, however, Meier has shown that כה אמר + personal name typically functions in the Old Testament as a *citation* formula, without necessarily implying any "messenger" activity.[129]

The ensuing simile, כתאנים הטובת האלה כן אביר את גלות...לטובה, forms the hermeneutical crux of the chapter.[130] Since the two named elements in this

---

bzw. jüngere Offenbarung, die dem Propheten zu Teil wurde, nachdem sich die 'früheren' mit der Exilierung Jojakins erfüllt hatten."

124. Cf. Susan Niditch, *The Symbolic Vision in Biblical Tradition* (HSM 30; Chico, Calif.: Scholars Press, 1980), 60–61: "Had the date segment begun Jeremiah 24, we might have considered it an original part of the vision...[however] we must assume that a redactor placed the indication of date within the initial description of the vision in order to make it *seem more a part of the whole*" (italics mine). This rather gives the game away; a simpler explanation is that it *was* part of the whole.

125. McKane, *Jeremiah 1*, 608.

126. Bright, *Jeremiah*, 193.

127. Duhm, *Jeremia*, 197; Thompson, *Jeremiah*, 507–8; Craigie, Kelley and Drinkard, *Jeremiah 1–25*, 358. In Deut 26:1–11, the worshipper is told to place the firstfruits in a basket, and set it before YHWH. But the terminology is different: טנא ("basket," vv. 2, 4), נוח Hiph. ("set down," vv. 4, 10) and ראשית פרי ("firstfruit," vv. 2, 10). Moreover, the offering is set לפני מזבח יהוה (v. 4) rather than לפני היכל יהוה.

128. Craigie, Kelley and Drinkard, *Jeremiah 1–25*, 358.

129. Samuel A. Meier, *Speaking of Speaking: Marking Direct Discourse in the Hebrew Bible* (VTSup 46; Leiden: Brill, 1992), 277–91.

130. With most scholars, I take לטובה as the complement of אביר, with מן המקום אשר שלחתי הזה ארץ כשדים being parenthetical. Arguably, however, לטובה relates syntactically to שלחתי, thereby emphasizing God's good purpose in sending these Judeans to Babylon; so A. C. Welch, *Jeremiah: His Time and His Work* (Oxford: Blackwell, 1951), 165; Pohlmann, *Studien*, 22.

analogy are the "good figs" and the exiles in Babylon, the point of similarity might be thought to lie in the goodness of both, a reading encouraged by the double use of טוב.[131] Consequently, אכיר is sometimes rendered "I regard as, count as."[132] There are, however, serious difficulties with this interpretation. First, although נכר Hiph. (like its LXX counterpart, ἐπιγνώσομαι) is semantically quite flexible, the meaning "regard as, count as" (for which חשב would be more likely)[133] is unattested for it. A more natural translation would be "regard, take note of" (2 Sam 3:36) or "give favourable attention to" (Ruth 2:10, 19; Ps 142:5).[134] Indeed, given the emphasis in v. 6 on the positive things YHWH will do for the exiles, אכיר may even carry the sense "I will show preference for" (a nuance that usually has a negative connotation; cf. Deut 1:17).[135] This suggests, however, that the analogy is more precisely between how people *view* ripe figs and how YHWH *views* the exiles—that is, with pleasure and favour.[136] Secondly, טובה is better taken as a noun, with לטובה meaning "for good, for a good purpose."[137] Not only is this nominal sense for לטובה characteristic of Jeremiah (15:11; 21:10; 39:16; 44:27), it is exactly what we find in the following verse. Once again, therefore, the text of Jer 24 contains an unexpected twist. The fact that v. 5 is cast in the form of a simile (כ...כן), leads us to expect that the exiles (like the figs), will be designated as good; instead, it is the disposition and intention of YHWH that is described this way. Nowhere is this related to the virtues of the *Golah* community.[138]

v. 6. ושמתי עיני עליהם לטובה are epexegetical, removing any ambiguity as to what was promised in v. 5.[139] The expression ושמתי עיני ("I will set my eye")

131. Brueggemann, *Exile and Homecoming*, 218, states that "the exiles are regarded as 'good' by Yahweh," though he adds, "their goodness does not rest in themselves, but in sovereign assertions of Yahweh, who announces them to be good." See too McKane's translation of the text, *Jeremiah 1*, 605: "I will acknowledge (the exiles) to be like these good figs."

132. Brueggemann, *Exile and Homecoming*, 218; R. K. Harrison, *Jeremiah and Lamentations: An Introduction and Commentary* (TOTC; Leicester: IVP, 1979), 124; also RSV, NIV, REB.

133. Note especially חשב ל, "to count one thing as another" (Gen 38:15). Nor is נכר ever used in parallel with חשב.

134. Cf. the paraphrases of Giesebrecht, *Jeremia*, 134 ("Ich will mich sorgend um sie kümmern zum Heile") and Thompson, *Jeremiah*, 508 ("Yahweh looks on these as the ones singled out for favour"). Craigie, Kelley and Drinkard, *Jeremiah 1–25*, 356, translate "I will regard for good"; *HALOT* 2, s.v. נכר, translates "I will regard favourably."

135. John H. Walton, "Vision Narrative Wordplay and Jeremiah XXIV," *VT* 39 (1989): 508–509 (508): "Just as one would show partiality toward the good figs, so the Lord intends to show partiality toward those who have gone into exile."

136. Cf. Hos 9:10: כענבים במדבר מצאתי ישראל כבכורה בתאנה בראשיתה ראיתה אבותיכם "I found Israel like [one finding] grapes in the desert; I saw your fathers like [one seeing] early fruit on the fig tree."

137. Raitt, "Jeremiah's Deliverance Message," 171: "The 'good' finds its primary rootage in the intention of God's action."

138. So Rudolph, *Jeremia*, 135; H. Graf Reventlow, *Liturgie und prophetische Ich bei Jeremia* (Gütersloh: Gütersloher Verlaghaus, Gerd Mohn, 1963), 91–92; Kilpp, *Niederreißen*, 36; Jones, *Jeremiah*, 320. Somewhat alone, Duhm, *Jeremia*, 198, insists that "good" denotes both the piety of the exiles and YHWH's purpose for them.

139. Calvin, *Jeremiah and Lamentations 3*, 225: "He confirms what he said in the last verse, but in other words"; similarly Pohlmann, *Studien*, 22.

means "to adopt a fixed attitude or disposition."[140] It is infrequent in the Old Testament, but note Jer 40:4, ואשים את עיני עליך, and especially Amos 9:4, ושמתי עיני עליהם לרעה ולא לטובה.

ובניתים ולא אהרס ונטעתים ולא אתוש echoes a refrain that occurs throughout Jeremiah, though its varied formulation raises complex hermeneutical questions.[141] Here, for the first time, the emphasis is on the promise of building and planting, rather than destruction and uprooting (cf 1:10), implying that for the exiled community a new salvific era has begun. Already in 18:7–9, however, YHWH has declared that his threats of destruction (לנתש ולנתוץ ולהאביד, v. 7) and promises of blessing (לבנת ולנטע, v. 9) are reversible, being contingent on the response of those addressed. The question thus arises as to whether the apparently unconditional nature of the promise in 24:6 is a distinctive aspect of the new era, or whether it should be understood as qualified by 18:7–9. The closest parallel to our verse is in 42:10: ובניתי אתכם ולא אהרס ונטעתי אתכם ולא אתוש. There, however, the promise is for those who had remained in Judah after 587—that is, precisely those people who in ch. 24 are excluded from any such hope.

v. 7. ונתתי להם לב לדעת אתי occurs only here in Jeremiah, though elements occur elsewhere; see 9:23, כי כולם ידעו אותי; 31:34, וידעו אותי כי אני יהוה; 32:39, ונתתי להם לב אחד לדרך ליראה אותי. The promise of 24:7 thus combines knowledge of YHWH with YHWH's gift of a heart.[142] Outside Jeremiah, Deut 29:3 offers the closest parallel: ולא נתן יהוה לכם לב לדעת ועינים לראות ואזנים לשמע עד היום הזה. Against this background, the climactic nature of 24:7 becomes clear: what Israel had failed to receive even under the leadership of Moses, YHWH now promises to give the exiles.

כי (אני יהוה) (like OG, ὅτι; Targ., ארי; Vulg., *quia*) can be taken as causal ("*because* I am YHWH") or resultative ("*that* I am YHWH").[143] The latter seems more likely; the words just cited in Deut 29:3, that YHWH had not given Israel "a heart to know," are followed by the statement that he had miraculously provided for them, למען תדעו כי אני יהוה אלהיכם (v. 5).[144]

140.　McKane, *Jeremiah 1*, 605, paraphrases as "I will mark them out for favour."

141.　For a full listing and discussion, see Marion Ann Taylor, "Jeremiah 45: The Problem of Placement," *JSOT* 37 (1987): 79–98.

142.　See Pohlmann, *Studien*, 23: "Eigenartig ist nicht nur, daß die Erkenntnis Jahwes von der Verleihung eines (neuen?) Herzens abhängig gemacht wird, was sonst nirgends im AT der Fall ist; merkwürdig ist ebenso die Kombination der zwei hauptsachlichen alttestamentlichen Redeweisen von der Erkenntnis Jahwes, die in ihrem Streuungsbereich sonst reinlich geschieden sind."

143.　Taking the former option here are McKane, *Jeremiah 1*, 605; Unterman, *Repentance to Redemption*, 76–80; Craigie, Kelley and Drinkard, *Jeremiah 1–25*, 359. For the latter, see Giesebrecht, *Jeremia*, 134; Volz, *Jeremia*, 247; A. Condamin, *Le Livre de Jérémie: Traduction et Commentaire* (3d ed.; Études Bibliques; Paris: Gabalda et Cie, 1936), 189; Bright, *Jeremiah*, 192; Thompson, *Jeremiah*, 506; Holladay, *Jeremiah 1*, 658.

144.　For the use of כי in a double accusative, see *GKC* §117h; Bruce K. Waltke and M. O'Connor, *An Introduction to Biblical Hebrew Syntax* (Winona Lake: Eisenbrauns, 1990), 644. The declaration וידעתם (ידעו) כי אני יהוה, "Then you (they) will know that I am YHWH," is of course very common in Ezekiel (6:7, 10, etc.), though here it does not involve a double accusative.

והיו לי לעם ואנכי אהיה להם לאלהים. The covenant formula first occurs in the Old Testament in Exod 6:7, ולקחתי אתכם לי לעם והייתי לכם לאלהים, where, significantly, it is followed immediately by וידעתם כי אני יהוה. Elsewhere in Jeremiah it occurs (with variations) in 7:23; 11:4; 30:22; 31:1, 33; 32:38. Craigie et al. note that in the first two of these, the promise is conditional on human response, while in the others YHWH's initiative is to the fore. They conclude that "this passage bridges both contexts; it is a restoration oracle, but it is also conditional as the next phrase indicates."[145] This, however, depends on how we take v. 7b.

כי ישבו אלי בכל לבם constitutes a *crux interpretum*, since the Hebrew particle can be understood here either as causal ("*for*"), conditional ("*if*"), or temporal ("*when*").[146] Most scholars prefer the first option (cf. OG, ὅτι),[147] although many of them take the very similar כי תדרשני בכל לבבכם (29:12) as conditional. Even if a causal reading is correct, however, this by itself does not preclude all contingency from the text. As Unterman notes, the statement "for they shall return to me with all their heart" leaves open the question of whether this is a free act of the people or the result of YHWH's initiative.[148] Taking the former view, he concludes that repentance is "an act of the exiles' will which becomes the rationale for all the promises of restoration in vv. 6-7."[149]

Conversely, Nicholson argues that Jer 24:5–7 marks an advance on other Deuteronomistic texts (e.g. Deut 4:29–31; 30:1–10; 1 Kgs 8:46–50) by affirming the priority of YHWH's redemptive action over repentance:

> Whilst it is still Israel's "turning again" which will secure forgiveness and restoration, such a "turning again" is now assured by Yahweh himself who now takes the initiative so that Israel will "turn again"... That is to say, the conditional "if" has now receded and the element of promise has come to the forefront of the kerygma.[150]

The fact that YHWH's promise of "a heart to know me" precedes the reference to the exiles seeking him "with all their heart" suggests that Nicholson's emphasis on divine initiative is correct. But to say that Israel's repentance is thereby

---

145. Craigie, Kelley and Drinkard, *Jeremiah 1*, 359–60.

146. Aejmelaeus, "Function and Interpretation," 202–8, argues that when a כי clause follows the main clause (as in Jer 24:7), it only rarely has a conditional or temporal aspect. However, she adds that exceptions to the rule are characteristic of Deuteronomy, "and these are always to be found in the same type of context, Israel's obedience as a condition for promises concerning the future" (pp. 207–8).

147. E.g. Volz, *Jeremia*, 247; Rudolph, *Jeremia*, 137; Artur Weiser, *Das Buch des Propheten Jeremia* (NGB; Göttingen: Vandenhoeck & Ruprecht, 1955), 219; Bright, *Jeremiah*, 192; Thompson, *Jeremiah*, 506; Holladay, *Jeremiah 1*, 659; McKane, *Jeremiah 1*, 609; Stipp, "Zedekiah," 648 n. 43. Preferring "if" are Giesebrecht, *Jeremia*, 34; Welch, *Jeremiah*, 163; Craigie, Kelley and Drinkard, *Jeremiah 1*, 360.

148. Unterman, *Repentance to Redemption*, 81.

149. Ibid., 81.

150. Nicholson, *Preaching*, 81; similarly, Raitt, "Jeremiah's Deliverance Message," 174; McKane, *Jeremiah 1*, 609; H. Lalleman-de Winkel, *Jeremiah in Prophetic Tradition: An Examination of the Book of Jeremiah in the Light of Israel's Prophetic Traditions* (CBET 26; Leuven: Peeters, 2000), 148.

assured is an overstatement. Rather, Jer 24:6–7 sees salvation as entailing *both* a prior act of Y‌HWH (the gift of a new heart) *and* a response on the part of the exiles ("to turn with all their heart") on which their salvation is indeed contingent.[151] The precise choreography of redemption is not spelt out, but McKane is probably right to describe Y‌HWH's role in the people's response as one of "enabling."[152] On this basis, Jer 24:6–7 gladly and confidently anticipates the full restoration of the exiles; to see it as *guaranteeing* such restoration (in a deterministic sense) would be pushing the text beyond its intended function.

v. 8. כן אתן. Duhm suggested that OG παραδώσω reflects אניר (Hiph. נגר, "hand over"), thereby forming a neat paronomasia with אכיר (v. 5).[153] The linguistic evidence is not compelling (in LXX παραδίδωμι routinely represents נתן), but Duhm's proposal was partly motivated by his dislike for the idea (implied by MT) that Y‌HWH is exclusively responsible for Zedekiah's fate. It may be that נתן...כ, which usually means "make (something) like (something else)" (1 Kgs 10:27; Ruth 4:11; Jer 19:12, etc.), should here be rendered "treat as" (Gen 42:30; possibly Ps 44:12 [11]).[154] Even so, the fact remains that there is no reason given for such a judgment. רע no more describes the moral condition of those in Jerusalem than טוב does those in Babylon.

הישבים בארץ מצרים. Most commentators see here a predictive allusion to the Judean remnant which fled to Egypt after 586 (43:4–7).[155] Some have argued that the words refer to an earlier migration—possibly when Jehoahaz was taken to Egypt in 609 (2 Kgs 23:34), or when Judah became a vassal state to Nebuchadnezzar (603)[156]—but the evidence for a colony there before 587 is slight.[157] Consequently, some scholars view the phrase as redactional.[158] Syntactically, however, it is well integrated in the sentence, הישבים בארץ מצרים balancing הנשארים בארץ הזאת and both being sub-divisions of שארית ירושלם. The remnant of Jerusalem will comprise those who remain in Judah and those who flee to Egypt. As a result, this reference to those in Egypt has been seen as evidence for the lateness of the entire chapter.[159] However, it is not unlikely that Jeremiah

---

151.   In fact, the same may be said for Deut 30:1–10 (though not Deut 4:29–31 or 1 Kgs 8:46–50). Here the tension is reflected in the structure of the passage, with the exhortations of v. 1, כי תשמע בקול יהוה...כי תשוב, and v. 10, והיה כי יבאו עליך כל הדברים האלה...והשבת אל לבבך, framing the affirmation in v. 6, ומל יהוה אלהיך את לבבך...לאהבה אל יהוה אלהיך בכל לבבך (cf. Deut 10:16!). On this passage, see further McConville, *Deuteronomy*, 423–28.

152.   McKane, *Jeremiah 1*, 609.

153.   Duhm, *Jeremia*, 199.

154.   As it is by Rudolph, *Jeremia*, 134 ("behandle"), and Thompson, *Jeremiah*, 506.

155.   E.g. Duhm, *Jeremia*, 199; Nicholson, *Preaching*, 110; Thiel, *Redaktion 1–25*, 257; Niditch, *Symbolic Vision*, 61; Pohlmann, *Studien*, 26; Holladay, *Jeremiah 1*, 659; Carroll, *Jeremiah*, 486; McKane, *Jeremiah 1*, 610.

156.   E.g. Condamin, *Jérémie*, 189; Bright, *Jeremiah*, 193; Thompson, *Jeremiah*, 508–9; Jones, *Jeremiah*, 320.

157.   See Thiel, *Redaktion 1–25*, 256–57, and Pohlmann, *Studien*, 25–26 n. 40.

158.   So Volz, *Jeremia*, 247; Holladay, *Jeremiah 1*, 659; so too McKane, *Jeremiah 1*, 611, though he rejects the authenticity of the whole chapter.

159.   E.g. Thiel, *Redaktion 1–25*, 257; Pohlmann, *Studien*, 26–27; Carroll, *Jeremiah*, 486.

should have foreseen that some of his compatriots would flee to Egypt in the crisis to come, especially if some had already done so.

v. 9. ונתתים ל clearly means "I will make them" (for this meaning of נתן ל, see Jer 9:10; Deut 28:13; Ezek 7:20, etc.). Thus, just as v. 6 is epexegetical of v. 5, so is v. 9 of v. 8: YHWH will deal with the people by making them a curse.

בכל המקמות אשר אדיחם שם. The idea of YHWH pursuing the Judeans to other lands is often thought to conflict with the point being made otherwise in vv. 9–10, that the people will die in their own land.[160] Thus it is argued that this phrase is secondary, influenced by Deut 28:37 (והיית לשמה למשל ולשנינה בכל העמים) and 1 Kgs 9:7 (אשר ינהגך יהוה שמה והיה ישראל למשל ולשנינה בכל העמים). Such a verdict rests on a false antithesis; perishing from the land is hardly incompatible with being banished from it, and indeed, בכל המקמות אשר אדיחם שם neatly counter-balances לכל ממלכות הארץ (v. 9a).

4.4. *Coherence and Redaction*

Scholarly assessments both of the authenticity and integrity of Jer 24 differ widely. Even those who see it as accurately recording a visionary experience of Jeremiah generally accept the presence of at least some secondary elements.[161] As we have seen, particular suspicion has fallen on the historical note (v. 1), the messenger formula (vv. 5, 8), the reference to those in Egypt (v. 8) and certain phrases in vv. 7–10 judged to be Deuteronomistic glosses. Thus far, I have argued that there is no compelling reason for deleting the first three of these. That a clear family likeness exists between the language of vv. 7–10 and that of the Deuteronomistic corpus (especially Deut 28 and 30) is undeniable,[162] but knowing what inferences should be drawn from this is another matter. As anyone familiar with Jeremiah scholarship will know, the C material (of which such language is typical) may in principle be ascribed equally to the editors of the book, to the prophet's disciples or to the prophet himself.[163] In the absence of

---

160.   E.g. Volz, *Jeremia*, 241 n. 1; Rudolph, *Jeremia*, 134; Holladay, *Jeremiah 1*, 659; McKane, *Jeremiah 1*, 611; Carroll, *Jeremiah*, 482.

161.   See, e.g., Volz, *Jeremia*, 246–47; Rudolph, *Jeremia*, 134; Bright, *Jeremiah*, 192-94; Holladay, *Jeremiah 1*, 654–55; Jones, *Jeremiah*, 317–20.

162.   The data may be listed as follows: אלי בכל לבם (ישבו) (v. 7; cf. Deut 30:2, 10; 1 Sam 7:3; 12:20, 24; 1 Kgs 8:23, 48; 14:8; 2 Kgs 10:31; 23:25); ואנכי אהיה להם לאלהים והיו לי לעם (v. 7; cf. Deut 4:20; 7:6; 14:2; 26:18; 27:9); [ונתתים לזועה]...לבל ממלכות הארץ (v. 9; cf. Deut 28:25; 2 Kgs 19:15, 19); לחרפה ולמשל לשנינה ולקללה (v. 9; cf. Deut 28:37; 2 Kgs 22:19); בכל המקמות אשר אדיחם שם (v. 9; cf. Deut 28:37); נדח Hiph. (v. 9; cf. Deut 30:1); מעל האדמה אשר נתתי (v. 9; cf. Deut 28:11; 30:9), but its use in Jer 24 is quite distinctive; see Helga Weippert, *Die Prosareden des Jeremiabuches* (BZAW 132; Berlin: de Gruyter, 1973), 205–8; Raitt, "Jeremiah's Deliverance Message," 171–72.

163.   For a helpful review of critical discussion of the Jeremiah C material (up to 1986), see Louis Stulman, *The Prose Sermons of the Book of Jeremiah: A Redescription of the Correspondences with the Deuteronomistic Literature in the Light of Recent Text-Critical Research* (SBLDS 83; Atlanta: Scholars Press, 1986), 13–31. The links between Jeremiah C and Deut 28 are discussed by John V. M. Sturdy, "The Authorship of the 'Prose Sermons' of Jeremiah," in *Prophecy: Essays Presented to Georg Fohrer on his Sixty-Fifth Birthday, 6 September 1980* (ed. J. A. Emerton; Berlin: de Gruyter, 1980), 143–50.

a clear consensus on this issue (or, indeed, on the wider questions concerning Deuteronomistic influence in the Old Testament), it is hazardous to use the lexical data of vv. 7–10 as firm evidence for redaction.[164] In any case, we should note that the "building and planting" motif (v. 6) and the "sword, famine and plague" trilogy (v. 10)—both sometimes cited as Deuteronomistic—are in fact drawn from what is more accurately called the Jeremiah prose tradition, rather than from Deuteronomy or DtrH.

Others have questioned the integrity of Jer 24 on conceptual grounds. Böhmer and Kilpp note that whereas v. 5 leaves the time and nature of YHWH's salvation unstated, vv. 6–7 define it more precisely as return from exile and spiritual renewal.[165] Consequently, they identify these latter verses as Deuteronomistic redaction. Aware, perhaps, of the obvious response—namely, that precisely because of the lack of specificity in v. 5, there are no grounds for judging vv. 6–7 as secondary—Kilpp attempts to drive a sharper wedge between these verses: vv. 5, 8–10, he suggests, imply that salvation is simultaneous with the destruction of Judah, in which case it can only be experienced in a foreign land.[166] At this point, however, Kilpp concedes that his interpretation goes beyond the text.[167] In reality, no tension exists between v. 5 and vv. 6–7 that requires the latter to be seen as editorial. Kilpp has, though, rightly underscored the fact that the concept of salvation in Jer 24 is complex and multi-faceted, embracing YHWH's present goodwill towards the exiles, future acts of restoration to Judah and the gift of a new heart.

In short, it seems least problematic to regard Jer 24 as a unity, whether entirely authentic or entirely inauthentic.[168] Many who take the latter view believe that the text reflects a highly sectarian ideology from the post-exilic period, while displaying a striking lack of certainty as to the precise historical context.[169] The problem here lies in finding a post-exilic *Sitz im Leben* in which

164.   For samples of recent discussion, see R. J. Coggins, "What Does 'Deuteronomistic' Mean?," in Davies, Harvey and Watson, eds., *Words Remembered, Texts Renewed*, 135–48; Terence Collins, "Deuteronomist Influence on the Prophetical Books," in *The Book of Jeremiah and Its Reception* (ed. A. H. W. Curtis and T. Römer; BETL 128; Leuven: Leuven University Press, 1997), 15–26; Linda S. Schearing and Steven L. McKenzie, eds., *Those Elusive Deuteronomists: The Phenomenon of Pan-Deuteronomism* (JSOTSup 268; Sheffield: Sheffield Academic Press, 1999).

165.   S. Böhmer, *Heimkehr und neuer Bund. Studien zu Jeremia 30–31* (GTA 5; Göttingen: Vandenhoeck & Ruprecht, 1976), 32; Kilpp, *Niederreißen*, 39–41. Kilpp also believes that vv. 6–7 obscure the emphasis on judgment that was the real point of the original vision report (p. 37).

166.   Kilpp, *Niederreißen*, 40.

167.   Ibid.: "Allerdings wird dies im ursprünglichen Bericht nicht ausdrücklich gesagt."

168.   Classifying the entire passage as Deuteronomistic are May, "Objective Approach," 148–49; Hyatt, "The Deuteronomic Edition," 258; Thiel, *Redaktion 1–25*, 258–61; Carroll, *Jeremiah*, 482, 486. Pohlmann, *Studien*, 29, and Stipp, "Zedekiah," 642, also see Jer 24 as a late entry to the book, while refraining from styling its author "Deuteronomistic."

169.   The fifth-century conflicts depicted in Ezra are seen as a possible setting by Duhm, *Jeremia*, 196–97; May, "Objective Approach," 149; Stipp, "Zedekiah," 643. Noting the rivalry between exiles and non-exiles in the work of the Chronicler, Pohlmann, *Studien*, 190, places Jer 24 in the fourth century. See Robert P. Carroll's ambivalence on this point in "Deportation and Diasporic Discourses in the Prophetic Literature," in *Exile: Old Testament, Jewish and Christian*

the claims of the descendants of those exiled in 597—over against the descendants of those deported later—would have been a live issue.[170] Less problematic in this respect is the view that Jer 24 is an *exilic* text, reflecting disappointment with Zedekiah.[171]

Other scholars continue to accept Jer 24 as an authentic visionary experience of Jeremiah.[172] If it is, its message of hope certainly represents a remarkable shift from the earlier judgment oracles (e.g. 8:1–3 and 9:15–16), not least in regard to Jehoiachin (cf. 22:24–30). Equally, the *restriction* of salvation to the 597 exiles sits awkwardly alongside Jeremiah's words of assurance to the Judean community, both before and after 587 (27:12, 17; 42:9–11). Accepting the authenticity of Jer 24 does, however, solve the enigma of its exclusive focus on those deported in 597; the reason it says nothing about the 587 exiles is because 587 had not happened yet.

4.5. Judicial Differentiation in Jeremiah 24:1–10: גלות יהודה / שארית ירושלם
Even on a cursory reading, Jer 24:1–10 reveals a stark contrast in YHWH's stance towards the Jewish communities in Jerusalem and in Babylon in the aftermath of 597. As was noted earlier in conversation with Kilpp, however, the judgment pronounced on them has more than one dimension. On the one hand, it involves YHWH's present disposition; already he regards each community with either hostility or favour. On the other hand, judgment and salvation will be seen in his future actions. Those in Babylon will be restored to Judah as the covenant people of YHWH. For Zedekiah and his people in Jerusalem, only disaster awaits.

What reason (if any) does the text offer for this judicial distinction? Certainly not the moral or spiritual qualities of the respective communities. As we have seen, the key terms טוב and רע denote divine purpose rather than human character. This should be emphasized, since some commentators have argued for an ethical dimension to the rationale of this chapter. Volz and Rudolph, for example, connected YHWH's favour towards the exiles with the presence of innocent and upright people among them, such as the prophet Ezekiel.[173] Doubtless there were such, but there is no exegetical warrant for seeing this as the logic behind the pro-*Golah* stance of Jer 24. More recently, McKane has written that

---

Conceptions (ed. James M. Scott; JSJSup 56; Leiden: Brill, 1997), 63–85 (79), and "The Book of J: Intertextuality and Ideological Criticism," in Diamond, O'Connor and Stulman, eds., *Troubling Jeremiah*, 220–43 (238).

170.   A problem conceded by Duhm, *Jeremia*, 196; Pohlmann, *Studien*, 189; McKane, *Jeremiah 1*, 614; Stipp, "Zedekiah," 642–43.

171.   Thiel, *Redaktion 1–25*, 261; Applegate, "Fate of Zedekiah, Part 1," 146.

172.   In addition to those cited earlier, see Skinner, *Prophecy and Religion*, 251; Thompson, *Jeremiah*, 507; Unterman, *Repentance to Redemption*, 58–59. S. Mowinckel, *Zur Komposition des Buches Jeremia* (Videnskapsselskapets Skrifter. II. Hist.-Filos. Klasse 5; Kristiania: Jacob Dybwad, 1914), 21, assigned all of 24:1–10 to the A source.

173.   Volz, *Jeremia*, 248; Rudolph, *Jeremia*, 137.

A concern to emphasize the aspect of "grace"...is not beside the point, but it should not be carried so far as to deny that the likening of Jehoiachin and his group to good figs is a statement about their worth (cf. Jerome) and the likening of Zedekiah and his group to bad figs is a statement about their worthlessness. The assigning of different destinies has a relation to desert and is not an exercise of bare sovereignty.[174]

Again, though, this seems to ignore the plain testimony of the text, which says nothing about desert at all. On the contrary, the differentiation of גלות יהודה and שארית ירושלם seems quite clearly to be rooted in YHWH's "bare sovereignty."

In fact, finding any further explanation for the judicial polarity of Jer 24 is possible only if we allow other texts to inform our interpretation. Precisely this strategy is adopted by Kilpp who, as was noted in Chapter 2, argues from a *combined reading* of Jer 24:1–10; 29:4–7 and 32:1–15 that the determining factor in Jeremiah's preaching of salvation was the experience or non-experience of exile.[175] For those on whom disaster had fallen, hope was again possible. Raitt, too, believes that the judgment and salvation oracles in Jeremiah and Ezekiel presuppose an underlying "theology of exile":

> The people's accountability for their sin together with God's attitude and intention toward them are radically shifted when the exile becomes a fact. The punishment itself creates an entirely new situation. If a message of *shalom* before the exile-punishment was false, then continued predictions of annihilatory judgment to those already in exile would be rigid fanaticism.[176]

It must be said that the hermeneutical manoeuvre employed here by Kilpp and Raitt—that is, drawing on multiple texts to posit a common theological mindset, and then using this to further elucidate those texts individually—is open to question. In particular, Kilpp's argument depends on the view (which would certainly be disputed) that most of Jer 24:1–10; 29:4–7 and 32:1–15 reflects a single mind, namely, that of the prophet Jeremiah.[177] Methodologically, it is safer to say that Jer 24 *allows* the rationale Kilpp and Raitt ascribe to it, but does not actually *require* it.[178]

Are any further judicial polarities possible *within* the two communities? On the surface, the text appears not to envisage any among the *Golah* who will not be saved, nor any in Jerusalem who will be spared. Some scholars, however, argue for a less black and white reading of the text. Applegate questions whether

---

174.   McKane, *Jeremiah 1*, 609.

175.   Kilpp, *Niederreißen*, 38: "Geht es nicht an erster Stelle um den Wohnort, sondern um das eingetroffene bzw. nicht eingetroffene Gericht."

176.   Raitt, "Jeremiah's Deliverance Message," 171.

177.   Regarding Jer 32:1–15, for example, Gunther Wanke, "Jeremias Ackerkauf: Heil im Gericht?," in *Prophet und Prophetenbuch. Festschrift für Otto Kaiser zum 65 Geburtstag* (ed. Volkmar Fritz et al.; BZAW 185; Berlin: de Gruyter, 1989), 265–76, argues that the original form of the narrative did not include v. 15; hence, Jeremiah's purchase of the field was a sign of judgment rather than salvation.

178.   Within Jeremiah, the idea of exile as the key to restoration finds its strongest support in 29:16, where YHWH's wrath against the Jerusalem community is explicitly attributed to the fact that "they did not go out with you into exile." However, since 29:16–20 is an MT plus, using it to elucidate the intended rationale of 24:1–10 is hazardous, to say the least.

YHWH's promise of restoration extends to the exiled king: "It is significant…
that no mention is made of Jehoiachin or his successors."[179] Indeed, as Rudolph
pointed out, one may not assume that *any* of those deported to Babylon would
enjoy the blessings promised in vv. 6–7.[180] More importantly, some have
suggested that even in its future dimensions, salvation may not be the experience
of all the exiles. Zimmerli writes:

> The whole passage gives…a disunited impression. The vision of the two baskets of figs
> seems at first to lead to an unconditional verdict in the situation of 597; for those in
> exile future salvation, for those remaining in the land and for those who escaped to
> Egypt…future condemnation. But then through the preaching of alternatives a condi-
> tional element is introduced…in that the announcement of salvation to the exiles is
> linked to the condition of their conversion.[181]

If Zimmerli is correct, the judicial polarity reflected in Jer 24 would take on a
more nuanced aspect: judgment for the Judeans/judgment or salvation for the
exiles. This might even permit judgment and salvation on an individual basis. At
this point, though, one should recall the exegesis of vv. 6–7, and especially the
phrase כי ישבו אלי בכל לבם. What is emphasized here is YHWH's initiative; on
this basis, the text clearly anticipates the exiles' salvation. This does not mean,
however, that it guarantees salvation. In other words, while Jer 24 does not
envisage a negative nor divided response, it nevertheless affirms that YHWH's
plans are yet to be fulfilled, and that they will require the exiles' wholehearted
response. In so doing, it creates conceptual space in which new, internal polarities among the *Golah* may emerge.

5. *Conclusions: Judicial Differentiation in Jeremiah 21–24*

In this chapter, three messages of salvation and judgment in Jer 21–24 have
been examined. In the first (21:1–10), Jeremiah announces that YHWH is hand-
ing Jerusalem over to the Babylonians, but that any who abandon the city before
it falls will live. The second (23:1–8) states that YHWH will punish Israel's
leaders for their misrule of the now-dispersed people, whom he will bring back
to the land under a new king. In the third (24:1–10), YHWH promises the exiles
in Babylon a new heart and homecoming, but total destruction for all those
remaining in post-597 Jerusalem.

179. Applegate, "Fate of Zedekiah, Part 1," 146. Even Seitz, *Theology in Conflict*, 214,
concedes that ER was not able to rehabilitate Jehoiachin personally.
180. Rudolph, *Jeremia*, 135: "Braucht Kap. 24 nicht so verstanden zu werden, als ob dieselben
Leute, die 598 fort mußten, wiederkehren werden (es ist von der Gola als Gesamtbegriff die Rede)."
181. Walther Zimmerli, "Visionary Experience in Jeremiah," in *Israel's Prophetic Tradition:
Essays in Honour of Peter R. Ackroyd* (ed. R. J. Coggins et al.; Cambridge: Cambridge University
Press, 1982), 95–118 (111). For the idea that Jer 24 reflects the Deuteronomistic doctrine of
alternatives, see Siegfried Herrmann, *Die prophetischen Heilserwartungen im Alten Testament.
Ursprung und Gestaltwandel* (BWANT 5; Stuttgart: Kohlhammer, 1965), 165–66, and Thiel, *Redaktion 1–25*, 254–57; this is flatly denied by Pohlmann, *Studien*, 29, and Kilpp, *Niederreißen*, 36–37.

Each passage, therefore, configures its salvation/judgment message around a particular polarity of inner-Judean groups, and with its own distinctive rationale. The question we can now ask is how these texts are related. Their close proximity in a specific literary unit strongly suggests some hermeneutical dialogue between them; but since they are not in chronological order, and address different situations, the nature of this dialogue remains obscure.

One attempt to address this question comes from Pohlmann. He argues that 21:1–10 and 24:1–10—both created by the editor of GR—stand in a "question and answer" relationship, the latter passage categorically destroying the glimmer of hope that was (artificially) raised in the former.[182] The present study of these passages, however, does not support this. While ch. 21 affirms (as emphatically as ch. 24) the disaster about to befall Jerusalem, vv. 8–9 explicitly promise "life" for those who surrender to the Babylonians. This promise may be modest, but it still provides a clear alternative to the prospect of sword, famine and plague that dominates 24:8–10. For ch. 24 to serve the purpose Pohlmann attributes to it, it would need to show how the offer made in 21:8–9 was not actually taken up. In fact, it does not address the issue—unsurprisingly, given that it appears to be set several years before the siege of 588–587.

A very different reading of 21:1–10 and 24:1–10 is offered by Applegate, who argues that the latter passage actually serves to moderate the severity of the former: "Although Jer xxiv.8–10 threatens to drive the Judahites into exile by sword, famine and pestilence, it does not threaten total extermination, and so attenuates the extreme predictions of xxi.5–7. Annihilation is replaced by exile."[183] This too, though, is unconvincing; there is no mention of exile in 24:8–10, and the words "till they perish from the land" look very much like a prophecy of total extermination.

In fact, the hermeneutical relationship between these two frame passages may be simpler than Pohlmann or Applegate imply. When allowance is made for their differences in historical context (587/sometime post-597), genre (prophetic oracle/vision report) and audience (Jerusalem/Jeremiah), it seems most likely that ch. 24 functions as a *general summary* of YHWH's stance towards Jerusalem, which is stated more precisely in 21:1–10. True, it is curious that the more specific (and chronologically later) passage is placed first. This, however, may be due to the shape of the book when both passages were added. As I noted at the start of this chapter, 21:1–10 picks up key motifs from chs. 19–20 (siege, Babylon, "strike with the sword"), making its present setting highly appropriate. Meanwhile, the vision report of ch. 24 continues the motif of divine revelation that figures prominently in 23:16–40; see, for instance, the references to "standing in the council of YHWH" (עמד בסוד יהוה, 23:18, 22), and the rebuke of prophets who dream (חלם, 23:25–32).

---

182. Pohlmann, *Studien*, 42: "Jer 21,1–10 versetzt den Leser gleichsam in eine Erwartungshaltung, indem hier implizit die Frage nach her Möglichkeit eines weiteren künftigen Heilshandelns aufgeworfen wird. Jer 24 gibt darauf die Antwort und stellt fest, daß die Heilsgeschichte allein die Gola zum ziel haben wird."

183. Applegate, "Fate of Zedekiah, Part 1," 150.

The hermeneutical relationship between 23:1–8 and 24:1–10 is more problematic. Whereas 21:1–10 defines salvation merely in terms of personal survival, 23:1–8 and 24:1–10 both speak in terms of restoration to the land and spiritual renewal. Yet while 24:1–10 restricts this promise to the exiles in Babylon, 23:1–8 sees geographical and historical details as immaterial; the two-fold מכל הארצות אשר הדחתי(ם) (שם) (אתם) (23:3, 8) is emphatically comprehensive. The two texts thus define salvation similarly, but diverge regarding its recipients.[184]

Now it is a curious feature of Pohlmann's study that, despite his description of Jer 21–24 as a frame composition, he ignores everything between 21:10 and 24:1, including the oracle of 23:1–8. It is the opening and concluding sections alone that are programmatic for the rest of Jeremiah.[185] Since we do not read chs. 21 and 24 without also reading ch. 23, this is a serious methodological weakness. Seitz also says little about the prophecy of 23:1–8, but in a brief parenthetical comment he ascribes it (along with 24:4–7 and other passages) to the Exilic Redaction, since it "focuses on a future involving the return of the exiles."[186] In so doing, however, he blurs the distinction between the universality of 23:1–8 and the particularity of 24:1–10.

What if, as an alternative to Pohlmann's approach, we were to give 23:1–8 the last word in this unit? There are, indeed, good reasons for doing so. First, its position at the centre of the unit obviously suggests its conceptual importance. Secondly, of all the three passages we have examined, 23:1–8 has the broadest historical horizon. Since it is stated that YHWH has *already* scattered the people (23:3), the textual perspective is clearly from sometime *after* the disaster predicted in chs. 21 and 24. Consequently, 23:1–8 has the capacity to accommodate the judgment of 587, recognizing the reality of disaster but asking "what then?."

Giving 23:1–8 this privileged role significantly colours our reading of ch. 24. First, the "leader/people" polarity of 23:1–4 implies that the promises of 24:5–7 do not extend to Jehoiachin, nor perhaps to others of the former ruling elite. Secondly, YHWH's promise to restore the people מכל הארצות אשר הדחתי אתם שם (v. 3) anticipates his warning in 24:9 that those in Jerusalem will be a byword and a curse בכל המקמות אשר אדיחם. By means of this verbal parallel, those whom YHWH will scatter in ch. 24 are effectively included among those whom he will restore in ch. 23. Consequently, 23:1–8 serves to relativize 24:1–10. That is to say, while it recognises that YHWH has scattered his people, it also looks ahead to their restoration—a restoration that will include the deportees of 597 and 587 and even those who "dwell in the land of Egypt" (24:8).

One way, therefore, to bring Jer 21:1–10; 23:1–8 and 24:1–10 into hermeneutical relationship would be by giving 23:1–8 the dominant voice. Such a strategy is facilitated by the "silences" of the two frame units. Jeremiah 21:1–10 does not *say* what will happen to those who leave the city (other than that they will live), thereby allowing them to be accommodated within the salvation

---

184. As discussed in the next chapter, a similar tension arises in the MT plusses of 29:14, 16–20.

185. Pohlmann, *Studien*, 30.

186. Seitz, *Theology in Conflict*, 224; see too his brief comments concerning chs. 22–23 in general (pp. 226–27).

oracle of 23:3–8. Jeremiah 24:1–7 does not *say* whether Jehoiachin is among those whom YHWH will restore, thereby leaving room for him to be judged along with the other leaders of Israel in 23:1–2. Jeremiah 24:8–10 does not *say* what will happen to the people of Judah after they are scattered, thereby enabling them to be subsumed within the scattered people whom YHWH promises to restore in 23:3–4. In other words, 23:1–8 takes as its starting point a scenario not addressed by the other two passages. This may (or may not) violate their original intention, but allows us to read Jer 21–24, not as privileging the 597 exiles to the exclusion of all others (so Pohlmann), but rather as offering hope to the entire *Diaspora*—minus their leaders.

At the same time, it may be felt that giving 23:1–8 the controlling voice results in a rather flat, one-sided interpretation of the unit, rather than a genuine hermeneutical dialogue. Is it possible instead to bring these three passages into a more open interpretative relationship, in which they are heard as equal voices in debate? I suggest that it is, if they are seen as contributing to a discussion concerning divine judgment and human culpability, and I conclude this chapter by outlining the basis for such an interpretation.

As we have seen, although 21:1–10 and 24:1–10 are not completely univocal, they share the view that YHWH's wrath is against all Jerusalem: its king, officials, people and even animals. Precisely because of the totality of the disaster coming upon the city, only those who flee its walls may hope to live. By contrast, 23:1–8 focuses entirely upon the nation's leaders as deserving of YHWH's punishment, in contrast to the ordinary people. We thus have two perspectives in tension with one another. However, as was noted earlier in this chapter, sandwiched between 21:1–10, 23:1–8 and 24:1–10 are two further blocks of material, each containing a collection of oracles (21:11–22:30 and 23:9–40). I will now try to show how these two anthologies function as a bridge between these three passages, thereby bringing them into dialogue.

As its superscription לבית מלך יהודה (21:11) suggests, the first section contains warnings and criticisms of several kings and their officials, culminating in a scathing attack on Jehoiakim. Here too, therefore, the text places the burden of guilt on Judah's leaders. This specificity is sharpened by references to socially vulnerable groups whom the kings are expected to defend: the victim of robbery (גזול), the alien (גר), the orphan (יתום) and the widow (אלמנה) (21:12; 22:3)—groups which, elsewhere in the Old Testament, YHWH pledges to rescue and vindicate. Consequently, in its allocation of moral responsibility, the text implicitly distinguishes between Judah's leaders and her people.

Elsewhere in this section, however, the identity of the addressee is more ambiguous. In contrast to the message to the royal house in 21:12, the feminine participle ישבת in vv. 13–14 suggests that here it is "lady Jerusalem"—that is, the whole city—who is in mind.[187] Consistent with this is the fact that the charge is now one of complacency, rather than social injustice. Similarly, while 22:6 is

---

187. Cf. McKane, *Jeremiah 1*, 512–13: "There is an allusion to the strong, defensive position of Jerusalem and to the defiant confidence which this awakens in its inhabitants who feel secure against every threat of military attack and penetration" (p. 513).

initially directed על בית מלך יהודה, the oracle that follows (22:6b–7) envisages the destruction of the whole city, which it explains in terms that strongly suggest the entire nation is in mind: עזבו את ברית יהוה אלהיהם וישתחוו לאלהים אחרים ויעבדום (22:9). Again, after the oracle against Jehoiakim (22:13–19), 22:20–23 reverts to feminine singular language,[188] thus addressing all Jerusalem.[189] In other words, 21:10–22:30 oscillates between singling out Judah's leaders for criticism, and indicting the whole city.

A similar ambiguity can be observed in the section headed לנבאים (23:9–32). Here, the moral focus is on the religious leaders of Israel—chiefly its prophets, although priests are also mentioned in v. 11. By their immoral conduct and false messages of hope, they mislead (תעה Hiph., vv. 13, 32) the people, who are (as in 23:1–8) described as "my people" (עמי, vv. 13, 22, 27, 32). Nevertheless, throughout it is made clear that the rest of the people are also guilty; they despise (נאץ) YHWH (v. 17) and "walk in the stubbornness of their hearts" (הלך בשררות לבו, v. 17). Their ways and deeds are evil (רע, v. 22b). This shifting focus from prophets to people is particularly evident in vv. 13–14, which begin by castigating the prophets of Jerusalem. Not only do they commit adultery and falsehood (נאוף והלך בשקר, v. 14b) but they also fail to turn others from their wickedness (איש מרעתו, v. 14c). There is thus some ambiguity in YHWH's comment, היו לי כלם כסדם (v. 14d). Are "they" the prophets or the people? The uncertainty is removed only in the following clause: וישביה כעמרה. Jerusalem as a whole is like Gomorrah. Indeed, in the final section (vv. 33–39), the people appear to be positively colluding with the prophets. Overall, the perspective of the entire passage seems to be well summed up in v. 15: כי מאת נביאי ירושלם יצאה חנפה לכל הארץ.

Consequently, these two sections—B and B' in the earlier outline—create a degree of continuity between the frame units and the centre. On the one hand, by focussing on the evils of the kings and the prophets and acknowledging the existence of the poor and the weak, they modify the indiscriminate condemnation of Zedekiah and his people in chs. 21 and 24. On the other hand, they retain, more clearly than 23:1–8, the awareness that the entire land is guilty, as well as its leaders.

We have thus seen in Jer 21–24 three salvation/judgment oracles, each with its own configuration of judgment: those who stay in Jerusalem, and those who go out to Babylon; the shepherds and the flock; and the 597 exiles and the remnant of Jerusalem. What is clear, however, is that nowhere are these groups sub-divided further. No distinctions are made (although they are not necessarily excluded) among those who do not abandon Jerusalem, or among those deported to Babylon in 597. As we will see, subsequent sections of Jeremiah introduce precisely such inner-differentiations.

---

188.   Cf. the imperatives צעקי, חני, עלי (v. 20); the verbs תבשי ונכלמתי (v. 22); and the nouns מאהביך, "your lovers" (vv. 20, 22), שלותיך, "your security" (v. 21), דרכך מנעוריך, "your way from youth" (v. 21; cf. 2:1!), רעתך, "your evil" (v. 22) and רעיך, "your neighbours" (v. 22).

189.   "Your neighbours" are then either other Judean princes and their cities (Rudolph, *Jeremia*, 123) or, more likely, foreign nations with whom Judah had formed alliances (Schmid, *Buchgestallten*, 338).

Chapter 5

JUDICIAL DIFFERENTIATION IN JEREMIAH 27–29

1. *Introduction to Jeremiah 27–29*

1.1. *The Literary Setting of Jeremiah 27–29*

Both in MT and OG, Jer 27–29 (34–36) constitutes the first sub-section of the macro-unit 26–45 (33–51). Despite its diversity of contents and lack of chronological order, this is a unit which appears to have been arranged according to a particular pattern. Of special significance in this respect are the narratives set in the reign of Jehoiakim (chs. 26, 35, 36, 45), which form the structural pillars for the entire macro-unit.[1] Of the intervening chapters, all except chs. 30–31 (widely seen as a late addition to the book) relate to events during or after the reign of Zedekiah.[2] Before focussing on chs. 27–29 themselves, therefore, it is worth giving some attention to this broader literary framework.

The four "pillar" chapters form two corresponding pairs, 26/35 and 36/45. Both pairs, I suggest, depict *YHWH's judgment on Judah in transition*, as it moves from being conditional to certain.[3] Hence, the initial chapters in each pair (26 and 36) begin by summarizing YHWH's word to the people: YHWH is planning disaster (26:6; 36:3) and his wrath is great (36:7). Nevertheless, there is still hope, as indicated by the term אולי (26:3; 36:3, 7); perhaps the people will listen and repent, in which case YHWH will turn from bringing disaster (26:3) and forgive them (36:3). Both chapters then highlight the divided response of those who hear this message (26:16; 36:24–25),[4] before focussing on the figure of Jehoiakim, whose relentless pursuit of the prophet Uriah (26:20–23) anticipates his contemptuous burning of Baruch's scroll (36:21–26).[5]

---

1. Lundbom, *Jeremiah*, 107–8, sees the Jehoiakim material in chs. 25, 26, 35, 36 as chiastically arranged.

2. Even chs. 32–33, which in many ways form an extension to the Book of Consolation (chs. 30–31), begin with the story of Jeremiah's purchase of the field in the tenth year of Zedekiah's reign (32:1) and are set against the backdrop of the Babylonian siege (32:24–29; 33:1–5).

3. According to Martin Kessler, "Jeremiah Chapters 26–45 Reconsidered," *JNES* 27 (1968): 81–88 (84), "the profound difference between [Jer 26 and 36] is that the רעה mentioned in 26.3 is represented as contingent there, but in 36.3 as inevitable, as a result of the people's failure to hear Yahweh's prophet." But this overlooks the fact that judgment is still contingent at the start of ch. 36, and underestimates the significance of the *king's* failure to listen.

4. Noted by John Applegate, "'Peace, Peace, When There is No Peace': Redactional Integration of Prophecy of Peace into the Judgement of Jeremiah," in Curtis and Römer, eds., *The Book of Jeremiah and Its Reception*, 51–90 (73).

5. Winfried Thiel, *Die deuteronomistische Redaktion von Jeremia 26–45. Mit einer Gesamtbeurteilung der deuteronomistischen Redaktion des Buches Jeremias* (WMANT 52; Neukirchen–Vluyn:

By contrast, chs. 35 and 45 portray a situation in which the time for repentance has passed and judgment is certain. YHWH's promise of blessing on the Rechabites (35:18–19) contrasts with his declaration, "I am bringing on Judah and all the inhabitants of Jerusalem all the evil I spoke against them" (35:17), a warning repeated after Jehoiakim's burning of the scroll (36:31). The reference back to this event in 45:1 also interprets YHWH's threat to "overthrow what I have built and uproot what I have planted" (45:4) as referring to his judgment on Judah in the time of Jehoiakim. In its present form, therefore, Jer 26–45 is best viewed as comprising two sub-sections, chs. 26–35 and 36–45.[6] Both are made up mostly of material from the time of Zedekiah, but are framed by narratives which identify the actions of Jehoiakim as decisive in Judah's downfall.

Characterizing these four framing chapters is a pronounced interest in questions of judgment and culpability. On the first point, we find here the same emphasis on the *totality* of judgment that was seen in Jer 1–20. Jeremiah addresses his call for repentance to the nation ("all the cities of Judah," 26:2; "the house of Judah," 36:3), and it is the nation that stands under YHWH's wrath (35:17; 36:31b; 45:4–5). Granted, YHWH promises the Rechabites that they will always have a man to stand before him (35:19), but they appear to be an external foil for Judah, rather than a genuinely exceptive element within it;[7] hence, they are commended for obeying their forefather, rather than YHWH and his prophets.

On the question of culpability, however, the four frame chapters are more ambiguous. Jeremiah 35 concludes with the unqualified statement, "this people has not listened to me" (35:17), a charge repeated in 36:31. A more nuanced picture emerges, however, in chs. 26 and 36, which are careful to note the varied responses to Jeremiah's message, and to lay chief blame at the feet (or hands) of Jehoiakim. When Jeremiah is arrested for prophesying against Jerusalem (26:10–11), "some of the elders of the land" recall how Hezekiah had responded to Micah's warning of disaster by seeking YHWH's favour (26:17–19), while Ahikam son of Shaphan also comes to Jeremiah's defence (26:24). In 36:25, Jehoiakim's officials Elnathan, Delaiah and Gemariah urge (פגע Hiph.) the king not to burn Baruch's scroll. Taken together, therefore, these four chapters affirm that while Judah has not listened to YHWH, certain individuals have.

Neukirchener, 1981), 101, argues that Jehoiakim's response is "paradigmatisch für die des Volkes." Yet while his action is decisive for the fate of the nation, the narrator emphasizes that there were other voices urging a different response.

6. For a similar analysis in detail, see Rietzschel, *Urrolle*, 95–122, though he limits this second *Überlieferungsblock* to Jer 36–44. Also seeing ch. 36 as *introducing* what follows are Rudolph, *Jeremia*, xvii, and Thiel, *Redaktion 26–45*, 102. Most scholars see it as a *conclusion*: e.g. Volz, *Jeremia*, xliii–xlv; Kessler, "Jeremiah Chapters 26–45 Reconsidered," 83; Nicholson, *Preaching*, 106–7; Thompson, *Jeremiah*, 30; Hobbs, "Some Remarks," 193; Carroll, *Jeremiah*, 510; Holladay, *Jeremiah 2*, 254; McConville, *Judgment and Promise*, 111. Others remain uncertain on this question; cf. Jones, *Jeremiah*, 337; Brueggemann, *Exile and Homecoming*, 338 n. 1.

7. The precise identity of the Rechabites remains obscure; 1 Chr 2:55 identifies them as a Kenite clan. See further Gerald L. Keown, Pamela J. Scalise and Thomas G. Smothers, *Jeremiah 26–52* (WBC 27; Dallas: Word, 1995), 195–96.

This depiction of YHWH's word creating an inner-Judean division marks a significant development within the book. On ch. 26, Stulman comments: "For the first time in the book, the message of Jeremiah receives an ambivalent reception... Such conflict and ambivalence foreshadow the texture and ethos of the second scroll as a whole. A faithful few will hear and be receptive to the words of the prophet, while the multitudes remain defiant and recalcitrant."[8] Hobbs makes a similar observation in regard to chs. 26–36:

> In these chapters, the focus of attention seems to be the personnel of the city of Jerusalem, who had been generally attacked in the first section. Now the accusations become more specific, and the reaction of various groups within the capital city to the prophet and his word becomes clear as the section progresses.[9]

In fact, it is doubtful whether the second scroll *as a whole* does portray the divergent reactions that Stulman and Hobbs believe it does. A closer reading reveals that chs. 26 and 36 are unique in depicting one group responding positively to YHWH's word while another responds negatively. Nevertheless, the generalizing/differentiating perspectives in these frame chapters provide a significant hermeneutical context for what lies in between, including chs. 27–29.

1.2. *Jeremiah 27–29 as a Literary Unit*

Within the broader unit of Jer 26–45, the delineation of chs. 27–29 as a self-contained literary unit is widely accepted.[10] Indeed, some scholars believe that it circulated independently before being combined with other Jeremiah traditions.[11] A number of features give these three chapters internal coherence, while also setting them apart from the rest of the book. These are well-documented and can be summarized as follows.

(i) *Orthography*. The spelling נבוכדנאצר (27:6, 8, 20; 28:3; 29:1, 3) is here preferred to the form נבוכדראצר found elsewhere in Jeremiah (and Ezekiel). Other proper names, which elsewhere consistently have the long ending יהו, take here the short ending יה; for example, ירמיה (27:1; 28:5, etc.; 29:1), חנניה (28:1, 5, etc), יכניה (28:4, 20; 29:2), צדקיה (27:12; 28:1; 29:3). However, this pattern breaks down in 29:21–32, where long and short forms appear.[12]

---

8. Stulman, *Order Amid Chaos*, 65.
9. Hobbs, "Some Remarks," 193.
10. In addition to those cited below, see Volz, *Jeremia*, 255; Thomas W. Overholt, *The Threat of Falsehood: A Study in the Theology of the Book of Jeremiah* (SBT 16; London: SCM, 1970), esp. 27–30; Thompson, *Jeremiah*, 528; Holladay, *Jeremiah 2*, 114.
11. E.g. Rudolph, *Jeremia*, 147 ("als Kampfschrift gegen falsche Propheten"); Heinz Kremers, "Leidensgemeinschaft mit Gott im Alten Testament. Eine Untersuchung der 'biographischen' Berichte im Jeremiabuch," *EvT* 13 (1953): 129–30; Nicholson, *Preaching*, 93; Thiel, *Redaktion 26–45*, 5 n. 1; Gunther Wanke, *Untersuchungen zur sogennanten Baruchschrift* (BZAW 122; Berlin: de Gruyter, 1971), 58 n. 62; Carroll, *Jeremiah*, 523–54; Emanuel Tov, "The Literary History of the Book of Jeremiah in the Light of its Textual History," in *Empirical Models for Biblical Criticism* (ed. Jeffrey H. Tigay; Philadelphia: Fortress, 1985), 211–37; Keown, Scalise and Smothers, *Jeremiah 26–52*, 35–36. But see to the contrary Schmid, *Buchgestalten*, 236 n. 165.
12. But note the long forms צדקיהו (27:3) and יאשיהו (27:1).

(ii) *Vocabulary*. Although the designation of Jeremiah as הנביא is a feature of the MT rather than the Hebrew *Vorlage* of the OG, both texts repeatedly employ the title for Jeremiah's opponents (OG paraphrases with ψευδοπροφήτης). Also prominent is the verb שלח (לא), which seems to function like a catchword; it is linked to YHWH's word (29:19), the prophets (27:15; 28:15; 29:9, 31), people (29:3, 20) and various messages (27:3; 29:1, 25, 28, 31); cf. also the threat הנני משלח (28:16; 29:17). Daniel L. Smith has noted how the motif of prison, yokes and restraint also pervades these chapters.[13]

(iii) *Historical context*. Despite textual problems in MT 27:1 and 28:1, the events of chs. 27–28 appear to be set in the fourth year (בשנת הרבעית) of Zedekiah, that is, 594/3. The date of the correspondence in ch. 29 is less specific (אחרי צאת יכניה המלך והגבירה מירושלם), but it is evidently some time between 597 and 587. No other material in Jeremiah is dated to this period. This historical setting may account for the undercurrent of speculation about the early return of the exiles and the possibility of revolt.[14] The Babylonian Chronicle records a domestic revolt against Nebuchadnezzar in late 595/early 594, which may have been seen by Judah and its neighbours as an opportunity to rebel.[15]

(iv) *Theme*. The conflict between true and false prophecy is widely seen as *the* theme of Jer 27–29.[16] In ch. 27, Jeremiah urges his hearers to reject the message of their own prophets (vv. 9–10, 14–15, 16). Chapter 28 describes the confrontation between Jeremiah and Hananiah (both of whom are described as prophets) regarding who has the word of YHWH. Without pre-empting this study of ch. 29, it is clear that Jeremiah is here in conflict with the Judean prophets in Babylon. There is a corresponding stock of expressions: YHWH has not sent (לא שלח, 27:15; 28:15; 29:9, 32; cf. 28:9) the prophets; the people are not to listen (אל תשמעו, 27:9, 14, 16, 17; 29:8) to them, because they are prophesying lies (שקר נבאים, 27:10, 15, 16; 29:9, 21; cf. 29:23). Though found regularly in Jeremiah, these terms are especially concentrated in chs. 27–29.

(v) *Depiction of Jeremiah*. After the dominant impression of him as broken, marginalized and ignored in the first scroll of the book, Jeremiah appears in these three chapters as a more powerful, authoritative figure. Carroll writes:

> In this cycle he is clearly the leader of both communities, advising, condemning and encouraging the social leaders of the people in Jerusalem and Babylon... His role, therefore, in the cycle is that of an authoritative figure moving about Jerusalem, advising

13. Daniel L. Smith, *The Religion of the Landless: The Social Context of the Babylonian Exile* (Bloomington: Meyer Stone, 1989), 128. Jones, *Jeremiah*, 346, also sees "the theme of the yoke" as uniting these three chapters.

14. So Volz, *Jeremia*, 255–56; Holladay, *Jeremiah 2*, 118; Keown, Scalise and Smothers, *Jeremiah 26–52*, 36; see, however, Carroll, *Jeremiah*, 530.

15. Attempts to correlate Jer 27–28 with the Babylonian Chronicle are complicated, however, by the textual corruption of 27:1 and 28:1. See further Keown, Scalise and Smothers, *Jeremiah 26–52*, 47–48.

16. E.g. Volz, *Jeremia*, 255; Rudolph, *Jeremia*, 147; Nicholson, *Preaching*, 94–95; Thiel, *Redaktion 26–45*, 5; and especially Overholt, *Threat of Falsehood*, 24–48. See, however, William McKane, *A Critical and Exegetical Commentary on Jeremiah*. Vol. 2, *Commentary on Jeremiah XXVI–LII* (ICC New Series; Edinburgh: T. & T. Clark, 1996), cxxxviii–cxxxix. Conversely, Kessler, "Jeremiah 26–45 Reconsidered," 83, sees chs. 27–29 as unified by the theme of peace.

foreign nations of foreign policy (27), confronting an anti-Babylonian prophet (28), and proclaiming a policy of co-operation with the Babylonians to the Judaeans now living in Babylon.[17]

Consequently, Overholt's conclusion, that "in both style and content these chapters form a coherent, self-contained unit of narrative material,"[18] seems well-founded.

This is not to say that they were composed as a unity. Although chs. 27 and 28 both describe Jeremiah's confrontation with the prophets in Jerusalem, 27:2–28:1 is written in the first person while 28:2–17 is in the third person. Chapter 29 stands apart from both, by virtue of its audience (the exiles in Babylon) and genre (written, rather than oral, prophecy). We should probably assume, therefore, that this unit has been compiled from different sources.[19] Jones sums up the matter well: "The differences are just sufficient to demand some such variety of origin; but the homogeneity of them equally points to a single redactor who has stamped the whole with the singleness of his own purpose."[20] I will discuss questions of composition and redaction for chs. 27–28 and 29 in more detail when I look at these respective sections.

It might be argued that Jer 26 also belongs within this sub-section. According to Jones, "the editorial unity of chs. 26–29 in general and ch. 29 in particular is shown…by the pervasive theme of false prophecy and the prose of the familiar prose tradition."[21] Certainly, the picture of the Judean community divided over Jeremiah's words in ch. 26 foreshadows the question underlying chs. 27–28, namely, whom will the people believe? However, while these links with ch. 26 are certainly significant, chs. 27–29 are clearly demarcated by being set in the reign of Zedekiah, rather than of Jehoiakim. It is thus probably more accurate to consider ch. 26 as a preface to chs. 27–29.[22] Additional evidence for regarding chs. 27–29 as a redactional unit lies in its literary structure, to which we now turn.

17. Carroll, *Jeremiah*, 555. This view of Jeremiah as an *authoritative* figure is less obvious in ch. 28, where Hananiah appears to win the duel (cf. v. 11); but even here, Jeremiah is subsequently vindicated (vv. 12–17).

18. Overholt, *Threat of Falsehood*, 27.

19. For surveys of opinion, see Keown, Scalise and Smothers, *Jeremiah 26–52*, 36–37; Theodor Seidl, *Texte und Einheiten in Jeremia 27–29* (ATSAT 2; Munich: Eos St Ottilien, 1977), 21–22 n. 5. However, Carroll, *Jeremiah*, 523, sees the cycle as "a literary creation rather than historical records or reflections," and dates it no earlier than the fifth century.

20. Jones, *Jeremiah*, 346.

21. Ibid., 360; similarly, Clements, *Jeremiah*, 153. J. Gordon McConville, "Jeremiah," in *The New Bible Commentary: 21st Century Edition* (ed. D. A. Carson, R. T. France, J. A. Motyer and G. J. Wenham; Leicester: IVP, 1994), 671–708 (692), brackets all four chapters together under the heading "Jeremiah becomes a prophet of salvation," but it is hard to see how this thought plays a prominent role in ch. 26.

22. So Carroll, *Jeremiah*, 529. Duhm, *Jeremia*, 217 (cf. xxi–xxii), saw chs. 26–29 (minus interpolations) as having been added *en bloc* from Baruch's scroll into Jeremiah, but doubted whether ch. 26 originally introduced chs. 27–29: "Der zeitliche Abstand zwischen den in Cap 26 und in Cap 27f. erzählten Begebenheiten zu gross ist und andere Erzählungen vorhanden sind, die vor Cap 27f. zu stehen beanspruchen."

1.3. *The Literary Structure of Jeremiah 27–29*

Whatever the origins of the material in Jer 27–29, the editor has carefully structured it in such a way that ch. 29 parallels chs. 27–28. Initial evidence for this lies in certain verbal and conceptual echoes. Chapters 27 and 29 both begin with Jeremiah sending a message (שלח...ביד) to the foreign kings and the Jewish exiles respectively, thereby acting as a prophet to the nations (1:10).[23] Moreover, while the term נבאים ("prophets") is ubiquitous in this unit, the reference in 27:9 to קסמים and חלמות ("diviners" and "dreamers") recurs only in 29:8, אל ישיאו לכם...קסמיכם ואל תשמעו אל חלמתיכם. Meanwhile, chs. 28 and 29 conclude with pronouncements of judgment on specific prophets, Hananiah and Shemaiah.[24] The charges against them are almost identical: לא שלחך יהוה לא שלחתיו ויבטח אתכם על שקר (28:15) and ואתה הבטחת את העם הזה על שקר (29:31). MT heightens this parallel with the comment that both prophets have spoken rebellion against YHWH. (סרה דבר אל יהוה, 28:16; 29:32). Finally, Overholt notes that chs. 27–28 and 29 show the same pattern of conflict: Jeremiah's message about Babylon/A negative response from the prophets/ Resolution: a curse on the prophets.[25] He thus entitles these two sections, "Confronting the problem of false prophecy at home" and "Confronting the problem of false prophecy in Babylon."[26]

In fact, the structure of chs. 27–29 is more nuanced than this, as will become clear if we consider the rhetorical interaction of Jeremiah, prophets and people. In ch. 27, Jeremiah warns the foreign envoys, Zedekiah and the priests and the people against listening to "the prophets," a group consistently referred to only in the third person (vv. 9, 14–15, 16–18). In ch. 28, however, this situation is reversed; Jeremiah confronts Hananiah, while the priests and the people observe (vv. 1, 5, 7, 11). This pattern is repeated in ch. 29. Though Jeremiah's letter is addressed to כל הגולה (v. 4), vv. 8–9 clearly distinguish between its intended audience and the prophets: אל ישיאו לכם נביאיכם...כי בשקר הם נבאים לכם. Even when Ahab and Zedekiah appear in vv. 21–23, they are differentiated from those to whom Jeremiah is speaking: נתן אתם ביד מלך בבל והכם לעיניכם (v. 21). The rhetorical shift occurs in vv. 24–32. Although the text is confused, in its present form the MT represents Jeremiah as confronting another prophet, just as it does in ch. 28. Moreover, in MT v. 25 Shemaiah's audience includes "all the people in Jerusalem" and "all the priests," the same groups mentioned in chs. 27–28. I suggest, therefore, that chs. 27–29 are structured according to the following pattern:

---

23. 27:3 reads ושלחתם ("and send *them*"), the object being, presumably, replicas of the yoke bars Jeremiah has made. However, the text says nothing about additional yokes, and some scholars emend to שלחת ("send") implying a message as object. Either way, however, it is clear from the context that Jeremiah does send a message to the foreign kings, whether or not model yokes were also part of the delivery.

24. Shemaiah is not formally designated a prophet (נבא), but cf. 29:31, יען אשר נבא לכם שמעיה.

25. Overholt, *Threat of Falsehood*, 29–30.

26. Ibid., 30.

A: Jeremiah's message to the non-exiles about the prophets (27:1–22)
B: Jeremiah's confrontation with the prophet Hananiah (28:1–17)
A':   Jeremiah's message to the exiles about the prophets (29:1–23)
B':   Jeremiah's confrontation with the prophet Shemaiah (29:24–32).[27]

Consequently, the structure of chs. 27–29 serves to establish two *audience-critical* distinctions. On the one hand, Zedekiah's people in Judea are distinguished from the exilic community in Babylon. In both places, however, there is a crucial distinction between prophets and people. This is highlighted not only by the alternation of address, but also by the public nature of Jeremiah's confrontation with Hananiah, which is described as taking place in the sight (בעיני, 28:1, 5) and hearing (באזני, 28:7) of all the people. Indeed, the interaction between Jeremiah, prophets and people in these three chapters suggests that their theme is not simply true and false prophecy, but rather the interplay between prophets and people, prophecy and response, in the fate of the entire community.

2. Jeremiah 27–28 (34–35)

2.1. *Text*

בראשית ממלכת יהויקם בן יאושיהו מלך יהודה היה הדבר הזה אל ירמיה מאת יהוה לאמר	1	
כה אמר יהוה אלי עשה לך מוסרות ומטות ונתתם על צוארך	2	1 οὕτως εἶπε κύριος ποίησον δεσμοὺς καὶ κλοιοὺς καὶ περίθου περὶ τὸν τράχηλόν σου
ושלחתם אל מלך אדום ואל מלך מואב ואל מלך בני עמון ואל מלך צר ואל מלך צידון ביד מלאכים הבאים ירושלם אל צדקיהו מלך יהודה	3	2 καὶ ἀποστελεῖς αὐτοὺς πρὸς βασιλέα Ιδουμαίας καὶ πρὸς βασιλέα Μωαβ καὶ πρὸς βασιλέα υἱῶν Αμμων καὶ πρὸς βασιλέα Τύρου καὶ πρὸς βασιλέα Σιδῶνος ἐν χερσὶν ἀγγέλων αὐτῶν τῶν ἐρχομένων εἰς ἀπάντησιν αὐτῶν εἰς Ιερουσαλημ πρὸς Σεδεκιαν βασιλέα Ιουδα
וצוית אתם אל אדניהם לאמר כה אמר יהוה צבאות אלהי ישראל כה תאמרו אל אדניכם	4	3 καὶ συντάξεις αὐτοῖς πρὸς τοὺς κυρίους αὐτῶν εἰπεῖν οὕτως εἶπε κύριος ὁ θεὸς Ισραηλ οὕτως ἐρεῖτε πρὸς τοὺς κυρίους ὑμῶν
אנכי עשיתי את הארץ את האדם ואת הבהמה אשר על פני הארץ בכחי הגדול ובזרועי הנטויה ונתתיה לאשר ישר בעיני	5	4 ὅτι ἐγὼ ἐποίησα τὴν γῆν ἐν ἰσχύι μου τῇ μεγάλῃ καὶ ἐν τῷ ἐπιχείρῳ μου τῷ ὑψηλῷ καὶ δώσω αὐτὴν ᾧ ἐὰν δόξῃ ἐν ὀφθαλμοῖς μου
ועתה אנכי נתתי את כל הארצות האלה ביד נבוכדנאצר מלך בבל עבדי וגם את חית השדה נתתי לו לעבדו	6	5 ἔδωκα τὴν γῆν τῷ Ναβουχοδονοσαρ βασιλεῖ Βαβυλῶνος δουλεύειν αὐτῷ καὶ τὰ θηρία τοῦ ἀγροῦ ἐργάζεσθαι αὐτῷ
ועבדו אתו כל הגוים ואת בנו ואת בן בנו עד בא עת ארצו גם הוא ועבדו בו גוים רבים ומלכים גדלים	7	

---

27.   Admittedly, this section concludes by foregrounding the exiles once more, with Jeremiah writing to them concerning Shemaiah (vv. 30–32).

וַהיה הגוי והממלכה אשר לא יעבדו אתו את נבוכדנאצר מלך בבל ואת אשר לא יתן את צוארו בעל מלך בבל בחרב וברעב ובדבר אפקד על הגוי ההוא נאם יהוה עד תמי אתם בידו	8	6	καὶ τὸ ἔθνος καὶ ἡ βασιλεία ὅσοι ἐὰν μὴ ἐμβάλωσι τὸν τράχηλον αὐτῶν ὑπὸ ζυγὸν βασιλέως Βαβυλῶνος ἐν μαχαίρᾳ καὶ ἐν λιμῷ ἐπισκέψομαι αὐτούς εἶπε κύριος ἕως ἐκλίπωσιν ἐν χειρὶ αὐτοῦ
ואתם אל תשמעו אל נביאיכם יאל קסמיכם ואל חלמתיכם ואל ענניכם ואל כשפיכם אשר הם אמרים אליכם לאמר לא תעבדו את מלך בבל	9	7	καὶ ὑμεῖς μὴ ἀκούετε τῶν ψευδοπροφητῶν ὑμῶν καὶ τῶν μαντευομένων ὑμῖν καὶ τῶν ἐνυπνιαζομένων ὑμῖν καὶ τῶν οἰωνισμάτων ὑμῶν καὶ τῶν φαρμακῶν ὑμῶν λεγόντων οὐ μὴ ἐργάσθητε τῷ βασιλεῖ Βαβυλῶνος
בי שקר הם נבאים לכם למען הרחיק אתכם מעל אדמתכם יהדחתי אתכם ואבדתם	10	8	ὅτι ψευδῆ αὐτοὶ προφητεύουσιν ὑμῖν πρὸς τὸ μακρῦναι ὑμᾶς ἀπὸ τῆς γῆς ὑμῶν
והגוי אשר יביא את צוארו בעל מלך בבל ועבדו והנחתיו על אדמתו נאם יהוה ועבדה וישב בה	11	9	καὶ τὸ ἔθνος ὃ ἐὰν εἰσαγάγῃ τὸν τράχηλον αὐτοῦ ὑπὸ τὸν ζυγὸν βασιλέως Βαβυλῶνος καὶ ἐργάσηται αὐτῷ καὶ καταλείψω αὐτὸν ἐπὶ τῆς γῆς αὐτοῦ καὶ ἐργᾶται αὐτῷ καὶ ἐνοικήσει ἐν αὐτῇ
ואל צדקיה מלך יהודה דברתי בכל הדברים האלה לאמר הביאו את צואריכם בעל מלך בבל ועבדו אתו ועמו וחיו	12	10	καὶ πρὸς Σεδεκιαν βασιλέα Ιουδα ἐλάλησα κατὰ πάντας τοὺς λόγους τούτους λέγων εἰσαγάγετε τὸν τράχηλον ὑμῶν καὶ ἐργάσασθε τῷ βασιλεῖ Βαβυλῶνος
למה תמותו אתה ועמך בחרב ברעב ובדבר כאשר דבר יהוה אל הגוי אשר לא יעבד את מלך בבל	13		
ואל תשמעו אל דברי הנבאים האמרים אליכם לאמר לא תעבדו את מלך בבל כי שקר הם נבאים לכם	14	11	ὅτι ἄδικα αὐτοὶ προφητεύουσιν ὑμῖν
בי לא שלחתים נאם יהוה והם נבאים בשמי לשקר למען הדיחי אתכם ואבדתם אתם והנבאים הנבאים לכם	15	12	ὅτι οὐκ ἀπέστειλα αὐτούς φησι κύριος καὶ προφητεύουσι τῷ ὀνόματί μου ἐπ' ἀδίκῳ πρὸς τὸ ἀπολέσαι ὑμᾶς καὶ ἀπολεῖσθε ὑμεῖς καὶ οἱ προφῆται ὑμῶν οἱ προφητεύοντες ὑμῖν ἐπ' ἀδίκῳ ψευδῆ ὑμῖν
ואל הכהנים ואל כל העם הזה דברתי לאמר כה אמר יהוה אל תשמעו אל דברי נביאיכם הנבאים לכם לאמר הנה כלי בית יהוה מושבים מבבלה עתה מהרה כי שקר המה נבאים לכם	16	13	καὶ παντὶ τῷ λαῷ τούτῳ καὶ τοῖς ἱερεῦσιν ἐλάλησα λέγων οὕτως εἶπε κύριος μὴ ἀκούετε τῶν λόγων τῶν προφητῶν τῶν προφητευόντων ὑμῖν λεγόντων ἰδοὺ σκεύη οἴκου κυρίου ἐπιστρέφει ἐκ Βαβυλῶνος ὅτι ἄδικα αὐτοὶ προφητεύουσιν ὑμῖν
אל תשמעו אליהם עבדו את מלך בבל וחיו למה תהיה העיר הזאת חרבה	17	14	οὐκ ἀπέστειλα αὐτούς
ואם נבאים הם ואם יש דבר יהוה אתם יפגעו נא ביהוה צבאות לבלתי באו הכלים הנותרים בבית יהוה ובית מלך יהודה ובירושלם בבלה	18	15	εἰ προφῆταί εἰσι καὶ εἰ ἔστι λόγος κυρίου ἐν αὐτοῖς ἀπαντησάτωσάν μοι

Good Figs, Bad Figs

כי כה אמר יהוה צבאות אל העמדים ועל הים ועל המכנוה ועל יתר הכלים הנותרים בעיר הזאת	19	16 ὅτι οὕτως εἶπε κύριος καὶ τῶν ἐπιλοίπων σκευῶν
אשר לא לקחם נבוכדנאצר מלך בבל בגלותו את יכוניה בן יהויקים מלך יהודה מירושלם בבלה ואת כל חרי יהודה וירושלם	20	17 ὧν οὐκ ἔλαβε βασιλεὺς Βαβυλῶνος ὅτε ἀπῴκισε τὸν Ιεχονιαν ἐξ Ιερουσαλημ
כי כה אמר יהוה צבאות אלהי ישראל על הכלים הנותרים בית יהוה ובית מלך יהודה וירושלם	21	
בבלה יובאו ושמה יהיו עד יום פקדי אתם נאם יהוה והעליתים והשיבתים אל המקום הזה	22	18 εἰς Βαβυλῶνα εἰσελεύσεται λέγει κύριος
ויהי בשנה ההיא בראשית ממלכת צדקיה מלך יהודה בשנה הרבעית בחדש החמשי אמר אלי חנניה בן עזור הנביא אשר מגבעון בבית יהוה לעיני הכהנים וכל העם לאמר	1	καὶ ἐγένετο ἐν τῷ τετάρτῳ ἔτει Σεδεκια βασιλέως Ιουδα ἐν μηνὶ τῷ πέμπτῳ εἶπε μοι Ανανιας υἱὸς Αζωρ ὁ ψευδοπροφήτης ὁ ἀπὸ Γαβαων ἐν οἴκῳ κυρίου κατ' ὀφθαλμοὺς τῶν ἱερεῶν καὶ παντὸς τοῦ λαοῦ λέγων
כה אמר יהוה צבאות אלהי ישראל לאמר שברתי את על מלך בבל	2	οὕτως εἶπε κύριος συνέτριψα τον ζυγὸν βασιλέως Βαβυλῶνος
בעוד שנתים ימים אני משיב אל המקום הזה את כל כלי בית יהוה אשר לקח נבוכדנאצר מלך בבל מן המקום הזה ויביאם בבל	3	ἔτι δυο ἔτη ἡμερῶν καὶ ἐγὼ ἀποστρέψω εἰς τὸν τόπον τοῦτον τὰ σκεύη οἴκου κυρίου
ואת יכניה בן יהויקים מלך יהודה ואת כל גלות יהודה הבאים בבלה אני משיב אל המקום הזה נאם יהוה כי אשבר את על מלך בבל	4	καὶ Ιεχονιαν καὶ τὴν ἀποικίαν Ιουδα ὅτι συντρίψω τὸν ζυγὸν βασιλέως Βαβυλῶνος
ויאמר ירמיה הנביא אל חנניה הנביא לעיני הכהנים ולעיני כל העם העמדים בבית יהוה	5	καὶ εἶπεν Ιερεμιας πρὸς Ανανιαν κατ' ὀφθαλμοὺς παντὸς τοῦ λαοῦ καὶ κατ' ὀφθαλμοὺς τῶν ἱερέων τῶν ἑστηκότων ἐν οἴκῳ κυρίου
ויאמר ירמיה הנביא אמן כן יעשה יהוה יקם יהוה את דבריך אשר נבאת להשיב כלי בית יהוה וכל הגולה מבבל אל המקום הזה	6	καὶ εἶπεν Ιερεμιας ἀληθῶς οὕτως ποιῆσαι κύριος στῆσαι τὸν λόγον σου ὃν σὺ προφητεύεις τοῦ ἐπιστρέψαι τὰ σκεύη οἴκου κυρίου καὶ πᾶσαν τὴν ἀποικίαν ἐκ Βαβυλῶνος εἰς τὸν τόπον τοῦτον
אך שמע נא הדבר הזה אשר אנכי דבר באזניך ובאזני כל העם	7	πλὴν ἀκούσατε λόγον κυρίου ὃν ἐγὼ λέγω εἰς τὰ ὦτα ὑμῶν καὶ εἰς τὰ ὦτα παντὸς τοῦ λαοῦ
הנביאים אשר היו לפני ולפניך מן העולם וינבאו אל ארצות רבה ועל ממלכות גדלות למלחמה ולרעה ולדבר	8	οἱ προφῆται οἱ γεγονότες πρότεροί μου καὶ πρότεροί ὑμῶν ἀπὸ τοῦ αἰῶνος καὶ ἐπροφήτευσαν ἐπὶ γῆς πολλῆς καὶ ἐπὶ βασιλείας μεγάλας εἰς πόλεμον
הנביא אשר ינבא לשלום בבא דבר הנביא יודע הנביא אשר שלחו יהוה באמה	9	ὁ προφήτης ὁ προφητεύσας εἰς εἰρήνην ἐλθόντος τοῦ λόγου γνώσονται τὸν προφήτην ὃν ἀπέστειλεν αὐτόν κύριος ἐν πίστει

ויקח חנניה הנביא את המוטה	10	καὶ ἔλαβεν Ανανιας ἐν ὀφθαλμοῖς παντὸς τοῦ λαοῦ τοὺς κλοιοὺς ἀπὸ τοῦ τραχήλου Ιερεμιου καὶ συνέτριψεν αὐτούς
מעל צואר ירמיה הנביא וישברהו		
ויאמר חנניה לעיני כל העם	11	καὶ εἶπεν Ανανιας κατ' ὀφθαλμοὺς τοῦ λαοῦ λέγων οὕτως εἶπε κύριος οὕτως συντρίψω τὸν ζυγὸν βασιλέως Βαβυλῶνος ἀπὸ τραχήλου πάντων τῶν ἐθνῶν καὶ ᾤχετο Ιερεμιας εἰς τὴν ὁδὸν αὐτοῦ
לאמר כה אמר יהוה ככה אשבר		
את על נבוכדנאצר מלך בבל		
בעוד שנתים ימים מעל צואר כל		
הגוים וילך ירמיה הנביא לדרכו		
ויהי דבר יהוה אל ירמיה אחרי	12	καὶ ἐγένετο λόγος κυρίου πρὸς Ιερεμιαν μετὰ τὸ συντρῖψαι Ανανιαν τοὺς κλοιοὺς ἀπὸ τοῦ τραχήλου αὐτοῦ λέγων
שבור חנניה הנביא את המוטה		
מעל צואר ירמיה הנביא לאמר		
הלוך ואמרת אל חנניה לאמר	13	βάδιζε καὶ εἰπὸν πρὸς Ανανιαν λέγων οὕτως εἶπε κύριος κλοιοὺς ξυλίνους συνέτριψας καὶ ποιήσω ἀντ' αὐτῶν κλοιοὺς σιδηροῦς
כה אמר יהוה מוטת עץ שברה		
ועשית תחתיהן מטות ברזל		
כי כה אמר יהוה צבאות אלהי	14	ὅτι οὕτως εἶπε κύριος ζυγὸν σιδηροῦν ἔθηκα ἐπὶ τὸν τράχηλον πάντων τῶν ἐθνῶν ἐργάζεσθαι τῷ βασιλεῖ Βαβυλῶνος
ישראל על ברזל נתתי על צואר		
כל הגוים האלה לעבד את		
נבוכדנאצר מלך בבל ועבדהו		
וגם את חית השדה נתתי לו		
ויאמר ירמיה הנביא אל חנניה	15	καὶ εἶπεν Ιερεμιας τῷ Ανανια οὐκ ἀπέσταλκε σε κύριος καὶ πεποιθέναι ἐποίησας τὸν λαὸν τοῦτον ἐπ' ἀδίκῳ
הנביא שמע נא חנניה לא שלחך		
יהוה ואתה הבטחת את העם הזה		
על שקר		
לכן כה אמר יהוה הנני משלחך	16	διὰ τοῦτο οὕτως εἶπε κύριος ἰδοὺ ἐγὼ ἐξαποστέλλω σε ἀπὸ προσώπου τῆς γῆς τούτῳ τῷ ἐνιαυτῷ ἀποθανῇ
מעל פני האדמה השנה אתה מה		
כי סרה דברת אל יהוה		
וימת חנניה הנביא בשנה ההיא	17	καὶ ἀπέθανεν ἐν τῷ μηνὶ τῷ ἑβδόμῳ
בחדש השביעי		

2.2. *Textual Notes*
Chapter 27

v. 1. >OG. MT בראשית ממלכת יהויקם is clearly erroneous (cf. the subsequent references to Zedekiah), probably under the influence of 26:1.[28] Possibly יהויקם is itself a late gloss, with MT previously reading בראשית ממלכת צדקיה, as in 28:1. The verse is almost certainly an MT plus; note that, unlike the rest of the chapter, it refers to Jeremiah in the third person.

v. 3. MT ושלחתם and OG ἀποστελεῖς αὐτούς, "and send *them*" (the yoke bars) is surprising, since v. 2 need mean no more than one set of yokes. Emendation to שלחת, "send" (a message) is attractive,[29] but MT is supported by OG and also balances the preceding ונתתם.

---

28. So Wanke, *Untersuchungen*, 21; Janzen, *Studies*, 14.
29. So, e.g., Duhm, *Jeremia*, 217–18; Rudolph, *Jeremia*, 146; A. Graupner, *Auftrag und Geschick des Propheten Jeremia. literarische Eigenart, Herkunft und Intention vordeuteronomistischer Prosa im Jeremiabuch* (BTS 15; Neukirchen–Vluyn: Neukirchener, 1991), 63 n. 8; McKane, *Jeremiah 2*, 686.

OG εἰς ἀπάντησιν αὐτῶν >MT. OG suggests לִקְרָאתָם, but the resultant לִקְרָאתָם ירושלם אל צדקיהו is problematic. If לִקְרָאתָם is objective ("to meet *them*"), who are "they"? If it is subjective ("for them to meet"), it is awkwardly separated from "Zedekiah" by ירושלם אל (cf. Judg 4:18; 1 Sam 17:48; Isa 7:3). MT probably preserves an older reading.[30]

v. 6. MT כל הארצות האלה ביד; OG γῆν עην = אֶת הָאָרֶץ. Janzen observes that the global sense represented by OG follows neatly from v. 5.[31] But MT also provides a satisfying development ("I made the whole earth…so I am giving these lands").

MT עבדי; OG δουλεύειν αὐτῷ. Lemke argued that עבדי arose as a scribal error, leading to its addition in 25:9 and 43:10.[32] However, while ואל נבוכדראצר מלך בבל עבדי in 25:9 is an MT plus, here and in 43:10 עבדי is probably the more original reading, since לעבדו would entail an awkward repetition of לעבדו at the end of the verse. The translator may have misread י as ו, and read the final ל of בבל twice.[33] Unease at this description of a foreign king may also have encouraged an alternative reading.

v. 7. >OG. MT plus; cf. the very similar addition to MT in 25:14.[34] The idea that Babylon's rule will be limited in duration is not confined to MT (see 29:10), but it is heightened there; see too the prophecy of the return of the temple vessels in 27:22 (also an MT plus).

v. 9. MT חֲלֹמֹתֵיכֶם ("your dreams"); OG ἐνυπνιαζομένων ὑμῖν ("your dreamers") = חלמיכם. Since the context clearly implies a further group of people, there is much to be said for Ehrlich's revocalization of MT as חֹלְמֵיכֶם, "your dreamers," assuming a substantive חֹלוּם, "dreamer"; cf. 29:8.[35]

vv. 13–14. OG lacks v. 13 and most of v. 14, yielding the nonsensical "serve the king of Babylon, for they are prophesying a lie to you." The omission of the warning not to listen to the prophets (MT v. 14) is almost certainly due to haplography. OG καὶ ἐργάσασθε τῷ βασιλεῖ Βαβυλῶνος suggests a *Vorlage* that read ועבדו את מלך בבל; from there, the translator's eye could easily have skipped to תעבדו את מלך בבל (MT v. 14). Less certain is whether his *Vorlage* included the content of MT v. 13. The fact that similar material in v. 17 is an MT plus (see below) suggests the same is true here.

v. 15. MT הדיחי; OG πρὸς τὸ ἀπολέσαι = הדיח. The texts thus diverge over whether YHWH (MT) or the prophets (OG) will bring about Israel's ruin. Which

---

30. So Emanuel Tov, "Exegetical Notes on the Hebrew Vorlage of the LXX of Jeremiah 27 (34)," *ZAW* 91 (1979): 73–93 (82).

31. Janzen, *Studies*, 66; also preferring OG are Bright, *Jeremiah*, 199–200; Holladay, *Jeremiah 2*, 112.

32. Werner E. Lemke, "Nebuchadrezzar, My Servant," *CBQ* 28 (1966): 45–50; see the response by Thomas W. Overholt, "King Nebuchadnezzar in the Jeremiah Tradition," *CBQ* 30 (1968): 39–48.

33. So Tov, "Exegetical Notes," 83–84.

34. So Duhm, *Jeremia*, 220; Tov, "Exegetical Notes," 84–85; Louis Stulman, *The Other Text of Jeremiah: A Reconstruction of the Hebrew Text Underlying the Greek Version of the Prose Sections of Jeremiah with English Translation* (Lanham, Md.: University Press of America, 1986), 58.

35. So Ehrlich, *Randglossen*, 312–13; Paul Volz, *Studien zum Text des Jeremia* (Leipzig: Hinrichs, 1920), 213; Wanke, *Untersuchungen*, 22; Holladay, *Jeremiah 2*, 113.

reading is the more original is impossible to say; cf. 16:15, where OG reads
ἐξώσθησαν rather than MT הדיחם.

v. 17. OG οὐκ ἀπέστειλα αὐτούς = לא שלחתים; MT אל תשמעו אליהם עבדו
את מלך בבל וחיו למה תהיה העיר הזאת חרבה. OG probably reflects its *Vorlage*
accurately; we would then have a smooth flow of text concerning the prophets,
כי שקר המה נבאים לכם לא שלחתים ואם נבאים הם, similar to v. 15.[36] MT may
have been prompted by the similar question in v. 13.

v. 19. OG is usually thought to reflect a much shorter text, כי כה אמר יהוה
על יתר הכלים.[37] However, OG καὶ [τῶν ἐπιλοίπων] appears to represent (על)ו,
implying additional preceding wording.[38] OG haplography seems more likely
than an MT expansion.

Chapter 28
v. 1. MT gives two mutually exclusive dates, בראשית ממלכת צדקיה מלך יהודה
and בשנת הרבעית. The latter was probably added under the influence of 27:1.
OG ἐν τῷ τετάρτῳ ἔτει Σεδεκια βασιλέως Ιουδα reflects a shorter reading,
בשנה הרבעית לצדקיה מלך יהודה.

MT בשנה ההיא >OG. MT represents a conflation of two variants: בשנה A]
ההיא // בשנה ההיא (בראשית ממלכת) צדקיהו מלך יהודה ויהי // הרביעית ל B]. As Janzen
points out, A (which matches OG) is easily the superior reading; B arose after
the addition of 27:1.[39]

v. 7. MT שמע; OG ἀκούσατε. Possibly the OG *Vorlage* contained the plural
שמעו, but the ensuing reference to "the ears of all the people" may have
prompted the translator to make the change for the sake of consistency.

v. 13. MT ועשית; OG ποιήσω = ועשיתי. The second person form of YHWH's
statement in MT suggests a deed–consequence concept of judgment that we
might not have expected in this context; by his actions, Hananiah will bring
disaster upon himself.[40] YHWH's own judicial role is emphasized in OG, "I will
make."

v. 16. MT כי סרה דברת אל יהוה >OG. A probable MT plus, interpreting
Hananiah's actions and death in the light of YHWH's warning in Deut 13:6; cf.
Jer 29:32.

2.3. Exegesis
Chapter 27
v. 2. עשה לך מוסרות. The narrative begins with a sign act comparable to those in
13:1–11 (the linen belt) and 19:1–13 (the clay jar), the first of which is also
recounted in the first person.

36.   So Tov, "Exegetical Notes," 88; Stulman, *Other Text*, 59.
37.   So Duhm, *Jeremia*, 222; Rudolph, *Jeremia*, 148; H. Seebass, "Jeremias Konflikt mit Chananja," *ZAW* 82 (1970): 449–52 (450–51); Tov, "Exegetical Notes," 89; Stulman, *Other Text*, 59–60.
38.   Graupner, *Auftrag*, 65 n. 19, is almost alone in calling attention to this.
39.   Janzen, *Studies*, 15.
40.   "The sense of v. 13 is 'You have made a rebellious gesture (by breaking the wooden yoke) but you have thereby made for yourself an unyielding and unbreakable tyranny'" (McKane, *Jeremiah 2*, 713); contra Duhm, *Jeremia*, 226.

מוטה. In the Old Testament, מוטה ("yoke bar") is almost always a metaphor of oppression (foreign or social), and occurs either by itself (Isa 58:6, 9; Ezek 30:18) or in the phrase מטת על (Lev 26:13; Ezek 34:27). Each time, it is something that YHWH breaks (שבר) or urges his people to remove (אסר, נתק). Likewise, מוסרה ("strap") occurs in Jer 30:8 (//על), Nah 1:13 (//מוטה) and Ps 107:14 to symbolize foreign rule from which YHWH releases Israel. Only in Jer 27–28 do we read of YHWH *imposing* a yoke. Though the two words are similar in meaning, the ensuing narrative uses מוטה to denote the object worn by Jeremiah (28:10, 12, 13) and על to denote the power of Babylon (27:8, 11, 12; 28:2, 4, 11, 14).

v. 5. בכחי הגדול ובזרועי הנטויה. The phrase בזרוע הנטויה is commonly used in parallel with ביד חזקה (Deut 4:34; 5:15; Ps 136:12; Jer 21:5), especially in contexts describing YHWH's acts of redemption and judgment. Only in three other places, however, is it used with כח גדול (Deut 9:29; 2 Kgs 17:36; Jer 32:17), and only in the last of these is it used, as here, in relation to creation.

לאשר ישר בעיני. The phrase ישר בעיני, "pleasing in the eyes of (YHWH)," is also common in the Deuteronomistic literature (e.g. Deut 12:25; 21:9; 1 Kgs 11:33; 2 Kgs 10:30). There, however, as its collocation with עשה indicates, the emphasis is firmly on human conduct; here such considerations are absent, and the sense is rather "to whom I see fit" (cf. 18:4).[41]

v. 6. עבדי. YHWH's appellation of Nebuchadnezzar as "my servant" occurs also in MT 25:9 and 43:10, but is otherwise unparalleled in the Old Testament, though we should note the descriptions of Cyrus (Isa 44:28; 45:1) as YHWH's רע ("shepherd") and משיח ("anointed one"). Servanthood here clearly implies subordination to, rather than devotion to, YHWH; just as Judah and the nations will be Nebuchadnezzar's vassals, so he is YHWH's vassal.[42]

וגם את חית השדה נתתי לו לעבדו. The statement clearly emphasizes the extent of Nebuchadnezzar's dominion (cf. Dan 2:38). The reference to wild animals, however, may find added significance in the fact that the kings are told to "bow the neck to the yoke" (נתן את צואר בעל, vv. 8, 11, 12)—thereby implicitly likening them to domestic animals, and underlining the certainty of Nebuchadnezzar's rule over the nations.[43]

v. 10. למען הרחיק אתכם. Although the term למען usually has a final sense, "in order to" (Jer 32:14; 42:6; 43:3; 50:34; 51:39), it can also be resultative, "so that" (Lev 20:3; 2 Kgs 22:17; Amos 2:7; Jer 25:7; 32:35; Mic 6:16).[44] Since the subjects of the verb here (the prophets) are compatriots of the foreign envoys, a resultative sense seems clear.

---

41. So Thompson, *Jeremiah*, 529; McKane, *Jeremiah 2*, 684.
42. See Ziony Zevit, "The Use of ʿebed as a Diplomatic Term in Jeremiah," *JBL* 88 (1969): 74–77; Thompson, *Jeremiah*, 512–13.
43. So Holladay, *Jeremiah 2*, 119.
44. See *GBH 2*, §169g. Cf. BDB, s.v. מען: "Sometimes, in rhetorical passages, the issue of a line of action, though really undesigned, is represented by it [למען] ironically as if it were designed." BDB cites Jer 27:10 and 15 as examples of this ironic usage.

v. 11. והנחתיו על אדמתו...ועבדה וישב בה. The content of YHWH's promise for the nation that serves the king of Babylon is here spelt out. In Judg 2:23, YHWH allows the nations to remain (נוח Hiph.) in Canaan, but the most striking parallel to this phrase occurs in Gen 2:15, וינחהו בגן עדן לעבדה ולשמרה. This is the only other place in the Old Testament where נוח Hiph. is used in conjunction with עבד; the possibility that this is a deliberate echo of the Genesis passage is strengthened by the explicit reference to creation in v. 5.

v. 15. למען הדחתי אתכם. Jeremiah's message to Zedekiah concludes with a second למען clause. In the OG *Vorlage*, the subject is again the prophets, justifying a resultative interpretation. Arguably, since MT attributes the scattering to YHWH (הדיחי), למען could here have a final sense.[45] This would, however, go against the general tenor of Jeremiah's message.

v. 16. כלי בית יהוה. 2 Kgs 24:13 records that in 597 Nebuchadrezzar broke up the gold vessels made by Solomon; the present verse implies that some of the temple utensils were taken to Babylon, while others (v. 20) were left in Jerusalem. The emphasis on the return of these vessels may seem surprising, but as Ackroyd remarks, "restoration of the vessels implies re-establishment of that continuity of the cultus which was in some measure interrupted by the disaster of 597."[46]

v. 18. ואם יש דבר יהוה אתם. For similar expressions in relation to prophetic inspiration, see 5:13 (והדבר אין בהם) and 23:28 (ואשר דברי אתו).

יפגעו נא ביהוה. Some commentators believe that Jeremiah was being perfectly sincere at this point.[47] However, the tone of scepticism in ואם נביאים הם ואם יש דבר יהוה אתם is unmistakable. The fact that intercession was recognized as a distinctively prophetic activity makes Jeremiah's instruction to the exiles in 29:7 to pray on behalf (התפלל בעד) of Babylon the more striking.

v. 22. ושמה יהיו עד יום פקדי אתם. The significance of this MT plus should not be overlooked. The hitherto almost wholly negative meaning of פקד (see in more detail on 29:10) is reversed, as a favourable visitation from YHWH is predicted. Compare the very similar prophecy concerning Zedekiah in Babylon (32:5, also an MT plus).

Chapter 28

v. 4. ואת יכניה ואת גלות. Hananiah's prophecy of the return of the 597 exiles exceeds that of ch. 24 in two crucial respects; it supplies a time-frame (בעוד שנתים ימים, v. 3), and specifically lists Jehoiachin as among the returnees. As commentators have observed, the latter point would have presented an implicit challenge to Zedekiah.[48]

---

45.   The notion of YHWH sending false prophets in order to bring about disaster is not wholly alien to the Old Testament (1 Kgs 22:19–23).

46.   See Peter R. Ackroyd, "The Temple Vessels: A Continuity Theme," in *Studies in the Religious Tradition of the Old Testament* (ed. Peter R. Ackroyd; London: SCM, 1987), 46–60 (55).

47.   Keown, Scalise and Smothers, *Jeremiah 26–52*, 53: "He invites the other prophets to believe the word of God given through him and to intercede for that [*sic*] which he has been forbidden to pray. The possibility that the LORD might relent is implicit in this challenge."

48.   Carroll, *Jeremiah*, 543; Keown, Scalise and Smothers, *Jeremiah 26–52*, 54.

v. 6. אמן כן יעשׂה יהוה יקם יהוה את דבריך. Jeremiah's reply to Hananiah has long puzzled commentators, given his insistence in ch. 27 and elsewhere in ch. 28 that there would be no early return from Babylon. Explanations include irony or (more commonly) that Jeremiah was simply expressing his own desire as distinct from what he knew YHWH had decreed.[49] Both are plausible, and not necessarily mutually exclusive. Carroll notes that similar instances of a soft answer followed by אך (cf. v. 7) occur in v. 12 and 26:15: "General agreement with a situation or belief is expressed, but a few dissenting points may yet be made...These points usually constitute the heart of the matter and have a tendency to reverse the agreement expressed with the sentiments just enunciated."[50] For an unambiguous example of irony (also directed at the false prophets) in Jeremiah, see 23:28: הנביא אשׁר אתו חלום יספר חלום.

It may, however, be significant that Jeremiah makes no reference to Jehoiachin, whom Hananiah explicitly included among those whom YHWH would bring back in v. 4: "While the false prophet is hostile to the rule of Zedekiah and categorically demands the return of Jehoiachin to the throne, as an integral part of his party's political platform, Jeremiah intentionally skips over this problem."[51]

v. 9. הנביא אשׁר ינבא לשׁלום בבא דבר הנביא יודע. The implication of Jeremiah's words seems to be that since prophetic oracles are in the main of disaster (v. 8), the burden of proof is on the prophet of peace.[52] The final אשׁר בי באמת שׁלחני יהוה echoes 26:15, שׁלחו יהוה באמת.

v. 15. ואתה הבטחת את העם הזה על שׁקר. The same accusation is made against Shemaiah in 29:31; elsewhere, בטח Hiph. occurs only in 2 Kgs 18:30 = Isa 36:15. הבטחת is most naturally taken to mean "You have caused (this people) to trust (a lie)," an interpretation reflected in all the commentaries and EVV.[53] Yet while ch. 28 has carefully noted the presence of the people during Jeremiah's confrontation with Hananiah, nowhere has it reported their reaction. Equally, while in ch. 27 Jeremiah urges the people not to listen to the prophets, their response is left open. It is more probable that הבטחת here has the sense "you have *tried* to persuade." In the Old Testament, "try to" is usually expressed by בקשׁ + ל + inf. (Exod 2:15; Deut 13:11; 1 Sam 19:10)[54] or simply בקשׁ + inf. (Jer 26:21). Key to our passage, however, is Deut 13:2–6. Here, Moses warns the people that if a prophet or dreamer (נביא או חלם חלום) urges them to follow

---

49. For the former, see E. W. Nicholson, *The Book of the Prophet Jeremiah 26–52* (CBC; Cambridge: Cambridge University Press, 1975), 37; for the latter, Volz, *Jeremia*, 265; Rudolph, *Jeremia*, 152; Bright, *Jeremiah*, 201; Thompson, *Jeremiah*, 539.

50. Carroll, *Jeremiah*, 544.

51. Malamat, "Jeremiah and the Last Two Kings," 84.

52. Brueggemann, *Exile and Homecoming*, 252: "Hananiah is suspect because he does not say what prophets characteristically say. He is soft on the dangers of covenant disobedience." Similarly Thompson, *Jeremiah*, 540; Holladay, *Jeremiah 2*, 128.

53. Most use some such expression as "led, persuaded, made to believe." See especially Keown, Scalise and Smothers, *Jeremiah 26–52*, 58: "Hananiah (and Shemaiah, 29:31) had gone one step further and succeeded in making the people put their trust in a lie."

54. This construction often means "intend to"; however, in the instances cited above, it is clear that an attempt is made to do something.

other gods, they are not to listen (v. 4); rather, that prophet or dreamer must die, because he has spoken rebellion (דבר סרה) against YHWH, להדיחך מן הדרך אשר צוך יהוה אלהיך (v. 6). Here, although בקש is not used, להדיחך must mean "*to try to* seduce you"; the context makes it clear that the people resist the prophet's enticements (in MT v. 6, ובערת הרע מקרבך indicates that they themselves remove him).

v. 16. הנני משלחך מעל פני האדמה. In the situation confronting Jeremiah, however, YHWH will himself effect the death sentence. This phrase has no exact parallel in the Old Testament, although YHWH also expels (שלח Pi.) the man from the garden (Gen 3:23), and the nations from before (מפני) Israel (Lev 18:24; 20:23).

2.4. *Coherence and Redaction*

That *some* sort of editorial activity lies behind Jer 27–28 is clear enough from the shift from first person to third person speech in 28:2. There is, however, little consensus as to the nature of this redaction. The simplest hypothesis is that an editor has utilized two different, but historically reliable, sources. Thus Rudolph assigned ch. 27 to A (authentic sayings), with ch. 28 added later from B (Baruch's biography).[55] Jones also sees ch. 27 as the nucleus, to which an editor added ch. 28: "Without ch. 27, ch. 28 would lack its essential presupposition and clue. In particular, 28:10 presupposes 27:2."[56]

More commonly, it is held that the oldest material is found in ch. 28, while most of ch. 27 is secondary.[57] Those who take this view often identify the redactional material on the basis of its Deuteronomistic character, though as we saw in the previous chapter, such arguments tend to be inconclusive. Nicholson calls attention to the expressions בכחי הגדול ובזרועי הנמויה (27:5; Deut 9:29; 2 Kgs 17:36), הקם את דבר (28:6; Deut 9:5; 1 Sam 1:23; 1 Kgs 2:4; 6:12; 8:20) and דבר סרה אל יהוה (28:16; Deut 13:6).[58] As he acknowledges, however, the language is for the most part that of the Jeremiah prose tradition, rather than of DtrH.[59] To Nicholson's claim that the interest in true and false prophecy which dominates Jer 27–28 is typically Deuteronomistic, it may be replied that such an interest was probably widespread among Jews during and after the sixth century.[60]

Others have offered more complex analyses of Jer 27–28. Noting the shift from third person to second person address in 27:9, Wanke identifies all of

---

55. Rudolph, *Jeremia*, 147; cf. Volz, *Jeremia*, xlvi: "Hier lagen Baruch schriftliche Aufzeichnungen Jeremias vor, die aber nur eine Teil der Handlung umfaßten; das übrige ergänzt Baruch auf Grund von Mitteilungen Jeremia oder von Notizen Jeremias."

56. Jones, *Jeremiah*, 346.

57. Duhm, *Jeremia*, 216–17; Hyatt, "Jeremiah," 5:788–89; Thiel, *Redaktion 26–45*, 5–10.

58. Nicholson, *Preaching*, 95–97.

59. Ibid., 95–96; similarly Jones, *Jeremiah*, 22. Stulman, *Prose Sermons*, 89, draws the same conclusion in respect to ch. 27, pointing out that most of the Jeremiah prose language is in any case restricted to the MT plusses.

60. Nicholson, *Preaching*, 97.

27:9–22 as a late addition to the narrative.[61] In any case, he argues, their polemic against the false prophets is alien to the original meaning of the sign of the yoke.[62] Excising them reveals an older stratum comprising 27:2–8, 12b; 28:1–17. This has a coherent structure: action of Jeremiah (27:2–3, 12b); counter-action of Hananiah (28:1–4, 10–11); vindication of Jeremiah and sentence on Hananiah (28:12–17). Even here, however, Wanke finds redactional elements. Jeremiah 27:4–8 are verbose, overtly theological, and unconnected to the symbolic action. Also secondary are 28:1–9, 15–17, as shown by their heightened interest in the Babylonian exiles and by the fact that they presuppose the symbolic action of Hananiah. Consequently, the oldest core comprises 27:2–3, 12b; 28:10–14.[63]

While criticizing Wanke's argument at points, McKane takes essentially the same approach.[64] The warnings against false prophets are "only indirectly related to the message of the symbolic action."[65] Jeremiah 27:5–8 are clearly secondary, since "it was not a time to survey a grand theological structure which embraced the world."[66] The redactional nature of 27:12b–15 is shown by the fact that whereas v. 12a addresses Zedekiah, the subsequent verbs are plural. Like Wanke, McKane believes we should look for "a smaller core in which Jeremiah's action is explicated by a single meaning…a verse in which the tools of the symbolic action are preserved and in which the explanation sticks close to the concreteness of the metaphor."[67] Despite a painstaking analysis, however, McKane cannot decide whether this elusive verse is v. 11 or 12b. Meanwhile, ch. 28 contains two contrary views of שלום prophecy; that in vv. 6–9, where Jeremiah is content to let Hananiah's words be proved right or wrong by subsequent events, and that in v. 15, where he pronounces Hananiah a false prophet without further ado.[68]

Wanke and McKane have rightly highlighted the fact that Jer 27–28 deals with two distinct (though related) issues, namely, serving the king of Babylon and not listening to the prophets. Unfortunately, their conclusions illustrate the dangers of operating with fixed notions of what is relevant or superfluous in a text.[69] On what basis is it assumed that "this was not the time" for an affirmation

---

61. Wanke, *Untersuchungen*, 26–27.

62. Ibid., 26.

63. Ibid., 35. His analysis is partly shared by Graupner, *Auftrag*, 71–76.

64. McKane, *Jeremiah 2*, 695–704.

65. Ibid., 702.

66. Ibid., 700.

67. Ibid., 698.

68. Ibid., 719–20.

69. See too Wanke's treatment of 27:4. Despite conceding (*Untersuchungen*, 24) that this verse is syntactically well-integrated with vv. 2–3, he insists: "Eine solche umständliche Ausdrucksweise ist den Berichten über symbolische Handlungen im Jeremiabuch nicht *eigen*; mit v. 3 wäre schon alles gesagt, was zur Einführung der Deutung der Handlung *nötig* ist, und v. 4 ist damit praktisch *überflüssig*. Alles das weist darauf hin, daß man damit zu rechnen hat, daß in v. 4 eine Naht vorleigt, die zwei ursprünglich nicht zusammengehörige Stücke miteinander verbindet" (*Untersuchungen*, 25, italics mine).

of YHWH's worldwide sovereignty, when in fact it is precisely this which under-pins Jeremiah's message? On what basis is it assumed that the warnings against the prophets are a distraction, when their own words, "You will not serve the king of Babylon" (27:9, 14), directly contradict what Jeremiah is saying? On what basis is it assumed that Jeremiah's message must be "tightly" connected to the metaphor of the yoke? In any case, the claim that 27:4–12 are unconnected with the yoke symbol is seriously undermined by their triple use of the expression נתן/הביא את צואר בעל (vv. 8, 11, 12b). To argue, as Wanke does, that these have been inserted to *create* a link is little short of desperation.[70]

Nor are the arguments for multiple redactional layers in ch. 28 compelling.[71] The fact that Jeremiah accuses Hananiah of promoting lies (שֶׁקֶר, v. 15) in no way negates the test of time set out in vv. 7–8. Precisely because this criterion stands, Jeremiah makes no attempt to have Hananiah put to death by the com-munity (as prescribed in Deut 13:5). Instead, he predicts that YHWH himself will remove Hananiah "from the face of the earth" that same year (v. 16). In so doing, Jeremiah sets his own word against that of Hananiah. *Both* must now wait the test of time. As for Wanke's view that vv. 10–14 and vv. 1–9, 15–17 are from different authors, he himself supplies the best counter-argument: "Daß diese Einfügungen äußerst geschickt und dem vorliegenden Material entsprechend vorgenommen wurden, macht ihr Erkennen um so schwieriger."[72]

Granted, Jer 27–28 is not completely straightforward. Jeremiah's message in 27:12–18 implies the possibility of a peaceful existence for Judah, even under Babylonian rule (למה תמותו, v. 13; למה תהיה העיר הזאת חרבה, v. 17). Indeed, prophetic intercession may prevent still more of the temple vessels being taken away (v. 18). In vv. 19–22 (excluding the MT plus in v. 22), however, the mood changes. The temple vessels will, after all, be taken to Babylon. Consequently, many scholars see vv. 19–22 as reflecting a viewpoint quite different from that expressed in vv. 12–18.[73] According to Seitz, the prophecy concerning the tem-ple vessels "forms a redactional supplement to an otherwise coherent prophetic narrative."[74]

---

70. Ibid., 27.

71. Cf. Carroll, *Jeremiah*, 547: "Chapter 28 has been analysed without remainder and its interpretation appears to be unproblematical."

72. Wanke, *Untersuchungen*, 35. More convincing is the view of E. Jenni, *Die politischen Voraussagen der Propheten* (ATANT 29; Zurich: Zwingli, 1956), 59, which Wanke cites (*Unter-suchungen*, 35 n. 36): "Nur übertriebene rationalistische Kritik könnte die vv. 15–17 oder v. 17 allein als unechten Zusatz ablehnen."

73. Duhm, *Jeremia*, 222; Volz, *Jeremia*, 258; McKane, *Jeremiah 2*, 703–4. Even Jones, *Jeremiah*, 359, concedes that 27:16–22 "may or may not be original to the episode." But cf. Rudolph, *Jeremia*, 151: "Ein Widerspruch zu v. 18 ist nicht vorhanden: wenn die Propheten die Zukunft richtig wüßten wie Jer. selbst, täten sie Fürbitte, daß das von Jahwe Angedrohte nicht eintrifft. Denn das prophetische Drohwort gilt ja nie unbedingt, Jahwe kann seinen Plan immer noch ändern." See also Holladay, *Jeremiah 2*, 123.

74. Seitz, *Theology in Conflict*, 186. Seitz believes (pp. 207–14, 241) that Jer 27–29 contain the beginning of the Scribal Chronicle.

The apparent tension between the prophecy of vv. 19–22 and Jeremiah's invitation to the prophets in v. 18 to entreat (פגע) YHWH vanishes, however, if we understand v. 18 (like 28:6) as either ironic, or as expressing a wish rather than an expectation.[75] Nor is it necessary to see vv. 19–22 as conflicting with the conditional promise of life in vv. 13 and 17. The prediction that the temple vessels will be taken to Babylon is sobering, and serves to refute the optimism of the other prophets (v. 16), but it scarcely constitutes "an unqualified and unrelieved prophecy of doom."[76] Nor is it obvious how these three verses serve the function Seitz ascribes to them of foreclosing on what has gone before.[77] The option of ongoing life in a viable city still stands.

2.5. *Judicial Differentiation in Jeremiah 27–28:* / המלך הכהנים וכל העם חנניה הנביא

In the previous chapter, it was noted how at first sight Jer 21:1–10 appears to differentiate salvation and judgment along audience-critical lines (the king and the people). I argued, though, that despite those audience-markers, the issues of salvation and judgment were in fact correlated to the more basic issue of staying in the city and surrendering to the Babylonians. When we come to Jer 27–28 the matter is more complex. Here too we find very clear audience-critical notes in the text, which draw a sharp distinction between the Judean community as a whole (המלך הכהנים וכל העם) and their prophets (הנביאים). This time, however, the audience-critical distinction is matched by a judgment oracle against one of those prophets.

We can consider first Jeremiah's message in ch. 27 to the king, the priests and the people. This can be designated as one of *modest hope*; what is on offer, for Judah as for the other nations, is the chance to remain in the land and work it (27:11). Like other features of the chapter, this echoes the creation narrative from Genesis, and certainly entails more than the bare promise of survival in 21:9. It is emphasized in MT by a double invitation to serve the king of Babylon and live (חיה, 27:12, 17), so that Jerusalem may not become a ruin (27:17). I have argued that the prophecy concerning the temple vessels is not intended to foreclose on the possibility of life, but rather to refute the claims of the other prophets. Moreover, the offer presented in ch. 27 is still open at the end of ch. 28; as we have seen, the words ואתה הבטחת את העם הזה על שקר (28:15) do not imply that the people have in fact accepted Hananiah's message.

At the same time, this message of hope is highly restrained. In the first place, it is contingent upon the people accepting the sovereignty of the king of Babylon and serving him, which also means not listening to the prophets. Secondly, all that they are promised in return is the prospect of life in their own land; this is not elaborated, nor is there any word of personal blessing or assurance from

---

75.   Brueggemann, *Exile and Homecoming*, 248: "The prophet refutes his own playful invitation to the adversaries."

76.   As McKane, *Jeremiah 2*, 704, claims.

77.   Seitz, *Theology in Conflict*, 187.

YHWH (as there is, for example, in 42:9–12). In fact, there is greater emphasis on the results of disobedience, namely, removal from the land, scattering and perishing (vv. 10 and 15).[78] Thirdly, Jeremiah anticipates a further ransacking of the temple (27:19–22); the remaining temple vessels, national symbols of status and security, will be removed. The MT plus concerning the return of the temple vessels (v. 22b) looks beyond this, but does not negate it. Consequently, it is hardly surprising that in 28:9 Jeremiah distances himself from those who prophesy שלום.[79]

Clearly, this message of modest hope is presented to Judah as a single entity. Although 27:8 and 11 establish a (את המלך בבל) אשר עבד / אשר לא עבד polarity at an *international* level, so far as Judah is concerned Jeremiah's words imply that they will respond as one. Nowhere does he entertain the prospect of some serving the Babylonians and others refusing to do so, still less of what would happen if such a division occurred. To this extent, despite its rhetorical marginalizing of the prophets, Jer 27 actually follows the judicial model characteristic of Deuteronomy, namely, that of national salvation/judgment.

In Jer 28, however, this all-Judah perspective is dramatically modified by the judgment against Hananiah the prophet. Precisely because his message of hope and restoration is inimical to the welfare of the community (העם הזה, 28:15), YHWH will expel him (שלח Pi. ptc.) from the face of the earth (מעל פני האדמה, 28:16); that is, he will implement the sentence prescribed in Deut 13 for a member of the community who attempts to mislead his brothers. This specific and rapidly executed penalty is the more striking, since in ch. 27 the result of failing to serve the king of Babylon is that the prophets will be banished along with everyone else (27:15).

Consequently, Jer 27–28 may be said to reflect an inner-Judean judicial polarity of "all the people" and "Hananiah the prophet." Although a message of conditional hope is announced to the nation at large, it is one from which Hananiah is decisively excluded. Stulman's remark, that in Jeremiah "*bad insiders*—indigenous outsiders—pose a profound threat to those who adhere to social and cosmic restraints,"[80] finds in the prophet from Gibeon its prime exemplar. At the same time, however, this is not a rigid dichotomy. Undergirding Jeremiah's message in ch. 27 is what we might call a democratization of responsibility, that is, the assumption that it is the king, priests and people, rather than the prophets, who carry ultimate responsibility for the fate of the nation. It is *their* decision to listen or not to listen to the prophets which will determine their future. Hence, while Hananiah is singled out for judgment, accepting his message will result in *all* being scattered (27:15) and the city destroyed (27:17). Indeed, a hint of some blurring in the prophet/people distinction lies in the term

---

78. Compare 1 Sam 12:25, where Samuel concludes his appeal to the people to serve YHWH with the words ואם הרע תרעו גם אתם גם מלככם תספו. Though conditional, the final position of this clause ensures an ominous tone.

79. Contra Seebass, "Konflikt," 452.

80. Stulman, *Order Amid Chaos*, 128 (italics original).

נביאיכם, "your prophets" (27:9, 16), where the suffix suggests a degree of affinity between the two groups.[81]

This complex mode of judicial differentiation is quite distinctive. The hostile stance towards the prophets echoes the judgment oracles of 23:9–32, but there is no suggestion there that *other* groups or individuals might be saved; in fact, that passage is followed by a warning of judgment on the entire nation (23:33–39). The salvation promise of 21:8–10, like that of ch. 27, also includes an invitation to live (חיה, 21:9) dependent on submission to the Babylonians (יצא ונפל, 21:9), but this involves the exemption of individuals from national disaster, rather than of prophets from national blessing.[82] Jeremiah 23:1–8 prophesies judgment for Israel's leaders (who might include prophets) and salvation for the people; there, though, the latter are seen primarily as the victims of misrule, in contrast to the picture in chs. 27–28 of a community with democratized responsibility. Meanwhile in ch. 24, salvation and judgment are allocated (without explanation) to the exiled and non-exiled communities respectively. As we will see, however, the differentiation between people and prophets will be repeated in ch. 29.

3. *Jeremiah 29:1–32*

3.1. *Text*

ואלה דברי הספר אשר שלח ירמיה הנביא מירושלם אל יתר זקני הגולה ואל הכהנים ואל הנביאים ואל כל העם אשר הגלה נבוכדנאצר מירושלם בבל	1	καὶ οὗτοι οἱ λόγοι τῆς βίβλιου οὓς ἀπέστειλεν Ιερεμιας ἐξ Ιερουσαλημ πρὸς τοὺς πρεσβυτέρους τῆς ἀποικίας καὶ πρὸς τοὺς ἱερεῖς καὶ πρὸς τοὺς ψευδοπροφήτας ἐπιστολὴν εἰς Βαβυλῶνα τῇ ἀποικίᾳ καὶ πρὸς πάντα τὸν λαον
אחרי צאת יכניה המלך והגבירה והסריסים שרי יהודה וירושלם והחרש והמסגר מירושלם	2	ὕστερον ἐξελθόντος Ιεχονιου τοῦ βασιλέως καὶ τῆς βασιλίσσης καὶ τῶν εὐνούχων καὶ παντὸς ἐλευθέρου καὶ δεσμώτου καὶ τεχνίτου ἐξ Ιερουσαλημ
ביד אלעשה בן שפן וגמריה בן חלקיה אשר שלח צדקיה מלך יהודה אל נבוכדנאצר מלך בבל בבלה לאמר	3	ἐν χειρὶ Ελεασα υἱοῦ Σαφαν καὶ Γαμαριου υἱοῦ Χελκιου ὃν ἀπέστειλε Σεδεκιας βασιλεὺς Ιουδα πρὸς βασιλέα Βαβυλῶνος εἰς Βαβυλῶνα λέγων
כה אמר יהוה צבאות אלהי ישראל לכל הגולה אשר הגליתי מירושלם בבלה	4	οὕτως εἶπε κύριος ὁ θεὸς Ισραηλ ἐπὶ τὴν ἀποίκιαν ἣν ἀπῴκισα ἀπὸ Ιερουσαλημ
בנו בתים ושבו ונטעו גנות ואכלו את פרין	5	οἰκοδομήσατε οἴκους καὶ κατοικήσατε καὶ φυτεύσατε παραδείσους καὶ φάγετε τοὺς καρποὺς αὐτῶν

---

81. In 27:16 (34:13), OG reads simply τῶν προφητῶν, "of the prophets." In the previous verse, on the other hand, OG reads ὑμεῖς καὶ οἱ προφῆται ὑμῶν, while MT reads simply אתם והנביאים. See too 29:8.

82. On this type of distinction, see further Kilpp, *Niederreißen*, 61. It will be remembered that Seitz sees both Jer 21:1–10 and 27–28 (prior to redaction) as reflecting the "submit and live" outlook of the Scribal Chronicle.

Hebrew		Greek

קחו נשים והולידו בנים ובנות
וקחו לבניכם נשים ואת בנותיכם
תנו לאנשים ותלדנה בנים ובנות
ורבו שם ואל תמעטו

6 καὶ λάβετε γυναῖκας καὶ τεκνοποιήσατε υἱοὺς
καὶ θυγατέρας καὶ λάβετε τοῖς υἱοῖς ὑμῶν
γυναῖκας καὶ τὰς θυγατέρας ὑμῶν ἀνδράσι
δότε καὶ πληθύνεσθε καὶ μὴ σμικρυνθῆτε

ודרשו את שלום העיר אשר
הגליתי אתכם שמה והתפללו
בעדה אל יהוה כי בשלומה
יהיה לכם שלום

7 καὶ ζητήσατε εἰς εἰρήνην τῆς γῆς εἰς ἣν
ἀπῴκισα ὑμᾶς ἐκεῖ καὶ προσεύξασθε περὶ
αὐτῶν πρὸς κύριον ὅτι ἐν εἰρήνῃ αὐτῶν ἔσται
εἰρήνη ὑμῖν

כי כה אמר יהוה צבאות אלהי
ישראל אל ישיאו לכם נביאיכם
אשר בקרבכם וקסמיכם ואל
תשמעו אל חלמתיכם אשר אתם
מחלמים

8 ὅτι οὕτως εἶπε κύριος μὴ ἀναπειθέτωσαν ὑμᾶς
οἱ ψευδοπροφῆται οἱ ἐν ὑμῖν καὶ μὴ
ἀναπειθέτωσαν ὑμᾶς οἱ μάντεις ὑμῶν καὶ μὴ
ἀκούετε εἰς τὰ ἐνύπνια ὑμῶν ἃ ὑμεῖς
ἐνυπνιάζεσθε

כי בשקר הם נבאים לכם בשמי
לא שלחתים נאם יהוה

9 ὅτι ἄδικα αὐτοὶ προφητεύουσιν ὑμῖν ἐπὶ τῷ
ὀνόματι μου καὶ οὐκ ἀπέστειλα αὐτούς

כי כה אמר יהוה כי לפי מלאת
לבבל שבעים שנה אפקד אתכם
והקמתי עליכם את דברי הטוב
להשיב אתכם אל המקום הזה

10 ὅτι οὕτως εἶπε κύριος ὅταν μέλλῃ πληροῦσθαι
Βαβυλῶνι ἑβδομήκοντα ἔτη ἐπισκέψομαι ὑμᾶς
καὶ ἐπιστήσω τοὺς λόγους μου ἐφ' ὑμᾶς τοῦ
ἀποστρέψαι τὸν λαὸν ὑμῶν εἰς τὸν τόπον
τοῦτον

כי אנכי ידעתי את המחשבת
אשר אנכי חשב עליכם נאם יהוה
מחשבות שלום ולא לרעה לתת
לכם אחרית ותקוה

11 καὶ λογιοῦμαι ἐφ' ὑμᾶς λογισμὸν εἰρήνης καὶ
οὐ κακὰ τοῦ δοῦναι ὑμῖν ταῦτα

וקראתם אתי והלכתם
והתפללתם אלי ושמעתי אליכם

12 καὶ προσεύξασθε πρός με καὶ εἰσακούσομαι
ὑμῶν

ובקשתם אתי ומצאתם כי
תדרשני בכל לבבכם

13 καὶ ἐκζητήσατέ με καὶ εὑρήσετέ με ὅτι ζητήσετέ
με ἐν ὅλῃ καρδίᾳ ὑμῶν

ונמצאתי לכם נאם יהוה ושבתי
את שביתכם וקבצתי אתכם מכל
הגוים ומכל המקומות אשר הדחתי
אתכם שם נאם יהוה והשבתי אתכם
אל המקום אשר הגליתי אתכם משם

14 καὶ ἐπιφανοῦμαι ὑμῖν

כי אמרתם הקים לנו יהוה
נבאים בבלה

15 ὅτι εἴπατε κατέστησεν ἡμῖν κύριος προφήτας
ἐν Βαβυλῶνι

כי כה אמר יהוה אל המלך
היושב אל כסא דוד ואל כל העם
היושב בעיר הזאת אחיכם אשר
לא יצאו אתכם בגולה

16

כה אמר יהוה צבאות הנני משלח
בם את החרב את הרעב ואת הדבר
ונתתי אותם כתאנים השערים אשר
לא תאכלנה מרע

17

ורדפתי אחריהם בחרב ברעב
ובדבר ונתתים לזועה לכל
ממלכות הארץ לאלה ולשמה
ולשרקה ולחרפה בכל הגוים אשר
הדחתים שם

18

תחת אשר לא שמעו אל דברי
נאם יהוה אשר שלחתי אליהם את
עבדי הנבאים השכם ושלח ולא
שמעתם נאם יהוה

19

ואתם שמעו דבר יהוה כל הגולה
אשר שלחתי מירושלם בבלה

20

21

כה אמר יהוה צבאות אלהי
ישראל אל אחאב בן קוליה ואל
צדקיהו בן מעשיה הנבאים לכם
בשמי שקר הנני נתן אתם ביד
נבוכדראצר מלך בבל והכם
לעיניכם

οὕτως εἶπε κύριος ἐπὶ Αχιαβ καὶ ἐπὶ Σεδεκιαν ἰδοὺ ἐγὼ δίδωμι αὐτοὺς εἰς χεῖρας βασιλέως Βαβυλῶνος καὶ πατάξει αὐτοὺς κατ' ὀφθαλμοὺς ὑμῶν

22

ולקח מהם קללה לכל גלות
יהודה אשר בבבל לאמר ישמך
יהוה כצדקיהו וכאחב אשר קלם
מלך בבל באש

καὶ λήμψονται ἀπ' αὐτῶν κατάραν ἐν πάσῃ τῇ ἀποικίᾳ Ιουδα ἐν Βαβυλῶνι λέγοντες ποιήσαι σε κύριος ὡς Σεδεκιαν ἐποίησε καὶ ὡς Αχιαβ οὓς ἀπετηγάνισε βασιλεὺς Βαβυλῶνος ἐν πυρὶ

23

יען אשר עשו נבלה בישראל
וינאפו את נשי רעיהם וידברו
דבר בשמי שקר אשר לוא צויתם
ואנכי הוידע ועד נאם יהוה

δι' ἣν ἐποίησαν ἀνομίαν ἐν Ισραηλ καὶ ἐμοιχῶντο τὰς γυναῖκας τῶν πολιτῶν αὐτῶν καὶ λόγον ἐχρημάτισαν ἐν τῷ ὀνόματί μου ὃν οὐ συνέταξα αὐτοῖς καὶ ἐγὼ μάρτυς

24

ואל שמעיהו הנחלמי תאמר לאמר

καὶ πρὸς Σαμαιαν τὸν Νελαμίτην ἐρεῖς

25

כה אמר יהוה צבאות אלהי
ישראל יען אשר אתה שלחה
בשמכה ספרים אל כל העם אשר
בירושלם ואל צפניה בן מעשיה
הכהן ואל כל הכהנים לאמר

οὐκ ἀπέστειλά σε τῷ ὀνόματί μου καὶ πρὸς Σοφονιαν υἱὸν Μαασαιου τὸν ἱερέα εἰπεῖν

26

יהוה נתנך כהן תחת יהוידע
הכהן להיות פקדים בית יהוה
לכל איש משגע ומתנבא ונתתה
אתו אל המהפכת ואל הצינק

κύριος ἔδωκέ σε ἱερέα ἀντὶ Ιωδαε τοῦ ἱερέως γενέσθαι ἐπιστάτην ἐν οἴκῳ κυρίου παντὶ ἀνθρώπῳ προφητεύοντι καὶ παντὶ ἀνθρώπῳ μαινομένῳ καὶ δώσεις αὐτὸν εἰς τὸ ἀπόκλεισμα καὶ εἰς τὸν καταρράκτην

27

ועתה למה לא גערת בירמיהו
הענתתי המתנבא לכם

καὶ νῦν διὰ τί οὐκ ἐλοιδορήσατε Ιερεμιαν τὸν ἐξ Αναθωθ τὸν προφητεύσαντα ὑμῖν

28

כי על כן שלח אלינו בבל
לאמר ארכה היא בנו בתים ושבו
ונטעו גנות ואכלו את פריהן

οὐ διὰ τοῦτο ἀπέστειλε πρὸς ἡμᾶς εἰς Βαβυλῶνα λέγων μακράν ἐστιν οἰκοδομήσατε οἰκίας καὶ κατοικήσατε καὶ φυτεύσατε κήπους καὶ φάγεσθε τὸν καρπὸν αὐτῶν

29

ויקרא צפניה הכהן את הספר
הזה באזני ירמיהו הנביא

καὶ ἀνέγνω Σοφονιας τὸ βιβλίον εἰς τὰ ὦτα Ιερεμιου

30

ויהי דבר יהוה אל ירמיהו לאמר

καὶ ἐγένετο λόγος κυρίου πρὸς Ιερεμιαν λέγων

31

שלח על כל הגולה לאמר כה
אמר יהוה אל שמעיה הנחלמי יען
אשר נבא לכם שמעיה ואני לא
שלחתיו ויבטח אתכם על שקר

ἀπόστειλον πρὸς τὴν ἀποικίαν λέγων οὕτως εἶπε κύριος ἐπὶ Σαμαιαν τὸν Νελαμίτην ἐπειδὴ ἐπροφήτευσεν ὑμῖν Σαμαιας καὶ ἐγὼ οὐκ ἀπέστειλα αὐτὸν καὶ πεποιθέναι ἐποίησεν ὑμᾶς ἐπ' ἀδίκῳ

32

לכן כה אמר יהוה הנני פקד על
שמעיה הנחלמי ועל זרעו לא יהיה
לו איש יושב בתוך העם הזה ולא
יראה בטוב אשר אני עשה לעמי
נאם יהוה כי סרה דבר על יהוה

διὰ τοῦτο οὕτως εἶπε κύριος ἰδοὺ ἐγὼ ἐπισκέψομαι ἐπὶ Σαμαιαν καὶ ἐπὶ τὸ γένος αὐτοῦ καὶ οὐκ ἔσται αὐτῷ ἄνθρωπος ἐν μέσῳ ὑμῶν τοῦ ἰδεῖν τὰ ἀγαθά ἃ ἐγὼ ποιήσω ὑμῖν

3.2. *Textual Notes*

v. 1. MT יתר >OG. Cf. 27:19 (34:16), where OG renders with ἐπιλοίπος. The enigmatic meaning of the term in association with זקני may account for OG omission, but an MT plus seems more likely.

v. 6. ותלדנה בנים ובנות >OG. This breaks the pattern of two-verb clauses elsewhere in vv. 5–6. It may be an MT plus, making explicit the three-generational duration of the exile. However, Janzen suggests inner-Greek haplography;

if OG read δοτε ἀνδράσι καὶ τεκνοποιήσατωσαν καὶ θυγατέρας καὶ πληθύνεσθε, the repetition of ρασ(ι) καὶ could have caused a copyist's mistake.[83]

v. 7. MT העיר; OG τῆς γῆς. OG is often preferred on the grounds of being more realistic (the exiles were not restricted to one city), but Jeremiah's letter was probably intended specifically for the community in Babylon.[84] Berlin finds support for MT in the correspondence between vv. 6–7 and Deut 20:5–10; both contain the sequence בנה בתים ("build houses"), נטע גנות / כרם ("plant vine-yards/gardens"), לקח אשה ("marry wives") and שלום העיר ("the peace of the city").[85] However, while this is unlikely to be coincidental, it is text-critically inconclusive.

v. 8. MT אל ישיאו לכם נביאיכם אשר בקרבכם וקסמיכם; OG μὴ ἀναπειθέτωσαν ὑμᾶς οἱ ψευδοπροφῆται οἱ ἐν ὑμῖν καὶ μὴ ἀναπειθέτωσαν ὑμᾶς οἱ μάντεις ὑμῶν. OG implies a *Vorlage* longer than MT: אל ישיאו לכם הנביאים אשר בקרבכם ואל ישיאו לכם קסמיכם.[86] This has the virtue of greater parallelism. With its posses-sive suffix, MT נביאיכם strengthens the association between the people and the prophets.

MT חלמתיכם אשר אתם מחלמים; OG τὰ ἐνύπνια ὑμῶν ἃ ὑμεῖς ἐνυπνιάζεσθε = חלמתיכם אשר אתם חלמים. MT ("your dreams which you cause to dream") is awkward. Since חלם Hiph. is otherwise unknown in Old Testament, some scholars follow OG and emend to חלמים ("your dreams which you are dream-ing"); the מ could have arisen by dittography.[87] However, the preceding and following clauses concern a third party, and Soggin notes that a personal referent is also implied by אל תשמעו.[88] Good sense can be made of the MT consonantal text if, as in 27:9, we vocalize as חֲלֹמֹתֵיכֶם, "your dreamers."[89]

v. 10. MT אתכם; OG τὸν λαὸν ὑμῶν = עמכם. OG (and perhaps its *Vorlage*) indicates that it is not the addressees themselves who would return. Whether MT intends such a meaning, however, is doubtful; since in v. 6 it emphasizes the three-generational duration of the exile, אתכם should probably be read repre-sentatively.

v. 11. MT אנכי ידעתי את המחשבת אשר >OG. Probably lost due to haplography (repetition of אנכי). חשב מחשבת is an established idiom in the Old Testament (2 Sam 14:14; Jer 11:19; 18:11, 19; 49:20, 30; Ezek 38:10; Dan 11:24, 25).

MT אחרית ותקוה; OG ταῦτα. OG may be defective for τὰ μετὰ ταῦτα (so LXX[Luc]), reflecting a *Vorlage* that read simply אחרית (cf. 5:31).[90] MT maintains

83. Janzen, *Studies*, 103. Also favouring MT is Seidl, *Texte und Einheiten*, 92 n. 146.

84. Others have argued for MT by reading עיר in a general sense, "any city"; so Giesebrecht, *Jeremia*, 155; Klaas A. D. Smelik, "Letters to the Exiles: Jeremiah 29 in Context," *SJOT* 10 (1996): 282–95 (291).

85. Adele Berlin, "Jeremiah 29:5–7: A Deuteronomic Allusion," *HAR* 8 (1984): 3–11 (6).

86. So Stulman, *Other Text*, 70.

87. So GKC §53o; Giesebrecht, *Jeremia*, 155; S. R. Driver, *The Book of the Prophet Jeremiah: A Revised Translation with Introductions and Short Explanations* (London: Hodder & Stoughton, 1908), 170; Keown, Scalise and Smothers, *Jeremiah 26–52*, 62.

88. J. Alberto Soggin, "Jeremiah 29,8b," in *Old Testament and Oriental Studies* (BO 29; Rome: Biblical Institute, 1975), 238–40 (239).

89. So Volz, *Studien*, 217; Wanke, *Untersuchungen*, 39; Holladay, *Jeremiah 2*, 132.

90. So Holladay, *Jeremiah 2*, 133; Keown, Scalise and Smothers, *Jeremiah 26–52*, 62.

the parallelism present in the rest of the verse (המחשבת אשר אנכי חשב; מחשבת
שלום ולא לרעה).

vv. 12–13. MT וקראתם אתי והלכתם >OG. Possible haplography, arising from
a confusion of לתת לכם (v. 11) and הלכתם. The similarity is not great, however,
and the additional words in MT disturb an otherwise balanced construction in
these two verses. Carroll suggests that והלכתם reflects the practice of prayer in
the second temple period.[91]

MT התפללתם...ובקשתם; OG προσεύξασθε...ἐκζητήσατε. The imperatives in
OG point to a *Vorlage* reading התפללו...ובקשו (as in v. 7).

v. 14. MT ונמצאתי; OG ἐπιφανοῦμαι = ונראיתי ("I will be seen by you") or
perhaps ונגלתי ("I will reveal myself to you").[92]

MT נאם יהוה...משם >OG. A probable MT plus,[93] alluding to YHWH's promise
of restoration in Deut 30:3. Formally, MT broadens the scope of YHWH's promise
to include the entire *Diaspora*; see, however, my comments below, "Exegesis."

vv. 16–20 >OG. These verses interrupt an otherwise smooth progression from
v. 15 to v. 21, again suggesting they are MT plus, although haplography (repetition of בבלה, vv. 15 and 20) is not impossible (cf. the much longer omission in
OG of 39:4–13).[94]

v. 19. MT ולא שמעתם. The switch from third to second person is abrupt, and
some scholars emend to ולא שמעו.[95] The second person form may be deliberate,
however, especially given the following verse.

MT הנבאים בכם בשמי שקר >OG. MT plus, especially since the reason given for
their condemnation in v. 22 is quite different.

v. 23. MT הוידע >OG. The *Ketiv* may be defective for the *Qere* היודע ("I am
the one who knows") or for הוא ידע ("I myself know"). MT plus, possibly due to
conflation of ואנכי העד and ואנכי היודע.

vv. 24–28. All the principal textual witnesses diverge here, and none is
satisfactory.[96] The chief problem is in vv. 24–25. MT יען אשר (v. 25) lacks
apodosis, unless we relate it to the לכן of v. 32, where, however, it is the exiles
rather than Shemaiah who are addressed. The picture is still more confused in

---

91. Carroll, *Jeremiah*, 553,

92. For the latter proposal, see Jones, *Jeremiah*, 366.

93. Contra Thiel, *Redaktion 2*, 16, who posits deliberate omission by OG. Welch, *Jeremiah*,
174, and Holladay, *Jeremiah 2*, 133, believe the translator's *Vorlage* included שבתי את שביתכם.

94. So May, "Objective Approach," 152; Hyatt, "Jeremiah," 5:1020; Janzen, *Studies*, 118.
Holladay, *Jeremiah 2*, 135, posits haplography in the OG *Vorlage*. However, Thiel, *Redaktion 26–
45*, 17, believes the omission was deliberate.

95. So Giesebrecht, *Jeremia*, 157–58; Holladay, *Jeremiah 2*, 134. Bright, *Jeremiah*, 206,
transposes all of v. 19 into the second person, but notes that this still leaves a "scarcely grammatical"
switch from v. 18.

96. The Syriac *Peshitta* reads: "And Shemaiah the Nehelamite said, 'Thus has said YHWH the
God of Israel'; and he sent in his name a letter to all the people who are in Jerusalem and to
Zephaniah son of Maaseiah the priest and to the priests" (Holladay's translation, *Jeremiah 2*, 136).
The problem here is the lack of an oracle in v. 25. We could either shorten the text to "Shemaiah the
Nehelamite sent to Zephaniah the son of Maaseiah" (McKane, *Jeremiah 2*, 727), or assume that
Shemaiah's oracle has been lost (Holladay, *Jeremiah 2*, 136–37).

OG, which contains two oracles (οὐκ ἀπέστειλά σε τῷ ὀνόματί μου, v. 24; καὶ πρὸς Σοφονιαν υἱὸν Μαασαιου τὸν ἱερέα εἰπεῖν, v. 25), neither of which prepares us for the reference to τὸ βιβλίον in v. 29. Moreover, if in v. 27 we read οὐκ ἐλοιδορήσατε (LXX^Q),[97] we have the absurdity of YHWH rebuking Sophonias for not rebuking Jeremiah. It may be that vv. 24–25 were originally cast as a narrative ("But Shemaiah the Nehelamite sent in his own name a letter to Zeph-aniah the priest…"), rather than an oracle, the confusion arising when אל שמעיהו ("concerning Shemaiah") was misinterpreted as "to Shemaiah" (cf. v. 31).[98]

v. 25. MT אל כל העם אשר בירושלם; אל כל הכהנים ואל כל העם >OG. Both MT plusses, since the ensuing message is addressed only to Zechariah. Given these additional audience groups, MT ספרים should be interpreted as a genuine plural.

v. 26. MT פקדים; OG ἐπιστάτης. Again, the singular form in OG is probably the more original (cf. Targ., למהוי ממנא סגן כהניא, "to be an appointer of chief priests").

v. 32. MT ולא יראה; OG τοῦ ἰδεῖν = לראות.[99] MT retains the focus on Shem-aiah, while OG makes "his seed" the subject of the last part of the sentence.

MT בתוך העם הזה; OG ἐν μέσῳ ὑμῶν = בתוככם; MT לעמי; OG ὑμῖν = לכם. In MT, the recipients of YHWH's promise are addressed less directly in third person terms, the emphasis being on their relationship to YHWH.

αὐτῷ ἄνθρωπος (LXX^Q; Ziegler) = MT לו איש; αὐτῶν ἄνθρωπος (LXX$^{B, A}$; Rahlfs). The latter, which has the stronger support, reads "there will not be (a single) man of them," referring to Samaias *and* his descendants.

MT כי סרה דבר על יהוה >OG. MT plus, influenced by Deut 13:6; cf. Jer 28:16.

3.3. *Exegesis*

v. 1. אל יתר זקני הגולה ואל הכהנים ואל הנביאים ואל כל העם. This includes the same three groups—priests, prophets and people—which have appeared in chs. 27–28 (27:16; 28:1, 5). The phrase זקני הגולה is otherwise unattested (cf. זקני העם, 19:1; זקני הארץ, 26:17) but may reflect the growing social importance of the elders among the exiles in Babylon (cf. Ezek 8:1; 14:1; 20:1).[100]

---

97. The problem is avoided if we follow LXX$^{B, A}$, διὰ τί συνελοιδορήσατε (Rahlfs); but this indictment of Sophonias for opposing Jeremiah makes his willingness to read the letter to him (v. 29) very odd.

98. So Duhm, *Jeremia*, 234–5; Rudolph, *Jeremia*, 158; Thiel, *Redaktion 26–45*, 12; Wanke, *Untersuchungen*, 39; Kilpp, *Niederreißen*, 43 n. 9; Graupner, *Auftrag*, 89; McKane, *Jeremiah 2*, 731. For a fresh attempt to make sense of these verses, see Christoph Hardmeier, "Jer 29, 24–32— 'eine geradezu unüberbietbare Konfusion'? Vorurteil und Methode in der exegetischen Forschung," in *Die Hebräische Bibel und ihre zweifache Nachgeschichte. Festschrift für Rolf Rendtorff zum 65 Geburtstag* (ed. E. Blum, C. Macholz and E. W. Stegemann; Neukirchen–Vluyn: Neukirchener, 1990), 301–17.

99. So Janzen, *Studies*, 202 n. 78; Rudolph, *Jeremia*, 158; Wanke, *Untersuchungen*, 39–40; contra McKane, *Jeremiah 2*, 734 ("τοῦ ἰδεῖν is probably the result of a quest for neatness on the part of the Greek translator"); Graupner, *Auftrag*, 92 n. 112.

100. So Walther Eichrodt, *Ezekiel: A Commentary* (trans. C. Quin; OTL; London: SCM, 1970), 121; cf. A. R. C. Leaney, *The Rule of Qumran and Its Meaning: Introduction, Translation and Commentary* (NTL; London: SCM, 1966), 187.

יֶתֶר usually means "remainder." Possibly the term reflects unrest in Babylon, leading to arrest or execution of some of the elders (cf. vv. 21–22).[101] Streane's proposal, that these were the elders who had survived the journey to Babylon, also has merit.[102] Alternatively, on the basis of Gen 49:3, some scholars translate as "pre-eminent."[103] This would be consistent with the emphasis in this verse that it was the cream of society that had been deported.

v. 2. Like the historical note in 24:1, this is often judged redactional due to its parenthetical nature.[104] Compare however 27:19–21, which, like 29:1–3, contains (1) an introduction to a prophetic message, with a four-fold list of referents, (2) a subordinate clause referring to Nebuchadnezzar's exiling of Jehoiachin and (3) the resumption of the prophetic message, using the messenger formula.

v. 4. אֲשֶׁר הִגְלֵיתִי. Elsewhere in Jeremiah, whenever גלה means "exile" the subject is consistently human (20:4; 22:12; 27:20; 39:9; 43:3; 52:15, 28, 30), a pattern reflected generally in the Old Testament. It is thus remarkable that three times in ch. 29 (vv. 4, 7, 14), גלה is predicated of YHWH. The use of this verb (rather than שלח, פוץ or נדח) emphasizes YHWH's sovereignty over the political dimensions of deportation.

vv. 5–7. The language here takes up the refrain of building and planting found throughout Jeremiah, but is also redolent of other Old Testament passages. The paired imperatives of vv. 5–6, including the command רבו ("increase"), echo the creation mandate of Gen 1:28 (cf. 9:1).[105] Similar language also occurs in Ps 107:36–38; Isa 65:21–23, but more especially Deut 28:30–32, where Moses warns Israel of the curses that will result from disobedience:

> You will betroth a wife and another man will lie with her. You will build a house but you will not live in it. You will plant a vineyard but you will not enjoy its use… Your sons and daughters will be given to another people.

Read against this backdrop, 29:5–7 is announcing that the curses are rescinded; the exiles may once again enjoy YHWH's blessing on their day to day activities.[106] However, Berlin and Smith see an even closer parallel with Deut 20:5–10, a passage that lists exemptions from military service.[107] As Berlin notes,

101.   So Duhm, *Jeremia*, 228; Bright, *Jeremiah*, 208; Thompson, *Jeremiah*, 545. McKane's objection, *Jeremiah 2*, 727, that "there is a lack of evidence that Jewish communities in Babylon were subject to persecution or suppression," is unfounded; see D. L. Smith-Christopher, "Reassessing the Historical and Sociological Impact of the Babylonian Exile (597/587–539 BCE)," in Scott, ed., *Exile*, 7–36.

102.   A. W. Streane, *The Book of the Prophet Jeremiah Together with the Lamentations* (CB; Cambridge: Cambridge University Press, 1885), 192.

103.   E.g. Holladay, *Jeremiah 2*, 140.

104.   So Thiel, *Redaktion 26–45*, 11; Thompson, *Jeremiah*, 545.

105.   Holladay, *Jeremiah 2*, 138.

106.   The uprooted and orphaned exiles are invited to invest their lives in this new realm of blessing" (Keown, Scalise and Smothers, *Jeremiah 26–52*, 72); similarly Kilpp, *Niederreißen*, 57. This rescinding theology will dominate Jer 30–33.

107.   Berlin, "Jeremiah 29:5–7," 3–6; Daniel L. Smith, "Jeremiah as Prophet of Nonviolent Resistance," *JSOT* 43 (1989): 95–107 (100–102).

while the combination "build/plant" occurs frequently in the Old Testament, the series "build/plant/wives/children" is much less common. In addition, Deut 20:10 shares with Jer 29:7 the terms שלום and העיר. Consequently, "in addition to encouraging settlement, Jeremiah is also subtly counselling against revolt. Do those things, he tells the exiles, for which Deuteronomy permits a man to refrain from going to war."[108]

התפלל בעד occurs several times in Jeremiah to denote prophetic intercession (7:16; 11:14; 14:11; 37:3; 42:2), while דרש is used by Zedekiah in requesting prayer on behalf of Jerusalem (21:1; cf. the complaint against Jeremiah in 38:4, איננו דרש לשלום לעם הזה כי אם לרעה). What makes v. 7 remarkable, however, is that so far the prophet himself has been forbidden by Yhwh to pray for his people (7:6; 11:14; 14:11).

The promise of שלום also marks a turning point in the book. Hitherto, Jeremiah has emphasized the absence of שלום from Judah (14:19; 15:5; 16:5), in contrast to other prophets whom Yhwh has not sent (6:14; 8:11; 14:13; 23:17; 28:9). Now, for the first time in the book, Yhwh promises שלום (albeit conditionally and indirectly) to his people;[109] this theme will be developed in v. 11, and again in 33:6, 9.

v. 10. The construction לפי + infinitive probably implies "*only* when."[110] It thereby serves to qualify the salvation oracle that follows.

The much-debated phrase שבעים שנה occurs here for the second time in Jeremiah.[111] In 25:11–12 Yhwh announces that Judah and the surrounding lands will be subjugated to another nation for seventy years.[112] There, however, the fulfilment of that period will be followed by Yhwh's punishment of their oppressor; here, it will herald his salvation of the exiles in Babylon.

Although it can be argued that שבעים שנה refers to the actual duration of Judah's exile,[113] most scholars interpret it as in some sense metaphorical.[114]

---

108. Berlin, "Jeremiah 29:5–7," 4; similarly Smith, "Jeremiah as Prophet," 102.

109. Sisson, "Jeremiah and the Jerusalem Conception of Peace," 440: "Having called upon the exiles to seek a *šālôm* oracle on behalf of the city of Babylon, Jeremiah then indicated that the divine response to that plea would be favourable."

110. So Rudolph, *Jeremia*, 156; Bright, *Jeremiah*, 205; Holladay, *Jeremiah 2*, 141; Keown, Scalise and Smothers, *Jeremiah 26–52*, 60. Kilpp, *Niederreißen*, 62, argues that כי relates to אפקד (cf. Num 9:17, ולפי העלת הענן מעל האהל).

111. For surveys of the debate and bibliographies, see Ackroyd, *Exile and Restoration*, 240–41 n. 27; Keown, Scalise and Smothers, *Jeremiah 26–52*, 74–75, and John Applegate, "Jeremiah and the Seventy Years in the Hebrew Bible: Inner-Biblical Reflections on the Prophet and his Prophecy," in Curtis and Römer, eds., *The Book of Jeremiah and Its Reception*, 92–93.

112. MT and OG diverge significantly in 25:9–12. In contrast to OG's enigmatic prediction that the Lord will bring "the family from the north" (τὴν πατριὰν ἀπὸ βορρᾶ), MT explicitly identifies the invader as Babylon and highlights its role.

113. Duhm, *Jeremia*, 230, related the figure to the period of Babylonian supremacy, that is, from the defeat of Nineveh (612 BC) to the overthrow by Cyrus (539 BC). See too C. F. Whitley, "The Term Seventy Years Captivity," *VT* 4 (1954): 60–72, and "The Term Seventy Years: A Rejoinder," *VT* 7 (1957): 416–18.

114. For Volz, *Jeremia*, 269, "es ist die Vorstellung der geschichtlichen Epochen"; for Hyatt, "Deuteronomic Edition," 263, "it is a vague number—probably two generations or 'the days of one king' as in Isa. 23:15."

It may be a round number for "a lifetime" (cf. Ps 90:10), that is, a long time; cf. Shemaiah's interpretation of Jeremiah's message in v. 28, ארכה היא.[115] More likely, it represents three generations; this would conform to the prophecy in 27:7 that Nebuchadnezzar's domination would end with his grandson, and also to the three generation perspective of 29:6.[116] However, an inscription of Esarhaddon in which Marduk decrees seventy years of punishment for Babylon has led some to conclude that "seventy years" was a conventional description in the ancient Near East for a deity's judgment on a nation (cf. Isa 23:15–17).[117]

Up until this point in Jeremiah, the meaning of פקד has been almost entirely ominous, namely, "to punish."[118] Here, however, the connotation is clearly favourable. Aside from the MT plus of 27:22, only once previously has פקד signified YHWH's benevolent care, namely, in 15:15, where the prophet asks YHWH, זכרני ופקדני. Henceforth, it will mostly signify the punishment of Israel's enemies (30:2; 46:25; 49:8; 50:18, 31; 51:44, 47, 52). As with the term שלום, therefore, the use of פקד in Jer 29 seems to mark a turning point in the book.

v. 11. המחשבת אשר אנכי חשב עליכם. The benevolence of these plans is made explicit in what follows, מחשבות שלום ולא לרעה. Here again, we have a striking re-use of language that is otherwise consistently negative in Jeremiah. By itself, the noun מחשבות signifies humanity's evil inclinations (4:14; 6:19; 18:12), while חשב is used in conjunction with YHWH's plan for judgment (18:8; 26:3; 36:3) or human plans for evil (23:27; 48:2). Likewise, the expression חשב מחשבה (מחשבות) is consistently ominous, whether the subject is human (11:19; 18:18) or divine (18:11; 49:20, 30; 50:45; 51:29). Only here is this expression used positively.

vv. 12–13. והתפללתם...שמעתי...ובקשתם...ומצאתם. The use of indicatives in MT (cf. the imperatives in OG) does not necessarily eliminate any idea of contingency; the verses can still be translated, "If you call...I will listen... If you seek...you will find."[119] MT does however give YHWH's words a promissory and forward-looking aspect; this is also present in Deut 4:29, ובקשתם משם את יהוה אלהיך ומצאת כי תדרשנו בכל לבבך, to which Jer 29:13 alludes. As in 24:7, interpretation of the final clause כי תדרשני בכל לבבכם hinges on whether כי should be read as conditional, temporal or causal. Unlike the earlier verse, however, where the context sufficiently emphasized divine initiative to leave the question open, the strong accent on Israel's responsibilities in 29:12–13

---

115. So Clements, "Jeremiah: Prophet of Hope," 125.

116. So Rudolph, *Jeremia*, 157; Thiel, *Redaktion 26–45*, 17; Thompson, *Jeremiah*, 547 n. 21; McKane, *Jeremiah 2*, 689.

117. See Moshe Weinfeld, *Deuteronomy and the Deuteronomic School* (Oxford: Oxford University Press, 1972), 144–46; Applegate, "Jeremiah and the Seventy Years," 93.

118. Jer 1:10; 5:9, 29; 6:6, 15; 9:8, 24; 11:22; 13:21; 14:10; 15:3; 21:14; 23:2, 34; 25:12; 27:8; also 36:31; 44:13, 29. פקד does have a benevolent sense in its first occurrence in 23:2, but here the subject is human, and the reference is to the care which they have *failed* to provide.

119. For this use of the perfect consecutive in the protasis and apodosis of a conditional clause, see *GKC* §112 ff, kk.

indicates that כי should here be accorded the conditional sense that it also has in Deut 4:29.[120]

v. 14. YHWH's promise, ושבתי את שביתכם וקבצתי אתכם מכל הגוים ומכל המקומות אשר הדחתי אתכם שם forms a further echo of Deuteronomy, this time 30:3: ושב יהוה אלהיך את שבותך ורחמך ושב וקבצך מכל העמים אשר הפיצך יהוה אלהיך שמה. It is usually assumed that at this point the focus is no longer on the exiles in Babylon, but rather on the entire Jewish *Diaspora*. However, the use of גלה Hiph. in the final clause, המקום אשר הגליתי אתכם משם, points back to (and forms an *inclusio* with) כל הגולה אשר הגליתי מירושלם בבלה (v. 4), which obviously relates to the exiles of 597. I suggest, therefore, that the global language of v. 14 is being used with specific application to the *Golah* community in Babylon.[121] On this point, see further "The Significance of the MT Plusses of Jeremiah 29" (p. 130, below). Given the similarity of Jer 29:14 to Deut 30:3, it may even be that the author is referring to the latter passage as known scripture and applying it to the exiles.[122]

שוב שבות occurs here for the first time in Jeremiah, and is repeated a further seven times in chs. 30–33. For a long time the expression was rendered "restore the captives," based on an assumed derivation of the *Ketiv* שביתכם from שבה ("take captive").[123] However, E. L. Dietrich argued that it was in fact a cognate accusative of שוב: literally, "turn a turning," or more idiomatically, "restore the fortunes."[124] This is now generally accepted for most cases of שוב שבות in the Old Testament, including those in Jer 29 and 30.[125] Its scope is thus wider than "restoring the captives," although in certain contexts (such as Jer 29:14), this might be its implication.

---

120.   So most commentators; see too Aejmelaeus, "Function and Interpretation," 208 n. 46. A rare exception is McKane, *Jeremiah 2*, 726, who translates it as "for." כי is also rendered "if" in Deut 4:29 by Driver, *Deuteronomy*, 73; Gerhard von Rad, *Deuteronomy: A Commentary* (trans. D. Barton; OTL; London: SCM, 1966), 47; Craigie, *Deuteronomy*, 138; McConville, *Deuteronomy*, 110.

121.   See too Jer 46:27–28, where YHWH's pledge not to destroy Israel בכל הגוים אשר הדחתיך שמה seems to have particular application to the Jews in Egypt. Likewise, in Ezek 11:17 YHWH promises וקבצתי אתכם מן העמים ואספתי אתכם מן הארצות אשר נפצותם בהם, before taking Ezekiel to deliver this message to the exiles in Babylon (vv. 24–25).

122.   Deut 30 is often seen as a late addition to DtrH, influenced by Jeremiah and Ezekiel; see, e.g., Hans Walter Wolff, "Das Kerygma des deuteronomistischen Geschichtswerks," ZAW 73 (1961): 171–86 (180–83); Lust, '"Gathering and Return,"' 125; A. D. H. Mayes, *Deuteronomy* (NCB; Grand Rapids: Eerdmans, 1987), 367–68; Marc Z. Brettler, "Predestination in Deuteronomy 30:1–10," in Schearing and McKenzie, eds., *Those Elusive Deuteronomists*, 177–96 (187). However, Unterman, *Repentance to Redemption*, 67–74, and McConville, *Judgment and Promise*, 162–63, argue that Jer 29 draws on Deut 30.

123.   So E. Preuschen, "Die Bedeutung von שוב שבות im Alten Testamente," ZAW 15 (1895): 1–74, and E. L. Baumann, "שוב שבות, Eine exegetische Untersuchung," ZAW 47 (1929): 17–44; see too BDB, s.v. שבית, שבה.

124.   E. L. Dietrich, *Die endzeitliche Wiederherstellung bei den Propheten* (BZAW 40; Giessen: Töpelmann, 1925), 36–37.

125.   See, e.g., John M. Bracke, "šûb šᵉbût: A Reappraisal," ZAW 97 (1985): 233–44 (244); J. A. Thompson and Elmer A. Martens, s.v. שוב, *NIDOTTE* 4:55–59.

v. 15. כי אמרתם could be understood in an indirect explicative sense, "(I say this) because you have said…"[126] In this case, v. 15 would conclude the literary unit beginning in v. 10, with הקים לנו יהוה נבאים forming an *inclusio* with והקמתי עליכם את דברי הטוב. More probably, however, כי indicates that the exiles' words are the reason for what is to follow; cf. Isa 28:15–16, which also begins with כי אמרתם. Since vv. 16–20 (MT plus) address Jerusalem rather than Babylon, it is likely that v. 15 originally introduced the oracle against Ahab and Zedekiah (vv. 21–23).

הקים לנו יהוה נבאים echoes Moses' assurance in Deut 18:15, נביא מקרבך: מאחיך כמני יקים לך יהוה (cf. Deut 18:18). For the author of Jer 29, therefore, the exiles are applying a valid promise to the wrong people.

v. 16. אחיכם אשר לא יצאו אתכם בגולה indicates censure of those in Jerusalem for failing to act in unison with their fellow Israelites; see the use of אחיכם in Lev 25:46; Deut 3:18; Josh 1:14; 1 Kgs 12:24, and so on, to remind Israel of such obligations.[127] Similar bitterness in the post-exilic community is reflected in Isa 66:5, where "those who tremble at YHWH's word" (החרדים אל דברו) are differentiated from "your brothers who hate you" (אחיכם שנאיכם).

v. 19. ולא שמעתם. If, as I suggested above, we retain this reading rather than emending to ולא שמעו, the primary purpose of this pericope becomes clear: to rebuke the exiles for failing to listen to YHWH's prophets. It thereby complements vv. 8–9, which rebuke the exiles for listening to their own prophets. This reading also makes sense of the ensuing ואתם שמעו דבר יהוה (v. 20).

v. 23. יען אשר עשו נבלה בישראל. To "commit folly in Israel" is a technical expression denoting "a class of acts which bring appalling suffering in their wake because they disrupt the sexual harmony of the community."[128] Rape (Gen 37:7) and pre-marital intercourse (Deut 22:21) fall into this category, as does breach of rules regarding sacred property in holy war (Josh 7:15). The charge of adultery (וינאפו את נשי רעיהם) against Ahab and Zedekiah is not part of the normal rhetoric against false prophets in these chapters, but echoes the accusation against the prophets of Jerusalem in 23:14, נאוף והלך בשקר.

YHWH's self-description as witness (עד) may gain additional significance from the custom in other ancient Near Eastern letters of finishing with a reference to witnesses.[129] This impression of v. 23 as marking a formal conclusion is

---

126. Calvin, *Jeremiah and the Lamentations 3*, 439, thought this interpretation of כי was "not unsuitable." According to Aejmelaeus, "Function and Interpretation," 203, "it is characteristic of the indirect causal expressions that they do not state the cause for what is actually said in the main clause but rather the reason for saying it." She cites as examples Gen 32:21; 1 Sam 26:15; 1 Kgs 1:24–25.

127. The expectation of fraternal solidarity is highlighted in Judges, which begins with the tribe of Judah fighting alongside Simeon "his brother" (אחיו, 1:3, 17) and ends with the grim irony of the Israelites slaughtering the Benjamites "my brother" (אחי, 20:23, 28; cf. 21:6).

128. Carroll, *Jeremiah*, 560.

129. See Dennis Pardee et al., eds., *Handbook of Ancient Hebrew Letters: A Study Edition* (SBLSBS 15; Chico, Calif.: Scholars Press, 1982), 177, who note parallels with *pap. Mur* 42 (signatories of witnesses) and with *pap. Mur* 43 (oath formula with *m⁽yd*).

strengthened by the switch of address from the exiles (vv. 4–23) to Jeremiah
(v. 24).

v. 24. הנחלמי may be a word-play, being the Niph. ptc. of חלם ("the
dreamer").[130] This would suggest that Shemaiah is being depicted as one of the
dreamers mentioned in v. 8.

3.4. *Coherence and Redaction*
The textual and literary evidence indicates at least three stages in the composition of Jer 29: (1) the writing of the original letter; (2) the setting of the
letter in a narrative framework; and (3) expansion in MT. Defining the precise
contents of each stage is more difficult, however, and some would argue for
further redactional layers between (2) and (3).

The letter is widely agreed to comprise, at very least, vv. 5–7, with the
possible exception of ותלדנה בנים ובנות (>OG).[131] These verses possess unity of
theme (the call to peaceful life under YHWH's blessing in Babylon) and style
(semi-poetic parallelism).

The narrative framework includes the prologue (vv. 1–3) and the story of
Shemaiah's response (vv. 24–32). Regarding the former, it may be that v. 1
originally mentioned only "the elders of the exile" as the addressees, with "the
prophets and people" added later due to their prominence in chs. 27–28.[132] The
confused flow of the text in vv. 24–32 suggests that this narrative was later
partly reworked into an oracle; this would also explain the orthographic variations with proper names.[133]

The chief questions surround vv. 8–9, 10–14aα and 21–23.[134] In particular, it
is often argued that the warnings against false prophets (vv. 8–9 and 21–23) are
extraneous to the purpose of the original letter.[135] Likewise, the promise of
return from exile (vv. 10–14aα) is thought to undermine the practical, present-
oriented focus of vv. 5–7: "A prophet who is endeavouring to destroy expectations of a swift return to Jerusalem by urging exiles to cast away feverish

---

130. So L. Yaure, "Elymas—Nehelamite—Pethor," *JBL* 79 (1960): 297–314.

131. That there *was* a letter from Jeremiah to the exiles is seldom disputed, though Carroll,
Jeremiah, 552, and Smelik, "Letters to the Exiles," 284–85, remain unconvinced.

132. So too Duhm, *Jeremia*, 228; Kilpp, *Niederreißen*; 44–45; contra Graupner, *Auftrag*,
77–78.

133. Jeremiah's name reverts to its normal form ירמיהו (vv. 27, 29, 30), but both references to
Zephaniah (vv. 25, 29) use the short form צפניה. Shemaiah's name is long (שמעיהו) in v. 24, but
short (שמעיה) in vv. 31–32.

134. All these verses are seen as secondary by Duhm, *Jeremia*, 228–33; Nicholson, *Preaching*,
98–100; Wanke, *Untersuchungen*, 57–59; Thiel, *Redaktion 26–45*, 14–19; Carroll, *Jeremiah*, 556–
60; Kilpp, *Niederreißen*, 61–67; Graupner, *Auftrag*, 82–87. Hyatt, "Jeremiah," 5:1017, restricts
redaction to vv. 10–14aα and 21–23. Welch, *Jeremiah*, 171–74, sees vv. 8–9 alone as secondary;
Volz, *Jeremia*, 267–75, and Böhmer, *Heimkehr und neuer Bund*, 33–34, see vv. 10–14aα as the sole
addition.

135. Graupner, *Auftrag*, 83, describes vv. 8–9 as "Die nach V 5–7 überraschende Propheten-
polemik," while McKane, *Jeremiah 2*, 738, refers to the need to "disengage a theme which is
extensively represented in ch. 29, namely, false prophecy."

excitement and to cultivate composure does not undo his single-mindedness by inviting those whom he addresses to engage in a more distant kind of expectation," writes McKane.[136] Attention is also called to the presence of Deuteronomistic terminology in these verses; for example, נביאים and חלמים (who are further described as בקרבכם/בקרבך, vv. 8–9; cf. Deut 13:2–4), הקים דבר יהוה (v. 10; cf. Deut 9:5; 1 Kgs 2:4; 6:12; 12:15) and בכל לבם (v. 13; cf. 1 Sam 12:20; 1 Kgs 8:23; 14:8; 2 Kgs 10:31). Consequently, many scholars believe that all or some of the above verses are secondary, added with the narrative framework or at some other stage.

Without ruling out some expansion of the text, however, it is not obvious that vv. 8–9, 10–14aα and 21–23 are incompatible with vv. 5–7.[137] The claim that Jeremiah's warnings against false prophets do not belong to the original letter is valid only if one assumes an extraordinarily one-dimensional author. Dogmatic statements as to what a prophet in sixth-century Judah would or would not do are best avoided, but it is hard to see why the dampening of false hopes (implied in vv. 5–7) is incompatible with the affirmation of a more realistic hope in vv. 10–14.[138] As for the Deuteronomistic language in vv. 8–9 and 10–14, this is (once again) easier to observe than to interpret. It *may* indicate redaction, though the fact that vv. 5–7 themselves echo Deut 20:5–10 and 28:30–32 gives us pause.[139] Moreover, the injunction אל ישיאו לכם is absent from Deuteronomy, and occurs only twice in DtrH (2 Kgs 18:29; 19:10); it is more frequent in Jeremiah (Jer 4:10; 37:9; 49:16).

The third stage in the composition of Jer 29 is reflected in the longer text of MT, covering most of v. 14 and all of vv. 16–20, plus other minor additions. This material has the appearance of commentary on the preceding text, prompted by other passages in Jeremiah (especially 24:8–10) and by Deut 30. As was pointed out in Chapter 2 of the present study, however, these MT plusses belong not merely to a further phase in the literary growth of the book, but rather to a different edition of it.

Whatever the literary history of the text, interpretation must take seriously its present shape. Both in OG and MT, the prophetic letter is represented as covering all of vv. 4–23.[140] This is emphasized by YHWH's statement ואני עד (v. 23), which, as we noted earlier, echoes the conventional ending in ancient Near Eastern letters. Even the MT plus of vv. 16–20, announcing judgment on those in

---

136. McKane, *Jeremiah 2*, 737.

137. The integrity of these verses with vv. 5–7 is accepted by Rudolph, *Jeremia*, 154–57; Weiser, *Jeremia*, 261–64; Bright, *Jeremiah*, 208–9; Holladay, *Jeremiah 2*, 139–40; Jones, *Jeremiah*, 362–67. Even Wanke, *Untersuchungen*, 59, refers to "Der trotz dieser verschiedenen Erweiterungen immer noch einigermaßen gute Textzusammenhang."

138. So Rudolph, *Jeremia*, 156–57; Applegate, "Jeremiah and the Seventy Years," 97.

139. Berlin ("Jeremiah 29:5–7," 8) notes that "the deuteronomic echo in our verses is different, in a way that I am not sure I can adequately express, from the kinds of deuteronomic editorial additions usually pointed out. It is somehow more organic to the passage, more a part of the fabric of the text." However, as she herself points out (p. 7), if the allusion is intentional it demonstrates Jeremiah's familiarity with the contents of Deuteronomy.

140. So Holladay, *Jeremiah 2*, 137; cautiously, Brueggemann, *Exile and Homecoming*, 256 n. 32.

Jerusalem, has been formally integrated with the letter; as is shown by the phrases שמעו דבר יהוה (v. 19) and לא שמעתם (v. 16), אחיכם אשר לא יצאו אתכם כל הגולה (v. 20), it is still the exiles who are being addressed.

3.5. *Judicial Differentiation in Jeremiah 29:* כל הגולה בבבל / הנביאים

We can now consider what model of judicial differentiation is presented in Jer 29. In this and the following section I will focus on the text common to OG and MT, before asking how the additional material in MT affects the picture.

Jeremiah's letter to the exiles in Babylon contains a series of startling salvation promises, relating both to the present and the future. The promises of fertility and growth in vv. 5–7 not only echo the creation mandate of Gen 1:28, but also imply that the curses of Deut 28 have been lifted. Moreover, in a remarkable reversal of Jeremiah's own experience, the *Golah* are invited to pray and be heard. For the first time in the book, YHWH offers his people שלום, even if this is mediated through, and depends on, the שלום of Babylon. Further, future dimensions of salvation emerge in vv. 10–14aα. YHWH will visit (פקד) his people, not to bring disaster (as before) but to restore their descendents to Judah (v. 10). The prospect of שלום is repeated, but now as a direct gift. Above all, YHWH's salvation will involve his personal relationship with the exiles: ונראיתי (or ונגלתי) לכם (v. 14aα). Already, however, his goodwill towards them is evident from the fact that he is planning this salvation (the positive use of חשב מחשבה is in stark contrast to its threatening connotations elsewhere in Jeremiah).

As in ch. 24, no reason is given for YHWH's benevolent attitude. His promises seem to arise purely from his own initiative, arbitrary or otherwise. That his favour is in no sense *merited* is emphasized by the stern rebuke handed out to the exiles for colluding with the wrong prophets.[141] Granted, the statement about Shemaiah, ויבטח אתכם על שקר (v. 31), need only mean that he had attempted to mislead them (as in 27:15). However, in v. 8 (whether we follow OG or MT), it is clear that the exilic community *as a whole* is culpable for encouraging its dreamers. Likewise, their enthusiastic claim, הקים יהוה לנו נבאים בבלה (v. 15), is quickly refuted (vv. 21–23); the fact that in future they will regard Ahab and Zedekiah as cursed simply shows how misguided is their current opinion.

Nevertheless, although YHWH's benevolence is unrelated to the character of the exiles, his salvation also has future aspects which depend on their response. The paired imperatives in vv. 5–6 imply that the outworking of his blessing on their lives in Babylon remains conditional.[142] Similarly, the more future-oriented promises in vv. 10–14aα are contingent upon (כי, v. 13) the exiles praying and seeking him. To this extent, ch. 29 appears to develop the *potential* for future differentiation that was observed in ch. 24.

At the same time, ch. 29 goes further than ch. 24 by depicting an existing judicial polarity among the *Golah* community. Certain individuals among them

141.   Indeed, in terms of *blame*, ch. 29 blurs the people/prophets distinction much more than chs. 27–29. The Judean prophets in Babylon, it seems, were having more success than their colleagues in Jerusalem.

142.   See *GKC* §110c.

are already excluded from YHWH's salvation. Granted, Jeremiah addresses the exiles as one (אל הגולה אשר הגליתי מירושׁלם, v. 4), and this broad designation is repeated in v. 20. Yet, as I noted earlier, Jeremiah's rhetoric in this chapter serves to render the prophets as "others." Although they are described as "among you" (בקרבכם, v. 8), and even as "your prophets" (נביאיכם, v. 8), they are spoken of in the third person (vv. 8–9, 21–23, 32) or addressed separately (vv. 24–32). Moreover, like Hananiah, they stand under YHWH's judgment. Ahab and Zedekiah will be given over to Nebuchadrezzar to be burnt alive, and their names will become a curse לכל הגלות יהודה בבבל (vv. 21–22). The exact nature of Shemaiah's fate is not stated, but it is made clear (v. 32) that he too will be excluded from the community that will see YHWH's salvation (פקד here reverts to its customary negative meaning). Consequently, we find that Jer 29 presents the same judicial polarity of prophets and hearers that we saw in chs. 27–28.

4. *Judicial Differentiation in Jeremiah 27–29:* הגולה בבבל / הישבים בירושׁלם

Having seen the same form of selective judgment among the exiled and non-exiled Judeans, we can now ask if, and how, these two communities are differentiated from each other. While it is clear that ch. 29 proclaims salvation to the *Golah*, some uncertainty attaches to how this compares with the message of hope for those in Judah in ch. 27. Some commentators see in ch. 29 the same bias to the *Golah* that we find in ch. 24: "The exiles in Babylon," writes Carroll, "are presented as Yahweh's *special* concern in 24:4–7; 29:4–7, 10–14."[143] Similarly, Rubinger believes that ch. 29 reflects "Jeremiah's profound conviction about the inherent superiority of the Judean center in Babylon."[144]

This interpretation of Jer 29 is disputed, however. Notably, Seitz argues that if the MT plusses are set aside, what we find is the same principle of "submit and live" that is held out to the Judeans in ch. 27, with Jeremiah's message being in fact decidedly cool. The long term perspective of vv. 4–7 "was doubtless unpopular,"[145] while vv. 15, 21–32 contain "strong words to the exilic community and its prophets."[146] Indeed, Seitz concludes that "in the broader literary context of ch. 29, the 'good' which Yahweh promises to do for his people arguably includes the 'good' he does for those in Judah as much as the "good" he has in store for the exiles."[147] Similarly, Keown et al. claim that "the LORD's word through Jeremiah to the Judean exiles was the same as the divine message

---

143.   Carroll, *Jeremiah*, 532 (italics mine).
144.   Naphtali J. Rubinger, "Jeremiah's Epistle to the Exiles and the Field in Anathoth," *Judaism* 26 (1977): 84–91 (87).
145.   Seitz, *Theology in Conflict*, 210.
146.   Ibid., 212.
147.   Ibid., 211. Seitz believes the original letter + introduction comprises vv. 1–9, 15, 20–32. Kilpp, *Niederreißen*, 61, also interprets העם הזה in v. 32 as referring to the Jerusalem community, but assigns this latter part of the chapter to later redaction.

to Zedekiah and the others remaining in Jerusalem after 597, 'Serve the king of Babylon and you will live.'"[148] Sommer goes even further in describing the message of Jer 29 as "unremittingly bleak from the viewpoint of the individuals who received it,"[149] and emphasizing that the promises of vv. 10–14 are for the distant future.

These scholars are certainly right to highlight the less than glowing comments to the exiles in this chapter. However, my exegesis has shown that even in the shorter text represented by OG, the scope of YHWH's salvation in ch. 29 considerably exceeds that found in chs. 27–28. While the reference to remaining in and working the land in 27:11 may allude to the creation account of Gen 2:15, the injunctions of 29:5–6 go much further in both commanding and promising prosperity. If they subtly counsel against revolt, they also rescind the covenant curses; we thus have a picture of fruitfulness under divine blessing that contrasts markedly with the modest hope of ch. 27. Moreover, the invitation to pray for the good of Babylon (29:7) opens up for the exiles a vocation hitherto denied even to the prophet, and certainly not granted to those in Judah. The promise of שלום (29:7), indirect as it is, is the more striking given Jeremiah's dismissive attitude towards שלום prophecy in 28:9. Needless to say, the physical and spiritual restoration promised in vv. 10–14—that is, in the *shorter text reflected by OG*—is unparalleled in chs. 27–28. Seitz appears to attribute all of vv. 10–14, 16–20 to the Exilic Redaction, but in so doing blurs the distinction between ER and MT plus.[150] A final contrast with the salvation promised in chs. 27–28 comes in 29:32, where YHWH speaks of (ה)טוב אשר אני עשה לכם.

This disparity between the messages to the two communities is also clear from the greater emphasis on divine initiative in Jer 29. Granted, the exiles' prosperity in Babylon and their future restoration is contingent on their response. Nevertheless, the very fact that such options are open implies a prior decision on YHWH's part—a decision that Brueggemann calls "Yahweh's fresh turn towards Israel."[151] We have seen evidence for precisely such a turn in the way that ch. 29 relates to the rest of the book: reversing the prohibition on prayer (התפלל בעד), inverting an earlier expression of wrath (שלום ולא לרעה), redefining words that elsewhere signify judgment (חשב מחשבה ,פקד) and introducing a key salvific term (שוב שבות). This idea of salvation for the exiles as a divine *plan* is of course made explicit in 29:11. Consequently, whereas those in Judah are warned that listening to their prophets will mean disaster for the nation, YHWH's promises

---

148.   Keown, Scalise and Smothers, *Jeremiah 26–52*, 72.

149.   Benjamin D. Sommer, "New Light on the Composition of Jeremiah," *CBQ* 61 (1999): 646–66 (662). Cf. Holladay, *Jeremiah 2*, 144: "The words are words of judgment on the exiles for now, but words of salvation after a lapse of seventy years."

150.   Seitz, *Theology in Conflict*, 210 n. 8: "Jer 29,10–14 appears to have entered the text together with the clearly supplemental 29,16–19…vv. 11–14 are remarkably similar to the language and overall thrust of Deut 30,1–10 and 1 Kgs 8,33–34, passages which clearly presuppose the exile and point to the likelihood of an exilic author, working from the same perspective as the exilic redaction of Jeremiah."

151.   Walter Brueggemann, *Theology of the Old Testament: Testimony, Dispute, Advocacy* (Minneapolis: Fortress, 1997), 440–42.

to the exiles appear to stand *despite* the charge that they are doing precisely this (29:8, 15).

It is clear, then, that Jeremiah's message of hope to the remnant in Judah (chs. 27–28) is by no means analogous to his message of hope to the exiles in Babylon (ch. 29). A rather austere exhortation to serve the king of Babylon is replaced by an encouragement to prosper and multiply. Pure conditionality gives way to a greater emphasis on divine initiative. And, most of all, the focus on serving the king of Babylon moves to seeking YHWH for Babylon, with an underlying assurance of YHWH's accessibility and responsiveness.

5. *The Significance of the MT Plusses of Jeremiah 29*

We turn now to consider how this picture of judicial differentiation is altered or modified by the MT plusses in Jer 29:14, 16–20. This is due not simply to their length, but also to their relevance to the question of group differentiation in chs. 27–29.

In v. 14, YHWH pledges, וקבצתי אתכם מכל הגוים ומכל המקומות אשר הדחתי אתכם שם. The language is similar to that of 23:3; note especially the repetition of קבץ and נדח Hiph. Unlike the earlier passage, though, 29:14 does not even exclude Israel's leaders from the promised restoration. Consequently, scholars without exception assume that MT is here broadening the horizon from the exiled community in Babylon to a general Jewish *Diaspora* (the focus of chs. 30–33).[152] I suggest, however, that this interpretation needs to be reconsidered. If the author of the MT plus in v. 14 *did* intend to broaden his scope in this way, he has created an anachronism of which he could hardly have been unaware, given what follows: כי אמרתם הקים לנו יהוה נבאים בבלה (v. 15). Indeed, with its reference to אחיכם אשר לא יצאו אתכם בגולה, even the MT plus of vv. 16–20 keeps the focus on the Babylonian exiles. Furthermore, as I argued above, the final words of v. 14, המקום אשר הגליתי אתכם משם, appear to refer back to the geographically and historically specific כל הגולה אשר הגליתי מירושלם בבלה in v. 4. It thus seems more likely that the MT plus in 29:14 is applying the promise of general restoration to a particular group (the exiles in Babylon).

Jeremiah 29:16–20 is a judgment oracle in which YHWH announces his wrath on all those in post-597 Jerusalem: אל המלך היושב אל כסא דוד ואל כל העם היושב בעיר הזאת (v. 16). The language of vv. 17–18, and especially the fig imagery, closely parallels that of 24:8–10, though the tone is still more ferocious. Even Zedekiah's name is eschewed, while the expression כתאנים השערים (v. 17) is stronger than כתאנים הרעות (24:8). Consequently, vv. 16–20 seem to be reiterating the geographical גלות יהודה / שארית ירושלם polarity of ch. 24 (cf. Ezek 11:1–21).[153]

152.　See especially Yohanan Goldman, *Prophétie et royauté au retour de l'exil. Les origines littéraires de la forme massorétique du Livre de Jérémie* (OBO 118; Freiburg; Universitätsverlag; Göttingen: Vandenhoeck & Ruprecht, 1992), 74–75.

153.　E.g. Unterman, *Repentance to Redemption*, 84. Thiel, *Redaktion 26–45*, 17–18, argues that this was precisely the reason for the addition: "Versetzt man 15 vor 8f., schließen 16–19 direkt

On the other hand, whereas Jer 24 gives no explanation for YHWH's wrath against those in Judah, 29:16–20 supplies a two-fold rationale. The first point lies in v. 16: ‏ואל כל העם היושב בעיר הזאת אחיכם אשר לא יצאו אתכם בגולה‎.

The language here echoes the ‏ישב/יצא‎ polarity of 21:1–10, where those who stayed in Jerusalem would die, while those who surrendered would live. Unlike ch. 21, however, where the fate of the people turns on their actions during the siege of 587 and is still in the balance, in 29:16 their fate turns on their actions during the deportation of 597, and is thus settled. Salvation entails acceptance of YHWH's judicial act of exile. Not only have Zedekiah and his people refused to do so, they have not shown solidarity with their brothers who did. We may note, in passing, that by focussing on the (disobedient) actions of those in Jerusalem (‏ישב...לא יצאו‎), the author of vv. 16–20 has implicitly highlighted the (obedient) actions of the exiles: ‏לא יצאו אתכם בגולה‎. This of course contrasts with the emphasis in the rest of ch. 29, that the exiles are in Babylon due to YHWH's action (‏הגליתי‎, vv. 4, 14).[154]

The second reason for YHWH's wrath is given in v. 19: ‏תחת אשר לא שמעו אל דברי אשר שלחתי אליהם את עבדי הנבאים‎. This, of course, is a standard indictment of Israel and Judah in the Old Testament. Intriguingly, however, the final words of this verse, ‏ולא שמעתם‎, restore the focus to the *Golah* community, followed by the call, ‏ואתם שמעו דבר יהוה כל הגולה‎. The effect of this is to underline the spiritual obduracy of the exiles themselves. Despite having gone into exile, they are no better at hearing YHWH's word than their brothers in Jerusalem. Consequently, the MT plus of 29:16–20, as much as the rest of the chapter, emphasizes that while the exiles are privileged so far as YHWH's plans are concerned, they are in no position to congratulate themselves. To this extent, the verdict upon the exiles in ch. 29 echoes that in ch. 24.

On the other hand, there is clearly a major difference in perspective between 29:16–20 (also 24:1–10) and 27:12–22. In the latter, as we have seen, Jeremiah sees ongoing life for the Judean remnant as an option; the critical issue is not one of going into exile but rather submitting to Babylon. Not surprisingly, many consider it impossible to attribute both passages to the same person. The difficulty is real, though it is uncertain how optimistic Jeremiah himself was in ch. 27 that his audience would, in fact, listen to his message. Nor should the distinction between private revelation to the prophet (24:1–10) and public preaching of the prophet (27:12–22) be overlooked. Consequently, while the vision of disaster expressed in 29:16–20 may not have been apparent to Jeremiah when he delivered his "submit and live" message, it could represent a natural development of his thinking.

---

an 10–14 an, so daß eine durchgehende Parallelität zu 24,4–10 entsteht…D stellt hier wie in K. 24 Heil für die Exilierten und Gericht für die Zurückgebliebenen einander gegenüber."

154.   Of course, we do not know whether those deported in 597 (or 587) had any choice in the matter.

6. *Conclusions*

It is now possible to summarize and reflect on this study of judicial differentiation in Jer 27–29. Unlike Jer 21–24, which contains three quite distinct judicial polarities, these carefully counterbalanced chapters have yielded a more complex picture, one in which salvation and judgment are configured around two intersecting polarities.

The first is that of the two post-597 Judean communities: the remnant under Zedekiah and the exiles in Babylon. Although Jeremiah announces hope to both, the nature of this hope differs significantly. For those in Judah, there is the option of ongoing life in their own land, under the suzerainty of Babylon. The exiles, by contrast, are called to a life marked by שׁלום; even now they may prosper and pray to YHWH, while anticipating spiritual renewal and restoration to the land. Reading these words in the wider context of Jeremiah underlines their salvific importance.

Matching this disparity between the contents of the two messages is a significant difference in rationale. The entirely contingent nature of YHWH's word to Judah is clear from the alternatives, "Whoever serves the king of Babylon/Whoever does not serve the king of Babylon" (27:8, 11). Since this is bound up with the issue of prophecy, it could be reformulated as "Whoever listens to their prophets/Whoever listens to Jeremiah." Salvation depends upon obedience to YHWH and submission to Babylon. By contrast, ch. 29 lays more stress on divine initiative, while still calling the exiles to seek YHWH.

The other judicial polarity in Jer 27–29 is one of people and prophets. Partly, this is expressed through audience-critical distinctions; by being addressed separately, the prophets are rhetorically isolated. In addition, however, the named prophets Hananiah, Ahab, Zedekiah and Shemaiah receive YHWH's sentence of death. Consequently, just as elsewhere in Jeremiah individuals are exempted from disaster, so here individuals are exempted from a message of hope.[155]

The MT plus of 29:16–20 radicalizes the contrast between the exiled and non-exiled communities, so that it is now seen in the absolute terms of 24:1–10. Far from envisaging a positive future for those still in Judah, YHWH declares his wrath against them for remaining in the land. All distinctions between people and prophets here vanish; the only prophets mentioned are those whom YHWH has sent and to whom they have *not* listened. In context, however, the primary function of these verses is to rebuke the exiles themselves for failing to hear YHWH's word.

What significance do these findings have for our study of judicial differentiation in the Old Testament? Here we may highlight two points. First, bearing in mind the comments of Koenen noted earlier, it is important to emphasize that

155. I noted earlier Kilpp's observations on this point (*Niederreißen*, 61). Kilpp sees the exclusion (*die Aussonderung*) of Shemaiah from salvation in ch. 29 as a unique case in Jeremiah; however, Ahab, Zedekiah and Hananiah offer some sort of parallel, even though the nature of salvation in ch. 27 is different from that in ch. 29.

the polarity of "Salvation for the people/ Judgment on the prophets" is *in part* ethically grounded. For while at no point does Jeremiah affirm the goodness of the people (quite the opposite in ch. 29), his verdict upon the prophets is explicitly based on their words and conduct. Hananiah and Shemaiah have attempted to "make the people believe a lie" (28:15; 29:31) and have "preached rebellion against YHWH" (28:16; 29:32 MT). Ahab and Zedekiah have "preached lies in my name" (29:21) and "committed folly in Israel" (29:23). It may be the case (especially in ch. 29) that the people are encouraging them, but the text clearly implies that these prophets carry a singular degree of guilt.

Secondly, a comparison of Jeremiah's message to the two communities reveals that biblical texts are capable of depicting judicial differentiation in surprising ways. The prophetic message in Jer 27 would not normally be classified as one of judgment; on the contrary, it is one of qualified hope. When read alongside Jer 29, however, it becomes clear that Zedekiah's people are in fact *excluded* from salvation in its fullest sense. The Judean remnant, unlike the exiles, have not yet experienced "YHWH's fresh turn."

Chapter 6

JUDICIAL DIFFERENTIATION IN JEREMIAH 37–45

1. *Introduction to Jeremiah 37–45*

As I noted at the start of the previous chapter, Jer 26–45 is unanimously recognized as the second macro-unit of the book, comprising two major sub-sections: chs. 26–35(36) and 36(37)–45. This next chapter will focus on the second of these. Clearly, its length precludes discussion of every verse or even every pericope. As I will seek to show, however, the contents and structure of chs. 37–45 are such that the question of YHWH's selective judgment can be studied with reference to four passages: 38:1–3, 14–23; 39:15–18; 42:1–43:7; 45:1–5. At the same time, due account will be taken of the remaining material. As in previous chapters, I will begin by setting out the basis for viewing chs. 37–45 as a distinct unit, and this will provide a broad framework for the subsequent analysis of specific passages.

1.1. *Jeremiah 37–45 as a Literary Unit*

In the previous chapter, I argued that the story of Jehoiakim's burning of the scroll in Jer 36 marks the start, rather than the conclusion, of a literary unit.[1] In *narrative* terms, however, it is clear that a new section begins in ch. 37. Here, for the second time in the book, we move from the reign of Jehoiakim to that of Zedekiah (v. 1; cf. 27:1), with v. 2 giving an advance verdict upon both him and the nation: ולא שמע הוא ועבדיו ועם הארץ אל דברי יהוה אשר דבר ביד ירמיהו הנביא.[2] Less certain, however, is where this unit concludes. Since ch. 45 begins by referring back to Baruch's writing of the scroll in the fourth year of Jehoiakim, and since it has no *necessary* connection with the story of the Jews' flight to Egypt (chs. 43–44), it is seen by some as distinct from chs. 37–44.[3] Others argue that ch. 45 must be read in conjunction with what precedes. This is true

---

1. Alone in rejecting both options is Elmer A. Martens, "Narrative Parallelism and Message in Jeremiah 34–38," in *Early Jewish and Christian Exegesis. Studies in Memory of William Hugh Brownlee* (ed. Craig A. Evans and William F. Stinespring; Atlanta: Scholars Press, 1987), 33–49. He argues that "chaps. 34–38 comprise a unit *as the material now stands*" (p. 38, italics original).

2. Sean McEvenue, "The Composition of Jeremiah 37.1 to 44.30," in *Studies in Wisdom Literature*, special issue of *OTWSA* 15–16 (ed. W. C. van Wyk; Pretoria, 1972), 59–67, sees chs. 37–44 as depicting the outworking of this opening statement.

3. So McEvenue, "Composition of Jeremiah," 65; Holladay, *Jeremiah 2*, 282; Keown, Scalise and Smothers, *Jeremiah 26–52*, 209–11.

not only of those who view it as the final episode of Baruch's "passion narrative" (*Leidensgeschichte*),[4] but also of others who see it as an appropriate conclusion (if not continuation) of the story.[5] Scholarly ambivalence on this point is reflected in descriptions of the unit as chs. 37–44(45).[6]

Let us consider first the case for the unity of Jer 37–44. On the one hand, these eight chapters present an extended, chronologically arranged story, in two parts. Chapters 37–39 describe events leading up to the fall of Jerusalem in 587, while chs. 40–44 depict its aftermath, including Gedaliah's governorship of Judah, his assassination by the Ammonite-backed Ishmael, and finally the Judeans' flight to Egypt. Bearing in mind how earlier sections of Jeremiah have oscillated between the reigns of Jehoiakim, Jehoiachin and Zedekiah, the sustained historical sequence of chs. 37–44 is striking. "Here," writes Jones, "the reader is conscious of moving into a different and unique section of the book... They need to be read as a whole."[7]

At the same time, chs. 37–44 are more than a historical chronicle. Different perspectives and emphases notwithstanding, when read as a whole they convey a particular theological message, namely, the disobedience of the entire nation of Judah to YHWH and the disaster that thus befalls them. As was seen in Chapter 2 of this study, this point has been underlined especially by Pohlmann, who sees in this narrative the fulfilment of the prophecy of 24:8–10:

> Im blick auf Jer 21,1–10/Jer 24 enthalten die Kapitel Jer 37–44 zudem den Nachweis, daß sich diese Prophetenworte erfüllt haben. Denn der für die jetzige Textgestalt von Jer 37–44 zuständige Verfasser (oder Redaktor) kommt in seiner Darstellung der Geschichte Judas nach der Eroberung Jerusalem zu dem Ergebnis, daß schließlich das Land gänzlich verlassen und ohne Bewohner war (vgl. Jer 24,10) und der nach Ägypten abgewanderte Rest des Volkes (vgl. Jer 24,8) sich selbst disqualifiziert hat. Jer 21,1–10/Jer 24 und Jer 37–44 sind folglich nach dem Schema "Weissagung und Erfüllung" aufeinander abgestimmt.[8]

It will be noted that Pohlmann does not try to incorporate Jer 45 within this theological schema, and indeed, he has very little to say about this chapter. Two other scholars, who do in fact include ch. 45 in the literary unit, nonetheless accept Pohlmann's interpretation of chs. 37–44. Nicholson sees their unifying theme as the rejection of YHWH's word, the consequences of which for Jerusalem are set out in 37:1–40:6 and for the Judean remnant in 40:7–44,[9] while McConville describes these chapters as "essentially an application of the theology of chs. 21 and 24 to the events that lead up to and into the exile."[10]

---

4.   Notably Kremers, "Leidensgemeinschaft," 130–31 (but see further below).

5.   See especially Carroll, *Jeremiah*, 669–70, 745; also Kessler, "Jeremiah Chapters 26–45 Reconsidered," 85; Nicholson, *Preaching*, 107; Hobbs, "Some Remarks," 193; Thompson, *Jeremiah*, 631; McConville, *Judgment and Promise*, 111, 122; Stulman, *Order Amid Chaos*, 72–73, 88–93.

6.   E.g. Pohlmann, *Studien*, 48; Jones, *Jeremiah*, 36.

7.   Jones, *Jeremiah*, 36; similarly, Nicholson, *Preaching*, 18.

8.   Pohlmann, *Studien*, 185.

9.   Nicholson, *Preaching*, 104–13; see too Clements, *Jeremiah*, 203, 228.

10.   McConville, *Judgment and Promise*, 112. He adds that ch. 45 "stands somewhat aside from the main argument of the preceding discussion" (p. 121).

Thus, considerations of narrative and theme appear to demarcate Jer 37–44 as a literary unit. This analysis would seem to be confirmed by ch. 45 itself. As has been said, 45:1 explicitly locates the oracle to Baruch in the time of Jehoiakim, and refers us back to ch. 36. Moreover, its character as a personal salvation oracle stands in contrast to the preceding chapters, which focus on YHWH's judgment on Judah as a whole. Consequently, a good case can be made for treating chs. 37–44 as a self-contained unit, and regarding chs. 36 and 45 as "the brackets and boundaries which contain the entire narrative."[11] Indeed, this point was tacitly conceded by Kremers; on the one hand, he terms chs. 37–45 an *Erzählungszyklus*,[12] to which the oracle to Baruch is the conclusion, but then, noting that 45:1 refers back to 36, adds, "dadurch ist sein Erzählungszyklus von Kap. 36 und Kap. 45 wie von einer Klammer umgeben."[13]

There is, however, one very strong argument for treating Jer 45 as an integral part of chs. 37–44. As has often been noted, it forms a striking parallel with another individual salvation oracle, namely, that to Ebed-Melech in 39:15–18. Apart from their similarity of genre, both conclude with the promise of "life as booty" (39:18; 45:5) for their respective recipients. Indeed, these two brief oracles seem to be counter-balanced, so that 39:15–18 concludes the account of the fall of Jerusalem, and 45:1–5 the story of the flight to Egypt. This suggests that both are crucial for the interpretation of chs. 37–44 in their final form. Consequently, I will take chs. 37–45 as a meaningful literary entity within the final form of the book.[14]

It is, of course, accepted that this unity of narrative and theology relates to chs. 37–45 *in this present form*. Few would deny that the editor has utilized and adapted earlier material. As we will see later, chs. 37 and 38 are seen by many as doublets, as are the two accounts of the release of Jeremiah. In the first (39:11–14), he is released from the courtyard of the guard directly into the care of Gedaliah; in the second (40:1–6), he is set free at Ramah after being rounded up with the other Judean captives.[15] Immediately after this second release account, we have an extended narrative (40:7–41:18) describing Gedaliah's fledgling community, and the turmoil that follows his assassination; oddly, this makes no mention of Jeremiah.[16] "The simplest explanation," write Keown et al., "is to suggest the incorporation into the larger narrative of historical information that

---

11.   Brueggemann, *Exile and Homecoming*, 338. Similarly, Thiel, *Redaktion 26–45*, 102, notes that "Anfang und Ende dieser großen Einheit verweisen durch Datierung und inhaltlichen Kontrast aufeinander." See too Stulman, *Order Amid Chaos*, 89.

12.   Kremers, "Leidensgemeinschaft," 130.

13.   Ibid., 131.

14.   One must therefore question Pohlmann's exclusion of ch. 45 from his analysis of chs. 37–44. It is also noticeable that he has little to say about 39:15–18, describing it simply as a late interpolation (*Studien*, 99).

15.   Thompson, *Jeremiah*, 648: "It is thus clear that the editor had two stories before him both of which were included in the book."

16.   Nor is Jeremiah mentioned in the account of the fall of Jerusalem (39:1–10), but as he is imprisoned during this time, this is less surprising.

originally had no connection with Jeremiah."[17] Chapter 44, containing Jeremiah's speech to the Jews in Egypt, is somewhat disconnected from the preceding narrative (note the introductory formula, הדבר אשר היה אל ירמיהו, v. 1a) and reads as a postscript.[18] And, as we shall see, even within smaller sections scholars detect different voices.

2. *Jeremiah 38(45):1–3, 14–23*

2.1. *Text*

וישמע שפטיה בן מתן וגדליהו	1	καὶ ἤκουσε Σαφατιας υἱὸς Ματθαν καὶ
בן פשחור ויוכל בן שלמיהו		Γοδολιας υἱὸς Πασχωρ καὶ Ιωαχαλ υἱὸς
ופשחור בן מלכיה את הדברים		Σελεμιου τοὺς λόγους οὓς Ιερεμιας ἐλάλει
אשר ירמיהו מדבר אל כל העם לאמר		ἐπὶ τὸν ὄχλον λέγων
כה אמר יהוה הישב בעיר הזאת	2	οὕτως εἶπε κύριος ὁ κατοικῶν ἐν τῇ πόλει
ימות בחרב ברעב ובדבר והיצא		ταύτῃ ἀποθανεῖται ἐν ῥομφαίᾳ καὶ ἐν
אל הכשדים יחיה והיתה לו נפשו		λιμῷ καὶ ὁ ἐκπορευόμενος πρὸς τοὺς
לשלל וחי		Χαλδαίους ζήσεται καὶ ἔσται ἡ ψυχὴ
		αὐτοῦ εἰς εὕρεμα καὶ ζήσεται
כה אמר יהוה הנתן תנתן העיר	3	ὅτι οὕτως εἶπε κύριος παραδιδομένη
הזאת ביד חיל מלך בבל ולכדה		παραδοθήσεται ἡ πόλις αὕτη εἰς χεῖρας
		δυνάμεως βασιλέως Βαβυλῶνος καὶ
		συλλήμψεται αὐτήν
וישלח המלך צדקיהו ויקח את	14	καὶ ἀπέστειλεν ὁ βασιλεὺς καὶ ἐκάλεσεν
ירמיהו הנביא אליו אל מבוא		αὐτὸν πρὸς ἑαυτὸν εἰς οἰκίαν ασελισηλ
השלישי אשר בבית יהוה ויאמר		τὴν ἐν οἴκῳ κυρίου καὶ εἶπεν αὐτῷ ὁ
המלך אל ירמיהו שאל אני אתך		βασιλεύς ἐρωτήσω σε λόγον καὶ μὴ
דבר אל תכחד ממני דבר		κρύψῃς ἀπ' ἐμοῦ ῥῆμα
ויאמר ירמיהו אל צדקיהו כי	15	καὶ εἶπεν Ιερεμιας τῷ βασιλεῖ ἐὰν
אגיד לך הלוא המת תמיתני וכי		ἀναγγείλω σοι οὐχὶ θανάτῳ με
איעצך לא תשמע אלי		θανατώσεις καὶ ἐὰν συμβουλεύσω σοι οὐ
		μὴ ἀκούσῃς μου
וישבע המלך צדקיהו אל	16	καὶ ὤμοσεν αὐτῷ ὁ βασιλεὺς λέγων ζῇ
ירמיהו בסתר לאמר חי יהוה את		κύριος ὃς ἐποίησεν ἡμῖν τὴν ψυχὴν ταύτην
אשר עשה לנו את הנפש הזאת אם		εἰ ἀποκτενῶ σε καὶ εἰ δώσω σε εἰς χεῖρας
אמיתך ואם אתנך ביד האנשים		τῶν ἀνθρώπων τούτων
האלה אשר מבקשים את נפשך		
ויאמר ירמיהו אל צדקיהו כה	17	καὶ εἶπεν αὐτῷ Ιερεμιας οὕτως εἶπε
אמר יהוה אלהי צבאות אלהי		κύριος ἐὰν ἐξελθὼν ἐξέλθῃς πρὸς
ישראל אם יצא תצא אל שרי מלך		ἡγεμόνας βασιλέως Βαβυλῶνος ζήσεται ἡ
בבל וחיתה נפשך והעיר הזאת לא		ψυχή σου καὶ ἡ πόλις αὕτη οὐ μὴ
תשרף באש וחיתה אתה וביתך		κατακαυθῇ ἐν πυρί καὶ ζήσῃ σὺ καὶ ἡ οἰκία
		σου

---

17. Keown, Scalise and Smothers, *Jeremiah 26–52*, 242. According to Carroll, *Jeremiah*, 701, Jeremiah's absence "is inexplicable except on the grounds that 2 Kgs 25:22–26 has no place for him either." But see Wanke, *Untersuchungen*, 113.

18. Keown, Scalise and Smothers, *Jeremiah 26–52*, 262, describe it as "a self-standing oracle."

ואם לא תצא אל שרי מלך בבל ונתנה העיר הזאת ביד הכשדים ושרפוה באש ואתה לא תמלט מידם	18	καὶ ἐὰν μὴ ἐξέλθῃς δοθήσεται ἡ πόλις αὕτη εἰς χεῖρας τῶν Χαλδαίων καὶ καύσουσιν αὐτὴν ἐν πυρί καὶ σὺ οὐ μὴ σωθῇς
ויאמר המלך צדקיהו אל ירמיהו אני דאג את היהודים אשר נפלו אל הכשדים פן יתנו אתי בידם והתעללו בי	19	καὶ εἶπεν ὁ βασιλεὺς τῷ Ιερεμια ἐγὼ λόγον ἔχω τῶν Ιουδαίων τῶν πεφευγότων πρὸς τοὺς Χαλδαίους μὴ δώσι με εἰς χεῖρας αὐτῶν καὶ καταμωκήσονταί μου
ויאמר ירמיהו לא יתנו שמע נא בקול יהוה לאשר אני דבר אליך וייטב לך ותחי נפשך	20	καὶ εἶπεν Ιερεμιας οὐ μὴ παραδῶσί σε ἄκουσον λόγον κυρίου ὃν ἐγὼ λέγω πρὸς σέ καὶ βέλτιον ἔσται σοι καὶ ζήσεται ἡ ψυχή σου
ואם מאן אתה לצאת זה הדבר אשר הראני יהוה	21	καὶ εἰ μὴ θέλεις σὺ ἐξελθεῖν οὗτος ὁ λόγος ὃν ἔδειξέ μοι κύριος
והנה כל הנשים אשר נשארו בבית מלך יהודה מוצאות אל שרי מלך בבל והנה אמרות הסיתוך ויכלו לך אנשי שלמך הטבעו בבץ רגלך נסגו אחור	22	καὶ ἰδοὺ πᾶσαι αἱ γυναῖκες αἱ καταλειφθεῖσαι ἐν οἰκίᾳ βασιλέως Ιουδα ἐξήγοντο πρὸς ἄρχοντας βασιλέως Βαβυλῶνος καὶ αὗται ἔλεγον ἠπάτησάν σε καὶ δυνήσονταί σοι ἄνδρες εἰρηνικοί σου καὶ καταλύσουσιν ἐν ὀλισθήμασι πόδας σου ἀπέστρεψαν ἀπὸ σοῦ
ואת כל נשיך ואת בניך מוצאים אל הכשדים ואתה לא תמלט מידם כי ביד מלך בבל תתפש ואת העיר הזאת תשרף באש	23	καὶ τὰς γυναῖκάς σου καὶ τὰ τέκνα σου ἐξάξουσι πρὸς τοὺς Χαλδαίους καὶ σὺ οὐ μὴ σωθῇς ὅτι ἐν χειρὶ βασιλέως Βαβυλῶνος συλλημφθήσῃ καὶ ἡ πόλις αὕτη κατακαυθήσεται

2.2. *Textual Notes*

v. 14. MT ויקח את ירמיהו הנביא; OG καὶ ἐκάλεσεν αὐτόν. The proper name and title are typical MT plusses. OG probably read ויקחהו (as in 37:17), rather than ויקרא לו/אתו. Pohlmann remarks that the sequence וישלח...ויקח (Gen 20:2; 2 Sam 9:5; 1 Kgs 7:13) is just as possible as וישלח...ויקרא (Gen 31:4; Exod 9:27; Num 16:12).[19]

v. 19. MT אני דאג; OG ἐγὼ λόγον ἔχω. This usage of ἔχειν λόγον ("to take account of, have regard for") to render דאג recurs in 42(49):16.

MT והתעללו בי; OG καταμωκήσονται μου. In contrast to καταμωκάομαι ("to mock"), עלל Hith. usually implies a more violent form of abuse (1 Sam 31:4 = 1 Chr 10:4; Judg 19:25). However, the idea of mockery is present in Num 22:29 (the only instance of עלל Hith. in the Pentateuch), where LXX translates with παίζω ("to play, to jest").

v. 22. MT הטבעו בבץ רגלך; OG καταλύσουσιν ἐν ὀλισθήμασι πόδας σου. MT takes רגלך as the subject and points the verb as Hoph. הָטְבְּעוּ, "your foot is sunk." In OG, πόδας (accusative) indicates that the ἄνδρες εἰρηνικοί σου are the subject, with הטבעו being read as Hiph. הִטְבִּעוּ, "they made your feet sink down." If the latter reading is accepted, v. 22 has a single subject, the "men of your peace"; having misled Zedekiah and dragged him into the mud, they abandon him (סוג, v. 22bβ).

19. Pohlmann, *Studien*, 85 n. 167.

v. 23. MT תִּשָׂרֵף, "You will burn (this city)"; OG κατακαυθήσεται, "(This city) will be burnt." MT yields an interesting reading, but we should probably repoint to תִּשָּׂרֵף.[20]

2.3. *Exegesis*

v. 14. שֹׁאֵל אֲנִי אֹתְךָ דָּבָר. Like בקשׁ and דרשׁ, the term שֹׁאֵל can denote seeking an oracle through a prophet (1 Sam 28:16) and this may be the case here.[21] However, the combination שֹׁאֵל...דָּבָר suggests simply "ask you something";[22] cf. 2 Sam 14:18, אַל נָא תְכַחֲדִי מִמֶּנִּי דָּבָר אֲשֶׁר אָנֹכִי שֹׁאֵל אֹתָךְ. Even in 37:17 (וַיִּשְׁאָלֵהוּ הַמֶּלֶךְ...וַיֹּאמֶר הֲיֵשׁ דָּבָר מֵאֵת יהוה), Zedekiah is asking Jeremiah whether he has received an oracle, rather than asking him to consult YHWH for one.

אַל תְּכַחֵד. This too implies that Zedekiah believes Jeremiah already knows what YHWH's word is. Pohlmann notes that the phrase is used when unpleasant news is expected (Josh 7:19; 1 Sam 3:17, 18; 2 Sam 14:18).[23]

v. 15. כִּי אַגִּיד לְךָ...וְכִי אִיעָצֶךָ. Some commentators see the prophet's hesitation as surprising (and perhaps indicative of redactional activity), since his rough treatment so far has been at the hands of the שָׂרִים (37:14–16; 38:4–6), from whom Zedekiah has twice acted to protect him (37:21; 38:10).[24]

v. 16. חַי יהוה אֲשֶׁר עָשָׂה לָנוּ אֶת הַנֶּפֶשׁ הַזֹּאת. This oath formula is otherwise unattested in the Old Testament. For Rudolph, its significance is that "wer in Gott den Schöpfer des Lebens ehrt, kann nicht eines seiner Geschöpfe ums Leben bringen."[25] From the narrator's point of view, however, it may be significant that Zedekiah does not respond to the second part of Jeremiah's prediction, לֹא תִשְׁמַע אֵלָי (cf. 37:2).

הָאֲנָשִׁים הָאֵלֶּה can only be the שָׂרִים who placed Jeremiah in the cistern (v. 6). A clear antecedent is provided by Ebed-Melech's protest to Zedekiah in v. 9, הֵרֵעוּ הָאֲנָשִׁים הָאֵלֶּה, though at this point OG reads quite differently (ἐπονηρεύσω ἃ ἐποίησας = הֲרֵעוֹת אֵת אֲשֶׁר עָשִׂיתָ).

v. 17. אִם יָצֹא תֵצֵא. The use of the infinitive absolute emphasizes the requirement, and provides a point of variation from Jeremiah's similar declarations to the people (21:9; 38:2). Cf. Jeremiah's ultimatum to the remnant in 42:10, אִם שׁוֹב תֵּשְׁבוּ.

v. 19. אֲנִי דֹאֵג אֶת הַיְּהוּדִים אֲשֶׁר נָפְלוּ אֶל הַכַּשְׂדִּים פֶּן יִתְּנוּ אֹתִי בְּיָדָם. The term דאג occurs again in 42:16 (otherwise in Jeremiah only in 17:8). Exactly why Zedekiah would have feared those who had gone over to the Babylonians is

20. So Giesebrecht, *Jeremia*, 207; Rudolph, *Jeremia*, 228; Bright, *Jeremiah*, 228; Thompson, *Jeremiah*, 641 n. 4; Holladay, *Jeremiah 2*, 268; McKane, *Jeremiah 2*, 961; contra Streane, *Jeremiah*, 255.

21. Bright, *Jeremiah*, 231; Thompson, *Jeremiah*, 642; cautiously, Carroll, *Jeremiah*, 684.

22. So Holladay, *Jeremiah 2*, 290 ("I have something to ask you").

23. Pohlmann, *Studien*, 85 n. 170.

24. Pohlmann, *Studien*, 85; Holladay, *Jeremiah 2*, 290. Granted, Jeremiah may not have been aware that his rescue by Ebed-Melech was sanctioned by the king, but neither need he have known of the king's assent to the actions of the שָׂרִים in the first place (38:5).

25. Rudolph, *Jeremia*, 207.

unstated, but reprisals may have come from those who resented the suffering caused by the siege, as well as long-term political opponents.[26]

v. 20. וייטב לך. Here too, Jeremiah's promise to Zedekiah exceeds what was said to the people of Jerusalem. What "it will go well with you" means in practical terms is unspecified. In 40:9, the phrase seems to signify a peaceful life under Babylonian rule, but it also occurs on the lips of the military officers in 42:6. There, as here, the hope that "it will go well" is not considered incompatible with receiving a "bad" word from YHWH.

v. 21. זה הדבר אשר הראני יהוה. As Pohlmann notes, הראני יהוה with דבר as object occurs also in Num 23:3 and Ezek 11:25.[27] However, especially when seen in its wider context, the phrase also recalls Micaiah's words to Ahab and Jehoshaphat, ראיתי את כל ישראל נפצים (1 Kgs 22:17). Although not qualified by an "if" clause, a conditional aspect seems to be implied by the kings' question, הנלך אל רמת גלעד למלחמה אם נחדל (v. 15a). Only in vv. 19–23 does it emerge that their decision to go to war, and so to suffer disaster (רעה), is certain; and with this latter point, we may compare how the hypothetical scenario of Jer 38:21–22 becomes more certain in v. 23.[28]

v. 22. כל הנשים אשר נשארו בבית מלך יהודה. The identity of these people is unclear, though Pohlmann detects an allusion to the deportation of Jehoiachin's wives in 2 Kgs 24:15.[29]

והנה אמרות. The tone of the women's song is debated.[30] Rudolph resists the idea that it forms a taunt: "Warum sollten die Frauen über das Unglück ihres geliebten Herrn oder ihres Gebieters spotten, das doch ihr eigenes war?"[31] Certainly, הסיתוך ויכלו לך אנשי שלמך *can* be read as mockery (cf. Obad 7).[32] On the other hand, Jeremiah uses similar language of himself in his final lament: כל אנוש שלומי שמרי צלעי אולי יפתה ונוכלה לו (20:10). Ultimately, what settles the matter in favour of the taunt-interpretation is the wider context of the verse; since the advice of the trusted friends stands in opposition to that of YHWH's prophet, Zedekiah's downfall is due to culpable folly, rather than misfortune. This is emphasized if the writer intends us to see in אנשי שלמך an allusion to the prophets of שלום (27–28; 37:19).[33]

---

26. Cf. Duhm, *Jeremia*, 306; Rudolph, *Jeremia*, 207; Thompson, *Jeremiah*, 642; Brueggemann, *Exile and Homecoming*, 367; Keown, Scalise and Smothers, *Jeremiah 26–52*, 225. Either way, it was hardly a "strange excuse," as Skinner, *Prophecy and Religion*, 257, thought.

27. Pohlmann, *Studien*, 89 n. 190.

28. McKane, *Jeremiah 2*, 958, claims that "a 'hypothetical vision' seems to teeter on the edge of nonsense," adding that "Cornill's justification of the 'hypothetical vision,' that the setting out of alternatives is a formality, and that the vision contains Jeremiah's foreknowledge of the outcome, is a move out of the frying pan into the fire" (p. 959). Reflection on the Micaiah story might have led to a different conclusion. In fact, it is surprising that few commentators connect the two passages.

29. Pohlmann, *Studien*, 89 n. 192.

30. Holladay, *Jeremiah 2*, 290: "Outwardly a lament, inwardly it is a taunt-song."

31. Rudolph, *Jeremia*, 207; similarly, A. S. Peake, *Jeremiah and Lamentations*. Vol. 2, *Jeremiah XXV to LII, Lamentations* (CB; Edinburgh: T. & T. Clark, 1911), 173.

32. Cf. NIV's rendering of this phrase, "they overcame you, those trusted friends of yours."

33. McKane, *Jeremiah 2*, 960.

הטבעו בבץ רגלך. The fate envisaged for Zedekiah mirrors that suffered by
Jeremiah in 38:6, ויטבע ירמיהו בטיט.

2.4. Coherence and Redaction

Jeremiah 38:14–23 presents Zedekiah's second interview with the prophet, the
first having been reported in 37:17–21. The relationship between these two
interviews, and indeed between the two chapters, is open to different interpretations. Some scholars see in chs. 37–38 a continuous sequence of events, and find
it quite plausible that Zedekiah held two separate audiences with the prophet.[34]
There is a problem in that the second interview begins with Jeremiah being
brought from the courtyard of the guard (38:13) but ends with him pleading not
to be sent back (שוב Hiph.) to the house of Jonathan (38:26–27); Volz attempts
to solve this by relocating 38:24–28 to immediately after 37:17–21.[35]

On the other hand, Skinner's proposal that chs. 37 and 38 contain duplicate
accounts of the same sequence of events has more recently gained wider acceptance (though with varying descriptions of these chapters as "contradictory" or
"complementary").[36] As Bright observes, "everything seems to happen to
Jeremiah twice!"[37] On this view, 38:14–23 offers an alternative (and considerably longer) version of Jeremiah's advice to Zedekiah to that given in 37:17.

As regards the verses with which we are concerned, the cohesion and
integrity of 38:1–3 is unquestioned. On the other hand, considerable debate
surrounds vv. 14–23. Pohlmann believes the original text consisted of vv. 14,
17, 19–22,[38] the purpose of which was to show "daß Jahwe bis zuletzt durch
seinen Propheten die Möglichkeit angeboten hatte, der drohenden Katastrophe
zu entgehen."[39] However, while the emphasis is on Zedekiah's personal salvation, Pohlmann notes that his response to Jeremiah's message is depicted as
having wider significance. Regarding v. 17 he writes: "Es handelt sich um eine
an eine Bedingung geknüpfte Heilszusage. Die Erfüllung der Bedingung ist
allein Sache des Königs. Entsprechend gilt zunächst die anschließende Heilszusage dem König, dann aber auch 'dieser Stadt' (והעיר הזאת לא תשרף) und
abschließend wieder dem König und 'seinem Hause.'"[40] In fact, there is a further
reference to the king's house in v. 22. Pohlmann is uncertain, however, whether
the reference to "this city" in v. 17b should be retained as original, since the fate

---

34. Volz, *Jeremia*, 335–45; Rudolph, *Jeremia*, 204; Holladay, *Jeremiah 2*, 282. According to
Hyatt, "Jeremiah," 1076, "It is not at all improbable that the king, in his nervous state, did summon
the prophet twice."

35. Volz, *Jeremia*, 336; similarly Rudolph, *Jeremia*, 207, and Hyatt, "Jeremiah," 5:1078.

36. So Skinner, *Prophecy and Religion*, 258–59 n. 1; Bright, *Jeremiah*, 233–34; Thompson,
Jeremiah, 636–37; Carroll, *Jeremiah*, 679; McKane, *Jeremiah 2*, 968–71; Jones, *Jeremiah*, 455;
Clements, *Jeremiah*, 220.

37. Bright, *Jeremiah*, 233.

38. See Pohlmann, *Studien*, 84–89, 92.

39. Ibid., 92. He notes that v. 19 "hat kompositions- und erzähltechnisch eine retardierende
Aufgabe und ist für die folgenden Ausführungen des Propheten wichtig," (88) while vv. 20–22
"unbedingt erforderlich sind" after v. 19 (p. 89).

40. Ibid., 87; see too 88 n. 189.

of Jerusalem is otherwise mentioned only in the redactional vv. 18, 23. I will
return to this point shortly.

As for secondary elements, Pohlmann judges the depiction of Jeremiah as
fearful of the king (vv. 15–16) to be inconsistent with vv. 7–13 (where Zedekiah
acts on his behalf), and at odds with the character portrayal in vv. 19–22. Also
problematic is the change in Jeremiah's demeanour, from being hesitant (v. 15)
to insistent (vv. 17–18). Pohlmann concludes that vv. 15–16 have been added in
the light of 38:1–6. At first sight, v. 18 appears to be an integral part of
Jeremiah's reply to Zedekiah, but it is in fact redundant given of vv. 20–21:
"Diese zweifache Erörterung der Folgen einer möglichen Weigerung Zedekias
kann nicht ursprünglich sein."[41] Finally, like many scholars Pohlmann deems
v. 23 a redactional comment on v. 22: "Ein späterer Bearbeiter vermißte hier die
Erwähnung der Söhne des Königs, ferner eine noch einmal verdeutlichende
Festellung, daß Zedekia sich nicht retten werde, besonders aber die ausdrück-
liche Einbeziehung der vollkommenen Zerstörung Jerusalems."[42]

A somewhat similar approach is taken by Seitz, who sees in ch. 38 material
from the Scribal Chronicle and the Exilic Redaction.[43] Belonging to the former
are vv. 1–3, the outlook of which is "perfectly consistent with [Jeremiah's] post-
597 counsel,"[44] and vv. 16–22; here too, Jeremiah's words are "consistent with
his earlier statements, though the alternatives are now more pronounced (38.17–
18/19–22)."[45] Supplementation by ER occurs only in v. 15 (which depicts
Zedekiah, rather than the princes, as hostile to Jeremiah), and v. 23, which "does
away with the question of alternatives and the possibility of submission."[46]
Thus, while Seitz accepts more of 38:15–23 as original than does Pohlmann,
both take vv. 15 and 23 as secondary.[47]

In response, I suggest that the entire passage is best read as a coherent whole.
This is not to deny elements of surprise and ambiguity in the text, but rather to

---

41.   Ibid., 88. Pohlmann seeks to strengthen his case (pp. 87–88) by contrasting the "purely
theoretical" anticipation of Zedekiah's refusal to surrender in v. 18, with that in vv. 19–21, where it
has a more concrete basis in his fear of the Jews. The argument is weak; the shift to greater
specificity enables the dialogue to unfold in artistic fashion (see further below).

42.   Pohlmann, *Studien*, 89; so too Duhm, *Jeremia*, 307; Volz, *Jeremia*, 343; Thiel, *Redaktion
26–45*, 54; Wanke, *Untersuchungen*, 94 n. 9.

43.   Seitz, *Theology in Conflict*, 238–39, 261–63. Unlike Pohlmann, Seitz retains v. 16 in the
original text (262 n. 150).

44.   Ibid., 260.

45.   Ibid., 262.

46.   Ibid., 262. Earlier (p. 224), however, Seitz lists vv. 21–22 among ER material, pressing for
"the inevitability of further disobedience and the necessity of a judgment which will bring about the
final elimination of the post-597 remnant." In fact, he acknowledges (257 n. 137) that he has
modified his view on 38:22. However, his conclusion regarding vv. 21–22 has important implications for his overall approach, for it implies that the distinction between SC and ER is not so clear-
cut as he elsewhere maintains. SC, apparently, can sound as ominous a note concerning Zedekiah
as ER.

47.   For his part, McKane, *Jeremiah 2*, 966, regards v. 22 as "a message of unconditional doom"
and therefore incompatible with vv. 17–18.

see them as contributing to a skilfully narrated story.[48] Thus, Jeremiah's initial hesitation, and the response which this elicits (vv. 15–16), serve to delay what will in fact be YHWH's final word to the king, thereby heightening the suspense.[49] Moreover, Zedekiah's oath, though solemn, is flawed by what it omits; Jeremiah will be protected, but not necessarily heeded. The reader is thereby given a hint of the outcome (v. 24), as well as an echo of the opening statement in 37:2. What, then, of v. 23? While this does indeed foreclose on the conditional hope set out in vv. 17–22, this does not necessarily mark it out as redactional. Two other Old Testament passages may be relevant here.

The first is the story of Micaiah in 1 Kgs 22, to which reference was made earlier. Here, his initial oracle to Ahab and Jehoshaphat is wholly positive: "Go up, and be successful, for YHWH will give [Ramoth-gilead] into the king's hand" (v. 15). Reminded to speak only what YHWH tells him, however, Micaiah abruptly changes his message: "I saw all Israel scattered on the hills, like sheep without a shepherd" (v. 17). At this stage, it is still possible to construe his vision as hypothetical, contingent upon whether the kings go to war or not. Only then does Micaiah announce what YHWH has shown him in a vision: that YHWH has sent a lying spirit to speak through the other prophets, and so lead Israel and Judah to disaster (vv. 19–23).

The second passage is the account of Samuel's speech to Israel in 1 Sam 12:1–25. Here, Samuel openly denounces their demand for a king as evil (vv. 12, 17, 20). Now that they have got their wish, however, what of their future? The prophet's message seems to offer hope. If the people and their king serve YHWH, all will be well (vv. 14, 22–24); if they reject his commands, his hand will be against them (v. 15). Ostensibly, their future is open and conditional upon their obedience. But, as several commentators have noted, the tone of the entire speech is heavily coloured by its closing words: ואם הרע תרעו גם אתם גם מלככם תספו (v. 25).[50] While formally this does no more than set out a possible future scenario, its placement right at the end of the speech, with no further comment, serves as a broad hint to the reader as to what will happen.

There are of course major differences between these two passages and Jer 38:14–23. Yet what they all have in common is the use of irony and ambiguity in prophetic speeches which purport to offer their hearers genuinely live options. Micaiah presents two contradictory messages, before revealing that the issue is foreclosed. Samuel depicts obedience and blessing as a viable option, but leaves us in little doubt that it will not happen. I suggest, then, that to regard Jer 38:23 as redactional on the grounds that it forecloses on what Jeremiah has previously said is to miss the point.

---

48. Carroll, *Jeremiah*, 685–86, notes a number of distinctive features in this unit, such as the setting of the dialogue, the oath and the poetic fragment, adding that they "make for a more interesting exchange of opinions between king and prophet and indicate some of the story-teller's skills" (686). See too Brueggemann, *Exile and Homecoming*, 364–65.

49. Pohlmann (*Studien*, 88) makes a similar point in regard to v. 19: "V. 19 hat kompositions- und erzähltechnisch eine retardierende Aufgabe."

50. See David M. Gunn, *The Fate of King Saul: An Interpretation of a Biblical Story* (JSOTSup 14; Sheffield: JSOT, 1980), 65; Gordon, *1 and 2 Samuel*, 130.

2.5. *Judicial Differentiation in Jeremiah 38:1–3, 14–23:* / הישבים / היצאים / המלך צדקיהו

However we explain the idea of Jeremiah speaking to all the people (38:1) after having been placed in the courtyard of the guard (37:21), his proclamation in 38:1–3 clearly reiterates the simple differentiation we have already encountered in 21:1–10, namely, salvation for היצאים and judgment for הישבים. His ultima-tum in v. 2, הישב בעיר הזאת ימות בחרב ברעב ובדבר והיצא אל הכשדים יחיה והיתה לו נפשו לשלל, repeats 21:9 almost verbatim, while his declaration in v. 3 that YHWH was giving the city over to the Babylonians summarizes 21:4–7.

At first sight, Jeremiah's message to Zedekiah in vv. 14–23 seems identical to this. He too must choose whether or not to go out to the Babylonians (אם יצא תצא...ואם לא תצא, vv. 17–18). If he does, he will live (וחיתה נפשך, v. 17); if he refuses, he will not escape (לא תמלט) from the hands of the Babylonians (v. 18). Thus, Keown et al. insist, "It is not a new word, only a reemphasis of the con-sistent message delivered by the prophet to the king and the people."[51] In similar vein, Jones writes that "the message (vv. 17–25) is only an amplification of the divine message in its basic form, such as had been proclaimed openly both to the people and to the king."[52]

In fact, the situation is more complicated than this. For one thing, only now is the option of staying in the city or leaving presented directly to Zedekiah. Hitherto, Jeremiah has reserved this choice for a group identified simply as "the people" (21:8; 38:1), while his word to the king has been purely one of judg-ment (21:3–7; 32:3–5; 34:2–3; 37:6–10, 17b). As we saw in Chapter 2 of this study, this audience-critical distinction emerges most clearly in 21:1–10. Discuss-ing that passage, I noted Brueggemann's view that the respective messages of judgment and hope were correlated to those two audiences. In response, I argued that YHWH's wrath is against the city rather than any particular group, and that Zedekiah himself is ignored rather than explicitly precluded from the offer of surrender. Nevertheless, the fact remains that he *is* ignored, and this point has remained a constant in Jeremiah—that is, up until now. This diversity of opinion regarding the fate of Zedekiah may, at one level, reflect competing traditions;[53] within the final form of the book, however, the postponement of the offer of surrender until the final interview is unlikely to be coincidental.[54]

Before considering the significance of this, however, a second observation should be made, which is that Jeremiah's message to Zedekiah is *not* identical with his message to the people. An initial indication of this is the way that

---

51.   Keown, Scalise and Smothers, *Jeremiah 26–52*, 224–25.
52.   Jones, *Jeremiah*, 462; similarly, Thompson, *Jeremiah*, 642; Brueggemann, *Exile and Homecoming*, 366.
53.   On this, see John Applegate, "The Fate of Zedekiah. Part 1," and "The Fate of Zedekiah: Redactional Debate in the Book of Jeremiah. Part 2," *VT* 48 (1998): 301–8.
54.   So McConville, *Judgment and Promise*, 114: "The paradoxical effect of the 'last offer,' as it were, with its surface implication that the king's demise is not after all inevitable, is to seal its inevitability. It does so by revealing the real resistance of Zedekiah to the word... For all his craven toying with the word of YHWH, he will never hear it."

אם יצא חצא varies slightly from the wording in 21:9 and 38:2. Moreover, a close reading of the text shows that Zedekiah is offered rather more than bare survival. The term לשלל, which emphasizes the minimalistic nature of the life offered to the citizens of Jerusalem, is omitted; instead, the king is assured that "it will go well with you" (וייטב לך, v. 20). Again, whereas the scope of the promise in 21:9 and 38:2 is wholly individualistic (והיתה לו נפשו לשלל), for Zedekiah it has a corporate dimension. As Pohlmann noted, his actions will determine the welfare of his entire household (בית, v. 17), namely, his wives and sons (נשים, בנים, vv. 22–23). Especially striking is the assurance that the city itself may be saved (והעיר הזאת לא תשרף באש, v. 17), reversing earlier statements (21:10; 34:2; 37:10).[55]

The most distinctive aspect of Jeremiah's message to Zedekiah, however, is the way it is subverted in v. 23. The revelation that the king's decision and its consequences are already known to YHWH and his prophet casts an ironic light over all that has gone before. Against Pohlmann and Seitz, I have argued that it is unnecessary to see this verse as redactional; similar ambiguity and subtlety can also be seen on the lips of Samuel and Micaiah. It might, of course, be argued that this ironic interpretation has only been achieved secondarily by the addition of v. 23. This cannot be ruled out, although the king's failure to promise that he will listen to Jeremiah (v. 16), and the questioning tone of אם יצא תצא (v. 17), seem to provide advance clues as to the outcome. Given the presence of several verbal and conceptual links between 38:14–23 and Jeremiah's speech to the remnant in ch. 42, I will return to this question after having looked at the latter passage.

Either way, as it stands, ch. 38 presents what we might call a double judicial differentiation. To the people, Jeremiah reiterates the basic polarity of היצאים and הישבים (vv. 1–3). Those who remain in the city will die; but to those who go out, the promise of "life as booty"—meagre as it is—still stands. To Zedekiah, conversely, the prophet presents what seems to be a rather more hopeful message; but not without revealing that its rejection by the king is already known.

3. *Jeremiah 39(46):15–18*

3.1. *Text*

ואל ירמיהו היה דבר יהוה	15	καὶ πρὸς Ιερεμιαν ἐγένετο λόγος κυρίου ἐν
בהיתו עצור בחצר המטרה לאמר		τῇ αὐλῇ τῆς φυλακῆς λέγων
הלוך ואמרת לעבד מלך הכושי	16	πορεύου καὶ εἰπὸν πρὸς Αβδεμελεχ τὸν
לאמר כה אמר יהוה צבאות אלהי		Αἰθίοπα οὕτως εἶπε κύριος ὁ θεὸς Ισραηλ
ישראל הנני מבי את דברי אל		ἰδοὺ ἐγὼ φέρω τοὺς λόγους μου ἐπὶ τὴν
העיר הזאת לרעה ולא לטובה		πόλιν ταύτην εἰς κακά καὶ οὐκ εἰς ἀγαθά
והיו לפניך ביום ההוא		

---

55. These variations in message are perhaps unsurprising, given that it is the king who is being addressed. *His* surrender might well achieve for others and for the city what the surrender of ordinary citizens could not; he might even hope to receive slightly preferential treatment.

והצלתיך ביום ההוא <u>נאם יהוה</u>	17	καὶ σώσω σε ἐν τῇ ἡμέρᾳ ἐκείνῃ καὶ οὐ μὴ
ולא <u>תנתן</u> ביד האנשים אשר אתה		δώσω σε εἰς χεῖρας τῶν ἀνθρώπων ὧν σὺ
יגור מפניהם		φοβῇ ἀπὸ προσώπου αὐτῶν
כי מלט אמלטך ובחרב לא תפל	18	ὅτι σῴζων σώσω σε καὶ ἐν ῥομφαίᾳ οὐ μὴ
והיתה לך נפשך לשלל כי בטחת		πέσῃς καὶ ἔσται ἡ ψυχή σου εἰς εὕρεμα ὅτι
בי נאם יהוה		ἐπεποίθεις ἐπ᾽ ἐμοί φησὶ κύριος

3.2. *Textual Notes*

v. 16. MT והיו לפניך ביום ההוא >OG. MT plus; perhaps dittography from והצלתיך ביום ההוא at the start of v. 17.[56] The implied sense is, "they will be fulfilled before your eyes."

v. 17. MT ולא תנתן; OG καὶ οὐ μὴ δώσω σε = ולא נתתיך. OG may reflect a content variant in its *Vorlage*. Other instances of the expression "(not) give into the hand of" in Jeremiah show a striking correspondence between נתן Niph. and (παρα)δίδωμι passive (21:10; 32[39]:4, 24, 25, 36, 43; 34[41]:3; 37[44]:17; 38[45]:3, 18; 46[26]:24), and נתן Qal and (παρα)δίδωμι active (22:25; 32[39]:3; 38[45]:16).

v. 18. MT לשלל; OG εἰς εὕρεμα ("for a prize, a godsend"). OG offers a rather loose translation; cf. εἰς σκῦλα ("for spoil") in the parallel expression in 21:9.

3.3. *Exegesis*

v. 15. בחצר המטרה. References to Jeremiah in the courtyard of the guard occur also in 32:2, 8; 33:1; 37:21; 38:13, 28; 39:14. The exact nature of his confinement here is unclear; it was evidently preferable to the בית הכלא ("prison house") into which he is thrown by the שרים in 37:15, 18, and may even have entailed some degree of protection. However, chs. 32 and 33 portray the חצר המטרה negatively, emphasizing the aspect of confinement (כלא, 32:2, 3; עצור, 33:1), and attributing Jeremiah's presence there to Zedekiah's irritation at his message (32:3).

v. 16. עבד מלך הכושי has previously appeared in 38:7–13, where he takes the initiative in rescuing Jeremiah from the cistern. עבד מלך is probably a proper name (as in OG, Αβδεμελεχ; contrast Targ., עבד דמלכא); nevertheless, it underlines his role as a palace official,[57] so that his story stands in contrast with the statement that opens the entire narrative: ולא שמע (צדקיהו) ועבדיו ועם הארץ אל דברי יהוה (37:2).[58]

הנני מביא את דברי. Elsewhere in Jeremiah, בוא Hiph. with דבר as object occurs only in 11:8 and 25:13; much more common is בוא + רעה Hiph. The sense would seem to be "to fulfil one's word,"[59] as is occasionally expressed by בוא + דבר Qal (Judg 13:12, 17; Jer 28:9; Ps 105:19).

---

56. So Duhm, *Jeremia*, 312; Rudolph, *Jeremia*, 210; cautiously, Graupner, *Auftrag*, 127; McKane, *Jeremiah 2*, 982. Wanke, *Untersuchungen*, 105, suggests it is a gloss referring to the intervening events.

57. Holladay, *Jeremiah 2*, 289: "It sounds like the kind of *ad hoc* name given to a slave whose original name no one could pronounce."

58. As noted by Seitz, *Theology in Conflict*, 261.

59. Rudolph, *Jeremia*, 210: "Lassen in Erfüllung gehen"; this is preferable to "I am *sending* my words" (Keown, Scalise and Smothers, *Jeremiah 26–52*, 227).

v. 17. והצלתיך. Hitherto, נצל Hiph. as spoken by YHWH has occurred just four times, in two key contexts: 1:8, 19; 15:20, 21.[60] In each case, the beneficiary of the promise is Jeremiah, his adversaries being the people of Judah who will oppose him (כל הארץ, 1:18; העם הזה, 15:20). Subsequently, it will occur only in 42:11, as part of YHWH's conditional promise to the Judean remnant.

ולא תנתן ביד. The phrase נתן ביד is characteristic of judgment oracles in Jeremiah. The central chapters state that YHWH will give into the hands of the Babylonians all Judah (20:4), Jehoiakim (22:25), Zedekiah (32:4; 34:21), the prophets Ahab and Zedekiah (29:21), Jerusalem (32:3, 24–25; 38:3, 18) and its wealth (20:5). Similar warnings will be made later against Egypt (44:30; 46:24, 26).[61] Only here, however, do we have the negative לא נתן ביד.

האנשים אשר אתה יגור מפניהם. The identity of these people is uncertain. Possibly the Judean שרים are in mind;[62] cf. Zedekiah's oath in 38:16 not to give Jeremiah ביד האנשים האלה אשר מבקשים את נפשך. Ebed-Melech's support for Jeremiah, plus the fact that he was a foreigner (and a suspected quisling?), could well have made him a target for reprisals. Others believe he feared those Judeans who had deserted to the Babylonians;[63] cf. Zedekiah's confession in 38:19, אני דאג את היהודים אשר נפלו אל הכשדים. Probably, however, the reference is to the Babylonians themselves.[64] For one thing, 39:17 has a striking counterpart in 22:25, ונתתיך ביד מבקשי נפשך אשר אתה יגור מפניהם (the only other instance of יגור in the Old Testament), and here, those whom Jehoiachin fears are explicitly identified as הכשדים. Moreover, v. 18, בחרב לא תפל והיתה לך נפשך לשלל, seems to set Ebed-Melech's deliverance in a context of military conflict.[65] In any case, whatever its original literary context, 39:15–18 must now be read in conjunction with 39:4–14 (note the repetition of ביום ההוא, vv. 10, 17) and 40:1–6, both of which emphasize how Nebuzaradan protected Jeremiah while the Babylonians razed the city and deported its citizens.

v. 18. מלט אמלטך. Although מלט Pi. occurs frequently with a human subject, especially in the idiom מלט את נפש (e.g. 1 Sam 19:11; 1 Kgs 1:12; Jer 48:6; Amos 2:14; Ps 89:49), it is less often predicated of God (Isa 46:4; Pss 41:2; 107:20; 116:4; Job 22:30). Especially noteworthy are the parallels with Ps 41:2, ביום רעה ימלטהו יהוה, which continues with the assurance ואל תתנהו בנפש איביו

---

60.   נצל Hiph. is used *of* YHWH in Jer 20:13, where the beneficiaries are the needy (אביון).

61.   Though the identity of the enemy is here less clear: ביד איביו וביד מבקשי נפשו (44:30); ביד עם צפון (46:24). Only in 44:26 (MT plus) are they identified as the Babylonians; cf. 34:20, where YHWH warns that he will give Judah's leaders and people ביד איביהם.

62.   So Bright, *Jeremiah*, 232; Hannelis Schulte, "Baruch und Ebedmelech: Persönliche Heils-orakel im Jeremiabuche," *BZ* 32 (1988): 257–65 (259–60); cautiously, Thompson, *Jeremiah*, 649. Thompson notes that Ebed-Melech had accused the princes of acting wickedly (38:9), though this pertains only to MT; in OG, he directs the accusation against the king.

63.   So Jones, *Jeremiah*, 466.

64.   So, cautiously, McKane, *Jeremiah 2*, 982. Carroll, *Jeremiah*, 696, is unpersuaded by either view, arguing that the princes could have killed Ebed-Melech already, and that the Babylonians would have had no reason to harm him. The second point somewhat overlooks the treatment of Zedekiah and his sons by the Babylonians in 39:5–7.

65.   So McKane, *Jeremiah 2*, 982.

(v. 3). The promise מלט אמלטך forms a striking double contrast between Ebed-Melech and Zedekiah; while the king is repeatedly warned that he will not escape (מלט Niph.; 32:4; 34:3; 38:18, 23) from the Babylonians, his servant will "be escaped" (מלט Pi.) by YHWH.

ובחרב לא תפל. As with ולא תנתך ביד in v. 17, here too we have the sole instance of the negating of a formulaic expression of judgment; נפל בחרב (note the reverse order) occurs in oracles against the people of Judah (19:7; 20:4) and the remnant in Egypt (44:12).

כי בטחת ב׳. Nowhere else in Jeremiah is someone said to trust in (בטח ב) YHWH. In the first part of the book, the people of Judah are denounced for trusting in fortified cities (5:17), deceptive words (7:8), the temple (7:14), lies (13:25) and human kind (17:5), a list that leads up to YHWH's declaration, ברוך הגבר אשר יבטח ביהוה והיה יהוה מבטחו (17:7). Later chapters will indict Egypt, Moab and Ammon for trusting in Pharaoh (46:25) and in riches (48:7; 49:4). Within the final form of the book, therefore, Ebed-Melech is presented as the only figure who answers to the requirement of 17:7, a textual claim all the more remarkable given his non-Israelite status.

3.4. *Coherence and Redaction*

In view of its brevity, it is not surprising that most commentators regard Jer 39:15–18 as a unity and as either an authentic salvation oracle or a late and wholly fictional interpolation.[66] A few, however, have attempted to separate out an authentic kernel from later redaction. Thiel identifies as original the introductory material in vv. 15a, 16aα, and the promise מלט אמלטך ובחרב לא תפל (v. 18a); the remainder he assigns to the Deuteronomistic editor.[67] His analysis is accepted by Kilpp and Graupner.[68] Underlying their approach, however, is the same flawed methodology that has been noted in previous chapters, that is, citing language as Deuteronomistic which is more typical of Jeremiah than of DtrH.[69] Indeed, Graupner designates כי בטחתי בי as Deuteronomistic despite conceding that "die Wendung בטח ב ist zwar für die dtr. Bearbeiter nicht typisch."[70] The argument becomes still more precarious when it is claimed that since v. 17a, והצלתיך ביום ההוא, refers back to the "redactional" v. 16a, it too must be secondary—despite the use of והצלתיך in the (poetic) 15:21.[71] Stulman points out that the only clearly Deuteronomistic phrase in 39:15–18 is the MT plus in v. 16, יהוה צבאות אלהי ישראל.[72]

---

66. For the former, see Volz, *Jeremia*, 348; Rudolph, *Jeremia*, 212–13; Weiser, *Jeremia*, 357; Holladay, *Jeremiah 2*, 290–91; Thompson, *Jeremiah*, 649. Taking the latter view are Duhm, *Jeremia*, 312–13; Mowinckel, *Jeremia*, 44; Hyatt, "Jeremiah," 1081–82; Wanke, *Untersuchungen*, 110–12; Pohlmann, *Studien*, 99; Carroll, *Jeremiah*, 696; McKane, *Jeremiah 2*, 991–92.

67. Thiel, *Redaktion 26–45*, 56–57.

68. Kilpp, *Niederreißen*, 88–90; Graupner, *Auftrag*, 126–28.

69. E.g. והיתה לך נפשך לשלל (21:9; 38:2); הנני מביא את דברי (11:8; 25:13; cf. Josh 23:15); אשר אתה יגור מפניהם (22:25; cf. Deut 28:60); לרעה ולא לטובה (21:10; 44:27).

70. Graupner, *Auftrag*, 127 n. 61.

71. Thiel, *Redaktion 26–45*, 56; Graupner, *Auftrag*, 127.

72. Stulman, *Prose Sermons*, 111–12. Stulman concludes (p. 112) that "the passage may be secondary from a literary point of view, but there is little basis for associating it with the C corpus."

A variant of Thiel's argument has been put forward by Schulte.[73] He agrees that with five separate promises the oracle is overladen, and that some of the language is Deuteronomistic. More particularly, Schulte argues that the promises relating to the destruction of Jerusalem (ובחרב לא תפל; והצלתיך ביום ההוא) are shown to be secondary by their *irrelevance*: "Für Ebedmelech ist…im Augenblick seine persönliche Bedrohung durch die Heerführer das eigentliche Problem."[74] This focus on what he perceives as "the real problem" is for Schulte the decisive criterion. Consequently, he accepts as original not only מלט אמלטך (v. 18) but also the promise לא תנתן ביד האנשים אשר אתה יגור מפניהם (v. 17b), which Thiel, Kilpp and Graupner reject. He also retains the final words והיתה לך נפשך לשלל כי בטחת בי (v. 18b). Schulte's refusal automatically to delete supposedly Deuteronomistic language is welcome, but it is by no means certain that Ebed-Melech's fate was unconnected with that of Jerusalem. Even if it was the שרים (rather than the Babylonians) who posed the threat to him, the chaos (and loss of royal protection?) attending the fall of the city would offer a clear opportunity for settling old scores.

The fact is that all attempts to separate kernel from redaction in 39:15–18 on the basis of terminology founder on the sheer profusion of verbal inter-connections with other parts of Jeremiah that are evident here.[75] I have already noted these separately, but can now list them together: הנני מביא את דברי (cf. 11:8; 25:13); והצלתיך (cf. 1:8, 19; 15:20, 21); האנשים אשר אתה יגור מפניהם (cf. 22:25); מלט אמלטך (cf. 32:4; 34:3; 38:18, 23); ובחרב לא תפל (cf. 19:7; 20:4; 44:12); כי בטחת בי (cf. 5:17; 7:8, 14; 13:25; 17:5; 46:25; 48:7; 49:4); והיתה לך נפשך לשלל (cf. 21:9; 38:3; 45:5).[76] Schulte's remark about "die Überfüllung" of the unit is thus in one sense quite correct, but it proves too much. Jeremiah 39:15–18 blends words and phrases from a variety of passages, which cannot all meaningfully be termed "Deuteronomistic." This suggests that we are dealing not with a single redaction of an authentic saying, but rather with a compositional unity—either by the prophet, utilizing his own prophetic utterances, or by a later author creating a literary pastiche.[77]

3.5. *Judicial Differentiation in Jeremiah 39(46):15–18:* עבד מלך הכושי / העיר הזאת

For all its brevity, Jer 39:15–18 provides arguably the most remarkable salvation oracle to be found in the entire book. Against the backdrop of the fall of Jerusalem, anticipated and described in chs. 37–39, one person—"a virtually anonymous foreigner"[78]—is promised YHWH's protection and rescue. Brueggemann

---

73. Schulte, "Persönliche Heilsorakel," 258–60.

74. Ibid., 259.

75. A point noted by Wanke, *Untersuchungen*, 111.

76. The idiom נתן ביד is so common in Jeremiah and the Old Testament generally that לא תנתן ביד can hardly be seen as alluding to any particular passage.

77. Carroll, *Jeremiah*, 696, describes 39:15–18 as "a midrash built out of phrases and motifs from the whole tradition." Duhm describes the author as "der Midraschist" (*Jeremia*, 313).

78. As Holladay, *Jeremiah 2*, 289, describes Ebed-Melech. Stulman, *Order Amid Chaos*, 112, describes Ebed-Melech as "this faithful outsider."

remarks: "The destruction of Jerusalem is sweeping and comprehensive (vv. 1–10). A critical exception is nonetheless made. Ebed-Melech constitutes an important remnant. The destruction wrought by God through Nebuchadnezzar is not morally indifferent or undifferentiated."[79]

In certain respects, the mode of judicial differentiation in 39:15–18 resembles that which we encountered in 21:1–10 and 38:1–3, namely, that of the "doomed city/saved individual." The words with which the oracle begins (מבי את דברי אל העיר הזאת לרעה ולא לטובה, v. 16), and the promise with which it concludes (והיתה לך נפשך לשלל, v. 18), unmistakably echo the language of those two earlier passages. The shared historical context, and the absence of any promise of future restoration, might also suggest that the same philosophy of differentiation underlies these three passages.

At the same time, however, in several respects the nature of the polarity in 39:15–18 differs markedly from that in chs. 21 and 38. For one thing, while in those two passages "life as booty" is contingent upon surrender (יצא) to the Babylonians, ch. 39 makes no such demand of Ebed-Melech. Indeed, since the story of his rescue of Jeremiah (38:7–13) *follows* the prophet's appeal for people to leave the city, the impression given is that he, like Jeremiah, remained (ישב) in Jerusalem. Instead, according to 39:18 the salvation of this Cushite official is due simply to his trust in YHWH.

Moreover, what he is promised bears only slight resemblance to what was offered to the inhabitants of Jerusalem. The assurances, "I will save you on that day…you will not be given into the hands of the men you fear…I will surely deliver you…you will not fall by the sword," while limited to the immediate crisis, are unparalleled in chs. 21 and 38, and render YHWH's promise to Ebed-Melech qualitatively different from that to the יוצאים. Salvation is not simply a function of escaping the doomed city—avoiding the disaster scene, so to speak —but of YHWH's personal protection in the midst of it. Putting this another way, Ebed-Melech's welfare is presented as YHWH's personal pledge (והצלתיך…מלט אמלטך) rather than as a somewhat detached prediction (cf. היצא אל המשדים יחיה, 21:9; 38:2). Together with the commendation בטחת בי, these promises give to 38:15–18 a note of divine favour that is wholly absent from 21:8–10 and 38:1–3.[80]

If, then, we are in a different type of configuration to that found in 21:1–10 and 38:1–3, who provides the foil for Ebed-Melech in this judgment and salvation oracle? At one level, the answer is clearly "this city" (העיר הזאת, v. 16). With no reference to any who might surrender to the Babylonians, Ebed-Melech appears as the one figure who will survive YHWH's wrath against Jerusalem. At the same time, the wording of vv. 17–18 suggests a more textured answer. As we have seen, two of the promises—ולא תנתן ביד האנשים אשר אתה יגור מפניהם and מלט אמלטך—are negations of earlier warnings against

---

79. Brueggemann, *Exile and Homecoming*, 374.
80. Ebed-Melech's relationship to those who go out to the Babylonians in chs. 37–39 could be compared to that of the exiles to their counterparts in Judah in chs. 27–28; the promises offered to each of the latter parties are more impersonal and modest than those held out to the former.

Jehoiachin and Zedekiah. Meanwhile, בחרב לא תפל exempts Ebed-Melech from YHWH's threat to the people of Judah (19:7; 20:4). This cluster of promises allows the figure of Ebed-Melech to take on new significance; the foreign official stands over and against not only his master Zedekiah,[81] but also Jehoiakim and indeed the whole land. Especially significant in this regard are the words כי בטחת בי, emphasized by their final position within the oracle. When read within the wider context of the book, this affirmation serves to demarcate Ebed-Melech from both Judeans and foreigners who trust in other things (5:17; 7:8, 14; 13:25; 17:5; 46:25; 48:7; 49:4). In particular, 39:18 recalls the promise of 17:7, ברוך הגבר אשר יבטח ביהוה.

This link with Jer 17:5–8 is significant, since the latter passage is one of only two Jeremianic texts included in Koenen's study (discussed in Chapters 1 and 2).[82] Koenen argues that these verses were added to modify Jeremiah's prophecy against all Judah in 17:1–4: "Sie gilt allen Gottlosen, nicht jedoch den frommen Jahwe-Verehrern."[83] He then considers the function of Jeremiah's confession in 17:14–18:

> Die psalmistisch geprägte Konfession vv. 14–18 erscheint im Licht von vv. 5–8 als Explikation der weisheitlichen Lehre dieser Verse. Jeremia wird damit auf einer sekundären Ebene als prototypischer Frommer verstanden und als solcher gerettet, während seine Gegner als Gottlose untergehen.[84]

While this understanding of 17:14–18 may well be valid, the fact that within the entire book only Ebed-Melech is actually said to trust in YHWH strongly suggests that he too is being presented as a prototypical pious man.[85] Nor would this be the only way in which 39:15–18 parallels Ebed-Melech and Jeremiah. Some sort of analogy between the two figures is implied by the setting of 39:15–18, sandwiched as it is between the two accounts of Jeremiah's release (39:11–14; 40:1–6).[86] Moreover, as we noticed earlier, YHWH's promise והצלתיך (v. 17) is otherwise applied only to the prophet himself (1:8, 19; 15:20, 21). This in turn strengthens the argument for seeing the underlying differentiation in 39:15–18 as between Ebed-Melech and the nation; for this is precisely how 1:17–19 and 15:19–20 configure the relationship between Jeremiah and the people of Judah (כל הארץ, 1:18; העם הזה, 15:20).

---

81. A point of contrast noted by Rudolph, *Jeremia*, 213.

82. Koenen, *Heil den Gerechten*, 189–200.

83. Ibid., 200.

84. Ibid.

85. Note too the affinities between Ebed-Melech and the blessed man of the Psalms. As well as the language of trust in YHWH, the promise of rescue (מלט) on the day (ביום ההוא) when YHWH brings evil (רעה) on Jerusalem echoes Ps 41:2, ימלטהו יהוה ביום רעה. Also, just as Ebed-Melech's salvation follows his rescue of Jeremiah (38:8–13), the promise of deliverance in Ps 41 is for "the one who has regard for the poor" (משכיל אל דל, v. 2 [1]).

86. One should not overlook the parallels between 39:15–18 and Nebuzaradan's speech in 40:2–4. Both are introduced as divine oracles to Jeremiah, and offer hope to individuals in the context of national judgment; cf. the balancing terms, מביא (39:16) and ויבא (40:3); ביום ההוא (39:17) and היום (40:4); רעה / טובה (39:16) and טוב / רע (40:4).

Some may question the validity of reading 39:15–18 within the wider context of the book. Or, putting the question another way, if the language of this unit does indeed dialogue with other parts of Jeremiah, what does this imply about its literary origins? To ask the question this way is of course to suggest one answer; namely, that the oracle to Ebed-Melech was incorporated into the book relatively late. As noted earlier, this view is held by a number of scholars. Evidence for this may lie in the fact that the passage appears to be out of place (cf. the reference to Jeremiah's confinement, v. 15a). Some have suggested that it has been moved from its original context (either after 38:13[87] or 38:28[88]), but even there it would have a slightly intrusive quality. As Jones remarks, "the fact is that it cannot be closely welded into the main theme of chs. 37–45."[89] Without prejudging its authenticity (a quite separate matter), therefore, there is reason to think that this oracle was added at a time when much of Jeremiah was already complete, so that allusions to earlier passages may well be intentional.

4. *Summary: Judicial Differentiation in Jeremiah 38–39*

We can now review our findings so far concerning the concept of judicial differentiation in Jer 37–45. As we have seen, the unit begins by restating the היצאים / הישבים polarity that we encountered in 21:1–10. The report of Jeremiah's interview with Zedekiah, however, nuances this. While the prophet's message appears to repeat 38:1–3, it turns out on closer inspection to diverge significantly. Zedekiah may save not only himself, but also his family and indeed the whole city; in addition, the promise "it will go well with you" sounds a note of optimism that is singularly absent in 21:9 or 38:2. At the same time, the invitation begins with a note of doubt and ends by making it clear that the option for Zedekiah is foreclosed.

What, then, is the relationship between Jer 21:1–10 and 38:1–3? In the first passage, salvation hinges on the question of affiliation to Jerusalem. However, since only the people are told of this offer, it is ambiguous as to whether Zedekiah can be one of the יצאים. In ch. 38, we find a different but equally ambiguous picture. The היצאים / הישבים polarity is reiterated, and this time Zedekiah is himself invited to surrender. Even he, then, is not excluded from YHWH's offer. Even before he makes his response, however, we learn that he will follow the counter-advice of his friends. His salvation (like that of the city) is no more than a theoretical possibility.

The oracle to Ebed-Melech (39:15–18) echoes the promise of 38:2, but also exceeds it, and does so towards an individual who has not fulfilled its requirements. Especially when read within the context of the whole book, it suggests that the critical distinction vis-à-vis YHWH's salvation is in fact אשר בטח ביהוה / אשר לא בטח ביהוה. To be sure, the הישבים / היצאים and אשר בטח ביהוה / אשר לא בטח ביהוה polarities are not mutually exclusive. On the one

---

87. Rudolph, *Jeremia*, 212–13.
88. Bright, *Jeremiah*, 229.
89. Jones, *Jeremiah*, 465.

hand, the issue of trust may be said to undergird the הישבים / היצאים distinction since, as I have argued, the issue at stake in Jer 21 is one of affiliation to Jerusalem. On the other hand, two of the objects which the Judeans are rebuked for trusting in (בטח ב) in the earlier chapters of the book are their fortified cities (5:17) and the temple (7:14). Nevertheless, it is clear that the oracle to Ebed-Melech frames the issue in a distinctive way. Consequently, it may be read as a claim that even those who were not exiles in 597 (ch. 24) and who did not go out to the Babylonians in 587 (21:8–10; 38:1–3) might yet receive divine favour.

5. *Jeremiah 42(49):1–43:7*

5.1. *Text*

ויגשו כל שרי החילים ויוחנן בן קרח ויזניה בן השעיה וכל העם מקטן ועד גדול	1	καὶ προσῆλθον πάντες οἱ ἡγεμόνες τῆς δυνάμεως καὶ Ιωαναν καὶ Αζαριας υἱὸς Μαασαιου καὶ πᾶς ὁ λαὸς ἀπὸ μικροῦ καὶ ἕως μεγάλου
ויאמרו אל ירמיהו הנביא תפל נא תחנתנו לפניך והתפלל בעדנו אל יהוה אלהיך בעד כל השארית הזאת כי נשארנו מעט מהרבה כאשר עיניך ראות אתנו	2	πρὸς Ιερεμιαν τὸν προφήτην καὶ εἶπαν αὐτῷ πεσέτω τὸ ἔλεος ἡμῶν κατὰ πρόσωπόν σου καὶ πρόσευξαι πρὸς κύριον θεόν σου περὶ τῶν καταλοίπων τούτων ὅτι κατελείφθημεν ὀλίγοι ἀπὸ πολλῶν καθὼς οἱ ὀφθαλμοί σου βλέπουσι
ויגד לנו יהוה אלהיך את הדרך אשר נלך בה ואת הדבר אשר נעשה	3	καὶ ἀναγγειλάτω ἡμῖν κύριος ὁ θεός σου τὴν ὁδόν ᾗ πορευσόμεθα ἐν αὐτῇ καὶ λόγον ὃν ποιήσομεν
ויאמר אליהם ירמיהו הנביא שמעתי הנני מתפלל אל יהוה אלהיכם כדבריכם והיה כל הדבר אשר יענה יהוה אתכם אגיד לכם לא אמנע מכם דבר	4	καὶ εἶπεν αὐτοῖς Ιερεμιας ἤκουσα ἰδοὺ ἐγὼ προσεύξομαι πρὸς κύριον θεὸν ὑμῶν κατὰ τοὺς λόγους ὑμῶν καὶ ἔσται ὁ λόγος ὃν ἂν ἀποκριθήσεται κύριος ἀναγγελῶ ὑμῖν οὐ μὴ κρύψω ἀφ' ὑμῶν ῥῆμα
והמה אמרו אל ירמיהו יהי יהוה בנו לעד אמת ונאמן אם לא כבל הדבר אשר ישלחך יהוה אלהיך אלינו כן נעשה	5	καὶ αὐτοὶ εἶπαν τῷ Ιερεμια ἔστω κύριος ἐν ἡμῖν εἰς μάρτυρα δίκαιον καὶ πιστὸν εἰ μὴ κατὰ πάντα τὸν λόγον ὃν ἂν ἀποστείλῃ σε κύριος πρὸς ἡμᾶς οὕτως ποιήσομεν
אם טוב ואם רע בקול יהוה אלהינו אשר אנו שלחים אתך אליו למען ייטב לנו כי נשמע בקול יהוה אלהינו	6	καὶ ἐὰν ἀγαθὰ καὶ ἐὰν κακόν τὴν φωνὴν κυρίου τοῦ θεοῦ ἡμῶν οὗ ἡμεῖς ἀποστέλλομέν σε πρὸς αὐτόν ἀκουσόμεθα ἵνα βέλτιον ἡμῖν γένηται ὅτι ἀκουσόμεθα τῆς φωνῆς κυρίου τοῦ θεοῦ ἡμῶν
ויהי מקץ עשרת ימים ויהי דבר יהוה אל ירמיהו	7	καὶ ἐγενήθη μετὰ δέκα ἡμέρας ἐγενήθη λόγος κυρίου πρὸς Ιερεμιαν
ויקרא אל יוחנן בן קרח ואל כל שרי החילים אשר אתו ולכל העם למקטן ועד גדול	8	καὶ ἐκάλεσε τὸν Ιωαναν καὶ τοὺς ἡγεμόνας τῆς δυνάμεως καὶ πάντα τὸν λαὸν ἀπὸ μικροῦ καὶ ἕως μεγάλου
ויאמר אליהם כה אמר יהוה אלהי ישראל אשר שלחתם אתי אליו להפיל תחנתכם לפניו	9	καὶ εἶπεν αὐτοῖς οὕτως εἶπε κύριος

אם שוב תשבו בארץ הזאת ובניתי אתכם ולא אהרס ונטעתי אתכם ולא אתוש כי <u>נחמתי</u> אל הרעה אשר עשיתי לכם	10	ἐὰν καθίσαντες καθίσητε ἐν τῇ γῇ ταύτῃ οἰκοδομήσω ὑμᾶς καὶ οὐ μὴ καθέλω καὶ φυτεύσω ὑμᾶς καὶ οὐ μὴ ἐκτίλω ὅτι <u>ἀναπέπαυμαι</u> ἐπὶ τοῖς κακοῖς οἷς ἐποίησα ὑμῖν
אל תיראו מפני מלך בבל אשר אתם יראים מפניו <u>אל תיראו ממנו</u> נאם יהוה כי אתכם אני להושיע אתכם ולהציל אתכם מידי	11	μὴ φοβηθῆτε ἀπὸ προσώπου βασιλέως Βαβυλῶνος οὗ ὑμεῖς φοβεῖσθε ἀπὸ προσώπου αὐτοῦ φησὶ κύριος ὅτι μεθ' ὑμῶν ἐγώ εἰμι τοῦ ἐξαιρεῖσθαι ὑμᾶς καὶ σώζειν ὑμᾶς ἐκ χειρὸς αὐτοῦ
ואתן לכם רחמים <u>ורחם</u> אתכם <u>והשיב</u> אתכם אל אדמתכם	12	καὶ δώσω ὑμῖν ἔλεος καὶ <u>ἐλεήσω</u> ὑμᾶς καὶ <u>ἐπιστρέψω</u> ὑμᾶς εἰς τὴν γῆν ὑμῶν
ואם אמרים אתם לא נשב בארץ הזאת לבלתי שמע בקול יהוה <u>אלהיכם</u>	13	καὶ εἰ λέγετε ὑμεῖς οὐ μὴ καθίσωμεν ἐν τῇ γῇ ταύτῃ πρὸς τὸ μὴ ἀκοῦσαι φωνῆς κυρίου
<u>לאמר לא</u> כי ארץ מצרים נבוא אשר לא נראה מלחמה וקול שופ־ לא נשמע וללחם לא נרעב ושב נשב	14	ὅτι εἰς γῆν Αἰγύπτου εἰσελευσόμεθα καὶ οὐ μὴ ἴδωμεν πόλεμον καὶ φωνὴν σάλπιγγος οὐ μὴ ἀκούσωμεν καὶ ἐν ἄρτοις οὐ μὴ πεινάσωμεν καὶ ἐκεῖ οἰκήσομεν
<u>ועתה</u> לכן שמעו דבר יהוה <u>שארית יהודה</u> כה אמר יהוה <u>צבאות אלהי ישראל</u> אם אתם שום תשמון פניכם <u>לבא</u> מצרים ובאתם לגור שם	15	διὰ τοῦτο ἀκούσατε λόγον κυρίου οὕτως εἶπε κύριος ἐὰν ὑμεῖς δῶτε τὸ πρόσωπον ὑμῶν εἰς Αἴγυπτον καὶ εἰσέλθητε ἐκεῖ κατοικεῖν
והיתה החרב אשר אתם יראים ממנה <u>שם</u> תשיג אתכם <u>בארץ</u> מצרים והרעב אשר אתם דאגים ממנו <u>שב</u> ידבק אחריכם מצרים ושם תמתי	16	καὶ ἔσται ἡ ῥομφαία ἣν ὑμεῖς φοβεῖσθε ἀπὸ προσώπου αὐτῆς εὑρήσει ὑμᾶς ἐν Αἰγύπτῳ καὶ ὁ λιμός οὗ ὑμεῖς λόγον ἔχετε ἀπὸ προσώπου αὐτοῦ καταλήμψεται ὑμᾶς ἐν Αἰγύπτῳ καὶ ἐκεῖ ἀποθανεῖσθε
ויהיו כל האנשים אשר שמו את פניהם <u>לבוא</u> מצרים לגור שם ימותו בחרב ברעב <u>ובדבר</u> ולא יהיה להם <u>שריד</u> ופליט מפני הרעה אשר אני מביא עליהם	17	καὶ ἔσονται πάντες οἱ ἄνθρωποι <u>καὶ πάντες οἱ ἀλλογενεῖς</u> οἱ θέντες τὸ πρόσωπον αὐτῶν εἰς <u>γῆν</u> Αἰγύπτου ἐνοικεῖν ἐκεῖ ἐκλείψουσιν ἐν ῥομφαίᾳ καὶ ἐν λιμῷ καὶ οὐκ ἔσται αὐτῶν οὐθεὶς σωζόμενος ἀπὸ τῶν κακῶν ὧν ἐγὼ ἐπάγω ἐπ' αὐτούς
כי כה אמר יהוה <u>צבאות אלהי</u> <u>ישראל</u> כאשר נתך אפי וחמתי על ישבי ירושלם כן תתך חמתי עליכם בבאכם מצרים והייתם <u>לאלה</u> ולשמה ולקללה ולחרפה ולא תראו עוד את המקום הזה	18	ὅτι οὕτως εἶπε κύριος καθὼς ἔσταξεν ὁ θυμός μου ἐπὶ τοὺς κατοικοῦντας Ιερουσαλημ οὕτως στάξει ὁ θυμός μου ἐφ' ὑμᾶς εἰσελθόντων ὑμῶν εἰς Αἴγυπτον καὶ ἔσεσθε εἰς ἄβατον καὶ <u>ὑποχείριοι</u> καὶ εἰς ἀρὰν καὶ εἰς ὀνειδισμὸν καὶ οὐ μὴ ἴδητε οὐκέτι τὸν τόπον τοῦτον
דבר יהוה עליכם שארית יהודה אל תבאו מצרים ידע תדעו כי <u>העידתי בכם היום</u>	19	<u>ἃ</u> ἐλάλησε κύριος ἐφ' ὑμᾶς τοὺς καταλοίπους Ιουδα μὴ εἰσέλθητε εἰς Αἴγυπτον <u>καὶ νῦν</u> γνόντες γνώσεσθε
כי <u>התעתים</u> בנפשותיכם כי <u>אתה שלחתם</u> אתי אל יהוה אלהיכם לאמר התפלל בעדנו אל יהוה <u>אלהינו</u> וככל אשר יאמר יהוה אלהינו <u>כן הגד לנו</u> ועשינו	20	ὅτι <u>ἐπονηρεύσασθε</u> ἐν ψυχαῖς ὑμῶν <u>ἀποστείλαντες</u> με λέγοντες πρόσευξαι περὶ ἡμῶν πρὸς κύριον καὶ κατὰ πάντα ἃ ἐὰν λαλήσῃ σοι κύριος ποιήσομεν
<u>ואגד לכם היום</u> ולא שמעתם בקול יהוה <u>אלהיכם ולכל</u> אשר־ שלחני אליכם	21	καὶ οὐκ ἠκούσατε τῆς φωνῆς κυρίου ἧς ἀπέστειλε με πρὸς ὑμᾶς

ועתה <u>ידעו תדעו כי</u> בחרב	22	καὶ νῦν ἐν ῥομφαίᾳ καὶ ἐν λιμῷ ἐκλείψετε ἐν
ברעב <u>ובדבר</u> תמותו במקום אשר		τῷ τόπῳ οὗ ὑμεῖς βούλεσθε εἰσελθεῖν
הפצתם לבוא לגור שם		κατοικεῖν ἐκεῖ
ויהי ככלות ירמיהו לדבר אל	1	καὶ ἐγενήθη ὡς ἐπαύσατο Ιερεμιας λέγων
<u>כל</u> העם <u>את</u> כל דברי יהוה		πρὸς τὸν λαὸν τοὺς πάντας λόγους κυρίου
<u>אלהיהם</u> אשר שלחו יהוה <u>אלהיהם</u>		οὓς ἀπέστειλεν αὐτὸν κύριος πρὸς αὐτοὺς
אליהם את כל הדברים האלה		πάντας τοὺς λόγους τούτους
ויאמר עזריה בן הושעיה ויוחנן	2	καὶ εἶπεν Αζαριας υἱὸς Μαασαιου καὶ
בן קרח וכל האנשים <u>הזדים</u> אמרים		Ιωαναν υἱὸς Καρηε καὶ πάντες οἱ ἄνδρες <u>οἱ</u>
אל ירמיהו שקר <u>אתה מדבר</u> לא		<u>εἴπαντες</u> τῷ Ιερεμια λέγοντες ψεύδη οὐκ
שלחך יהוה <u>אלהינו</u> לאמר לא		ἀπέστειλε σε κύριος πρὸς ἡμᾶς εἶπεῖν μὴ
תבאו מצרים לגור שם		εἰσέλθητε εἰς Αἴγυπτον οἰκεῖν ἐκεῖ
כי ברוך בן נריה מסית אתך בני	3	ἀλλ᾽ ἢ Βαρουχ υἱὸς Νηριου συμβάλλει σε
למען תת אתנו ביד הכשדים		πρὸς ἡμᾶς ἵνα δῷς ἡμᾶς εἰς χεῖρας τῶν
להמית אתנו ולהגלות אתנו בבל		Χαλδαίων τοῦ θανατῶσαι ἡμᾶς καὶ
		ἀποικισθῆναι ἡμᾶς εἰς Βαβυλῶνα
ולא שמע יוחנן <u>בן קרח</u> וכל	4	καὶ οὐκ ἤκουσεν Ιωαναν καὶ πάντες οἱ
שרי <u>החילים</u> וכל העם בקול יהוה		ἡγεμόνες <u>τῆς δυνάμεως</u> καὶ πᾶς ὁ λαὸς τῆς
לשבת בארץ יהודה		φωνῆς κυρίου κατοικῆσαι ἐν γῇ Ιουδα
ויקח יוחנן <u>בן קרח</u> וכל שרי	5	καὶ ἔλαβεν Ιωαναν καὶ πάντες οἱ ἡγεμόνες
החילים <u>את</u> כל שארית יהודה		<u>τῆς δυνάμεως</u> πάντας τοὺς καταλοίπους
אשר שבו <u>מכל הגוים אשר נדחי</u>		Ιουδα τοὺς ἀποστρέψαντας κατοικεῖν ἐν τῇ
<u>שם</u> לגור בארץ <u>יהודה</u>		γῇ
את <u>הגברים</u> ואת הנשים ואת <u>הטף</u>	6	τοὺς <u>δυνατοὺς</u> καὶ τὰς γυναῖκας καὶ τὰ
ואת בנות המלך ואת <u>כל</u> הנפש		<u>λοιπὰ</u> καὶ τὰς θυγατέρας τοῦ βασιλέως καὶ
אשר הניח נבוזראדן <u>רב טבחים</u>		τὰς ψυχάς ἃς κατέλιπε Ναβουζαρδαν μετὰ
את גדליהו בן אחיקם <u>בן שפן</u>		Γοδολιου υἱοῦ Αχικαμ καὶ Ιερεμιαν τὸν
ואת ירמיהו הנביא ואת ברוך		προφήτην καὶ Βαρουχ υἱὸν Νηριου
בן נריהו		
ויבאו <u>ארץ</u> מצרים כי לא שמעי	7	καὶ εἰσῆλθοσαν εἰς Αἴγυπτον ὅτι οὐκ
בקול יהוה ויבאו עד תחפנחס		ἤκουσαν τῆς φωνῆς κυρίου καὶ εἰσῆλθωσαν
		εἰς Ταφνας

5.2. *Textual Notes*
Chapter 42(49)

v. 10. אם שוב תשבו ("If returning you will dwell"); OG ἐὰν καθίσαντες καθίσητε ("If indeed you will remain") = אם ישוב תשבו. OG is supported by the versions and accepted by most scholars. Preferring MT, Holladay argues that "it is possible to have an infinitive absolute of one verb and a finite form of a second verb related by word-play."[90] He thus translates, "If you change your mind and stay." This is an attractive reading, but MT may have been secondarily influenced by the statement in 41:17 that the Jews already intended to go to Egypt.

MT נחמתי; OG ἀναπέπαυμαι. If נחם Niph. is understood to mean "grieve, be sorry for" (Gen 6:7; 1 Sam 15:11), then OG ("I have ceased from") yields a significantly different sense. Possibly the translator wanted to avoid the idea of God repenting. Others argue that נחם here means "relent, change course" (Isa

---

90. Holladay, *Jeremiah 2*, 274, 300; similarly, *DIHGS* §101. Rem. 1.

57:6; Jer 4:28; 18:8; 26:3; Ezek 24:14; Zech 8:14), thus reducing the difference with OG.[91] In almost all these latter references, however, a future scenario is in mind, whereas in Jer 42:10 (as in Gen 6:7; 1 Sam 15:11), YHWH is reviewing some past action. Probably, therefore, נחמתי here has an emotive sense—"sorry about," if not "sorry for."[92]

v. 12. MT ואתן...ורחם...והשיב; OG δώσω...ἐλεήσω...ἐπιστρέψω. The third person forms in MT after the initial ואתן are consistent with the use of נתן רחמים elsewhere in the Old Testament (Gen 43:14; Deut 13:18; 1 Kgs 8:50; Neh 1:11; Ps 106:46; Dan 1:9). In each case, the subject of נתן רחמים is YHWH, and in each case except Deut 13:18, his compassion involves moving other people (often captors of some sort) to show benevolence. Twice, the nature of their benevolence is then described more precisely: Gen 43:14, ושלח לכם את אחיכם, and 1 Kgs 8:50, ורחמים. Both these verses correspond to MT Jer 42:12, where ואתן לכם רחמים (subject: YHWH) is defined by ורחם אתכם והשיב אתכם (subject: Nebuchadrezzar).

MT הֵשִׁיב; OG ἐπιστρέψω. Both texts read the verb as שוב ("restore, return"); cf. Targ. (ויתיב) and Vulg. (*et habitare vos faciam*), presupposing ישׁב Hiph. Given the location of the remnant on the border of Judah (41:17), the agreed reading of MT and OG makes good sense. The Hiph. is best taken as permissive, "he will *allow* you to return."[93]

v. 17. OG πάντες οἱ ἀλλογενεῖς (= וכל זרים) >MT. The reading is odd, though several scholars have connected it with the MT plus כל האנשים הזדים in 43:2. Janzen proposes that זדים was an early marginal note on 42:17; this was incorporated into the MT tradition at 43:2, while in the OG *Vorlage* it was corrupted to זרים and added at 42:17.[94]

v. 19. MT דִּבֶּר יהוה; OG ἃ ἐλάλησε κύριος. Both MT and OG are awkward. While the use of דבר Pi. to introduce or conclude an oracle is well attested in the Old Testament, a bare דִּבֶּר יהוה is unparalleled. We could emend to זֶה דְבַר יהוה (cf. Zech 4:6);[95] the loss of זֶה may have been caused by the ending of v. 18, המקום הזה. However, OG implies a *Vorlage* reading אשר דבר, "this is that which."[96]

MT כי העידתי בכם היום >OG. Cf. Deut 4:26. Duhm believed that this was MT plus;[97] however, scribal error through homoiarchton (כי ה) seems more probable.[98]

91. E.g. Duhm, *Jeremia*, 321; Bright, *Jeremiah*, 255; McKane, *Jeremiah 2*, 1030; Holladay, *Jeremiah 2*, 300; Brueggemann, *Exile and Homecoming*, 390.
92. Cf. Bright, *Jeremiah*, 256; Thompson, *Jeremiah*, 666.
93. On the permissive use of Hiph., see *IBH* §157.
94. Janzen, 65; but see the response of McKane, *Jeremiah 2*, 1036–37.
95. So Duhm, *Jeremia*, 323; Wanke, *Untersuchungen*, 118.
96. Stulman, *Other Text*, 153. *GKC* §138b n. 2 notes the Jeremianic expression אשר היה דבר יהוה אל (14:1; 46:1; 47:1; 49:34), where אשר assumes an absolute sense, "this is that which."
97. Duhm, *Jeremia*, 324.
98. So Janzen, *Studies*, 118; Holladay, *Jeremiah 2*, 275.

v. 20. MT *Ketiv* התעתים בנפשתיכם; OG ὅτι ἐπονηρεύσασθε ἐν ψυχαῖς ὑμῶν. The *Ketiv* is impossible, and most follow *Qere*, התעיתם[99] (Hiph. תעה, "to err"). התעיתם is probably one of several "*inwardly transitive* or *intensive* Hiphils,"[100] all of which have a moral aspect (e.g חטא, תעב, יטב). By understanding the preposition as "ב of price" (cf. Jer 17:21), most scholars render the phrase in some such way as "you have wandered at the cost of your lives."[101] However, OG suggests הרעתם, "you did evil (in yourselves)." Duhm considered this more original, though his reasoning shows a strongly anti-theological bias.[102] More probably, the translator has substituted a known term for one that was obscure.

Chapter 43(50)
In addition to the witness of MT and OG, we also have a fragmentary text of Jer 43:2–10 in 4QJer[d]. Although reconstructions of this text are uncertain at points, it is clear that it mostly agrees with the text reflected by OG.[103]

v. 2. MT האנשים הזדים אמרים; OG οἱ ἄνδρες οἱ εἴπαντες...λέγοντες. Concerning אמרים, not only is the use of a participle to introduce direct speech unusual, but the plural form is inconsistent with the opening ויאמר (though it agrees with the number of people specified in the verse).[104] OG οἱ εἴπαντες implies האמרים, but this still conflicts with the opening ויאמר; moreover, since OG λέγοντες implies an original לאמר,[105] we would then have the syntactically awkward האנשים האמרים אל ירמיהו לאמר. A clue to a possible solution lies in MT הזדים, "insolent" (>OG). I noted above Janzen's suggestion that OG οἱ ἀλλογενεῖς in 42:17 and MT הזדים here are misreadings of a single marginal gloss, הזרים, "foreign."[106] Building on this, we could follow the suggestion that where MT now reads אמרים, the OG *Vorlage* read המרים "obstinate."[107] This would yield a natural word-pair, הזדים והמרים.

---

99. Not התעתם as given in Duhm, *Jeremia*, 324, and some editions of *BHS*. See the corrigenda in R. Wonneberger, *Understanding BHS: A Manual for the Users of the Biblia Hebraica Stuttgartensia* (SB 8; Rome: Pontifical Biblical Institute, 1990), 75.

100. *GKC* §53d (italics original).

101. E.g. Rudolph, *Jeremia*, 220; Thompson, *Jeremiah*, 665; Keown, Scalise and Smothers, *Jeremiah 26–52*, 246. However, Ehrlich, *Randglossen*, 348, and McKane, *Jeremiah 2*, 1038, see YHWH as its object.

102. Duhm, *Jeremia*, 324; so too Condamin, *Jérémie*, 281.

103. Emanuel Tov, "Three Fragments of Jeremiah from Qumran Cave 4," *RQ* 15 (1992): 531–41, is more ready than Janzen to identify points of agreement between 4QJer[d] and MT; but even Janzen, while affirming the "familial allegiance" of the OG *Vorlage* and 4QJer[d], surmises that "it represents a slightly different branch of the Egyptian family" (*Studies*, 183–84). See also George J. Brooke, "The Book of Jeremiah and its Reception in the Qumran Scrolls," in Curtis and Römer, eds., *The Book of Jeremiah and Its Reception*, 183–205 (187).

104. In any case, we should probably not expect ancient Hebrew writers to be any more consistent in their grammar than present-day English writers; see *DIHGS* §26 Rem. 5.

105. Rudolph, *Jeremia*, 218; Holladay, *Jeremiah 2*, 275; contra Stulman, *Other Text*, 157.

106. Janzen, *Studies*, 65; so too Holladay, *Jeremiah 2*, 275.

107. Volz, *Jeremia*, 358; Rudolph, *Jeremia*, 218; Holladay, *Jeremiah 2*, 275.

v. 5. It will be helpful here to compare the readings of MT, OG and 4QJer^d (line 4). The last of these, which is poorly preserved, has been reconstructed in two quite different ways.[108]

MT   אשר שבו מכל הגוים אשר נדחו שם לגור בארץ יהודה

OG   τοὺς ἀποστρέψαντας κατοικεῖν ἐν τῇ γῇ[109]
                = אשר שבו לגור בארץ

4QJer^d (Janzen)[110]   [אשר שבו לגור באר]ץ [מצר]ים

4QJer^d (Tov)[111]   [אשר שבו מכל הגוים אשר [נדחו] שם

OG non-representation of מכל הגוים אשר נדחו שם strongly suggests its absence from its *Vorlage*, especially since it also lacks the near-identical phrase in 40:12. There is no clear motive for deliberate omission, and no obvious cause of haplography. τοὺς ἀποστρέψαντας is not a literal rendering of אשר שבו (= οἱ ἀπεστρέψαν) but is unlikely to reflect a content variant in the *Vorlage*.

Determining the text of 4QJer^d is less straightforward. Janzen's reconstruction seems more probable, since it is doubtful whether the lacuna can contain all the wording that Tov proposes.[112] Tov concedes that לגור בארץ מצרים is possible, but objects that this would be "contextually difficult."[113] The problem is that כל שארית יהודה אשר שבו לגור בארץ מצרים (Janzen) is most naturally rendered as "the remnant of the Jews, who had returned (in order) to go to Egypt," an obviously implausible statement. However, perhaps we should see אשר שבו as parenthetical, and take לגור to complement ויקח יוחנן.

5.3. *Exegesis*
Chapter 42
v. 2. התפלל בעדנו. Carroll sees here a striking contrast with earlier passages (7:16; 11:14; 14:11) where Jeremiah is forbidden to intercede.[114] Here, however, intercession is for direction rather than for well-being.[115] See also 1 Sam 12:23, where Samuel pledges to intercede (התפלל בעד) for the people and to teach them the way (דרך).

v. 3. הדבר. Either "the thing, that which" or "the word" (i.e. the oracular message as such, rather than the directions contained in it). Especially in the light of 41:17, הדרך אשר נלך בה ("the way in which we should go") is probably

---

108.   These reconstructions are inevitably conjectural, with only the final *mem* being certain. Preceding that is the barest tip of a downward stroke, which could be a *yodh* (Janzen) or *shin* (Tov). At the end of the previous word, or the word before that, is what might be the tail of a *tsadeh* (Janzen) or *resh* (Tov).

109.   LXX^B, S. LXX^A adds Ιουδα, agreeing with MT.

110.   Janzen, *Studies*, 182–83; so too McKane, *Jeremiah 2*, 1053; Holladay, *Jeremiah 2*, 276.

111.   Tov, "Three Fragments," 538–40; so too Brooke, "Book of Jeremiah," 187.

112.   Janzen, *Studies*, 183.

113.   Tov, "Three Fragments," 539.

114.   Carroll, *Jeremiah*, 715.

115.   So McKane, *Jeremiah 2*, 1041.

intended literally. Elsewhere in the Old Testament, this phrase occurs sixteen times,[116] and only in Judg 2:17 and 2 Kgs 21:21 does it have a metaphorical use.

v. 5. יהי יהוה בנו לעד אמת ונאמן. The phrase עד אמת ונאמן ("faithful and true witness") occurs only here in the Old Testament; עד אמת occurs otherwise only in Prov 14:25. For לעד בנו meaning "a witness *against* (us)," see Num 5:13; Deut 31:19, 26; Josh 24:27; Mic 1:2. Again we have an echo of 1 Sam 12, where in response to Samuel's challenge עד יהוה בכם, the people affirm simply עד (1 Sam 12:5).

Formally impressive, the people's promise has the unmistakable nature of "rhetorical overkill."[117] As Nicholson notes, "the people's solemn undertaking…already alerts the reader to expect the subsequent conflict between the community and the prophet."[118] The overtones of 1 Sam 12 may point in the same direction.

v. 10. ובניתי אתכם ולא אהרס ונטעתי אתכם ולא אתוש. This language is paradigmatic in Jeremiah (cf. 1:10; 12:14–17; 18:7–9; 24:6; 31:28; 45:4), but the form in which it occurs here is particularly close to 24:6, which uses the same verbs in the same order: ונטעתים ולא אתוש ובניתם ולא אהרס.[119]

v. 11. אל תיראו מפני מלך בבל…כי אתכם אני להושיע אתכם ולהציל אתכם. The language of this salvation oracle is otherwise restricted in the book to two distinct audiences: to Jeremiah himself (אל תירא מפניהם כי אתך אני להצלך, 1:8; כי אתך אני להושיעך ולהצילך, 1:19; כי אתך אני…להצילך, 15:20) and to the *Diaspora* (אל תירא עבדי יעקב…כי אתך אני להושיעך, 30:10–11 = 46:27; cf. 23:6; 30:7). The only other recipient of an oracle involving נצל Hiph. is Ebed-Melech (39:17).

הציל מיד. Elsewhere, the expression usually denotes an act of deliverance involving military victory or escape. Here, however, resistance is out of the question, and escape to another land forbidden. Instead, as v. 12 explains, YHWH will rescue his people precisely by causing Nebuchadrezzar to be compassionate.[120] Compare Josh 24:10, where YHWH reminds Israel of how Balaam had intended to curse them, before adding, ולא אביתי לשמע לבלעם ויברך ברוך אתכם ואצל אתכם מידו. YHWH thus rescues Israel from a curse by forestalling it. Also significant is Gen 32, where, anticipating Esau's wrath (v. 6), Jacob prays for help: הצילני נא מיד אחי מיד עשו (v. 12). His hopes seem to lie either in a quick escape (vv. 7–8), or in placating Esau with a gift (v. 21). In the event, however, Esau receives his brother warmly (33:10), and in this we are probably meant to see God's answer to Jacob's prayer.

v. 12. והשיב אתכם אל אדמתכם. Following the reading reflected in MT and OG, some commentators have suggested that the wording betrays a later exilic

---

116.   Gen 35:3; 42:38; Deut 1:31, 33; 8:2; Josh 3:4; 24:17; Judg 2:17; 18:6; 1 Sam 9:6; 1 Kgs 13:9, 12, 17; 2 Kgs 21:21; Neh 9:12, 19.

117.   Holladay, *Jeremiah 2*, 299.

118.   Nicholson, *Jeremiah 26–52*, 142. Duhm, *Jeremia*, 323, also sees in v. 5 a hint that the people had already decided to go to Egypt.

119.   Taylor, "Jeremiah 45," 91.

120.   As Thiel remarks, *Redaktion 26–45*, 64, "v.12 präzisiert die Zusage."

perspective.[121] This is unnecessary, but there does seem to be a further echo of
24:6, והשבתים על הארץ הזאת.

v. 15. שארית יהודה. This is the regular designation of the Judean community
in this section of the narrative (40:11, 15; 42:19; 43:5; 44:12, 28); it occurs
nowhere else in the Old Testament. Until now, it has been used quite objec-
tively to describe the poor (העם הדלים) whom Nebuzaradan left with Gedaliah
(39:10), supplemented by Ishmael and his men (40:7–8) and those who returned
from other lands (40:11–12). From now on, however, it will carry heavily
pejorative overtones. In this passage, it seems to counter-balance ישבי ירושלם
(v. 18).

v. 19. כי העידתי בכם היום. Jeremiah's words echo those of Moses to the
Israelites in Deut 4:26 (העידתי בכם היום את השמים ואת הארץ), assuring them of
the dire consequences of idolatry.

Chapter 43

v. 3. כי ברוך בן נריה מסית אתך בנו. Baruch's appearance here is wholly unexpected, as is the charge that he is behind Jeremiah's counsel; previously (32:12–
14; 36:4–19) he has been presented in a subservient role to the prophet. Arguments that he is introduced here as a literary device, possibly representative of a
particular readership,[122] are less convincing than that the allegation was actually
made for reasons that are now unclear.

v. 5. אשר שבו. The reference is clearly to those who had returned to Judah
from other nations (40:12); this is made explicit in the MT plus, מכל הגוים
אשר נדחו שם, but is also implied in OG.[123] The *identification* of כל שארית יהודה
with the returnees from other lands is puzzling; we would expect it also to
include the original Mizpah community (cf. v. 6b).[124] Strictly speaking, however, this would require את אשר שבו.

v. 6. את הגברים ואת הנשים ואת הטף. Standing in apposition to the preceding
כל שארית יהודה אשר שבו, and with no initial ו, the phrase equates the first four
groups with the returnees from other lands in v. 5.[125] However, ואת כל הנפש
אשר הניח נבוזראדן את גדליהו clearly establishes the members of the Mizpah

---

121.   Bright, *Jeremiah*, 256; Jones, *Jeremiah*, 477.

122.   E.g. Carroll, *Jeremiah*, 722–23. Walter Brueggemann, "'The Baruch Connection':
Reflections on Jer 43:1–7," *JBL* 113 (1994): 413, treats Baruch as representative of "the scribal-
Deuteronomistic circles who enlisted Jeremiah's poetic-Yahwistic discernment for their own
purposes."

123.   This is worth emphasizing, since McKane, *Jeremiah 2*, 1053, attaches great significance
to the MT plus: "The group around Jonathan [*sic*] is made to consist not only of those taken from
Mizpah by Ishmael and rescued by Jonathan [*sic*], but also of those whose return from neighbouring
countries is reported at 40.11f." To support his argument, however, McKane also has to delete
אשר שבו.

124.   This is indeed how Pohlmann, *Studien*, 154, interprets MT. See too Bright's translation,
Jeremiah, 252: "Johanan…took the whole remnant of Judah: those who had returned to settle in the
land of Judah from the various countries to which they had been scattered; the men, the women, and
the children."

125.   Duhm, *Jeremia*, 325; see too McKane, *Jeremiah 2*, 1050, and RSV.

community as a separate group. Although, as the textual variants show, the wording and syntax of vv. 5–6 have become somewhat muddled in the course of transmission, the overall picture is clear enough.

5.4. *Coherence and Redaction*

That Jer 42:1 marks the start of a new episode is clear from a number of factors.[126] As fast-moving drama gives way to speech-dominated material, Jeremiah mysteriously reappears (42:1). Exactly where the section ends is less certain. From a narrative point of view, however, the obvious conclusion is v. 7, where, having rejected YHWH's final word, the Jews are found once more in Egypt, their former land of slavery.

The setting (vv. 1–9) describes how the people ask Jeremiah to intercede for them (vv. 2, 4) in order to obtain YHWH's direction. When he assents to their request, they swear to obey unreservedly whatever YHWH says. Although this interchange is recounted at some length (cf. the much briefer accounts in 21:2; 37:3), we need not suspect secondary expansion; in the light of their subsequent rejection of the oracle (43:2–3), it is more likely that the narrator wants to cast their request in an ironic light.[127]

The oracle (vv. 10–16) falls into two parts, each comprising a conditional clause (אִם שׁוֹב תֵּשְׁבוּ, v. 10; וְאִם...לֹא, v. 13) with a corresponding promise or warning. The first part (vv. 10–12) centres on the theme of living (יָשַׁב), which forms an *inclusio* (תֵּשְׁבוּ, v. 10a; הֵשִׁיב, v. 12).[128] Nevertheless, these verses are not one-dimensional. First, YHWH assures the people of his own favour, underlining this with the startling remark that he has "repented" (נִחַם, v. 10) from his anger. Secondly, he promises to save the people from the king of Babylon (v. 11) and cause him to show them mercy (v. 12).[129]

In the second half of the oracle (vv. 13–16), יָשַׁב is again the *leitmotif*. The remnant might decide not to live in this land (לֹא נֵשֵׁב בָּאָרֶץ הַזֹּאת, v. 13), but to flee to Egypt to escape war and famine, and live there (וְשָׁם נֵשֵׁב, v. 14). Such hopes are refuted in v. 16; especially striking is the final וְשָׁם תָּמֻתוּ, counterbalancing וְשָׁם נֵשֵׁב (v. 14).[130] Granted, v. 15 is repetitive, and interrupts an otherwise smooth flow from v. 14 to v. 16. Without it, vv. 10–14, 16 form an

---

126. Kremers, "Leidensgemeinschaft," 127, and Wanke, *Untersuchungen*, 119, see the previous section as ending at 41:15; however, the story of Johanan's rescue of the hostages clearly ends in v. 18.

127. As Nicholson, *Jeremiah 26–52*, 142, notes, "the people's solemn undertaking...already alerts the reader to expect the subsequent conflict between the community and the prophet." Duhm (*Jeremia*, 323) also sees in v. 5 a hint that the people had already decide to go to Egypt.

128. This holds true irrespective of whether we emend שׁוֹב to יָשׁוֹב in v. 10.

129. How useful it is to describe the נָתַשׁ / נָטַשׁ, הָרַס / בָּנָה refrain (v. 10; cf. 1:10; 18:7–9; 24:6; 31:28; 45:4) and the expression אֶתֵּן לָכֶם רַחֲמִים (v. 12) as Deuteronomistic (so Wanke, *Untersuchungen*, 125–27; Thiel, *Redaktion 26–45*, 64–65) is questionable. Weippert, *Prosareden des Jeremiabuches*, 197–98, shows that outside Jeremiah, the pairs הָרַס / בָּנָה and נָתַשׁ / נָטַשׁ occur (individually) only in post-Jeremianic and non-Deuteronomistic contexts. נָתַן רַחֲמִים occurs also in Gen 43:14; Neh 1:11 and Dan 1:9.

130. Wanke, *Untersuchungen*, 121–22, also notes how v. 16 counterbalances v. 14.

oracle comprising two parts of almost equal length, with "living/remaining" its consistent theme.[131]

Some scholars have questioned the place of vv. 11–12 in this section. Wanke sees them (along with vv. 15, 17–18) as part of a redactional strand in which salvation is unconditional.[132] By contrast, in vv. 10, 13–14, 16 salvation is contingent upon remaining in the land. But this is unconvincing; the function of vv. 11–12 is to elucidate and reinforce the message of v. 10. It is a bizarre hermeneutic that detaches vv. 11–12 from this mooring and then claims that they lack a conditional clause.[133] Pohlmann argues that vv. 11–12 disrupt the two אם clauses of vv. 10 and 13.[134] Indeed, vv. 11–12 themselves conflict, for why should YHWH need to rescue the people from Nebuchadrezzar, if the latter is well-disposed towards them?[135] But, as I argued earlier, without v. 12 the promise of v. 11 would be meaningless. As it is, these verses affirm that YHWH will rescue his people by causing Nebuchadrezzar to be compassionate.

A significant shift occurs in vv. 17–18. Whereas v. 16 predicts war and famine in a somewhat matter of fact fashion, vv. 17–18 refer to war, famine and plague, which they interpret in explicitly theological terms, that is, as aspects of YHWH's wrath.[136] The language strongly resembles that found in ch. 44; the warning ולא יהיה להם שריד ופליט (v. 17) is repeated almost verbatim in 44:14, while the analogy between YHWH's wrath on Jerusalem and on the remnant (v. 18) finds a parallel in 44:13. Notable too is the switch to third person speech in v. 17 (כל האנשים). All this may suggest that vv. 17–18 are redactional comment,[137] possibly from a Deuteronomistic source.[138] At the same time, since the rest of the sermon clearly presents going to Egypt as disobedience to YHWH (vv. 13, 19), a declaration that doing so would provoke his wrath is hardly incongruous. In sum, vv. 17–18 represent a different voice to that in vv. 10–16, but not necessarily a different speaker.

131.　According to Seitz, *Theology in Conflict*, 277, "the basic response of Jeremiah to the delegation can be isolated in vv. 9–12," since these verses deal with the point at issue, the people's fear of the Babylonians. By contrast, vv. 13–22 derive from ER. But the אם of v. 10 virtually demands the אם לא of v. 13. Duhm, *Jeremia*, 322, saw vv. 13–14, 19–21 as containing the only authentic material in this chapter.

132.　Wanke, *Untersuchungen*, 120–24.

133.　We should also note that the promise of v. 10, though contingent on the people's response, is also grounded in YHWH's independent volition: כי נחמתי אל הרעה אשר עשיתי לכם.

134.　Pohlmann, *Studien*, 132.

135.　Ibid., 132; likewise, Duhm, *Jeremia*, 322, and McKane, *Jeremiah 2*, 1034. In any case, v. 12 does not assert that the king *is* well-disposed towards the remnant, but that he *will be* so; we could paraphrase, "I will show you compassion *in that* he will show you compassion."

136.　As Pohlmann, *Studien*, 144, correctly observes.

137.　So Duhm, *Jeremia*, 322–23; McKane, *Jeremiah 2*, 1045 (though by ascribing v. 16 to the same redactor, both scholars obviate the distinction between vv. 16 and 17–18); Wanke, *Untersuchungen*, 120–22 (who sees vv. 17–18 as from the same hand as vv. 11–12, 15); contra Thiel, *Redaktion 26–45*, 63, who sees v. 17 as the sole authentic kernel in the entire sermon.

138.　Though this is disputed by Jones, *Jeremiah*, 474–75.

Verses 19–22 constitute a problem in that Jeremiah rebukes the people for rejecting YHWH's word before they have actually replied. Some scholars have transposed these verses with 43:1–3,[139] but לא שלחך יהוה אלהינו לאמר לא תבאו מצרים (43:2) clearly presupposes אל תבאו מצרים (42:19). Duhm took v. 22 as redactional, and for vv. 19–21 followed the shorter text of OG,[140] but even OG presupposes ולא שמעתם בקול יהוה. Wanke regards the words framed by ידע תדעו (vv. 19b, 22a) as redactional, precisely because they anticipate the flight to Egypt;[141] however, even the material he retains includes the description of Egypt as המקום אשר חפצתם לבוא לגור שם (v. 22b). Pohlmann regarded vv. 19–21 as a distinct redactional layer, added to prepare us for "die unerwartet ablehnende Reaktion gegenüber Jeremia"[142] in 43:1–3. But again, the people's protest, לא שלחך יהוה אלהינו לאמר לא תבאו מצרים (43:2), makes little sense without Jeremiah's explicit command אל תבאו מצרים (42:19).[143] In fact, in historical terms it is quite plausible that the prophet correctly anticipated the reaction of his audience.[144] In any case, so far from being a surprise, Jeremiah's declaration in vv. 19–22 fulfils the reader's expectations. As we have seen, the rhetorical overkill of the people's words in vv. 2–6 prepares us for a negative response to his message, while even within the body of the sermon, the tone has from v. 13 become progressively more ominous.[145] As in 38:17–23, therefore, 42:10–22 depicts Jeremiah subverting his own message of conditional salvation.

Jeremiah 43:1–7 reports the hostile reaction of the people to the prophet's message, and their decision to go to Egypt. In narrative terms, 43:7 brings the story to an end, with the arrival in Tahpanhes. At the same time, in several respects 43:5–7 stands apart from 42:1–43:4, showing more in common with 40:7–41:18. The focus reverts from speech to action, and Jeremiah recedes once more into the background (in v. 6 he seems almost to be an afterthought). Moreover, after the explicitly theological tenor of 42:1–43:4,[146] 43:5–7 assumes a more restrained tone; in 43:6, אשר הניח נבוזראדן רב טבחים את גדליהו recalls the subtle criticism of Ishmael's actions in ch. 41. The wording of 43:5, ויקח יוחנן בן קרח וכל שרי החילים את כל שארית יהודה, closely resembles 41:16a, and in both verses the remnant are then defined in more detail (41:16b; 43:6). Most significant of all, in 41:16 and 43:5 the remnant appear to be subject to the

139. Volz, *Jeremia*, 357–58, 361; Rudolph, *Jeremia*, 218–20; Bright, *Jeremiah*, 252, 256.
140. Duhm, *Jeremia*, 323–24.
141. Wanke, *Untersuchungen*, 123.
142. Pohlmann, *Studien*, 143.
143. As Wanke, *Untersuchungen*, 124, notes.
144. Thompson, *Jeremiah*, 667; Keown, Scalise and Smothers, *Jeremiah 26–52*, 252–53; see too Bright, *Jeremiah*, 256.
145. Cf. Seitz, *Theology in Conflict*, 277: "Developing the redactional motif at work in 21.7 and especially 24.8–10, Jer 42.13–22 reverses Jeremiah's words of promise as it anticipates a disobedient decision…to flee to Egypt."
146. Cf. Wanke's comment on 43:4 (*Untersuchungen*, 126): "Solcher Kommentar ist innerhalb der übrigen Erzählungen nirgends zu beobachten. Ihrem Stil entspricht es viel eher, sich auf die Mitteilung der Gespräche…und die Beurteilung des Verhaltens der handelnden Personen dem Leser zu überlassen."

actions of Johanan's men.[147] By contrast, 42:1, 8; 43:2, 4 depict the two groups as equal partners in seeking and then rejecting Jeremiah's advice.[148]

While certainty is impossible, these stylistic and conceptual variations between 40:7–41:18 and 43:5–7 on the one hand, and 42:1–43:4 on the other, probably reflect different literary sources. Seitz sees in 43:1–3 the conclusion of the Scribal Chronicle, while vv. 4–6 stem from the Exilic Redaction: "At the literary level, Jer 43.5–7 goes to great pains to portray the comprehensiveness of the contingent fleeing to Egypt... All Judah is there, and all are disobedient."[149] Similarly, Pohlmann argues that the editor has combined a story of how Johanan's group fled to Egypt (40:7–41:18) with one that told how "all the people from the smallest to the greatest" came to Jeremiah to seek direction. This, he believes, also solves the puzzle of why in 42:1 the people ask him to intercede for them, after the remark in 41:17 that they had already decided to go to Egypt.[150] In fact, Pohlmann's view that 42:1–22 originally made no mention of Johanan's contingent is questionable, requiring him to delete the references to the military officers in 42:1, 8 as glosses.[151] A more probable conclusion is that 40:7–41:18 is *historically* continuous but not *literarily* continuous with 42:1–22.[152] That is to say, the accounts are drawn from different sources, and use different terminology for the parties involved, but the parties are in reality the same and the events sequential.

Finally, we note that 42:1–43:7 displays a number of parallels, verbal and conceptual, with 38:5–23. The remnant, like Zedekiah, invoke YHWH in an oath in seeking his direction (חי יהוה אשר עשה לנו את; 42:5, יהי יהוה בנו לעד אמת, הנפש הזאת 38:16), while Jeremiah's promise, לא אמנע מכם דבר (42:4), echoes

---

147.   Contra P. A. H. de Boer, "Some Remarks Concerning and Suggested by Jeremiah 43:1–7," in *Selected Studies in Old Testament Exegesis* (ed. C. Van Duin; Leiden: Brill, 1970), 113–21 (118), who claims that "the verb לקה indicates that those who are taken with them are carried away; not, however, that the carrying away takes place against their will."

148.   See Wanke, *Untersuchungen*, 126 n. 26: "Der deuteronomistischen Bearbeitung entspricht auch gut die Ausdehnung des aktiven Personenkreises auf das ganze Volk (v. 4). Demgegenüber nennen 43.2, 5 nur die Heerführer. Die Verantwortung nur einzelnen Personen aufzubürden, liegt nicht im Sinne der deuteronomistischen Theologie, der es um das Volksganze geht."

149.   Seitz, *Theology in Conflict*, 278; see too de Boer, "Some Remarks," 120. By contrast, Wanke, *Untersuchungen*, 119–31, treats 43:1–7 as part of the literary unit 41:16 to 43:7, but concedes that there is redactional supplementation in 43:4, 5b and 6a.

150.   Pohlmann, *Studien*, 124–25. Pohlmann is highly critical of the psychological explanations of scholars like Rudolph, *Jeremia*, 218–19.

151.   Key to Pohlmann's argument is v. 8: ויקרא אל יחנן בן קרח ואל כל שרי החילים...ולכל העם. Whereas קרא ל means "summon, assemble," he argues, קרא אל means "call to," "wenn man sich in Rufnähe oder Sichtweite aufhält und direkter Kontakt möglich ist" (*Studien*, 128). Since ten days passed before YHWH's word came to Jeremiah (v. 7), he probably had to summon the people to hear it; thus, קרא ל is more appropriate than קרא אל. But this semantic distinction is questionable, since קרא אל can also mean "summon, gather together" (2 Sam 9:2; 14:33; 2 Kgs 4:22, 36; 6:11; 7:10; 10:19).

152.   Skinner, *Prophecy and Religion*, 282, refers to "an overlapping of two documents, of which the first (closing with ch. 41) gives a condensed account of the migration to Egypt, while the second (ch. 42) relates in amplified detail Jeremiah's unavailing opposition to the resolve of the military leaders."

the king's solemn אל תכחד ממנו דבר (38:14). The remnant, like Zedekiah, seem braced for bad news (אם טוב ואם רע, 42:6; cf. again אל תכחד ממני דבר, 38:15), but vow to obey "so that it may go well with us" (למען אשר ייטב לנו, 42:6), thereby echoing Jeremiah's וייטב לך (38:20). Jeremiah's message to each party is to submit to the Babylonians, with אם ישוב תשבו (42:10, if we follow OG) corresponding structurally to אם יצא תצא (38:17). Fear of the consequences of doing so is anticipated, in both cases with the unusual term דאג (38:19; 42:16). At the same time, what dominates his message is the counter-balancing negative clause, אם לא (38:18, 21; 42:13), which ends by predicting a negative response (38:21–23; 42:19–22).

5.5. *Judicial Differentiation in Jeremiah 42:1–43:7:* שבי / שארית יהודה ירושלם

Both in OG and MT, Jeremiah's message to the Judean remnant represents his final oracle within the borders of Judah. Those that follow in MT (46:27–28; 50:4–5; 20) will address an exiled audience. As we have seen, 42:10–22 configures the alternatives of salvation and judgment around the issue of where the people will live (ישב). If they remain in their land, they are assured of Nebuchadrezzar's goodwill and YHWH's blessing. If, however, they flee to Egypt, the very hardships they hope to escape will follow them, and they will suffer YHWH's judgment.[153] The choice presented to the remnant thus creates a straightforward distinction between הישבים בארץ הזאת and הישבים בארץ מצרים.

This by itself, of course, does not constitute selective judgment. Rather, it provides a set of alternatives, whereby a group or nation has to choose between two options. In this sense, the הישבים בארץ הזאת / הישבים בארץ מצרים polarity of ch. 42 resembles the אשר עבד / אשר לא עבד את מלך בבל polarity of ch. 27. In both cases, Jeremiah envisages his audience responding *as one*. This is empha-sized in ch. 42 by the fact that the remnant are consistently described in plural terms, either second person (ואם אמרים אתם...אם שוב תשבו, vv. 10, 13) or third person (כל האנשים אשר שמו את פניהם, v. 17), and are conceived of as thinking in the first person plural (לא נשב בארץ הזאת...כי ארץ מצרים נבוא...ושם נשב, vv. 13–14). This unitary view of the group is maintained even when the narrator acknowledges their diversity (43:4). Only in 43:5 does the picture become more complex, with Johanan and his officers *taking* (לקח, v. 5) the rest of the people (including Jeremiah and Baruch) to Egypt. I have suggested that a literary seam in the text is evident here.

Jeremiah's address does, however, establish one very significant judicial polarity. I noted earlier that throughout this narrative his audience are referred to as "the remnant of Judah" (שארית יהודה). This designation recalls, but is not identical with, the phrase used in 24:8 for those who will experience YHWH's wrath, "the remnant of Jerusalem" (שארית ירושלם). The hint of a subtle

---

153.   It may be significant that Jeremiah uses the term ישב in relation to Egypt when he is voicing the thoughts of the remnant (vv. 13, 14), but גור when he is voicing his own perspective (vv. 15, 17, 22).

distinction between these two groups suddenly becomes explicit with YHWH's warning in 42:18: ‫כאשר נתך אפי וחמתי על ישבי ירושלם...כן תתך חמתי עליכם‬. The polarity created as Jeremiah addresses this group, therefore, is between the ‫שארית ירושלם / ישבי ירושלם‬ of chs. 21 and 24, and the present ‫שארית יהודה‬.

This distinction is sharpened when we remember that in 24:8, the ‫שארית‬ ‫ירושלם‬ is further defined as ‫הנשארים בארץ הזאת והישבים בארץ מצרים‬. That is to say, for the remnant of Jerusalem "this land" and "Egypt" stand in parallel; those in either place will experience YHWH's wrath. For the remnant of Judah, on the other hand, "this land" and "Egypt" are alternatives; to flee to Egypt will incur judgment, but to remain in Judah will result in salvation. That is to say, 42:10–22 creates alternatives out of what in ch. 24 was a single entity. In this way, it reflects a mode of judicial differentiation that was described earlier; namely, it offers a choice to some that is not offered to others.

In fact, the textual depiction of the remnant in Jer 42 implies that, for the moment, they are judicially distinct from *both* groups in ch. 24. On the one hand, the promises ‫ובנתיתי אתכם ולא אהרס ונטעתי אתכם ולא אתוש‬ (v. 10) and ‫והשיב אתכם אל אדמתכם‬ (42:12) clearly echo YHWH's words in 24:6. The remnant of Judah may thus participate in the blessings promised to the exiles in Babylon. At the same time, they are warned that by going to Egypt they will die ‫בחרב ברעב ובדבר‬ (v. 17; cf. 24:10) and will be ‫לאלה ולשמה ולקללה ולחרפה‬ (v. 18; cf. 24:9). The allusion to 24:8–10 is underlined by YHWH's words in v. 18: ‫כאשר נתך אפי וחמתי על ישבי ירושלם כן תתך חמתי עליכם‬. Consequently, the text represents the ‫שארית יהודה‬ as distinct from the ‫שארית ירושלם‬ and the ‫גלות יהודה‬, but capable of identifying with either.

Indeed, the salvation promise of 42:10–12 goes further than that of 24:6. As we saw earlier, the exhortation ‫אל תיראו...כי אכתם אני להושיע אתכם ולהציל‬ ‫אתכם‬ (v. 11) is applied elsewhere only to the prophet and the *Diaspora*. The assurance ‫ואתן לכם רחמים‬ (v. 12) is unparalleled in Jeremiah. Both in their tone and content, therefore, these verses far exceed earlier promises of mere survival (21:9; 38:20), or even the hope of a viable community (27:2–18), that are offered to those who submit to the Babylonian yoke. The point is worth noting, not least because Seitz allocates all this material to the Scribal Chronicle.[154] It may be that they stem from a common source, but it should not be assumed that they present a uniform message. The voice that we hear in 42:10–12 sounds a note of hope for the remnant that is more akin to that sounded for the exiles in ch. 24 and for the prophet himself earlier in the book.[155]

The judicial polarity of ‫שארית יהודה / ישבי ירושלם‬ becomes more ambiguous, however, when we consider the rationale underlying the offer of salvation. The

---

154. On 42:10–12, Seitz (*Theology in Conflict*, 277 [see also 291]) writes: "Consistent with the prophet's counsel in the post-597 years (Jeremiah 27–29), especially as recorded prior to the events of 587 (Jeremiah 37–38), the leaders of the remnant are exhorted not to fear the Babylonians."

155. Cf. Thompson, *Jeremiah*, 665–66: "This remnant, like the one in Babylon, was being offered the same promise of renewal and restoration... But in a negative way it became clear, as it was declared positively elsewhere, that the future lay with the exiles in Babylon (chs. 24, 29) and not with those who fled to Egypt or those who remained in the land."

fact that the "remnant of Judah" is distinct from the "remnant of Jerusalem" suggests that YHWH is willing to show compassion to the former precisely because they are a separate group. On the other hand, YHWH himself gives a very different explanation: כי נחמתי אל הרעה אשר עשתי לכם (42:10). Salvation is possible because he is grieved over the judgment he has already inflicted. Here there seems to be a hint of the "theology of exile" which I discussed earlier in connection with the work of Kilpp and Seitz, and which comes to expression in Isa 40:1–2; salvation is open to those who have experienced judgment. However, the reference to הרעה אשר עשיתי לכם has the effect of blurring the distinction between the remnant of Judah and the remnant of Jerusalem; both alike, apparently, have experienced judgment. Thus, the textual construal of the people in 42:10–22 fluctuates between differentiating them from their counterparts in Jerusalem and Babylon, and seeing them as representative of Judah as a whole.

6. *Jeremiah 45:1–5 (51:31–35)*

6.1. *Text*

הדבר אשר דבר ירמיהו הנביא אל ברוך בן נריה בכתבו את הדברים האלה על ספר מפי ירמיהו בשנה הרבעית ליהויקים בן יאשיהו מלך יהודה לאמר	1 31	ὁ λόγος ὃν ἐλάλησεν Ιερεμιας ὁ προφήτης πρὸς Βαρουχ υἱὸν Νηρου ὅτε ἔγραφε τοὺς λόγους τούτους ἐν βιβλίῳ ἀπὸ στόματος Ιερεμιου ἐν τῷ ἐνιαυτῷ τῷ τετάρτῳ τῷ Ιωακιμ υἱῷ Ιωσια βασιλέως Ιουδα
כה אמר יהוה אלהי ישראל עליך ברוך	2 32	οὕτως εἶπε κύριος ἐπὶ σοί Βαρουχ
אמרת אוי נא לי כי יסף יהוד יגון על מכאבי יגעתי באנחתי ומנוחה לא מצאתי	3 33	ὅτι εἶπας οἴμμοι οἴμμοι ὅτι προσέθηκε κύριος κόπον ἐπὶ πόνον μου ἐκοιμήθην ἐν στεναγμοῖς ἀνάπαυσιν οὐχ εὗρον
כה תאמר אליו כה אמר יהוה הנה אשר בניתי אני הרס ואת אשר נטעתי אני נתש ואת כל הארץ היא	4 34	εἶπον αὐτῷ οὕτως εἶπε κύριος ἰδοὺ οὓς ἐγὼ ᾠκοδόμησα ἐγὼ καθαιρῶ καὶ οὓς ἐγὼ ἐφύτευσα ἐγὼ ἐκτίλλω
ואתה תבקש לך גדלות אל תבקש כי הנני מביא רעה על כל בשר נאם יהוה ונתתי לך את נפשך לשלל על כל המקמות אשר תלך שם	5 35	καὶ σὺ ζητήσεις σεαυτῷ μεγάλα μὴ ζητήσῃς ὅτι ἰδοὺ ἐγὼ ἐπάγω κακὰ ἐπὶ πᾶσαν σάρκα λέγει κύριος καὶ δώσω τὴν ψυχήν σου εἰς εὕρεμα ἐν παντὶ τόπῳ οὗ ἐὰν βαδίσῃς ἐκεῖ

6.2. *Textual Notes*

v. 3. OG ὅτι = כי >MT. Probably lost through haplography (repetition of ך from ברוך). An initial כי would be normal in this type of clause; cf. 29:15, 21.

MT יגעתי, "I have grown weary"; OG ἐκοιμήθην (Aor. Pass. κοιμάω), "I have gone to sleep." *BHS* suggests that OG is a corruption of ἐκόπωθην (Aor. Pass. κόπω), but Ziegler points out that κόπω occurs only twice in the LXX, both times in very late texts (Eccl 10:15; Jdt 13:1).[156] Ziegler also notes that while the alternative form κοπίαω is used for יגע in Jer 51(28):58; Lam 5:5 and Ps 6:7 (ἐκοπίασα ἐν τῷ στεναγμῷ μου), ἐκοπίασα could hardly have been confused with ἐκοιμήθην; we should thus either posit יצעתי ("spread out, lay [down]") in the *Vorlage* or assume a rather free translation.[157] The latter seems more probable.

v. 4. MT ואת כל הארץ היא >OG. MT plus. This is clearly intended as an interpretative gloss, "that is, the whole earth" (for this rendition of הארץ, see below). Although the use of את with a subject is grammatically awkward, it is not unparalleled where the subject is in apposition to a direct object (cf. 1 Kgs 2:32; Ezek 14:22).[158] Emendation may therefore be unnecessary.[159]

MT בניתי...נטעתי; OG ἐγὼ ᾠκοδόμησα...ἐγὼ ἐφύτευσα. Since OG renders the Hebrew participles with finite verbs, the personal pronouns are grammatically unnecessary, and thus emphatic. However, this is probably the implied sense of נטעתי and בניתי in MT also.[160]

6.3. *Exegesis*

v. 1. הדבר אשר דבר ירמיהו הנביא אל. The structure of this introductory formula occurs elsewhere in Jeremiah only in 51:59: הדבר אשר צוה ירמיהו הנביא את שריה. Noting other similarities between 45:1–5 and 51:59–64, and the fact that Baruch and Seraiah were brothers, Wanke argues that these two passages were originally transmitted together as an independent tradition.[161] He may, however, have overstated the parallels, which can in any case be explained in other ways.

הדברים האלה. The question of what "these words" denote is a *crux interpretum*. Clearly, the ensuing מפי ירמיהו בשנה הרבעית ליהויקים בן יאשיהו מלך יהודה relates them to Baruch's scroll (ch. 36), and many scholars accept this as the original meaning. One difficulty with this is that since ch. 36 does not actually cite the contents of the scroll, a logical antecedent for הדברים האלה is lacking.[162] This problem is solved if we accept Rietzschel's thesis that ch. 45 originally stood at the end of ch. 20 (note the repetition of יגון in 20:18 and 45:3), so that הדברים האלה referred to the scroll contained in Jer 1–20.[163] In its present context, however, the phrase seems to require a more immediate

156.   Ziegler, *Beiträge*, 35.

157.   Ibid.; the latter option is favoured by McKane, *Jeremiah 2*, 1098.

158.   See further *DIHGS* §94, and Rem. 6–7: "It seems more sensible to regard את accompanying subjects as (mildly) focussing or emphatic."

159.   Giesebrecht, *Jeremia*, 226, and Volz, *Jeremia*, 371, emend to אני מחריב or אחריב ("I will lay waste"). Volz suggests that ואת כל הארץ אחריב originally followed v. 5bα, הנני מביא רעה על כל בשר. G. R. Driver, "Linguistic and Textual Problems: Jeremiah," *JQR* 28 (1937–38): 97–129 (122–23), emends to אני מכה ("I will smite"); cf. Rudolph, *Jeremiah*, 226 (אכה).

160.   So Holladay, *Jeremiah 2*, 310.

161.   Wanke, *Untersuchungen*, 134, 140–42; his proposal is viewed sympathetically by Schulte, "Persönliche Heilsorakel," 259. But see Graupner's reply, *Auftrag*, 166–71.

162.   Noted by Graupner, *Auftrag*, 164.

163.   Rietzschel, *Urrolle*, 127–31; so too Lundbom, *Jeremiah 1–20*, 94 (cf. Holladay, *Jeremiah 2*, 308–9).

referent. Consequently, some scholars view מפי...יהודה as redactional and relate הדברים האלה to the preceding narrative of chs. 37–44.[164] It has even been argued that the phrase denotes the Oracles against the Nations (OAN) that immediately follow,[165] though of course this can apply only to Jer MT. I will return to this question below.

v. 3. אמרת. The prefacing of a prophetic message with the citation formula, "(Because) you said," often indicates that the cited words are in some way reprehensible; whether because they are arrogant (Isa 14:13; 28:15; 37:24; Ezek 27:3; 35:10), cynical (Mal 3:14), despairing (Ezek 33:10; cf. 37:11) or because they misconstrue reality (Jer 29:15; Ezek 11:5). Baruch's complaint will also earn a degree of censure.

אוי נא לי. The cry אוי ל is usually a response to national calamity, interpreted as divine judgment (Num 21:29; 1 Sam 4:7; Isa 3:9; Jer 4:13; 13:27; Hos 7:13; Lam 5:16).[166] Conversely, in 15:10 Jeremiah's אוי לי אמי כי ילדתני arises from the opposition of his compatriots. Indirectly, he also implicates YHWH (cf. 15:18b), since it is his preaching of YHWH's word that has caused this opposition. Here, however, Baruch directly attributes his suffering to YHWH (כי יהוה יסף).

אנחה...מכאוב...יגון. Found mostly in exilic and post-exilic poetic texts, these terms are especially characteristic of individual laments; for אנחה ("sighing"), see Pss 6:7; 31:11; 38:10; 102:6; Lam 1:22; Job 3:4, 24; for יגון ("sorrow, grief"), see Pss 13:2; 31:11; for מכאוב ("pain"), see Pss 38:17; 69:26; Lam 1:12, 18.[167] In addition, יגון occurs twice in the laments of Jeremiah (8:18; 20:18). The language is too general to permit conclusions as to the cause of Baruch's suffering (see further below). Duhm attributed Baruch's "pain" to the fate of his people, and his "sorrow" to his own circumstances,[168] but whether such a sharp

---

164. So Giesebrecht, *Jeremia*, 226; Duhm, *Jeremia*, 334–35; Graupner, *Auftrag*, 165 (though seeing הדברים האלה as itself secondary). S. Mowinckel, *Prophecy and Tradition: The Prophetic Books in the Light of the Study of the Growth and History of the Tradition* (Avhandlinger [Norske videnskaps-akademi i Oslo. II, Hist.-filos. klasse], 1946, no. 3; Oslo: Dybwad, 1946), 45, suggested that the reference was to the entire book.

165. So Ehrlich, *Randglossen*, 153; Seitz, "Canonical Shape," 21–23. Neither finds it necessary to delete the historical note in v. 1b; Seitz argues that a retrospective reference to Baruch's scroll is perfectly appropriate, since (according to 36:2) it included YHWH's words to the nations.

166. Isa 6:5 is the only exception. In Jer 4:31, אוי נא לי is uttered by Jerusalem.

167. Conventional language is not, of course, *de facto* inauthentic. On this point (though in relation to Jeremiah's laments), see John Bright, "Jeremiah's Complaints. Liturgy or Expressions of Personal Distress?," in *Proclamation and Presence: Old Testament Essays in Honour of Gwynne Henton Davies* (ed. J. I. Durham and J. R. Porter; Richmond, Vt.: John Knox, 1970), 189–214; Diamond, *Confessions*, 190; contra E. Gerstenberger, "Jeremiah's Complaints: Observations on Jer. 15:10–21," *JBL* 82 (1963): 393–408; Antonius H. J. Gunneweg, "Konfession oder Interpretation im Jeremiabuch," *ZTK* 67 (1970): 395–416 (412–14); Carroll, *From Chaos to Covenant*, 107–30; cf. 151.

168. Duhm, *Jeremia*, 335; similarly Peake, *Jeremiah & Lamentations 2*, 211; Artur Weiser, "Das Gotteswort für Baruch. Jer. 45 und die sogennante Baruchbiographie," in *Glaube und Geschichte im Alten Testmanent und andere ausgewählte Schriften* (ed. Artur Weiser; Göttingen: Vandenhoeck & Ruprecht, 1961), 321–29 (323).

distinction between these terms can be supported is doubtful.[169] Graupner argues
that the terminology signifies "ein bestimmtes Geschehen, das Gerichtshandeln
Jahwes, oder die Reaktion derer, die das Gericht erlebt haben";[170] however, this
overlooks Pss 13 and 31, where there is no obvious sense of divine judgment.

מנוחה. This is normally translated "rest" (as in Ruth 1:9; 2 Sam 14:17; 1 Kgs
8:56; Isa 28:12), that is, relief from the turmoil just described.[171] But מנוחה often
means "resting place" (e.g. Gen 49:15; Num 10:33; Deut 12:9; Ps 132:14; Isa
11:10; 32:18), and when Baruch's complaint is read in the light of his forced
migration to Egypt (43:4–7) and YHWH's promise to give him his life על כל
המקמות אשר תלך שם (v. 5), this overtone may also be intentional.

v. 4. כה תאמר אליו. The command for Jeremiah to speak *to* Baruch disrupts
the discourse structure of vv. 2–3, in which Jeremiah is addressing Baruch
directly; it is probably secondary.[172]

אשר בניתי אני הרס ואת אשר נטעתי אני נתש. This is the final instance of the
"build, plant" refrain in Jeremiah. Since in OG the oracle stands near the end of
Jeremiah, the use of these verbs in 1:10 and 51:34 creates a neat *inclusio* for the
entire book.

The clause is doubly ambiguous. First, *what* has YHWH built and planted?
Many scholars assume that the allusion is to Israel/Judah;[173] cf. YHWH's declaration to Israel in 2:21, "I planted you" (ואנכי נטעתיך), and his description of
Judah as "my house" (ביתי, 12:7) and "my vineyard" (כרמי, 12:10). On the
other hand, in 1:10 and 18:9 the language of building and planting is applied to
other nations; and in 25:31 YHWH's habitation (נוהו) includes the whole earth
(cf. v. 31).

Secondly, how should we understand the participles (cf. the finite and infinite
verbs in previous instances of this refrain)? Do they refer to what YHWH is/has
been doing, or anticipate a judgment still to come?[174] In OG, the setting of this
oracle at the end of the book suggests the former; v. 4 interprets all that we have
witnessed thus far, especially the overthrow of Judah and dispersal of its people
as narrated in chs. 44–51. In MT, however, the ensuing OAN allow the participles to have a forward-looking aspect, and thereby also support an international
interpretation of אשר בניתי...אשר נטעתי.

169. See Giesebrecht, *Jeremia*, 226 ("ein Unglück nach dem andern kommt über mich");
McKane, *Jeremiah 2*, 1097.
170. Graupner, *Auftrag*, 174.
171. E.g. Duhm, *Jeremia*, 335; Rudolph, *Jeremia*, 226; Bright, *Jeremiah*, 184; Holladay,
Jeremiah 2, 307; McKane, *Jeremiah 2*, 1096; Keown, Scalise and Smothers, *Jeremiah 26–52*, 270.
172. Contra Holladay, *Jeremiah 2*, 309. Having emended v. 3a to כי אמר ברוך, Duhm,
Jeremia, 335, is able to retain כה תאמר אליו in v. 4.
173. Duhm, *Jeremia*, 336; Bright, *Jeremiah*, 186; Thompson, *Jeremiah*, 684; McKane,
Jeremiah 2, 1097; Schulte, "Persönliche Heilsorakel," 262; Carolyn J. Sharp, "The Call of Jeremiah
and Diaspora Politics," *JBL* 119 (2000): 421–38 (426–27).
174. Scholars generally take the latter view; indeed, such a reading is often used to support a
pre-587 date for the oracle. But note Thiel's response: "doch beachte die Partizipialformulierungen!"
(*Redaktion 26–45*, 87). Brueggemann, *Exile and Homecoming*, 416, interprets these verbs as
embracing "the present and immediate future."

כל הארץ. This can be understood either as "the whole earth" or "all the land."[175] The latter is more usual in Jeremiah (1:18; 4:20; 8:16; 12:11; 15:10; 23:15; 25:11; 40:4), but in several places the context shows the whole world to be in view; for example, 4:27 (note the הארץ / השמים contrast in v. 23); 50:23; 51:25, 41, 49. On balance, a global sense seems likely here; if the glossator wanted to identify Judah as the referent, we might have expected ואת כל יהודה היא. This may therefore represent a reinterpretation of v. 4a,[176] but we have seen that אשר בניתי...אשר נטעתי is a semantically flexible phrase in the Jeremiah tradition.

v. 5. תבקש לך גדלות. Various interpretations have been offered of the "great things" Baruch was seeking. Plausible suggestions include his social/political advancement,[177] or simply his personal security amid YHWH's judgment.[178] The text (intentionally perhaps) scarcely permits a specific answer, though the collocation of בקש and לא מצא (v. 3) suggests we relate גדלות to מנוחה. De Boer argues that since גדלות elsewhere signifies YHWH's "wonderful deeds" (e.g. Deut 10:21; Job 5:9; Ps 106:21), what Baruch was seeking was an act of deliverance for Judah (cf. 21:2).[179] There is no reason to think that בקש here has intercessory significance,[180] but in any case de Boer's proposal comes to grief on the particle לך;[181] that this denotes some form of self-concern is clear from the "I–you" logic of vv. 4–5, אשר בניתי אני הרם...ואתה.

הנני מביא רעה. While the participles in v. 4 can be seen as retrospective, the use here of הנני points strongly in the direction of a future sense.[182]

175.   For the former, see Duhm, *Jeremia*, 336; Peake, *Jeremiah & Lamentations 2*, 211; Rudolph, *Jeremia*, 226; Weiser, *Jeremia*, 383; Thiel, *Redaktion 26–45*, 85; Thompson, *Jeremiah*, 683; McKane, *Jeremiah 2*, 1097. For the latter, see Volz, *Jeremia*, 371; Hyatt, "Jeremiah," 1103; Bright, *Jeremiah*, 184; Holladay, *Jeremiah 2*, 307; Carroll, *Jeremiah*, 744; Keown, Scalise and Smothers, *Jeremiah 26–52*, 270.

176.   Sharp, "Call of Jeremiah," 427: "It would seem that here are clear traces of a redactional struggle over the scope of the destruction prophesied in this oracle."

177.   So Carroll, *Jeremiah*, 745; Jack R. Lundbom, "Baruch, Seraiah, and Expanded Colophons in the Book of Jeremiah," *JSOT* 36 (1986): 89–104 (101); cautiously, Streane, *Jeremiah* 282; Skinner, *Prophecy and Religion*, 347; James Muilenburg, "Baruch the Scribe," in Durham and Porter, eds., *Proclamation and Presence*, 215–38 (237); Thompson, *Jeremiah*, 684; Brueggemann, *Exile and Homecoming*, 415 n. 103. Cf. Duhm, *Jeremia*, 335: "Es war für ihn…der als ספר in Ägypten wohl nicht leicht Verdienst fand, die Zukunft dunkel genug, dazu hatte ihm wenigstens einmal (s. 43.3) die jüdische Kolonie ihre Abneigung deutlich ausgesprochen."

178.   So Rudolph, *Jeremia*, 227; Peake, *Jeremiah & Lamentations 2*, 211; Holladay, *Jeremiah 2*, 310; Jones, *Jeremiah*, 483; Graupner, *Auftrag*, 177.

179.   P. A. H. de Boer, "Jeremiah 45, Verse 5," in Van Duin, ed., *Selected Studies*, 122–28 (124–26); followed by Schulte, "Persönliche Heilsorakel," 261. But as de Boer acknowledges (p. 125), גדלות can have other meanings, as in Ps 12:4 ("proud boasts") and Jer 33:3 ("inscrutable facts").

180.   As is assumed by de Boer, "Jeremiah 45, Verse 5," 126; Schulte, "Persönliche Heilsorakel," 261; and also Rudolph, *Jeremia*, 227. It is ironic that after criticizing others for their eisegesis of v. 4, de Boer (p. 126) interprets it as "a reaction to a prayer of Baruch *which has not been preserved*" (italics mine).

181.   De Boer's claim, "Jeremiah 45, Verse 5," 126, that this is an "ethical dative" is clutching at straws.

182.   *GKC* §116p; *GBH 2*, §121e.

על כל בשׂר. Although in a few instances כל בשׂר is shown by its context to refer solely to Israel/Judah (Jer 12:12; Ezek 20:48; 21:4, 5; Joel 2:28), for the most part it has genuinely universal significance (Gen 6:12, 13, etc; Isa 40:5; 66:16; Jer 25:31; 32:27; Job 12:10; 34:15), which is probably how it should be understood here.[183] In this way, 45:5 forms a neat *inclusio* with the reference to worldwide judgment in 36:2 (ועל כל הגוים) and (in MT) anticipates the OAN that follow.

ונתתי לך את נפשׁך לשׁלל. This represents a slight variant on the previous form of the promise, נפשׁו(נפשׁך) לשׁלל (21:9; 38:2; 39:18). It might be argued that the more personal ונתתי לך is appropriate in a context where YHWH is addressing his faithful servant, but the same could be said of 39:18, where he speaks to Ebed-Melech. There is, however, no basis for viewing the relationship of 45:5 to the earlier passages as one of authentic prototype and redactional copies.[184]

6.4. *Coherence and Redaction*

As with 39:15–18, most commentators view 45:1–5 as for the most part a literary unity containing an authentic lament and oracle.[185] Redaction is generally thought to be limited to v. 1b (see below), the prophetic formula in v. 4a, and the MT plus in v. 4b, ואת כל הארץ היא. In particular, the internal coherence of vv. 3–5 is rarely questioned. Wanke has shown that these verses possess a *formal* unity (both in literary structure and metrical balance) and also a unity of *content* (YHWH's declaration answering to Baruch's lament).[186]

A greater degree of redaction is detected by Thiel,[187] who sees the original core as comprising Baruch's lament (v. 3), the messenger formula in v. 4, and the two clauses in v. 5 which are directly relevant to Baruch: ואתה תבקשׁ D. ונתתי לך את נפשׁך לשׁלל על כל המקמות אשׁר תלך שׁם and לך גדלות אל תבקשׁ has added all of vv. 1, 2 (where the messenger formula is "out of place"), 4 (where the terms בנה, הרם, נטע, נתשׁ are typical of D) and the internationalizing הנני מביא רעה על כל בשׂר נאם יהוה in v. 5. Schulte also sees this last phrase as secondary, since it broadens the scope of the (original) v. 4,[188] while Sharp argues that v. 4 is secondary since it narrows the scope of the (original)

---

183. Contra Duhm, *Jeremia*, 336 (whose citation of Isa 66:23 is hardly decisive); B. Gosse, "Jérémie XLV et la Place du Recueil d'Oracles Contre les Nations dans le Livre de Jérémie," *VT* 40 (1990): 145–51 (148).

184. Contra Thiel, *Redaktion 26–45*, 86; Schulte, "Persönliche Heilsorakel," 261–62; Graupner, *Auftrag*, 163 n. 12.

185. Contra Wanke, *Untersuchungen*, 135–36, for whom the generality of Baruch's lament, and the lateness of its vocabulary, point in the opposite direction; cf. Seitz, "Canonical Shape," 22, who refers to "this redactionally composed and placed chapter." Carroll, *Jeremiah*, 746, is agnostic.

186. Wanke, *Untersuchungen*, 134–35. Volz, *Jeremia*, 371, also calls attention to the poetic metre of vv. 3–5.

187. Thiel, *Redaktion 26–45*, 82–88. Hyatt, "Jeremiah," 1102, sees Deuteronomistic redaction in vv. 1b, 4, 5b, while Kremers, "Leidensgemeinschaft," 129 n. 16, deletes v. 2 as superfluous and pedantic.

188. Schulte, "Persönliche Heilsorakel," 261.

v. 5.[189] There is no need here to rehearse the debate about the Deuteronomistic nature of the language in v. 4, but we should note Thiel's admission concerning the way that salvation for Baruch is "editorially" contrasted with judgment for the world: "Diese wirkungsvolle Kontrastierung erscheint an dieser Stelle als sachgemäß und als geschickt und organisch in den Kontext eingefugt, so daß wie selten sonst der Eindruck der Einheitlichkeit entsteht."[190] So organic, indeed, that one suspects the contrast was there from the beginning.[191]

The main problem, of course, relates to the placement of the oracle, and thus to the historical note in v. 1b which links it to Baruch's writing of the scroll in the year 604. As we saw earlier, many scholars accept the accuracy of this dating. It is argued that the very incongruity of v. 1b speaks in its favour, for why would such a reference be added to a passage that otherwise has no obvious connection with ch. 36?[192] Moreover, vv. 4–5 imply that judgment is still to come.[193] Naturally, the question, then, is why the oracle has been placed where it has.[194] This is explained, variously, as due to Baruch's modesty,[195] as his personal testimony (*Denkmal*) to God's grace,[196] or to the truth of the prophetic word,[197] as a mark of honour to Baruch by his editors,[198] or as an appropriate conclusion to Baruch's *Leidensgeschichte* of Jeremiah. According to Muilenburg, "it belonged with ch. 36, certainly, but it belonged even more profoundly at the point where he had completed the record of Jeremiah's trials and rejections, the end of the *via dolorosa* he had been fated to walk with the prophet."[199]

Others, however, reject an original connection between ch. 45 and the writing of the scroll. Apart from the difficulty v. 1b creates for the words הדברים האלה, Baruch's despair (v. 3) is thought to be unlikely as early as 604, when Judah's repentance was still hoped for. "Diese Klage bereits ein gerütteltes Maß leidvoller Erfahrungen voraussetzt und so auf einen viel späteren Zeitpunkt als 605 verweist," writes Thiel.[200] Consequently, some propose the period immediately before or after the fall of Jerusalem as a more plausible setting.[201] Thiel

---

189.   Sharp, "Call of Jeremiah" 427; she also accepts Thiel's view that v. 4 interrupts the focus on Baruch.

190.   Thiel, *Redaktion 26–45*, 88.

191.   For further criticisms of Thiel's argument, see Graupner, *Auftrag*, 161–63; McKane, *Jeremiah 2*, 1106.

192.   So Weiser, "Gotteswort," 322; Holladay, *Jeremiah 2*, 308; Jones, *Jeremiah*, 482; also Seitz, "Canonical Shape," 20, who, however, views the whole chapter as redactional.

193.   Volz, *Jeremia*, 372; Rudolph, *Jeremia*, 227; Weiser, "Gotteswort," 322.

194.   Of those who accept the integrity of v. 1b, only Bright, *Jeremiah*, lxxvii, believes that ch. 45 originally stood next to ch. 36. Most accept that its present position is original.

195.   Peake, *Jeremiah & Lamentations 2*, 209.

196.   Rudolph, *Jeremia*, 228.

197.   Weiser, "Gotteswort," 329.

198.   Kessler, "Jeremiah 26–45 Reconsidered," 87.

199.   Muilenburg, "Baruch the Scribe," 236; cf. Volz, *Jeremia*, 373: "Es ging dem Meister selbst wie dem Jünger."

200.   Thiel, *Redaktion 26–45*, 87.

201.   For the former view, see Schulte, "Persönliche Heilsorakel," 260–61; Graupner, *Auftrag*, 172–73. For the latter, see Giesebrecht, *Jeremia*, 226; Hyatt, "Jeremiah," 1102.

himself suggests that Baruch uttered this lament when he was taken off to Egypt (43:4–7), and that this was in fact its original setting in the book.[202] Duhm and Skinner situate it after his arrival in Egypt; according to Skinner, "it reads…like a farewell oracle, perhaps even a death-bed charge."[203]

In response, it must again be said that the language of v. 3 is too general to allow us to assign it with confidence to *any* particular event in Baruch's life. By the same token, however, there is no reason to judge it inappropriate to the setting given in v. 1b.[204] On balance, it would seem that the mainstream explanation is to be preferred; namely, that v. 1b accurately witnesses to the original setting of the oracle, which has achieved its present position secondarily.[205] For interpretative purposes, however, the question is somewhat sterile. If Baruch's lament was originally prompted by his forced migration to Egypt, it has been secondarily connected with the writing of the scroll; and if it was originally connected with the writing of the scroll, it has secondarily been connected with the flight to Egypt. Ultimately, Taylor's verdict must be accepted as correct: "Whereas the superscription functions as one hermeneutic guide, the reader is given many other hermeneutic clues which suggest that the historical referentiality is coded or symbolic in this chapter, so that a solely historical reading is inadequate."[206]

6.5. *Judicial Differentiation in Jeremiah 45:1–5:* כל בשׂר / ברוך בן נריה

Our final judicial polarity within Jeremiah has striking parallels with (though also important differences from) that found in 39:15–18. Just as Ebed-Melech will be saved when YHWH brings disaster upon the city, so Baruch is singled out from divine judgment on Judah and indeed all humanity. He too is promised his life "as booty." At the same time, however, the tone and content of the promise is more restrained than that given to the Ethiopian. Notably absent are any assurances that YHWH will "rescue" and "save" him (cf. 39:17–18). Indeed, according to Gunneweg, "Kap. 45 kein Heilswort für Baruch enthält, sondern die Abweisung seiner Klage."[207] For Baruch, as for Jeremiah, "bleibt nur noch die eine Hoffnung, die eigentlich keine Hoffnung ist, mit dem Leben davon zu

---

202.   Thiel, *Redaktion 26–45*, 87–88; similarly Graupner, *Auftrag*, 172–73, 181–82, who, however, argues that *historically* the oracle belongs shortly before 587.

203.   Duhm, *Jeremia*, 334–35; Skinner, *Prophecy and Religion*, 346.

204.   According to Bright, *Jeremiah*, 185, "it is quite possible that as [Baruch] heard the awful words of judgment which Jeremiah dictated to him…he became so oppressed by the horrors that the future had in store that all hope and joy died within him" (similarly Holladay, *Jeremiah 2*, 309). Such a comment should be recognized as speculative, but not dismissed as "psychologizing" (as it is by Taylor, "Problem of Placement," 80; Seitz, "Canonical Shape," 20)—as if Baruch had no psychology. In fact, as Seitz himself points out (p. 20), redactional theories such as those which delete the historical note in v. 1b are no less "psychologizing."

205.   There is little to be said for retaining בכתבו את הדברים האלה על ספר מפי ירמיהו but deleting בשׁנה הרבעית ליהויקים בן יאשׁיהו מלך יהודה. As Thiel remarks, *Redaktion 26–45*, 84, "die starke Entsprechung zu 36.1,4 macht es notwendig, 1b als Ganzes zu beurteilen."

206.   Taylor, "Problem of Placement," 94.

207.   Gunneweg, "Konfession oder Interpretation," 415 n. 64.

kommen, Leben unter dem Zorn des Deus absconditus, den diese Gerechten dennoch nicht verdient haben."[208] Only slightly more positive is the verdict of Carroll: "A moment of hope (strictly delimited) is allowed to penetrate the utter gloom. Communal devastation cannot be avoided, but in all the great slaughter named individuals survive as the booty of war."[209]

Nevertheless, it would be a mistake to miss the salvific elements in YHWH's address to Baruch. As the first person form of the promise וְנָתַתִּי לְךָ אֶת־נַפְשְׁךָ לְשָׁלָל (v. 5) implies, Baruch will keep his life due to YHWH's personal attention; the fact that this promise is valid עַל כָּל־הַמְּקֹמוֹת אֲשֶׁר תֵּלֶךְ־שָׁם (v. 5b) emphasizes this fact. For Baruch as for Ebed-Melech, what is at stake is not simply escape but the ongoing watchful protection of YHWH. As Parke-Taylor comments, this "is surely more than a promise of survival, and the additional phrase "in all places to which you may go" carries with it the assurance of protection."[210]

From whom is Baruch differentiated? The semantic fluidity of ch. 45 means that several answers are possible. Read in its immediate literary context, the announcement of judgment in v. 4 has application to the Judean remnant now in Egypt. It is from this group, therefore, that Baruch is singled out. Consequently, when read as a whole, chs. 42–45 present a form of double differentiation comparable to that in chs. 38–39. There, a choice is given to the people of Jerusalem; those who leave the city will live, but those who stay will die (38:1–3). The subsection concludes (39:15–18), however, with a salvation oracle for Ebed-Melech, for whom such issues are immaterial. Likewise, 42:9–18 sets two alternatives before the Judean remnant; to stay in the land will result in YHWH's blessing, but to go to Egypt will ensure his wrath. The latter scenario is confirmed in ch. 44. In ch. 45, however, we find that even among the fugitives to Egypt, an exemption will be made. Not only so, but by concluding with the assurance that Baruch will have his life as booty עַל כָּל־הַמְּקֹמוֹת אֲשֶׁר תֵּלֶךְ־שָׁם, ch. 45 expressly sets aside the issues of staying (יָשַׁב) and going (בּוֹא) which were so central to ch. 42. In contrast to the Judean remnant, where Baruch goes is utterly irrelevant.

When read within the wider book, the differentiation of Baruch from the Judean remnant in Egypt brings to an end a series of exemptive moves by YHWH. After the indiscriminate judgment of chs. 1–20, it suddenly emerges that there is, after all, a future for the 597 exiles (ch. 24). Although that particular configuration leaves no hope for any of Zedekiah's people, during the siege of Jerusalem Jeremiah announces that those who go out to the Babylonians will save their lives. In turn, that analysis seems to preclude hope for anyone else, but after the deportations of 587, the poor of the land and the returnees from the surrounding nations form a community. To this group, Jeremiah holds out the

208.	Ibid., 415.

209.	Carroll, *Jeremiah*, 749. Contrast the optimism of Clements, *Jeremiah*, 243. "This positive and reassuring message at first glance appears to be little enough. On reflection, however, we can see it has a wealth of meaning... Life itself is a precious gift and always provides a fundamental opportunity for the knowledge and service of God."

210.	Parke-Taylor, *Formation*, 202.

prospect of hope if they stay in the land. Now that community too has disobeyed by going to Egypt, but Baruch is singled out from among them.[211]

At the same time, the language of 45:3–5 implies that Baruch (like Ebed-Melech) is being aligned with the figure of Jeremiah—who, of course, also stands over against the whole nation. Their solidarity in opposition to the Judean remnant has, of course, already been signalled in the preceding narrative, when the people accuse Baruch of inciting Jeremiah against them (43:3). Moreover, the verbal and conceptual links we have observed between Baruch's lament in 43:3 and those of Jeremiah can scarcely be coincidental. As O'Connor notes, both individuals express woe (אוי נא לי; cf. 15:10) and complain of sorrow (יגון, cf. 8:18; 20:18), pain (מכאוב; cf. כאב, 15:18) and weariness (יגע; cf. לאה, 20:9). Both attribute their suffering to YHWH (יסף יהוה; cf. 15:18; 20:7–8). To both individuals, YHWH replies with a rebuke (45:4; cf. 12:5; 15:19) and uses language similar to that of the call narrative (45:4; cf. 1:10; 15:20).[212]

This being so, we might conclude that Baruch, like Jeremiah, is paradigmatic of the righteous sufferer. According to Brueggemann, "that Baruch finds "no rest" means that he has gotten the consequence appropriate to the wicked, but he himself is a righteous, obedient man. Thus, the complaint of Baruch voices a question of theodicy."[213] Taking up this last point, Clements suggests that, historically speaking, the *personae* of Jeremiah and Baruch articulate the outlook of a pious inner-community among the *Diaspora* Jews:

> If there was no hope at all for those who had fled to Egypt (42.22) then it would follow that even these two loyal worshippers taken there unwillingly could have no individual hope. Would this not then have been deeply unfair of God to deal with such loyal and righteous individuals wholly in terms of the two communities to which they now belonged?... The prophecy addressed to Baruch by Jeremiah in 45.4–5 deals with this issue... Baruch is presented here as representative of all the loyal Jewish citizens carried unwillingly into an alien and hostile world.[214]

At the same time, the fact that Baruch, unlike Ebed-Melech, is given no word of commendation should be taken seriously. In this respect also, he parallels his prophetic mentor, who, as we saw in Chapter 2, was given personal assurances of rescue while being called to repentance. Because Baruch (like Jeremiah)

211.   The relationship of the promise to Baruch to the wider picture of the book is noted by Taylor ("Problem of Placement," 93): "The promise is here given to one who is no longer a member of a group for which hope is still held out, that is, the group that remained in the land after the first exile (cf. 42.10), and those who are a part of the Babylonian exile (cf. 24.6). For the reader of ch. 45, the more comprehensive promises of future hope and salvation (cf. 31.4ff.) echo but faintly at this point."

212.   O'Connor, *Confessions*, 96.

213.   Brueggemann, *Exile and Homecoming*, 415; cf. Taylor, "Problem of Placement," 89.

214.   Clements, *Jeremiah*, 242–43. Alternatively, Seitz, "Canonical Shape," 16–18, concludes that "Ebed-Melech and Baruch are types modelled on Caleb and Joshua in the canonical movement of the Book of Jeremiah. All four figures are contrasted with the generations of which they were a part" (pp. 17–18). For Seitz, the textual emphasis on Baruch as scribe (ספר) indicates that he, like Caleb and Joshua, represent a new form of leadership among the scattered people in which prophecy gives way to *tôrāh*.

stands over against the disobedient nation, YHWH will indeed exempt him from wrath. But because Baruch (like Jeremiah) is capable of uttering "worthless words," he receives YHWH's rebuke. For both, a judicial polarity of "Salvation for the righteous / Disaster for the wicked" is insufficient, for they fit neither category. Taylor may therefore be correct to see Baruch as typifying the *disobedient righteous sufferer*:

> Even though the reader is not told why Baruch merited divine favour, the structure of the narrative may suggest that Baruch, like Ebed-melech, is rewarded because of his faith and obedience to the divine word. On the contrary, it could be argued that the lack of a merit clause in Baruch's oracle suggests that Baruch was given the promise despite the absence of the "truth" that Ebed-melech had. In any case, these men representing the faithful (or perhaps in the case of Baruch, the faithful servant who is presently so locked up in his own pain that he is not acting in faith) provide a telling foil to the flagrantly disobedient multitudes who will necessarily come under judgment.[215]

7. *Summary: Judicial Differentiation in Jeremiah 42–45*

We can now sum up our study of Jer 42–45. Though complex, it presents an overall *pattern* of judicial differentiation remarkably similar to that in chs. 38–39. In 42:10–22, Jeremiah addresses the remnant of Judah. By their actions (staying in Judah or fleeing to Egypt), they may align themselves with either the favoured exiles in Babylon or the doomed community in Jerusalem. While this can be seen as the preaching of alternatives, Jeremiah's message serves to distinguish the Judean remnant from both groups addressed in ch. 24. This illustrates a point made in Chapter 2, namely, that if some people are presented with alternatives while others are not, a genuine mode of judicial differentiation is implied. As was the case in 38:14–23, however, the prophet's message is rendered hypothetical by a pre-determined rejection of the offer.

Just as Jeremiah's message to Zedekiah was followed by a personal salvation oracle to Ebed-Melech, so his message to the Judean remnant is followed by a personal salvation oracle to Baruch (45:1–5). At one level, the placement of the passage clearly serves to differentiate Baruch from the people with whom he has come to Egypt. However, just as YHWH's promise of salvation for Ebed-Melech appears unrelated to the issue (crucial for Zedekiah) of staying or not staying in the city, so his promise of protection for Baruch is unrelated to the issue (crucial for the Judean remnant) of where he will go to live (45:5). Within the wider context of the book, however, Baruch (like Ebed-Melech) is depicted alongside Jeremiah, standing against an evil nation and exempt from YHWH's wrath upon it, even while he is subject to YHWH's displeasure.

---

215.   Taylor, "Problem of Placement," 93.

Chapter 7

UNDIFFERENTIATED SALVATION: JEREMIAH 30–31

1. *Introduction*

This study of judicial differentiation in Jeremiah has focussed on three literary units in the central section of the book (MT Jer 21–45). These units have been found to contain a *range* of polarities by which YHWH exercises selective judgment. Before reflecting on our findings, however, some brief comment is in order concerning two chapters which we have so far overlooked. We saw earlier that Jer 1–20 announces YHWH's undifferentiated judgment on Judah. As I will now show, Jer 30–31 counter-balances this with a message of undifferentiated salvation. It will be clear that what follows is intended as no more than a sketch of these two chapters.

2. *Jeremiah 30–31 as a Literary Unit*

With its forward-looking perspective and expansive message of salvation, including what for many is the high point of Old Testament theology (the new covenant prophecy in 31:31–34), the so-called Book of Consolation has been described as "the pivotal centre" and "the functional centre" of Jeremiah.[1] Admittedly, scholars differ as to its scope; some restrict the title to chs. 30–31,[2] while others apply it to all of chs. 30–33.[3] Certainly there are marked differences between the first two chapters (mostly poetic, and with a strongly ahistorical quality; Jeremiah is wholly absent) and the latter two (almost entirely prose, and set in the context of the Babylonian siege; Jeremiah is prominent throughout).

---

1. Clements, *Jeremiah*, 8, and Stulman, *Order Amid Chaos*, 78, respectively.
2. E.g. Duhm, *Jeremia*, 237; Christoph Levin, *Die Verheißung des neuen Bundes in ihrem theologiegeschichtlichen Zusammenhang ausgelegt* (FRLANT 137; Göttingen: Vandenhoeck & Ruprecht, 1985), 159; Jones, *Jeremiah*, 339; G. Fischer, *Das Trostbüchlein. Text, Komposition und Theologie von Jer 30–31* (SBB 26; Stuttgart: Katholisches Bibelwerk, 1993); Bob Becking, "Jeremiah's Book of Consolation: A Textual Comparison. Notes on the Masoretic Text and the Old Greek Version of Jeremiah XXX–XXXI," *VT* 44 (1994): 145–69 (148); Keown, Scalise and Smothers, *Jeremiah 26–52*, 82; Applegate, "'Peace, Peace,'" 74.
3. E.g. Bright, *Jeremiah*, 284; Thompson, *Jeremiah*, 551; Mark E. Biddle, "The Literary Frame Surrounding Jeremiah 30.1–33.26," *ZAW* 100 (1988): 409–13; McConville, *Judgment and Promise*, 92–95; Marvin A. Sweeney, "Jeremiah 30–31 and King Josiah's Program of National Restoration and Religious Reform," *ZAW* 108 (1996): 569–83 (569); Stulman, *Order Amid Chaos*, 78; Brueggemann, *Exile and Homecoming*, 264.

On the other hand, chs. 30–31 and 32–33 can be seen as counterbalancing each other; both include YHWH's promise of a covenant (ברית חדשה, 31:31; ברית עולם, 32:40), which includes the declaration, "I will be their God and they will be my people" (31:33; 33:38).[4] Also unifying all four chapters is the phrase שוב שבות ("render a restoration"). Though this phrase is present elsewhere in the Old Testament, Bracke observes that "by far the greatest concentration of occurrences is found in Jeremiah 29–33,"[5] adding that "while the phrase is used initially in Jer 29.14, the promises of which it is a part are not developed until Jer 30.3, where *šûb šᵉbût* is used in the heading of Jer 30–33."[6] Consequently, Biddle is probably right to speak of all four chapters possessing a certain unity "at the secondary level."[7] Here, however, I shall focus on the accepted core of the Book of Consolation, namely, chs. 30–31, and highlight four features of the text which emphasize the comprehensiveness of their vision of salvation.

3. Undifferentiated Salvation in Jeremiah 30–31

3.1. The Inclusion of Israel and Judah
Given the predominantly Judean focus of Jeremiah, the Book of Consolation is distinctive for its promise that both Israel and Judah will share in YHWH's salvation. Although only the introduction (30:3–4) and the new covenant prophecy (31:27–34) mention both kingdoms together, elsewhere we find two oracles addressed to Israel (31:3–6, 21–22), four to Israel/Jacob (30:5–7, 10–11; 31:7–9, 10–14), two to Judah (31:23–24, 38–40) and one to Zion (30:12–17).[8] This audience variation has often been explained by the hypothesis that 30:5–31:22 contains authentic oracles addressed to the former northern kingdom, supplemented with (post-)exilic material incorporating Judah into YHWH's salvation.[9] The theory is not without its merits, although its proponents differ in their assessments of how much is authentic. It is equally possible, however, that "Israel" (30:10; 31:2, 3, 7, 9, 10, 21) and "Jacob" (30:7, 10, 18; 31:7, 11) signify the entire *Diaspora*, as they do frequently in later biblical literature (Isa 40:27;

---

4. Other terms common to both sections are סלח ("forgive," 31:34; 33:8; elsewhere only in 5:1, 7; 36:3; 51:20); עלה ארכה ("bring healing," 30:17; 33:6; elsewhere only in 8:22); רפא ("heal," 30:17; 33:6) and יסר / מוסר ("discipline," 30:11; 31:18; 32:33). MT heightens the parallel with its second "creation guarantee" passage (33:19–26 >OG; cf. 31:35–37).

5. Bracke, "*šûb šᵉbût*," 236. The phrase occurs in 29:14; 30:3, 18; 31:23; 32:44; 33:7, 11, 26.

6. Ibid., 236. We might also note that עוד (לא) ("once more; no longer") finds one third of its fifty-four Jeremianic instances in chs. 30–33.

7. Biddle, "Literary Frame," 410.

8. There may also be a reference to Judah in 30:18, if the city (עיר) is Jerusalem, and ארמון the royal palace. However, these identifications are uncertain.

9. E.g. Volz, *Jeremia*, 284–302; Rudolph, *Jeremia*, 159; Bright, *Jeremiah*, 284–85; Böhmer, *Heimkehr und neuer Bund*, 81–85; Lust, " 'Gathering and Return,' " 132–33; Norbert Lohfink, "Der junge Jeremia als Propagandist und Poet. Zum Grundstock von Jer 30–31," in Bogaert, ed., *Le Livre de Jérémie*, 351–68; T. Odashima, *Heilsworte im Jeremiabuch. Untersuchungen zu ihrer vordeuteronomistischen Bearbeitung* (BWANT 125; Stuttgart: Kohlhammer, 1989), 130, 305; Kilpp, *Niederreißen*, 102–3, 133–72; Sweeney, "Jeremiah 30–31," 569–83.

41:8; 43:1; 49:5; cf. Pss 79:7; 147:19). In any case, even if we isolate the Israel/Jacob material from the Judah/Zion material, there is no hint of mutual polemicizing.[10]

3.2. *The Non-specific Nature of the Diaspora*

Unlike Jer 29, which is clearly addressed to the community exiled to Babylon in 597, chs. 30–31 are consistently ambiguous regarding the identity and location of their audience. In 30:10, YHWH pledges to rescue his people from "a distant place" (רחוק) and from "the land of their captivity" (ארץ שבים), even though he has scattered them "among all the nations" (בכל הגוים, v. 11). Jeremiah 31:8 anticipates their return from "a land of the north" (ארץ צפון) and "the ends of the earth" (ירכתי הארץ), while in 31:16, YHWH assures Rachel that her children will return from "an enemy land" (ארץ אויב). We may also note that 30:10–11 alternates between describing the place of *Diaspora* as singular (רחוק, ארץ שבים) and plural (בכל הגוים אשר הפצותיך שם). To be sure, it is possible that the writer is here using a plural idiom with a single referent; compare 46:27–28, where the same promise follows the oracle against Egypt, and 29:14, which I argued earlier applies מכל הגוים ומכל המקומות to Babylon. In 30:10–11, however, even if a particular exilic group is in mind, it is certainly not specified.[11]

Similarly, although Jer 30–31 refers to Israel's enemies, none are identified. Again, there is some variation as to whether *one* or *several* enemies are in view. Jeremiah 30:16 lists "all who devour you" (כל אכליך), "all your enemies" (כל צריך), "those who plunder you" (שאסיך), and "all who loot you" (כל בזזיך), while 30:20 refers to "all who oppress him" (כל לחציו). A single oppressor is implied, however, in 31:10–14, where YHWH will redeem Jacob "from the hand of one stronger than he" (מיד חזק ממנו, v. 11). Here, the other nations serve merely as witnesses to YHWH's salvation (31:10).

3.3. *The Personification of Israel*

As noted above, the significance of the names Jacob, Ephraim and Rachel in Jer 30–31 has often been sought in terms of their historical referents, that is, as ciphers for the former northern kingdom. At least as significant, however, is how these personifications function at a poetic level. For one of the most striking features of the Book of Consolation is its use of individual metaphors for its addressees.

---

10.   Note Rudolph's remark, *Jeremia*, 165, on the application of the term "Ephraim" to Israel in 31:9: "dieses Vorrecht Efraims wird hier nicht (wie 2 Sam. 19.44; LXX 1 Chr. 5.1f.) gegen Juda ausgespielt, das außerhalb des Blickfelds bleibt, sondern den anderen Völkern gegenüber betont (vgl. 7a.; 2.3; 3.19)." Schmid, *Buchgestalten*, 110–87, argues that while the Jacob, Rachel and Ephraim texts (30:5–7, 18–21; 31:15–22) anticipate the resettlement of Samaria *and* Judah, the Zion texts (31:6, 10–14) interpret the repopulation of Samaria merely as a prelude to its people coming to worship in Jerusalem. If this is correct, we would have to reckon with some tension between the different redactional layers over the centrality of Jerusalem, but the pan-Israel nature of YHWH's salvation would not be in dispute.

11.   Volz, *Jeremia*, 288, 290, and Rudolph, *Jeremia*, 161, take 30:10–11 to refer to the Israelite exiles in Assyria, while Bright, *Jeremiah*, 284–85, sees it as addressed to Judean exiles in Babylon. Cf. 31:8, which juxtaposes ארץ צפון with ירכתי הארץ.

Dominant among these is Jacob. The name first occurs in 30:5–7, where
ועת צרה היא ליעקב (v. 6) gives way to the corporate כל גבר ידיו על חלציו
כי הנני מושיעך מרחוק ואת זרעך (v. 7b). Similarly, while the promise ממנה יושע
מארץ שבים (30:10b) differentiates between the exiles and their children, both
groups are in the same verse addressed as Jacob (v. 10a, c).[12] In 31:7, Jacob is
equated with the שארית ישראל, whom YHWH will save, while in 31:11, the
statement פדה יהוה את יעקב וגאלו מיד חזק ממנו is followed in vv. 12–14 by
third person plural forms (ובאו ורננו).[13] In addition, the people are depicted as
Ephraim. In 31:9, the parallelism with Israel (כי הייתי לישראל לאב ואפרים בכרי
הוא) shows the entire nation to be in view, while in 31:18–19, Ephraim's
confession, אפרים מתנודד (v. 18), prompts YHWH's affirmation, הבן יקיר לי
אפרים (v. 20).

There are also two contrasting female metaphors for the scattered people.
Twice, they are described as a בתולה, an image that is itself semantically fluid;
this בתולה is YHWH's virgin bride,[14] dancing with tambourines (31:4), and also
his wayward daughter (31:21–22). Conversely, in 30:17 the speaker of the
preceding lament is described by her foes as a נדחה. The participle of נדח
(Niph.) usually denotes an exile or fugitive, but as the following דרש אין לה
implies, the picture here is more personal; this one whom YHWH has severely
chastised resembles an unloved, rejected woman.

In short, the trope of a single human figure is one of the primary means by
which Israel/Judah is conceptualized in chs. 30–31.[15] Although these personifications allow the people to be seen variously (as humiliated, wayward, pure,
etc.), they also serve to emphasize their unity, and undermine internal distinctions among them.

3.4. *The Listing of Groups*

In contrast to the point just made concerning personification, several oracles in
Jer 30–31 emphasize the undiscriminating nature of YHWH's salvation by highlighting the social diversity of the restored community. In 31:8, for example, the
great company (קהל גדול) whom YHWH will bring back expressly includes
vulnerable members of society: the blind and the lame (עור ופסח), the pregnant
woman and the one giving birth (הרה וילדת). In 31:13, despite the differences

12. Alternatively, in 30:10 "Jacob" may be the patriarch himself, with "your seed" the present
exiles (cf. 31:15–17, which addresses "Rachel" concerning her "children"). In this case, the thought
is that God's promise to Jacob is applicable to his descendants.

13. In MT 30:18 the equation of patriarch and people is weakened by the phrase אהלי יעקוב (cf.
Num 24:5; Mal 2:12); however OG ἐγὼ ἀποστρέφω ἀποικίαν Ιακωβ may reflect הנני שב שבות
יעקוב, thus retaining the Jacob metaphor.

14. See further John J. Schmitt, "The Virgin of Israel: Referent and Use of the Phrase in Amos
and Jeremiah," *CBQ* 53 (1991): 365–87, who argues that in Jer 31 "virgin" denotes the capital city
(Samaria)—which in turn, however, "may stand for that whole kingdom, indeed for the whole exiled
people of Israel" (p. 386).

15. Schmid, *Buchgestalten*, 150, sees the *Grundtext* of chs. 30–31 as alternating between poems
using the names of the patriarchs, and poems written in the second feminine singular. Whatever the
merits of this analysis, it illustrates the prominence of *singular* address.

between MT and OG, the picture is clearly one of young women, young men and old men rejoicing together. Again, 31:24 anticipates YHWH's renewed blessing of both urban and rural communities, though here MT and OG diverge somewhat.[16] While these are all conventional social categories, the listing of them, along with the term יחדו (31:8, 24; MT 31:13) emphasizes the broad scope of YHWH's salvation. This significance of this listing of groups increases when we recall that earlier in Jeremiah, the same rhetorical technique expressed the comprehensiveness of Judah's sin and YHWH's judgment.

4. *Israel and the Nations*

There is, though, one very explicit judicial polarity in the Book of Consolation, namely, in 30:18–24. Two oracles have been juxtaposed here. In the first (30:18–22), YHWH promises to "restore the fortunes of the tents of Jacob"; the city will be rebuilt and a new community established. At the same time, however, YHWH will act against those who oppress the people (ופקדתי על כל לחציו, v. 20). The prophecy might seem to echo 23:1–8, where Judah's kings are condemned for misruling the people. However, the assurance that Israel's future leader will be one of its own (מקרבו...ממנו, v. 21) clearly implies that in this context foreign oppressors are in view. The second oracle (30:23–24) prophesies YHWH's wrath breaking upon the wicked (הרשעים). Elsewhere in Jeremiah, הרשעים are the arrogant in Judean society who oppress the poor (e.g. 5:26; 12:1), while the almost identical passage, 23:19–20, identifies them as Judah's prophets. Consequently, several scholars have concluded that 30:23–24 constitutes a genuine case of selective judgment within Israel.[17] However, the term הרשעים can also denote foreign nations (Jer 12:14; Ezek 21:34; Ps 9:18 // גוים), and the preceding oracle suggests that this is also the case here.[18] This being so, the only form of judicial differentiation in the Book of Consolation involves Israel and the foreign nations.

5. *The Rationale for Salvation and the New Covenant*

The picture of all-Israel salvation in Jer 30–31, therefore, is in stark contrast to the message of national judgment that dominates chs. 1–20. Equally, however, it

---

16.　MT וישבו בה יהודה וכל עריו יחדו; OG καὶ ἐνοικοῦντες ἐν πόλεσιν Ιουδα καὶ ἐν πάσῃ τῇ γῇ αὐτου ἅμα = וישבי בערי יהודה ובכל ארצו יחדו. Since MT makes ארצו ובכל יהודה the subject of וישבי, the lack of a verb for the ensuing אברים is awkward. Also difficult is MT אברים ונסעו בעדר. LXXᵃ·ᵒ, Targ., Vulg., support an emendation to ונסעי, "those who set out with," but a finite verb is supported by OG, καὶ ἀρθήσεται ἐν ποιμνίῳ; this could mean "he will set out" (ויסע) or "he shall be lifted up" (ונשא).

17.　E.g. Duhm, *Jeremia*, 243; Volz, *Jeremia*, 279; Karl-Friedrich Pohlmann, *Die Ferne Gottes. Studien zum Jeremiabuch. Beiträge zu den "Konfessionen" in Jeremiabuch und ein Versuch zur Frage nach dem Anfängen der Jeremiatradition* (BZAW 179; Berlin: de Gruyter, 1989), 94; Koenen, *Heil den Gerechten*, 78 n. 7.

18.　So Rudolph, *Jeremia*, 163; Bright, *Jeremiah*, 280; Thompson, *Jeremiah*, 563; Odashima, *Heilsworte*, 53; Brueggemann, *Exile and Homecoming*, 279; Schmid, *Buchgestalten*, 181–82.

stands out from the rest of chs. 21–45, where YHWH judges and saves selectively. In the redemptive vision of the Book of Consolation, Judah and Israel are a single entity, distinguished only from other lands. As Keown et al. observe:

> Whatever the details of the history of redaction of these chapters…in their final form the contents have been "loosened from their original historical moorings." All of Israel and Judah, whether exiled in the eighth century B.C., the sixth century B.C., or not at all, and all of their descendants, hope in God through these promises. The distinctions present in chs. 2, 24 and 29 will have no significance in their future.[19]

Does the text offer any explanation for this new perspective? Unlike 23:1–8, there is no hint that the people are victims of their leaders' folly. Unlike 39:15–18, salvation is not promised as the reward for trusting in YHWH. On the contrary, Israel is a vacillating daughter (הבת השובבה, 31:22), whose guilt and sin is great (רב עונך, עצמו חטאתיך, 30:14, 15). Indeed, she is called to repent (31:18–19). In no way, however, is repentance the catalyst for salvation, for the promises are already being spoken. To this extent, chs. 30–31 share common ground with chs. 24 and 29, where YHWH's redemptive intention towards the exiles precedes their own actions. In the Book of Consolation, however, there are no exceptions, for all have now been exiled or made exiles in their own land.

Do the promises of Jer 30–31 therefore reflect the theology of exile that I discussed earlier in conversation with Kilpp and Raitt? In one sense yes, inasmuch as these chapters clearly assume a time when disaster has fallen on all. The question remains, however, as to *how* this has created a radically new situation in which salvation is now possible. We are still some way from the idea of recompense implied in Isa 40:2, namely, that Jerusalem "has received from the LORD's hand double for all her sins."[20]

In fact, Jer 30–31 offers an intriguing double rationale for its message of salvation. On the one hand, given Israel's continuing obduracy it is no surprise to find that YHWH is motivated by his own compassion, though the word has been blunted through ubiquity. In the thought world of the Book of Consolation, YHWH's compassion is instinctive and spontaneous, arising out of his own emotional turmoil:

> For as often as I speak against him,
> I surely remember him again.
> Therefore my heart stirs for him,
> I surely have compassion for him. (31:20)

In other words, YHWH's decision for mercy, his "fresh turn towards Israel," is neither rational nor predictable—certainly not to disobedient Israel, and *maybe not even to himself*.[21] Within the Old Testament, such an unpremeditated change of heart is paralleled only in Hos 11:8 (also, as it happens, addressed to Ephraim).

---

19. Keown, Scalise and Smothers, *Jeremiah 26–52*, 85; the quotation is from Childs, *Introduction*, 351.

20. For the legal background to this verse, see Brevard S. Childs, *Isaiah: A Commentary* (OTL; Louisville: Westminster John Knox, 2001), 297.

21. Among modern commentators, perhaps Brueggemann (*Exile and Homecoming*, 287–88) reads Jer 31:18–20 with most insight: "There is, on God's part, an inclination to reject wayward

The poem about wounded Zion (30:12–17) interprets salvation from a different angle. The initial cameo involves only two characters: Zion has sinned against YHWH (עונך...חטאתיך, vv. 14–15) and YHWH has punished Zion (הביתיך...אכזרי, v. 14b; עשיתי אלה לך v. 15b). Those who might have offered help are notable for their absence (כל מאהביך שכחוך; אין דן דינך למזור, v. 13aα; אותך לא ידרשו, v. 14a). The second part of the poem, however, makes the nations active participants in the drama; they, rather than YHWH, have afflicted Zion (כל אכליך...כל צריך...כל בזזיך, v. 16; cf. 30:8). The paradigm shift is crucial, since it allows Zion to be seen no longer as offender but as victim. She is thus reinterpreted as someone *eligible for salvation in the face of injustice*. And indeed, YHWH's response conforms precisely to this expectation: "I will heal your wounds…for they have called you an outcast" (v. 17).[22]

Although we are dealing here with a judicial polarity of Israel and the nations rather than of groups within Israel, it nevertheless touches on an issue that arose earlier in connection with the work of Koenen: namely, that of the relationship between divine judgment and human conduct. The Book of Consolation suggests that once again the answer is more complex than Koenen implied. Guilty Israel is saved only by YHWH's mercy (30:12–17). The wicked nations are punished according to their conduct (30:18–24). Yet since the nations are Israel's oppressors, divine mercy and human conduct necessarily coincide in Israel's salvation. Moreover, if YHWH's rescue of Israel is prompted by the nations' guilt, does it not also imply Israel's *relative* innocence? At the heart of the issue is the theological paradigm through which Israel is to be seen. Precisely this point emerges in 31:18–20, where Zion's redemption reflects the transformation of her status from offender to victim.

The Book of Consolation, therefore, announces undifferentiated salvation for Israel. All alike will resettle the land, governed justly by their own rulers and under YHWH's blessing. Indeed, the climactic prophecy of 31:29–34 goes further still. YHWH's gift of an internalized Torah will make possible a new covenant with his people, characterized by its immediacy and inclusiveness: "They will all know me, from the least of them to the greatest" (v. 34). How tantalizing, then, that the one possible chink in this optimism should appear in the immediately preceding verse: "Each one will die for his own sin" (v. 30). To be sure, the proverbial context suggests that the principle has generational rather

Israel, and to be done with such painful, exhausting recalcitrance. That inclination, however, is countered in the very heart of God. God's heart is profoundly torn… God is reduced to trembling yearning, and finally finds that mercy wins over rejection." See too his essay, "A Shattered Transcendence? Exile and Restoration," in his *Old Testament Theology: Essays on Structure, Theme and Text* (ed. Patrick D. Miller; Minneapolis: Fortress, 1992), 183–203, where he explores "the instant of the breaking of God's loyal love" in Isa 54:7–10 (p. 195).

22. Cf. Brueggemann, *Exile and Homecoming*, 277: "It is powerful irony that God's own verdict in v. 14 is now on the lips of the nations in v. 17. When that same verdict is sounded by the nations, however, it evokes in Yahweh a response of caring solidarity. Yahweh had been free to critique and condemn this people. However, when the nations do the same as Yahweh had done, Yahweh is made freshly aware of deep concern for Israel."

than individual application.[23] Consequently, it serves to liberate Jeremiah's audience by limiting to their fathers the results of their fathers' sin. And yet, while the outlook of the passage is wholly optimistic, the unmediated nature of YHWH's new covenant means that the doctrine of v. 30 might still cut the other way. In a manner akin to chs. 24 and 29, chs. 30–31 celebrate the prospect of comprehensive salvation, while leaving room for a different future. Jones captures the sense of the passage well: "In the new age there will no longer be a dead weight of the entail of the past, but with a new start, the individual will simply be responsible for his own transgression."[24]

---

23.   So ibid., 291; Keown, Scalise and Smothers, *Jeremiah 26–52*, 130. The principle of individual retribution also has a generational application in Ezek 18; see especially Paul Joyce, *Divine Initiative and Human Response in Ezekiel* (JSOTSup 51; Sheffield: JSOT, 1988), 35–60.

24.   Jones, *Jeremiah*, 375.

Chapter 8

CONCLUSIONS

1. *Review of Findings*

Does YHWH judge his people selectively? The book of Jeremiah answers with an emphatic "Yes." In particular, three literary units at the centre of the book offer a series of judicial polarities. Chapters 21–24 differentiate between those who remain in Jerusalem and those who surrender, between leaders and people, and between the exiles in Babylon and their compatriots in Judah. Chapters 27–29 contrast the Judean and *Golah* communities, while at the same time distinguishing between people and prophets. Chapters 37–45 begin by repeating the polarity of those who remain in the city and those who surrender, only to qualify it in the case of Ebed-Melech. Later, salvation and judgment turn on the issue of remaining in the land, only for this to be qualified in the case of Baruch. The importance of judicial differentiation as a motif in these chapters is unavoidable; indeed, I have argued that the literary structure of each of the above units serves to highlight the idea. Even in chs. 1–20, however, YHWH's wrath against Judah is not wholly indiscriminate. An exemption is made for Jeremiah himself, to whom YHWH promises salvation (1:8, 18–19; 15:19–21) in terms that anticipate what will later be said to Ebed-Melech and Baruch.

Yet, as this review shows, the concept of judicial distinctions is highly flexible. In part, this reflects the fact that salvation and judgment are themselves multi-faceted terms. For individuals, salvation may mean survival in time of disaster or life under the personal blessing of YHWH. For a community, salvation may mean continued existence in their own land, a blessed life in a foreign land, future homecoming, or a new relationship with YHWH. Equally, judgment may entail an individual death penalty, communal exile, or death by sword, famine and plague. However, the flexibility of the concept of judicial differentiation is further underlined by the diversity of polarities and of rationales.

2. *The Diversity of Perspectives on Judicial Differentiation*

2.1. *The Diversity of Polarities*
This study has demonstrated that judicial polarities can be created in a surprising number of ways. Most obviously, there are what in Chapter 1 I referred to as antithetical judgment oracles; that is to say, oracles which announce salvation

for one group or individual, and judgment for another group or individual. Most of the polarities I have studied come into this category: those who remain in the city and those who leave, the shepherds and the sheep, and so on.

In addition, however, I have seen that even when a prophetic message takes the form of dual alternatives, this nevertheless constitutes a mode of judicial differentiation *if it is not extended to everyone*. While the Judean community at large are given the option to submit and live, Hananiah receives YHWH's death penalty (chs. 27–28). Nor will Ahab, Zechariah and Shemaiah have the chance to respond to the *conditional* promises issued to their brothers in Babylon (ch. 29). To the Judean remnant in ch. 42, YHWH presents a clear choice; to the Jerusalem community in ch. 24, he announces only disaster.

A third type of judicial polarity, which is rarely recognized as such, is that of modest blessing over against rich blessing. This, I have argued, precisely describes Jeremiah's message to the Judean and Babylonian communities in chs. 27–29. Both are offered a word of hope; but the nature of that hope for those in Judah bears little comparison with the rich and dramatic promises to the exiles. Whatever the reason, YHWH is dealing with the two groups quite differently.

2.2. *The Diversity of Rationales*

If YHWH judges selectively, on what basis does he do so? Is the operating principle one of strict justice, arbitrary grace, or something else? Here too, the response given in Jeremiah is neither uniform nor simple. To be sure, chs. 1–20 provide an unambiguous rationale for judgment; the nation has been unfaithful to YHWH, as seen most clearly in its idolatry and social injustice. This indictment also serves as the implied rationale for the oracles of judgment in chs. 21–45, several of which lack any explanation of their own (21:4–7; 24:7–10; 45:4–5). In others, the basis of judgment is stated clearly: failure to care for the people (23:1–2), prophesying lies (28:16; 29:21–23, 32), immorality (29:23) and (in the MT plus of 29:16) refusal to go into exile. All this is to say that YHWH's wrath is related to the spiritual and ethical failures of his people. So far, no surprise.

The rationale for salvation, however, is more elusive. The clearest indication of a link with human piety comes in 39:15–18, where Ebed-Melech's salvation is attributed to the fact that he trusted in YHWH. Contextually, this trust has been shown not only by his courageous support for Jeremiah, but by the fact that (unlike the rest of Zedekiah's court) he recognized Jeremiah as the one bearing the divine word. A clearer spiritual/ethical rationale for salvation would be hard to find. Trust in YHWH may also be a factor in the offer of life for those who surrender to the Babylonians (21:8–10; 38:1–3), since such action entails the acceptance of YHWH's judgment on Jerusalem, and contrasts with the Judeans' inclination to trust in their cities (5:17) and the temple (7:14).

In other judicial polarities, however, the determining factor in salvation is YHWH's own gracious decision (23:3–8; 24:5–7; 29:4–14). To be sure, some might regard a decision which does not apply to everyone as arbitrary rather than gracious. The fact that all the oracles listed above are addressed to those in exile *may* indicate that the experience of judgment is the decisive criterion (so Seitz and Kilpp), although none of these oracles make this idea explicit (cf. 29:16). In any case, the question would remain as to *why* the experience of judgment should be so significant. The clearest expression of such a theology, in fact, comes in 42:10. Here, we may note, YHWH's new openness towards the people is based not on a retributive principle ("They've suffered enough"), but rather on his personal grief (cf. 31:18–20).

This study has shown, however, that the distinction between contingency and grace is not absolute. Rather, in many judicial polarities divine freedom *and* human conduct both play a role. In 23:3–8, for example, YHWH promises to save his flock because it is *his* flock. The very nature of the metaphor underlines his initiative and precludes human merit. But, one may ask, are not those shepherds whom YHWH will punish for their misdeeds also part of his flock? Implicitly, the oracle does seem to recognize human conduct as a factor in judgment and salvation, if only to the extent that the leaders are more culpable than the people. The same principle explains why the prophets in chs. 27–29 receive the death penalty, while their hearers receive only a verbal chastening (and the opportunity to respond). Even if human piety is not the *basis* for salvation, therefore, YHWH's judicial actions may still take account of the *relative guilt or innocence* of the parties concerned.

Perhaps this point is best illustrated by the two individuals with which the book begins and (in the LXX) ends. Jeremiah and Baruch are promised salvation from the disaster YHWH is bringing on Judah, contingent upon their faithful acceptance of his call (1:7–8, 17–19; 45:5). Although the book as a whole testifies to such a response, there are times when both the prophet and his assistant are portrayed as speaking foolishly and needing to repent (15:19; 45:3–5). Are they then to forfeit the promise of protection and suffer judgment with the rest? Evidently not. YHWH distinguishes between a disobedient servant and an obdurate nation.

A further reason for not making divine action and human conduct mutually exclusive emerges from the multi-faceted nature of salvation in 24:4–7 and 29:4–14. YHWH has turned to the exiles; by no merit of their own, they have entered a new era with new possibilities. Future homecoming and spiritual renewal is confidently expected. Nevertheless, the exiles must turn to YHWH, whose blessings will not be realized without their obedience. The invitation to build, plant and multiply (29:5–6) is simultaneously a call to repudiate alternative messages. The covenant relationship will require their wholehearted seeking of YHWH (24:6–7; 29:10–14); and even if this is *facilitated* by his gift of a new heart, it is not *guaranteed*. An element of conditionality remains.

As we saw in Chapter 2, Klaus Koenen's study of judicial differentiation was limited to those oracles in which salvation and judgment are strictly correlated with the ethical profile of the groups involved. My own investigation suggests that this criterion is somewhat artificial. Instead, by considering *all* the judicial polarities and their underlying rationales in Jeremiah, we have been able to see more clearly the complexity of judgment, salvation, obedience, guilt and grace.

3. *Dominant Perspectives on Judicial Differentiation*

Is it possible, however, to hear a unifying voice amid this chorus of perspectives? This study has shown that the text resists any easy synthesis. Granted, some tensions are more apparent than real. I have argued, for example, that the offer of life in 21:1–10 does no more than nuance the broad brushstrokes of 24:8–10. Again, while Ebed-Melech and Baruch do not meet the conditions for salvation set out in 38:1–3 and 42:10–18, their loyalty to YHWH adequately explains their exemption from judgment. On the other hand, 24:1–10 and 23:1–8 set out different judicial polarities (leaders and people; exiles and non-exiles), and operate with different criteria (ethical culpability; experience of judgment). The dual differentiation in chs. 27–29 (exiles and non-exiles; people and prophets) is coherent, but the invitation to the Judeans to submit and live is remarkable after the grim prophecy against the same people in 24:8–10 (repeated in MT 29:16–19). Meanwhile, Jeremiah's assurance to Zedekiah that by surrendering he will save all Jerusalem (38:17–18) is at odds with the basic principle of 21:1–10, that the city is doomed.

This diversity of theological analysis is no surprise. Some will attribute it to the different editorial hands that doubtless shaped the canonical book. Others will not find it difficult to believe that the historical and political maelstrom of early sixth-century Judah should have elicited such a range of responses from the prophet himself. In one sense, it matters little. The density of history is such as to render any one mode of judicial differentiation inadequate.[1] Indeed, according to Biddle, "the case could be made that the argument of the book lies in the contention that God's relationship with God's people defies resolution and systematization."[2] Guilt is universal, but not equal. People need a new relationship with YHWH, but they also need new leaders. Restoration is an act of grace from which some may still be excluded because of their conduct. Ebed-Melech will be saved because of his trust; Baruch will be saved in spite of his self-concern. Placing such diverse perspectives in a wider Old Testament context, Duguid comments:

> Many people…looked to the past and sought to identify the sins (and the sinners) that had brought them into exile… Similar thoughts are also at work in other biblical documents of the exilic and post-exilic period, such as the Deuteronomistic History. That each comes to different conclusions as to the causes and future remedies of the exile shows that history and its analysis is a complex and multi-faceted affair, especially when it comes to the apportionment of blame.[3]

---

1. Norman K. Gottwald, *The Politics of Ancient Israel* (LAI; Louisville: Westminster John Knox, 2001), 5, refers to "the realization that every telling of history is a fresh construal and that the political past embraces more than any single telling is capable of grasping."

2. Biddle, *Polyphony and Symphony*, 40. In similar vein, Stulman, *Order Amid Chaos*, 187, argues that the absence of conceptual uniformity in Jeremiah attests "to the wild and undomesticated God who refuses to be imprisoned by any closed system."

3. Duguid, *Ezekiel and the Leaders of Israel*, 2.

Nevertheless, as I review the chorus of judicial polarities in Jeremiah, it seems to me that two particular voices have been given prominence. In the first place, we saw in Chapter 5 that Jer 29 has a pivotal function within the book as a whole. Here, in a way that is striking and unlikely to be coincidental, earlier signs of judgment are reversed, negative terms redefined and salvific themes introduced. The positioning of this chapter immediately ahead of the Book of Consolation underlines its significance. This means, of course, that the judicial polarity of exiles and non-exiles comes to the foreground. But that is not all. Regarding the idea that the experience of judgment forms the decisive rationale for salvation in Jeremiah, I have already noted that neither in ch. 29 nor in ch. 24 is this idea explicitly stated. However, the role of ch. 29 as a turning point within the book would seem to offer *literary* evidence for this concept. In canonical terms, exile is where YHWH pauses and history turns a corner.

Secondly, the literary structure of Jeremiah clearly highlights the salvation oracles to Jeremiah and Baruch. This is especially true in OG, in which the oracle to Baruch virtually closes the book. In this way, the text underlines the conviction that YHWH does indeed differentiate between faithful individuals and their apostate contemporaries. In structuring the text in this way, it is unlikely that the editors were simply affirming YHWH's selective salvation of Jeremiah and Baruch; rather, in those two individuals they saw themselves and their own communities.

4. *Hermeneutical and Theological Reflections*

This study has underlined the role of models and metaphors in shaping biblical discourse about judgment and salvation. To take an obvious example, the metaphor of shepherds and sheep (23:1–4) inevitably implies the guilt of Judah's leaders and the unjust suffering of its people. Adopt such an interpretative framework, and YHWH's judicial actions are predictable enough.[4] Set against the nation, Jeremiah and Ebed-Melech are saved *because of* their faithfulness. Set before God, Jeremiah and Baruch are saved *in spite of* their failures.

Clearly, a plurality of paradigms can be fruitful in enabling different, but equally important, sets of ideas to be expressed. The *unitary* view of Judah in YHWH's message to the remnant—"I am sorry about the disaster I have brought upon you" (42:10)—provides the necessary rationale for hope; all have been judged. However, since these people must choose whether to accept YHWH's offer, the following verses (42:10–18) construe them as a *distinct group*. At times, though, the juxtaposition of alternative theological models creates logical tension. To say that YHWH exiled Jehoiachin's people (29:4) certainly grounds their salvation in divine initiative, but it offers no basis for judgment on those in Jerusalem. To say that Zedekiah's people *did not go* into exile (29:16) certainly establishes their guilt, but might imply some credit for their compatriots in Babylon.

---

4. In the world of apocalyptic, of course, it is not impossible that sheep could turn violent, debauched and drunk; Ezek 34:17–21 marks a step in this direction.

The extent to which biblical perspectives on judgment reflect different paradigms of the nation would form a rewarding study. In the Gospels, for example, we find Jesus construing the people in two quite different ways. They are "a wicked generation" (Matt 12:39–43 // Luke 11:29–32), under God's wrath. Yet the crowds who come to him for teaching are "like sheep without a shepherd," thereby eliciting his compassion (Matt 9:36 // Mark 6:34).[5] There is no reason to think these are separate groups of people; rather, they are the same people *seen differently*. Nevertheless, the different models inevitably generate different responses, namely, judgment and mercy.

The problem (or advantage) with interpretative models, of course, is that they are able to handle only a limited amount of data. As a result, they are also highly fluid; modifying one element alters the entire paradigm. The relevance of this to prophetic interpretations of judgment and salvation becomes especially clear when we consider the textual depiction of YHWH, Israel and the foreign nations. I noted in Chapter 1 that Habakkuk's analysis of Judah was modified when Babylon entered his field of vision, but the way in which the conduct of Israel and the nations shapes the Old Testament perception of YHWH's justice is complex.

In much of the prophetic corpus (e.g. Jer 1–20; 30:12–15), the dominant paradigm is that of "guilty Israel versus YHWH." Since judgment involves invasion and exile, the nations play the role of YHWH's allies. A hermeneutical crux is reached, however, when the nations come to be seen as unjust oppressors (Jer 30:16–17; 50:17–18, 33–34; Mic 4:11–13; Joel 3:1–3; Obad 8–18). In the polarity that results, of "guilty nations versus victim Israel," YHWH plays the role of Israel's ally. A further re-ordering of the paradigm (not reflected in Jeremiah) occurs when the focus on *one* nation as offender leads to a broadening of the "victim" category; the model is thus one of "guilty nation versus victim nations," in which YHWH judges on behalf of all the latter. Thus Nahum envisages worldwide joy at Assyria's downfall, "for who has not felt your endless cruelty?" (Nah 3:18–19). A similar judicial configuration appears in *4 Ezra* (first century CE), where Rome is singled out for divine wrath: "And so the whole earth, freed from your violence, shall be refreshed again, and hope for the judgment and mercy of the one that made her" (*4 Ezra* 11:85).

Here too, there would seem to be considerable scope for further study. Of special interest would be cases where two (or more) interpretative frameworks are brought together. How does each interpret the issues of guilt and justice, and how is the tension resolved? We have already seen how in 31:12–17 Zion moves from being the guilty offender justly punished to the desolate victim eliciting divine aid. Rather differently, Jer 50:6–7 characterizes Israel as misruled by its leaders (cf. 23:1–4) and oppressed by its enemies, while conceding (through the words of its enemies) the guilt of the whole nation. The book of Lamentations,

---

5. Then again, the "harvest field" logion to which Matthew adjoins this saying (Matt 9:37) is juxtaposed with a sheep metaphor of a different sort in Luke; here, Jesus' disciples are lambs and their hearers—or at least some of them—are wolves (Luke 10:2–3).

with its open confession of guilt *and* bitter protest against injustice, might make for a particularly fruitful study.

The process of redefining the lines along which YHWH would judge Israel continued long after the book of Jeremiah reached its present shape. As we saw in Chapter 1, passages in Trito-Isaiah and Malachi reflect a process towards more sectarian notions of who constituted the people of YHWH. Later still, of course, John the Baptist would announce an eschatological judgment in which personal repentance and baptism would override questions of ethnicity (Luke 3:7–14). Around the same time, the sectarians at Qumran were defining themselves as "the Sons of Light" who would be vindicated over against their wicked fellow-Israelites, "the Sons of Darkness."[6]

Such notions of inner-Israel judicial differentiation find certain parallels in the preaching of Jesus. Indeed, in several respects Jesus' message echoes concepts of judgment and salvation in Jeremiah. Just as Jer 24, 29 and 30–31 unilaterally announce a new era in salvation history, so (in Luke's Gospel) Jesus begins his ministry proclaiming "the year of God's favour" (Luke 4:19). Indeed, as N. T. Wright has emphasized, Jesus' entire ministry "was a sign that the real return from exile, the new age, the 'resurrection,' was coming into being."[7] Yet so far from guaranteeing national restoration, this eschatological event placed the whole of Israel in urgent need of conversion: "Jerusalem herself, and especially the Temple and its hierarchy, had become hopelessly corrupt, and was as ripe for judgment as it had been in the days of Jeremiah."[8] In the face of this crisis, Wright concludes, Jesus set out to redefine Israel by making personal loyalty to himself the sole criterion of membership. The scandal of his life was precisely this radical new criterion of judgment, in which previous identity markers were abolished, and his followers alone—"muddled and ambiguous"[9] as they were—would be saved. The wavering prophet from Anathoth, his dejected assistant and the foreigner Ebed-Melech would have found themselves in good company.

---

6. See the Qumran *War Scroll*, 1QM.

7. N. T. Wright, *Jesus and the Victory of God* (London: SPCK, 2004), 255. Wright's interpretation of Jesus' message is well encapsulated in Chapter 7 of his book (pp. 244–319). Note the frequent parallels between Jesus and Jeremiah contained in pp. 317–27.

8. Ibid., 317.

9. Ibid., 318.

BIBLIOGRAPHY

Abegg, Jr., Martin G. s.v. צמח. *NIDOTTE* 3:815–17.

Ackroyd, Peter R. *Exile and Restoration: A Study of Hebrew Thought of the Sixth Century B.C.* OTL. London: SCM, 1968.

———. "The Temple Vessels: A Continuity Theme." Pages 46–60 in *Studies in the Religious Tradition of the Old Testament*. Edited by Peter R. Ackroyd. London: SCM, 1987.

Aejmelaeus, Anneli. "The Function and Interpretation of כי in Biblical Hebrew." *JBL* 105 (1986): 193–209.

Anderson, A. A. *The Book of Psalms*. Vol. 1, *Psalms 1–72*. NCB. London: Marshall, Morgan & Scott, 1972.

Applegate, John. "The Fate of Zedekiah. Redactional Debate in the Book of Jeremiah. Part 1." *VT* 48 (1998): 137–60.

———. "The Fate of Zedekiah. Redactional Debate in the Book of Jeremiah. Part 2." *VT* 48 (1998): 301–8.

———. "Jeremiah and the Seventy Years in the Hebrew Bible: Inner-Biblical Reflections on the Prophet and his Prophecy." Pages 91–110 in Curtis and Römer, eds., *The Book of Jeremiah and Its Reception*.

———. " 'Peace, Peace, When There is No Peace': Redactional Integration of Prophecy of Peace into the Judgement of Jeremiah." Pages 51–90 in Curtis and Römer, eds., *The Book of Jeremiah and Its Reception*.

Auld, A.G. "Counting Sheep, Sins and Sour Grapes: The Primacy of the Primary History?" Pages 63–72 in *Sense and Sensitivity. Essays on Reading the Bible in Memory of Robert Carroll*. Edited by Alastair G. Hunter and Philip R. Davies. JSOTSup 348. London: Sheffield Academic Press, 2002.

Baker, David W. "Further Examples of the Waw Explicativum." *VT* 30 (1980): 129–36.

Baldwin, Joyce G. "Ṣemaḥ as a Technical Term in the Prophets." *VT* 16 (1964): 93–97.

Barstad, Hans M. *The Myth of the Empty Land: A Study in the History and Archaeology of Judah during the "Exilic" Period*. SOFSup 28. Oslo: Scandinavian University Press, 1996.

Baumann, E. L. "שוב שבות, Eine exegetische Untersuchung." *ZAW* 47 (1929): 17–44.

Becking, Bob. "Jeremiah's Book of Consolation: A Textual Comparison. Notes on the Masoretic Text and the Old Greek Version of Jeremiah XXX–XXXI." *VT* 44 (1994): 145–69.

Berlin, Adele. "Jeremiah 29:5–7: A Deuteronomic Allusion." *HAR* 8 (1984): 3–11.

Berridge, John M. *People, Prophet, and the Word of YHWH: An Examination of Form and Content in the Proclamation of the Prophet Jeremiah*. BST 4. Zurich: EVZ, 1970.

Biddle, Mark E. "The Literary Frame Surrounding Jeremiah 30.1–33.26." *ZAW* 100 (1988): 409–13.

———. *Polyphony and Symphony in Prophetic Literature: Rereading Jeremiah 7–20*. SOTI 2. Macon, Ga.: Mercer University Press, 1996.

Boer, P.A.H. de. "Jeremiah 45, Verse 5." Pages 122–28 in Van Duin, ed., *Selected Studies*.

————. "Some Remarks Concerning and Suggested by Jeremiah 43:1–7." Pages 113–21 in Van Duin, ed., *Selected Studies*.

Bogaert, P.-M. "De Baruch à Jérémie. Les Deux Rédactions Conservées du Livre de Jérémie." Pages 168–73 in Bogaert, ed., *Le Livre de Jérémie*.

————, ed. *Le Livre de Jérémie. Le Prophète et son Milieu, les Oracles et leur Transmission*. Leuven: Leuven University Press, 1981.

Böhmer, S. *Heimkehr und neuer Bund. Studien zu Jeremia 30–31*. GTA 5. Göttingen: Vandenhoeck & Ruprecht, 1976.

Bracke, John M. "*šûb šᵉbût*: A Reappraisal." *ZAW* 97 (1985): 233–44.

Brettler, Marc Z. "Predestination in Deuteronomy 30:1–10." Pages 177–96 in Schearing and McKenzie, eds., *Those Elusive Deuteronomists*.

Bright, John. *Jeremiah: Introduction, Translation and Notes*. AB 21. New York: Doubleday, 1965.

————. "Jeremiah's Complaints: Liturgy or Expressions of Personal Distress." Pages 189–214 in Durham and Porter, eds., *Proclamation and Presence*.

Brooke, George J. "The Book of Jeremiah and Its Reception in the Qumran Scrolls." Pages 183–205 in Curtis and Römer, eds., *The Book of Jeremiah and Its Reception*.

Brueggemann, Walter. "'The Baruch Connection': Reflections on Jer 43:1–7." *JBL* 113 (1994): 405–20.

————. *A Commentary on Jeremiah. Exile and Homecoming*. Grand Rapids: Eerdmans, 1998.

————. *The Land: Place as Gift, Promise and Challenge in Biblical Faith*. OBT. Philadelphia: Fortress, 1977.

————. *Old Testament Theology: Testimony, Dispute, Advocacy*. Minneapolis: Fortress, 1997.

————. "A Shattered Transcendence? Exile and Restoration." Pages 183–203 in Walter Brueggemann, *Old Testament Theology: Essays on Structure, Theme and Text*. Edited by Patrick D. Miller. Minneapolis: Fortress, 1992.

Budd, Philip J. *Numbers*. WBC. Waco: Word, 1984.

Butterworth, Mike. *Structure and the Book of Zechariah*. JSOTSup 130. Sheffield: JSOT Press, 1992.

Calvin, John. *Commentaries on the Book of the Prophet Jeremiah and the Lamentations*, Vol. 1. Translated by J. Owen. Edinburgh: Calvin Translation Society, 1852.

————. *Commentaries on the Book of the Prophet Jeremiah and the Lamentations*, Vol. 3. Translated by J. Owen. Edinburgh: Calvin Translation Society, 1852.

Carroll, Robert P. "The Book of J: Intertextuality and Ideological Criticism." Pages 220–43 in Diamond, O'Connor and Stulman, eds., *Troubling Jeremiah*.

————. "Deportation and Diasporic Discourses in the Prophetic Literature." Pages 63–85 in Scott, ed., *Exile*.

————. *From Chaos to Covenant: Uses of Prophecy in the Book of Jeremiah*. London: SCM, 1981.

————. *Jeremiah. A Commentary*. OTL. London: SCM, 1986.

Cazelles, H. "Israël du nord et arche d'alliance (Jér. III 16)." *VT* 18 (1968): 147–58.

————. "La Vie de Jérémie dans son Contexte National et International." Pages 21–39 in Bogaert, ed., *Le Livre de Jérémie*.

Childs, Brevard S. *Exodus. A Commentary*. OTL. London: SCM, 1974.

————. *Introduction to the Old Testament as Scripture*. London: SCM, 1979.

————. *Isaiah: A Commentary*. OTL. Louisville: Westminster John Knox, 2001.

Clements, Ronald E. "Jeremiah 1–25 and the Deuteronomistic History." Pages 107–22 in Clements, ed., *Old Testament Prophecy*.

————. *Jeremiah: A Bible Commentary for Teaching and Preaching*. Interpretation. Atlanta: Westminster John Knox, 1988.

———. "Jeremiah: Prophet of Hope." Pages 123–41 in Clements, ed., *Old Testament Prophecy*.

———, ed. *Old Testament Prophecy: From Oracles to Canon*. Louisville: Westminster John Knox, 1996,

Clines, David J. A. *The Theme of the Pentateuch*. JSOTSup 10. Sheffield: JSOT, 1978.

Clines, David J. A., and David M. Gunn. "Form, Occasion and Redaction in Jeremiah 20." *ZAW* 88 (1976): 390–409.

Coats, George W. *Rebellion in the Wilderness*. Nashville: Abingdon, 1968.

Coggins, R. J. "What Does 'Deuteronomistic' Mean?" Pages 135–48 in Davies, Harvey and Watson, eds., *Words Remembered, Texts Renewed*.

Collins, Terence. "Deuteronomist Influence on the Prophetical Books." Pages 15–26 in Curtis and Römer, eds., *The Book of Jeremiah and Its Reception*.

Condamin, A. *Le Livre de Jérémie. Traduction et Commentaire*. 3d ed. Études Bibliques. Paris: Gabalda et Cie, 1936.

Conrad, Edgar W. *Reading the Latter Prophets: Towards a New Canonical Criticism*. JSOTSup 376. London: Continuum, 2003.

Craigie, Peter C. *The Book of Deuteronomy*. NICOT. Grand Rapids: Eerdmans, 1976.

Craigie, Peter C., Page H. Kelley and Joel F. Drinkard, Jr. *Jeremiah 1–25*. WBC 26. Dallas: Word, 1991.

Crenshaw, James L. *A Whirlpool of Torment: Israelite Traditions of God as an Oppressive Presence*. OBT. Philadelphia: Fortress, 1984.

Croft, Stephen J. L. *The Identity of the Individual in the Psalms*. JSOTSup 44. Sheffield: JSOT, 1987.

Cross, Frank M. "The Evolution of a Theory of Local Texts." Pages 306–20 in *Qumran and the History of the Biblical Text*. Edited by Frank M. Cross and Shemaryahu Talmon. Cambridge, Mass.: Harvard University Press, 1975.

Curtis, A. H. W., and T. Römer, eds. *The Book of Jeremiah and Its Reception*. BETL 128. Leuven: Leuven University Press, 1997.

Davies, Eryl W. *Numbers*. NCB. London: HarperCollins, 1995.

Davies, Jon, Graham Harvey and Wilfred G. E. Watson, eds. *Words Remembered, Texts Renewed: Essays in Honour of John F.A. Sawyer*. JSOTSup 195. Sheffield: Sheffield Academic Press, 1995.

Dearman, J. Andrew. "My Servants the Scribes: Composition and Context in Jeremiah 36." *JBL* 109 (1990): 403–21.

DeVries, Simon J. *1 Kings*. WBC 12. Waco: Word, 1985.

Diamond, A. R. *The Confessions of Jeremiah in Context: Scenes of Prophetic Drama*. JSOTSup 45. Sheffield: JSOT, 1987.

Diamond, A. R. Pete, Kathleen M. O'Connor and Louis Stulman, eds., *Troubling Jeremiah*. JSOTSup 260. Sheffield: Sheffield Academic Press, 1999.

Dietrich, E. L. *Die endzeitliche Wiederherstellung bei den Propheten*. BZAW 40. Giessen: Töpelmann, 1925.

Driver, G. R. "Linguistic and Textual Problems: Jeremiah." *JQR* 28 (1937–38): 97–129.

Driver, S. R. *The Book of the Prophet Jeremiah: A Revised Translation with Introductions and Short Explanations*. London: Hodder & Stoughton, 1908.

———. *A Critical and Exegetical Commentary on Deuteronomy*. ICC. Edinburgh: T. & T. Clark, 1895.

Duguid, Iain M. *Ezekiel and the Leaders of Israel*. VTSup 56. Leiden: Brill, 1994.

Duhm, B. *Das Buch Jeremia*. KHAT. Tübingen: Mohr (Paul Siebeck), 1901.

Dumbrell, William J. *Covenant and Creation: A Theology of the Old Testament Covenants*. BTCL. Carlisle: Paternoster, 1997.

Durham, John I., and J. R. Porter, eds. *Proclamation and Presence: Old Testament Essays in Honour of Gwynne Henton Davies*. Richmond: John Knox, 1970.

Eaton, Michael A. *Ecclesiastes: An Introduction and Commentary*. TOTC. Leicester: IVP, 1983.

Ehrlich, A. B. *Randglossen zur Hebräischen Bibel: textkritisches, sprachliches und sachliches*. Vol. 4, *Jesia, Jeremia*. Leipzig: Hinrichs, 1912.

Eichrodt, Walther. *Ezekiel: A Commentary*. Translated by C. Quin. OTL. London: SCM, 1970.

———. *Theology of the Old Testament*, Vol. 2. Translated by J. A. Baker. OTL. London: SCM, 1967.

Emmerson, Grace I. *Isaiah 56–66*. OTG. Sheffield: Sheffield Academic Press, 1992.

Fischer, G. *Das Trostbüchlein. Text, Komposition und Theologie von Jer 30–31*. SBB 26. Stuttgart: Katholisches Bibelwerk, 1993.

Fox, Michael V. *A Time to Tear Down and a Time to Build: A Rereading of Ecclesiastes*. Grand Rapids: Eerdmans, 1999.

Fretheim, Terence E. "The Plagues as Ecological Signs of Historical Disaster." *JBL* 110 (1991): 385–96.

Gerstenberger, E. "Jeremiah's Complaints: Observations on Jer. 15:10–21." *JBL* 82 (1963): 393–408.

Giesebrecht, F. *Das Buch Jeremia, übersetzt und erklärt*. HKAT. Göttingen: Vandenhoeck & Ruprecht, 1894.

Goldman, Yohanan. *Prophétie et royauté au retour de l'exil. Les origines littéraires de la forme massorétique du Livre de Jérémie*. OBO 118. Freiburg: Universitätsverlag; Göttingen: Vandenhoeck & Ruprecht, 1992.

Gordis, Robert. *Koheleth: The Man and His World; A Study of Ecclesiastes*. New York: Schocken, 1968.

Gordon, Robert P. *1 and 2 Samuel: A Commentary*. Exeter: Paternoster, 1986.

———. "Curse, Malediction." *NIDOTTE* 4:491–93.

Gosse, Bernard. "Jérémie XLV et la Place du Recueil d'Oracles Contre les Nations dans le Livre de Jérémie." *VT* 40 (1990): 145–51.

Gottwald, Norman K. *The Hebrew Bible: A Socio-Literary Introduction*. Philadelphia: Fortress, 1985.

———. *The Politics of Ancient Israel*. LAI. Louisville: Westminster John Knox, 2001.

Graupner, A. *Auftrag und Geschick des Propheten Jeremia. literarische Eigenart, Herkunft und Intention vordeuteronomistischer Prosa im Jeremiabuch*. BTS 15. Neukirchen–Vluyn: Neukirchener, 1991.

Gray, John. *I and II Kings: A Commentary*. OTL. London: SCM, 1964.

Greenberg, Moshe. *Ezekiel 21–37: A New Translation with Introduction and Commentary*. AB 22A. New York: Doubleday, 1997.

Grisanti, Michael A. s.v. שְׁרִירוּת. *NIDOTTE* 4:253–54.

Gunn, David M. *The Fate of King Saul: An Interpretation of a Biblical Story*. JSOTSup 14. Sheffield: JSOT, 1980.

Gunneweg, Antonius H. J. "Konfession oder Interpretation im Jeremiabuch." *ZTK* 67 (1970): 395–416.

Haak, Robert D. *Habakkuk*. VTSup 44. Leiden: Brill, 1992.

Habel, Norman C. *The Land is Mine*. Minneapolis: Fortress, 1995.

Hardmeier, Christof. "Jer 29, 24–32—'eine geradezu unüberbietbare Konfusion'? Vorurteil und Methode in der exegetischen Forschung." Pages 301–17 in *Die Hebräische Bibel und ihre zweifache Nachgeschichte. Festschrift für Rolf Rendtorff zum 65 Geburtstag*. Edited by Erhard Blum, Christian Macholz and Ekkehard W. Stegemann. Neukirchen–Vluyn: Neukirchener, 1990.

Harrison, R. K. *Jeremiah and Lamentations: An Introduction and Commentary*. TOTC. Leicester: IVP, 1979.

Hayman, A. P. "The 'Original Text': A Scholarly Illusion." Pages 434–49 in Davies, Harvey and Watson, eds., *Words Remembered, Texts Renewed*.

Herrmann, Siegfried. *Die prophetischen Heilserwartungen im Alten Testament. Ursprung und Gestaltwandel*. BWANT 5. Stuttgart: Kohlhammer, 1965.

Hertzberg, H. W. *I and II Samuel: A Commentary*. Translated by J. S. Bowden. OTL. London: SCM, 1964.

Hobbs, T. R. "Some Remarks on the Composition and Structure of the Book of Jeremiah." Pages 175–91 in Perdue and Kovacs, eds., *A Prophet to the Nations*.

Holladay, William L. *Jeremiah: Spokesman Out of Time*. Philadelphia: United Church Press, 1974.

———. *Jeremiah 1: A Commentary on the Book of the Prophet Jeremiah, Chapters 1–25*. Philadelphia: Fortress, 1986.

———. *Jeremiah 2: A Commentary on the Book of the Prophet Jeremiah, Chapters 26–52*. Minneapolis: Fortress, 1989.

Houston, Walter. "What Did the Prophets Think They Were Doing? Speech Acts and Prophetic Discourse in the Old Testament." *Biblical Interpretation* 1, 2 (1993): 167–88.

Hyatt, J. Philip. "The Beginning of Jeremiah's Prophecy." *ZAW* 78 (1966): 204–14.

———. "The Book of Jeremiah." Pages 777–1142 in *The Interpreter's Bible*. Vol. 5, *Ecclesiastes, Song of Songs, Isaiah, Jeremiah*. Edited by G. A. Buttrick. Nashville: Abingdon, 1956.

———. "The Deuteronomic Edition of the Book of Jeremiah." Pages 247–67 in Perdue and Kovacs, eds., *A Prophet to the Nations*.

Janzen, J. Gerald. *Studies in the Text of Jeremiah*. HSM 6. Cambridge MA: Harvard University Press, 1973.

Jenni, E. *Die politischen Voraussagen der Propheten*. ATANT 29. Zurich: Zwingli, 1956.

Jones, Douglas Rawlinson. *Jeremiah*. NCB. London: Marshall Pickering, 1992.

Joyce, Paul. *Divine Initiative and Human Response in Ezekiel*. JSOTSup 51. Sheffield: JSOT, 1988.

———. "Individual and Community." Pages 74–89 in John Rogerson, ed., *Beginning Old Testament Study*. Rev. ed. London: SPCK, 1998.

Keil, C. F. *Biblischer Kommentar über den Propheten Jeremia und die Klageliede*. BKAT 2/3. Leipzig: Dörffling & Franke, 1872.

Kessler, Martin. "Jeremiah Chapters 26–45 Reconsidered." *JNES* 27 (1968): 81–88.

Keown, Gerald L., Pamela J. Scalise and Thomas G. Smothers. *Jeremiah 26–52*. WBC 27. Dallas: Word, 1995.

Kidner, Derek. *The Message of Jeremiah: Against Wind and Tide*. TBST. Leicester: IVP, 1987.

Kilpp, Nelson. *Niederreißen und aufbauen. Das Verhältnis von Heilsverheißung und Unheilsverkündigung bei Jeremia und im Jeremiabuch*. BTS 13. Neukirchen–Vluyn: Neukirchener, 1990.

Klein, Ralph W. *Textual Criticism of the Old Testament: From the Septuagint to Qumran*. Philadelphia: Fortress, 1974.

Koch, Klaus. "Is There a Doctrine of Retribution in the Old Testament?" Pages 57–87 in *Theodicy in the Old Testament*. Edited by James L. Crenshaw. Philadelphia: Fortress, 1983.

———. *The Prophets*. Vol. 1, *The Assyrian Period*. Translated by Margaret Kohl. London: SCM, 1982.

Koenen, Klaus. *Heil den Gerechten—Unheil den Sündern! Ein Beitrag zur Theologie der Prophetenbücher.* BZAW 229. Berlin: de Gruyter, 1994.

Kraus, H.-J. *Worship in Israel: A Cultic History of the Old Testament.* Translated by Geoffrey Buswell. Oxford: Blackwell, 1966.

Kremers, Heinz. "Leidensgemeinschaft mit Gott im Alten Testament. Eine Untersuchung der 'biographischen' Berichte im Jeremiabuch." *EvT* 13 (1953): 122–40.

LaSor, William Sanford, David Allan Hubbard and Frederic William Bush. *Old Testament Survey: The Message, Form and Background of the Old Testament.* Grand Rapids: Eerdmans, 1982.

Leaney, A. R. C. *The Rule of Qumran and Its Meaning: Introduction, Translation and Commentary.* NTL. London: SCM, 1966.

Lemke, Werner E. "Nebuchadrezzar, My Servant." *CBQ* 28 (1966): 45–50.

Levin, Christoph. *Die Verheißung des neuen Bundes in ihrem theologiegeschichtlichen Zusammenhang ausgelegt.* FRLANT 137. Göttingen: Vandenhoeck & Ruprecht, 1985.

Lindblom, J. *Prophecy in Ancient Israel.* Philadelphia: Fortress, 1962.

Loader, J. *Polar Structures in the Book of Qoheleth.* BZAW 152. Berlin: de Gruyter, 1979.

Lohfink, Norbert. "Der junge Jeremia als Propagandist und Poet. Zum Grundstock von Jer 30–31." Pages 351–68 in Bogaert, ed., *Le Livre de Jérémie.*

Long, Burke O. "Social Dimensions of Prophetic Conflict." *Semeia* 21 (1981): 31–53.

Lundbom, Jack R. "Baruch, Seraiah, and Expanded Colophons in the Book of Jeremiah." *JSOT* 36 (1986): 89–114.

———. *Jeremiah: A Study in Ancient Hebrew Rhetoric.* SBLDS 18. Missoula, Mont.: Scholars Press, 1975.

———. *Jeremiah 1–20: A New Translation with Introduction and Commentary.* AB 21A. New York: Doubleday, 1999.

———. *Jeremiah 21–36: A New Translation with Introduction and Commentary.* AB 21B. New York: Doubleday, 2004.

———. *Jeremiah 37–52: A New Translation with Introduction and Commentary.* AB 21C. New York: Doubleday, 2004.

Lust, J. "'Gathering and Return' in Jeremiah and Ezekiel." Pages 1197–42 in Bogaert, ed., *Le Livre de Jérémie.*

Malamat, A. "Jeremiah and the Last Two Kings of Judah." *PEQ* 83 (1951): 81–87.

Martens, Elmer A. "Narrative Parallelism and Message in Jeremiah 34–38." Pages 33–49 in *Early Jewish and Christian Exegesis: Studies in Memory of William Hugh Brownlee.* Edited by Craig A. Evans and William F. Stinespring. Atlanta: Scholars Press, 1987.

Mason, R. *Zephaniah, Habakkuk, Joel.* OTG. Sheffield: JSOT, 1994.

May, Herbert Gordon. "Towards an Objective Approach to the Book of Jeremiah: The Biographer." *JBL* 61 (1942): 139–53.

Mayes, A. D. H. *Deuteronomy.* NCB. Grand Rapids: Eerdmans, 1987.

McKenzie, Steven L., and Howard N. Wallace, "Covenant Themes in Malachi." *CBQ* 45 (1983): 549–63.

McConville, J. G. *Deuteronomy.* AOTC. Leicester: IVP/Apollos, 2002.

———. "Jeremiah." Pages 671–708 in *New Bible Commentary: 21st Century Edition.* Edited by D. A. Carson et al. Leicester: IVP, 1994.

———. *Judgment and Promise: An Interpretation of the Book of Jeremiah.* Winona Lake: Eisenbrauns, 1993.

McEvenue, Sean. "The Composition of Jeremiah 37.1 to 44.30." Pages 59–67 in *Studies in Wisdom Literature.* Special issue of *OTWSA* 15–16. Edited by W. C. van Wyk. Pretoria, 1972.

McKane, William. *A Critical and Exegetical Commentary on Jeremiah*. Vol. 1, *Introduction and Commentary on Jeremiah I–XXV*. ICC: New Series. Edinburgh: T. & T. Clark, 1986.

———. *A Critical and Exegetical Commentary on Jeremiah*. Vol. 2. *Commentary on Jeremiah XXVI–LII*. ICC: New Series. Edinburgh: T. & T. Clark, 1996.

Meier, Samuel A. *Speaking of Speaking: Marking Direct Discourse in the Hebrew Bible*. VTSup 46: Leiden: Brill, 1992.

Min, Y.-J. The Minuses and Pluses of the LXX Translation of Jeremiah as Compared with the Massoretic Text. Ph.D diss. Jerusalem, Hebrew University, 1977.

Mowinckel, S. *Zur Komposition des Buches Jeremia*. Videnskapsselskapets Skrifter. II. Hist.-Filos. Klasse 5. Kristiania: Jacob Dybwad, 1914.

———. *Prophecy and Tradition: The Prophetic Books in the Light of the Study of the Growth and History of the Tradition*. Avhandlinger (Norske videnskaps-akademi i Oslo. II, Hist.-filos. klasse), 1946, no. 3; Oslo: Dybwad, 1946.

Muilenburg, James. "Baruch the Scribe." Pages 215–38 in Durham and Porter, eds., *Proclamation and Presence*.

Murphy, Roland E. *Ecclesiastes*. WBC 23A. Dallas: Word, 1992.

Nicholson, E. W. *The Book of the Prophet Jeremiah 26–52*. CBC. Cambridge: Cambridge University Press, 1975.

———. *God and His People: Covenant and Theology in the Old Testament*. Oxford: Clarendon, 1986.

———. *Preaching to the Exiles: A Study of the Prose Tradition in the Book of Jeremiah*. Oxford: Blackwell, 1970.

Nielsen, E. "The Righteous and the Wicked in Habaqquq." *ST* 6 (1953): 54–78.

Niditch, Susan. *The Symbolic Vision in Biblical Tradition*. HSM 30. Chico, Calif.: Scholars Press, 1980.

Noth, Martin. *Numbers: A Commentary*. Translated by James D. Martin. OTL. London: SCM, 1968.

O'Connor, Kathleen M. *The Confessions of Jeremiah: Their Interpretation and Role in Chapters 1–25*. SBLDS 94. Atlanta: Scholars Press, 1988.

Odashima, T. *Heilsworte im Jeremiabuch. Untersuchungen zu ihrer vordeuteronomistischen Bearbeitung*. BWANT 125. Stuttgart: Kohlhammer, 1989.

O'Donovan, O. M. T. *The Desire of the Nations: Rediscovering the Roots of Political Theology*. Cambridge: Cambridge University Press, 1986.

Otto, E. "Die Theologie des Buches Habakkuk." *VT* 35 (1985): 274–95.

Overholt, Thomas W. "King Nebuchadnezzar in the Jeremiah Tradition." *CBQ* 30 (1968): 39–48.

———. *The Threat of Falsehood: A Study in the Theology of the Book of Jeremiah*. SBT 16. London: SCM, 1970.

Pardee, Dennis, et al., eds. *Handbook of Ancient Hebrew Letters: A Study Edition*. SBLSBS 15. Chico, Calif.: Scholars Press, 1982.

Parke-Taylor, Geoffrey H. *The Formation of the Book of Jeremiah: Doublets and Recurring Phrases*. SBLMS 51. Atlanta: Scholars Press, 2000.

Paterson, J. "Jeremiah." Pages 537–62 in *Peake's Commentary on the Bible* (ed. M. Black and H. H. Rowley; London: Thomas Nelson & Sons, 1962).

Peake, A. S. *Jeremiah and Lamentations*. Vol. 2, *Jeremiah XXV to LII, Lamentations*. CB. Edinburgh: T. & T. Clark, 1911.

Perdue, Leo G., and Brian W. Kovacs, eds. *A Prophet to the Nations: Essays in Jeremiah Studies*. Winona Lake: Eisenbrauns, 1984.

Pohlmann, Karl-Friedrich. *Studien zum Jeremiabuch. Ein Beitrag zur Frage nach der Entstehung des Jeremiabuches*. FRLANT 118. Göttingen: Vandenhoeck & Ruprecht, 1978.

———. *Die Ferne Gottes. Studien zum Jeremiabuch. Beiträge zu den "Konfessionen" in Jeremiabuch und ein Versuch zur Frage nach dem Anfängen der Jeremiatradition*. BZAW 179. Berlin: de Gruyter, 1989.

Preuschen, E. "Die Bedeutung von שבות שוב im Alten Testamente." *ZAW* 15 (1895): 1–74.

Provan, Iain W. *1 and 2 Kings*. NIBC. Carlisle: Paternoster, 1995.

Rabin, C., S. Talmon and E. Tov, eds. *The Hebrew University Bible: The Book of Jeremiah*. Jerusalem: Magnes, 1997.

Rad, Gerhard von. *Deuteronomy: A Commentary*. Translated by D. Barton. OTL. London: SCM, 1966.

———. *Genesis: A Commentary*. Translated by John H. Marks. OTL. London: SCM, 1972.

Raitt, Thomas M. "Jeremiah's Deliverance Message to Judah." Pages 166–85 in *Rhetorical Criticism: Essays in Honor of James Muilenburg*. Edited by J. J. Jackson and M. Kessler. PTMS 1. Pittsburgh: Pickwick, 1974.

———. *A Theology of Exile: Judgment / Deliverance in Jeremiah and Ezekiel*. Philadelphia: Fortress, 1977.

Reimer, David J. *The Oracles Against Babylon in Jeremiah 50–51: A Horror Among the Nations*. San Francisco: Mellen Research University Press, 1993.

———. "Political Prophets? Political Exegesis and Prophetic Theology." Pages 126–42 in *Intertextuality in Ugarit and Israel*. Edited by Johannes C. de Moor. Leiden: Brill, 1998.

———. s.v. צדק. *NIDOTTE* 3:744–69.

Reventlow, H. Graf. *Liturgie und prophetische Ich bei Jeremia*. Gütersloh: Gütersloher Verlaghaus, Gerd Mohn, 1963.

Rietzschel, Claus. *Das Problem der Urrolle. Ein Beitrag zur Redaktionsgeschichte des Jeremiabuches*. Gütersloh: Gerd Mohn, 1966.

Roberts, B. J. *The Old Testament Text and Versions. The Hebrew Text in Transmission and the History of the Ancient Versions*. Cardiff: University of Wales Press, 1951.

Robinson, H. Wheeler. *Inspiration and Revelation in the Old Testament*. Oxford: Oxford University Press, 1946.

Rofé, A. "The Arrangement of the Book of Jeremiah." *ZAW* 101 (1989): 390–98.

Rosenberg, Joel. "Jeremiah and Ezekiel." Pages 184–206 in *The Literary Guide to the Bible*. Edited by Robert Alter and Frank Kermode. London: Fontana, 1987.

Rubinger, Naphtali J. "Jeremiah's Epistle to the Exiles and the Field in Anathoth." *Judaism* 26 (1977): 84–91.

Rudolph, W. *Jeremia*. HAT. Tübingen: Mohr (Paul Siebeck), 1947.

Schearing, Linda S., and Steven L. McKenzie, eds. *Those Elusive Deuteronomists: The Phenomenon of Pan-Deuteronomism*. JSOTSup 268. Sheffield: Sheffield Academic Press, 1999.

Schmid, Konrad. *Buchgestalten des Jeremiabuches: Untersuchungen zur Redaktions- und Rezeptionsgeschichte von Jer 30–33 im Kontext des Buches*. WMANT 72. Neukirchen–Vluyn: Neukirchener, 1996.

Schmitt, John J. "The Virgin of Israel: Referent and Use of the Phrase in Amos and Jeremiah." *CBQ* 53 (1991): 365–87.

Schulte, Hannelis. "Baruch und Ebedmelech—Persönliche Heilsorakel im Jeremiabuche." *BZ* 32 (1988): 257–65.

Scott, James M. ed. *Exile: Old Testament, Jewish and Christian Conceptions*. JSJSup 56. Leiden: Brill, 1997.

Seebass, H. "Jeremia's Konflikt mit Chananja. Bemerkungen zu Jer 27 und 28." *ZAW* 82 (1970): 449–52.

Seidl, Theodor. *Texte und Einheiten in Jeremia 27–29*. ATSAT 2. Munich: Eos St Ottilien, 1977.

Seitz, Christopher R. "The Crisis of Interpretation Over the Meaning and Purpose of the Exile." *VT* 35 (1985): 78–97.

———. "Isaiah in Parish Bible Study. The Question of the Place of the Reader in Biblical Texts." Pages in 194–212 in *Word Without End: The Old Testament as Abiding Theological Witness*. Edited by Christopher R. Seitz. Waco: Baylor University Press, 2004.

———. "The Prophet Moses and the Canonical Shape of Jeremiah." *ZAW* 101 (1989): 3–27.

———. *Theology in Conflict: Reactions to the Exile in the Book of Jeremiah*. BZAW 176. Berlin: de Gruyter, 1989.

Sharp, Carolyn J. "The Call of Jeremiah and Diaspora Politics." *JBL* 119 (2000): 421–38.

Sheriffs, Deryck. *The Friendship of the Lord: An Old Testament Spirituality*. Carlisle: Paternoster, 1996.

Sisson, Jonathan Paige. "Jeremiah and the Jerusalemite Conception of Peace." *JBL* 105 (1986): 429–42.

Skinner, John. *Prophecy and Religion: Studies in the Life of Jeremiah*. Cambridge: Cambridge University Press, 1922.

Smelik, Klaas A. D. "Letters to the Exiles: Jeremiah 29 in Context." *SJOT* 10 (1996): 282–95.

Smith, Daniel L. "Jeremiah as Prophet of Nonviolent Resistance." *JSOT* 43 (1989): 95–107.

———. *The Religion of the Landless: The Social Context of the Babylonian Exile*. Bloomington: Meyer Stone, 1989.

Smith-Christopher, Daniel L. "Reassessing the Historical and Sociological Impact of the Babylonian Exile (597 / 587–539 BCE)." Pages 7–36 in Scott, ed., *Exile*.

Smith, Mark S. *The Laments of Jeremiah and Their Contexts: A Literary and Redactional Study of Jeremiah 11–20*. SBLMS 42. Atlanta: Scholars Press, 1990.

Soderlund, Sven. *The Greek Text of Jeremiah: A Revised Hypothesis*. JSOTSup 47. Sheffield: JSOT, 1985.

Soggin, J. Alberto. "Jeremiah 29,8b." Pages 238–40 in *Old Testament and Oriental Studies*. Edited by J. Alberto Soggin. BO 29. Rome: Biblical Institute, 1975.

Sommer, Benjamin D. "New Light on the Composition of Jeremiah." *CBQ* 61 (1999): 646–66.

Southwell, Peter J. M. "Habakkuk: Theology of." *NIDOTTE* 4:688–90.

Spencer, Aida Besancon. "שרירות as Self-Reliance." *JBL* 100 (1981): 247–48.

Stipp, Hermann-Josef. "Zedekiah in the Book of Jeremiah: On the Formation of a Biblical Character." *CBQ* 58 (1996): 627–48.

Streane, A. W. *The Book of the Prophet Jeremiah Together with the Lamentations*. CB. Cambridge: Cambridge University Press, 1885.

Stulman, Louis. *Order Amid Chaos: Jeremiah as Symbolic Tapestry*. BS 57. Sheffield: Sheffield Academic Press, 1998.

———. *The Other Text of Jeremiah: A Reconstruction of the Hebrew Text Underlying the Greek Version of the Prose Sections of Jeremiah with English Translation*. Lanham, Md.: University Press of America, 1986.

———. *The Prose Sermons of the Book of Jeremiah: A Redescription of the Correspondences with the Deuteronomistic Literature in the Light of Recent Text-Critical Research*. SBLDS 83. Atlanta: Scholars Press, 1986.

Sturdy, John V. M. "The Authorship of the 'Prose Sermons' of Jeremiah." Pages 143–50 in *Prophecy: Essays Presented to Georg Fohrer on his Sixty-Fifth Birthday, 6 September 1980*. Edited by J. A. Emerton. BZAW 150. Berlin: de Gruyter, 1980.

Sweeney, Marvin A. "Jeremiah 30–31 and King Josiah's Program of National Restoration and Religious Reform." *ZAW* 108 (1996): 569–83.

Swetnam, James. "Some Observations on the Background of צדיק in Jeremias 23, 5a." *Biblica* 46 (1965): 29–40.

Taylor, Marion Ann. "Jeremiah 45: The Problem of Placement." *JSOT* 37 (1987): 79–78.

Thiel, Winfried. *Die deuteronomistische Redaktion von Jeremia 1–25*. WMANT 41. Neukirchen–Vluyn: Neukirchener, 1973.

———. *Die deuteronomistische Redaktion von Jeremia 26–45. Mit einer Gesamtbeurteilung der deuteronomistischen Redaktion des Buches Jeremias*. WMANT 52. Neukirchen–Vluyn: Neukirchener, 1981.

Thiselton, Anthony C. *The Two Horizons: New Testament Hermeneutics and Philosophical Description with Special Reference to Heidegger, Bultmann, Gadamer and Wittgenstein*. Exeter: Paternoster, 1980.

Thomas, D. Winton. "A Note on מועדים in Jeremiah 24, 1." *JTS* 3 (1952): 55.

———. "The Root ידע in Hebrew." *JTS* 35 (1934): 298–306.

———. "The Textual Criticism of the Old Testament." Pages 238–59 in *The Old Testament and Modern Study: A Generation of Discovery and Research*. Edited by H. H. Rowley. Oxford: Oxford University Press, 1951.

Thompson, J. A. *The Book of Jeremiah*. NICOT. Grand Rapids: Eerdmans, 1980.

Thompson J. A., and Elmer A. Martens, s.v. שׁוב. *NIDOTTE* 4:55–59.

Tov, Emanuel. "Exegetical Notes on the Hebrew *Vorlage* of the LXX of Jeremiah 27 (34)." *ZAW* 91 (1979): 73–93.

———. "Some Aspects of the Textual and Literary History of the Book of Jeremiah." Pages 147–67 in Bogaert, ed., *Le Livre de Jérémie*.

———. "The Literary History of the Book of Jeremiah in the Light of Its Textual History." Pages 211–37 in *Empirical Models for Biblical Criticism*. Edited by Jeffrey H. Tigay. Philadelphia: Fortress, 1985.

———. "Three Fragments of Jeremiah from Qumran Cave 4." *RQ* 15 (1992): 531–41.

———. "Did the Septuagint Translators Always Understand Their Hebrew Text?" Pages 203–18 in *The Greek and Hebrew Bible: Collected Essays on the Septuagint*. Edited by Emanuel Tov. VTSup 72. Leiden: Brill, 1999.

Unterman, Jeremiah. *From Repentance to Redemption: Jeremiah's Thought in Transition*. JSOTSup 54. Sheffield: Sheffield Academic Press, 1987.

Van Duin, C., ed. *Selected Studies in Old Testament Exegesis*. OS 27. Leiden: Brill, 1970.

Volz, Paul. *Der Prophet Jeremia. Übersetzt und erklärt*. 2d ed. KAT. Leipzig: Deichert, 1928.

———. *Studien zum Text des Jeremia* (Leipzig: Hinrichs, 1920).

Waltke, Bruce K., and M. O'Connor. *An Introduction to Biblical Hebrew Syntax*. Winona Lake: Eisenbrauns, 1990.

Walton, John H. "Vision Narrative Wordplay and Jeremiah XXIV." *VT* 39 (1989): 508–9.

Wanke, Gunther. "Jeremias Ackerkauf: Heil im Gericht?" Pages 265–76 in *Prophet und Prophetenbuch. Festschrift für Otto Kaiser zum 65 Geburtstag*. Edited by Volkmar Fritz, Karl-Friedrich Pohlmann and Hans-Christoph Schmitt. BZAW 185. Berlin: de Gruyter, 1989.

———. *Untersuchungen zur sogennanten Baruchschrift*. BZAW 122. Berlin: de Gruyter, 1971.

Weinfeld, Moshe. *Deuteronomy and the Deuteronomic School*. Oxford: Oxford University Press, 1972.

———. "Jeremiah and the Spiritual Metamorphosis of Israel." *ZAW* 88 (1976): 17–56.

Weippert, Helga. "Jahwekrieg und Bundesfluch in Jer 21 1–7." *ZAW* 82 (1970): 396–409.

———. *Die Prosareden des Jeremiabuches*. BZAW 132. Berlin: de Gruyter, 1973.

Weiser, Artur. *Das Buch des Propheten Jeremia*. NGB. Göttingen: Vandenhoeck & Ruprecht, 1955.

———. "Das Gotteswort für Baruch. Jer. 45 und die sogennante Baruchbiographie." Pages 321–29 in *Glaube und Geschichte im Alten Testmanent und andere ausgewählte Schriften*. Edited by A. Weiser. Göttingen: Vandenhoeck & Ruprecht, 1961.

———. *Introduction to the Old Testament*. Translated by D. M. Barton. London: Darton, Longman & Todd, 1961.

———. *The Psalms: A Commentary*. Translated by H. Hartwell. OTL. London: SCM, 1962.

Welch, A. C. *Jeremiah. His Time and His Work*. Oxford: Blackwell, 1951.

Wells, Roy D. "The Amplification of the Expectations of the Exiles in the MT Revision of Jeremiah." Pages 272–92 in Diamond, O'Connor and Stulman, eds., *Troubling Jeremiah*.

Wenham, Gordon J. *Numbers: An Introduction and Commentary*. TOTC. Leicester: IVP, 1981.

Westermann, Claus. "Die Begriffe für Fragen und Suchen im Alten Testament." *KD* 6 (1960): 2–30.

Whitley, C. F. "The Term Seventy Years Captivity." *VT* 4 (1954): 60–72.

———. "The Term Seventy Years: A Rejoinder." *VT* 7 (1957): 416–18.

Williams, Tyler F. s.v. אֵיב. *NIDOTTE* 1:365–71.

Wilson, R. R. *Prophecy and Society in Ancient Israel*. Philadelphia: Fortress, 1980.

Lalleman-de Winkel, H. *Jeremiah in Prophetic Tradition: An Examination of the Book of Jeremiah in the Light of Israel's Prophetic Traditions*. CBET 26. Leuven: Peeters, 2000.

Wolff, Hans Walter. *Hosea: A Commentary on the Book of the Prophet Hosea*. Translated by Gary Stansell. Hermeneia. Philadelphia: Fortress, 1974.

———. *Joel and Amos. A Commentary on the Books of the Prophets Joel and Amos*. Translated by W. Janzen. Hermeneia. Philadelphia: Fortress, 1977.

———. "Das Kerygma des deuteronomistischen Geschichtswerks." *ZAW* 73 (1961): 171–86.

Wonneberger, R. *Understanding BHS: A Manual for the Users of the Biblia Hebraica Stuttgartensia*. SB 8. Rome: Pontifical Biblical Institute, 1990.

Wright, Christopher J. H. s.v., אָרַר. *NIDOTTE* 1:518–24.

———. s.v., יָרֵשׁ. *NIDOTTE* 2:547–49.

Wright, N. T. *Jesus and the Victory of God*. London: SPCK, 2004.

Yaure, L. "Elymas—Nehelamite—Pethor." *JBL* 79 (1960): 297–314.

Zevit, Ziony. "The Use of ʿebed as a Diplomatic Term in Jeremiah." *JBL* 88 (1969): 74–77.

Ziegler, J. *Beiträge zur Ieremias-Septuaginta. Nachrichten der Akademie der Wissenschaften in Göttingen*. Vol. 1, *Philologisch-Historische Klasse*. Göttingen: Vandenhoeck & Ruprecht, 1958.

— ed. *Septuaginta. Vetus Testamentum Graecum*. Vol. 15, *Ieremias, Baruch, Threni, Epistula Ieremiae*. Göttingen: Vandenhoeck & Ruprecht, 1957.

Zimmerli, Walther. *Ezekiel 1: A Commentary on the Book of the Prophet Ezekiel, Chapters 1–24*. Translated by Ronald E. Clements. Hermeneia. Philadelphia: Fortress, 1979.

———. "The Message of the Prophet Ezekiel." *Interpretation* 23 (1969): 131–57.

———. "Visionary Experience in Jeremiah." Pages 95–118 in *Israel's Prophetic Tradition: Essays in Honour of Peter R. Ackroyd*. Edited by R. J. Coggins, A. C. J. Phillips and M. A. Knibb. Cambridge: Cambridge University Press, 1982.

INDEXES

INDEX OF REFERENCES

INDEX OF AUTHORS